AF183163

AMERICAN LEGAL EDUCATION ABROAD

American Legal Education Abroad

Critical Histories

Edited by
Susan Bartie and David Sandomierski

NEW YORK UNIVERSITY PRESS
New York

NEW YORK UNIVERSITY PRESS
New York
www.nyupress.org

© 2021 by New York University
All rights reserved

References to Internet websites (URLs) were accurate at the time of writing. Neither the author nor New York University Press is responsible for URLs that may have expired or changed since the manuscript was prepared.

Library of Congress Cataloging-in-Publication Data
Names: Bartie, Susan, editor. | Sandomierski, David, editor.
Title: American legal education abroad : critical histories /
edited by Susan Bartie and David Sandomierski.
Description: New York : New York University Press, [2021] |
Includes bibliographical references and index.
Identifiers: LCCN 2020040682 (print) | LCCN 2020040683 (ebook) |
ISBN 9781479803583 (hardcover) | ISBN 9781479803644 (ebook) |
ISBN 9781479803606 (ebook)
Subjects: LCSH: Law—Study and teaching—United States. | Law—Study and teaching—American influences. | Law—American influences.
Classification: LCC KF272 .A475 2020 (print) | LCC KF272 (ebook) | DDC 40.071/173—dc23
LC record available at https://lccn.loc.gov/2020040682
LC ebook record available at https://lccn.loc.gov/2020040683

New York University Press books are printed on acid-free paper, and their binding materials are chosen for strength and durability. We strive to use environmentally responsible suppliers and materials to the greatest extent possible in publishing our books.

Manufactured in the United States of America

10 9 8 7 6 5 4 3 2 1

Also available as an ebook

CONTENTS

Introduction

Throughout the twentieth century, elite US law schools have been presented as sites of power, admiration, influence, and envy. Robert Stevens, in the opening of his seminal 1983 work *Law School*,[1] suggested that foreign lawyers looked wistfully at elite US law schools for two central reasons. First, they have held such commanding positions within American universities and the profession. Second, their law graduates went on to occupy privileged and influential posts that contributed to changing political and social ordering. To Stevens's foreign observers, mimicking or transplanting American models must have seemed the most promising way to create new bands of legal elites—highly educated lawyers with reformist orientations—in their own countries. Adding to the impression of American dominance, Gail Hupper and others have explained how some US law professors took to the task of spreading the model with missionary-like zeal.[2]

This collection of contributed essays investigates whether, in reality, the elite US models proved so attractive to foreigners and considers where the efforts of the American missionaries led. It explores whether the allure of the US law schools and the activities of their law professors contributed to the globalization, or homogenization, of legal education that Stevens envisaged. It examines the extent to which educators beyond the United States believed that the adoption of American models would lead to better legal education and scholarship, better legal systems, better lawyers, and better governance. And it reveals the importance of circumstances and individuals to the transmission and reception of US ideas, exploring the relationship between institutions and agency. It transcends questions of pedagogical method to consider the cultural and political significance of attempts to transplant US models.

We concentrate on the twentieth century, a time when US lawyers began in earnest to define their relationship with the rest of the world. While this collection does not pretend to be an exhaustive examination of the Americanization of legal education globally, it nonetheless provides a significant sample, examining the role of American ideas and practices in thirteen countries: Australia, Brazil, Canada, China, England, Estonia, France, Ghana, Israel, Japan, Nigeria, the Philippines, and Sweden.

The Americanization of Legal Education

All contributors adopt historical perspectives for understanding what the Americanization of legal education has meant in the regions studied. In keeping with this commitment, we did not begin with a set idea of what a standard, dominant, static, or universal American model (or models) of legal education entails. And we have not sought to compare the models of legal education practiced in each region with prevailing models of legal education practiced, at the same time, in the United States. Indeed, we hold considerable doubts over whether such definitions and comparisons are either useful or desirable. We consider that such starting points will necessarily misrepresent the nature of legal education, something that we believe is an ever-changing, socially and politically constructed and contested phenomenon—one that is neither inherently good nor bad. Further, understanding how the legal education models of these regions have fallen short, over time, of an American ideal would unduly privilege US perspectives and models, undermining one of the central aims of this exercise: to reveal the various ways that the regions have received, interpreted, and engaged with US educational ideas and practices and to understand what this has meant for those regions.

Put simply, our goal has been to understand what the "Americanization" of legal education has meant over time and space. To this end each contributor has explained various, and even conflicting, concepts or constructs of the Americanization of legal education through their historical studies of ideas, actors, and practices within their region, concentrating on critical explanatory moments across the twentieth century and sometimes reaching into the present. This approach has meant that in many cases the so-called American practices and ideas considered, rejected, or adopted in a region do not correspond with past or prevailing practices in the United States. In other words, even where people within a region believed that they were following or rejecting an

American model, in truth they were following or rejecting an imaginary American ideal, one that does not correspond with the daily practices of American law professors. As Jedidiah Kroncke observes in this collection in his piece on China, "[M]any domestic Chinese reformers were exposed only to the ideal type of American lawyering and legal education. They rarely confronted the reality that the ideal model of modern American legal education itself seldom fully reflected American legal education in practice."

This is not, of course, to say that the American models considered bear no correlation to any of the American ideas and practices. Contributors repeatedly reference well-known practices and ideas associated with elite US law schools from the late nineteenth century up until the twenty-first century. The best-known feature of US legal education is the Langdellian model associated with the case and Socratic methods, and several of our contributors consider how academic lawyers from their regions conceptualized, experimented with, or rejected this model. Some contributors also consider the reception of models based on thinking that challenged Langdellian formalism, for example, American Legal Realism, the Legal Process School, the law and society movement, socio-legal studies, critical legal studies, and the clinical legal education movement. In each case, contributors explain what academic lawyers in the region took to be the defining elements and philosophies underlying the models.

In one sense we use the expression "legal education" narrowly, in that it is limited to the instruction in law within universities and (largely) university law schools. While we accept William Twining's arguments that the bulk of learning about law occurs outside of these institutional settings, and agree that law professors ought to pay greater attention to their responsibility to lead the education of broader publics, his wider conception of legal education is beyond the scope of this project.[3] Anchoring the notion of legal education to universities and law schools allows the volume's contributors to concentrate on its unique dimensions, examining not only the teaching methods adopted in classrooms but also how they and the materials presented embody and seek to advance, either deliberately or inadvertently, broader philosophies about the role of law and lawyers in society and the future careers and lives of graduates.

Legal Education as a Global Activity

The United States has a well-established tradition of critical writing about legal education, including its history. This work has underscored the relationship among legal education, lawyering, law, legal consciousness, and local and national politics. It has also challenged rationalizations of the current state of legal education and encouraged law professors to view their situation differently. Beyond the United States it is rare to find a similarly large body of work that maps the origins, contours, and changing state of the discipline of law within a particular region.

In some countries the smaller size, shorter history, and fewer resources available to law schools have meant that teachers have had little opportunity to reflect on their endeavors. In others, ongoing and dramatic political instability has made it difficult to speak of traditions in legal education. The fraught link between legal education and politics has in some cases discouraged scholarship in this field. In some regions legal education has been framed as either a choice between, or the wholesale adoption of, certain European[4] and US models. This characterization implies that local legal scholars do not benefit from the intensive dialogue that exists in the United States and that, accordingly, the history of legal education in these other countries is largely nascent.

By scrutinizing the extent to which US models have homogenized legal education, examining how local conditions have either accommodated or repelled such models, and linking attempted transplants with broader political and intellectual histories, this project aims to provide rich insights into legal education as a local and transnational affair. It seeks to challenge common perceptions that the history of legal education beyond the United States is uninteresting and unexceptional. And, most important, by bringing together scholars from numerous countries, this collection provides the basis for comparative analysis and discussion about the role and effect of US models globally.

Returning to the definition of legal education, our point is not simply that not enough comparisons have been made between legal education cultures and practices. Nor do we merely argue that more work ought to be done so that ideas and practices that have sat at the periphery are given the seriousness and attention they deserve. Rather we consider that, until we compare and contrast the changing educational commitments and practices within a diverse range of regions, we cannot begin to understand either what legal education has been or what it might become. Legal education is not a "thing" but an activity, one that is practiced throughout the world by a diverse range of actors and is shaped by both them and their environments. Unless we study the actors, the institutions, and the broader social and political contexts, we are bound to misunderstand the enterprise.

Why the United States?

This collection begins with chapters from Bruce Kimball and David Sugarman. Together they provide an essential foundation for understanding some of the central factors and circumstances that made US models attractive and why some legal educators across the twentieth century thought of legal education as involving a choice between English and American models and traditions. Kimball, both in chapter 1 and in his other work on Harvard Law School,[5] helps us understand how and why Harvard gave birth to a model of legal education that would dominate elite US legal education for several decades, that would become known all over the world, and that many foreign legal educators would seriously consider or adopt. Kimball provides a robust explanatory framework for understanding why a large number of US law schools adopted the Langdell-inspired case method while others rejected it, and he extends his analysis to explain why two other disciplines—business and medicine—experimented with the case method. Had Langdell's case method not been spread so successfully within the United States, it seems doubtful that we would now be speaking of the Americanization of legal education in countries around the globe.

By identifying the key features that led to the dominance of an American model domestically, Kimball's work also provides us with a tool for identifying explanatory factors unique to the movement of American ideas internationally. For example, Kimball suggests that academic trends, particularly those from the master discipline of science, formed one of the early and central reasons for the rise of the case method in the United States. And yet only one of our contributors, Kjell Å Modéer in chapter 9 (on Sweden) suggests that American ideas and practices prospered due to academic trends beyond law. Instead our collection suggests that political, historical, cultural, and economic factors often trumped intellectual commitments as explanatory factors for the success and failure of American models.

David Sugarman's chapter 2 (England) also helps us understand why, speaking generally, US ideas and models proved more attractive than the English despite the existence of some prominent English jurists. It provides a vital foundation for understanding why, over the course of the twentieth century, some academic lawyers came to perceive two dominant yet distinctive educational models: an English model born from a conservative and narrow legal culture that subordinated legal education, and dynamic American models based on progressive ideas about the role of lawyers in society that elevated law professors and law schools within the legal and social hierarchy. While Sugarman explains that the relationship between American and English ideas and practices is more complicated than this simple dichotomy, with moments of continuity and divergence in traditions across the twentieth century, his piece generally supports the thesis that US law schools proved to be the more innovative, prestigious, and resourceful, laying down many more attractive educational practices for others to follow.

US and English Intellectual Traditions and Allegiances

Philip Girard's chapter 3 (Canada) provides interesting comparisons with the English experience and also presents an interesting puzzle: Why did Canadian law schools conduct some of the earliest experiments with Langdell's case method, outside of the United States, at a time when Canada's profession remained heavily wedded to English legal practices and culture? His chapter suggests that English conservatism has sometimes sat alongside, rather than precluded, American enthusiasms. As with their American counterparts, some Canadian legal educators clearly saw merit in the case method's ability to engage students and believed that it was a useful method to prepare their graduates for professional work as lawyers.[6] While in the second half of the twentieth century the American influence became much stronger, and ties to England in legal education diminished, Girard suggests that in the final few decades of that century many Canadian law professors drew more from the local context, most notably "Indigenous peoples, the trans-systemic study of law, and bilingualism (i.e., English-French)."

Susan Bartie's chapter 4 on Australian legal education suggests that many Australian legal scholars found US models more attractive than the English model. She explains how leading Australian legal scholars referred to the American model when expressing their aspirations for Australian legal educators to move away from English practices during a crucial formative period: the 1950s and 1960s. This was due to frustrations over educational methods rather than the belief that Australia ought to be entirely independent from Britain or should wholly adopt American practices. There is little evidence of such convictions among Australian law professors of the period. Bartie suggests that contemporaneous and historical accounts of legal education have tended to present Australian legal education as the product of a choice between caricatures of the two models, and the author argues this has stifled the recognition of distinctively Australian traditions and confused understandings of both Australian legal education and Australian law.

Political, Social, Economic, and Cultural Explanations

Kimball suggests that several early adopters of the case method in the United States did so to "elevate their status and enhance their legitimacy" by drawing an association between their law, business, or medical schools and Harvard. This might suggest that foreign educators would preference US models as a way of lending greater legitimacy and status to legal education in their region. However, our contributors suggest that the reputation of US law schools as compared to their English equivalents was often a less important explanatory factor than the political and cultural relationships between Britain, the United States, and the region under study, or the politics, history, and culture of those regions.

In chapter 5, John Harrington and Ambreena Manji explain that during a critical formative period following Ghana's independence in 1957, and then after the 1966 coup, key figures rejected a humanistic American model that facilitated interactive teaching in favor of a traditional British model. Although the British model maintained links with English professional legal culture, they argue that the rejection of American ideas cannot simply be attributed to broader societal or political attitudes toward English and American influence. They explain that the reception of educational models was influenced by "questions of African nationalism, development, and social progress, the ambivalent legacy of British rule, and the growing influence of the United States in these territories." And they further suggest that the form and location of legal education was at the center of complex debates over Ghana's political and economic identity and future.

In chapter 6, J. Jarpa Dawuni and Rebecca Badejogbin suggest that, while ongoing ties with Nigeria's colonial past and Britain's interest in Nigeria encouraged English forms of legal education (even postindependence), three central initiatives encouraged experimentation with American ideas and methods: US-trained lawyers teaching in Nigeria, opportunities for Nigerian lawyers to study and attend conferences in the United States, and broader initiatives designed to promote connections between educators in each country. Funding from US-based philanthropic organizations also proved crucial, and the authors place particular emphasis on the role of the Ford Foundation Staffing of African Institutions of Legal Education and Research.

Resisting US Ideas and Models

Political, social, and cultural factors play a strong role in the explanations given by our contributors for why American ideas and practices did not take a strong hold in China, Estonia, Sweden, and Japan. Jedidiah J. Kroncke, in chapter 7 on the role of American legal education in China following two key revolutionary points (1911 and 1978), proposes an analytic scheme for understanding attempts at educational reform that rest on foreign ideas and practices. Kroncke suggests that, when comparing and contrasting, or choosing between, educational practices grounded in a set of commitments about the role of law, it is important to consider not only the philosophies underpinning the model but to also appreciate that legal education does not stand apart from existing social and political environments. It is only these broader factors that explain why American ideas and models (although American legal education was known to Chinese educators and lawyers and efforts were made to adopt some of its features) did little overall to change the way Chinese lawyers were educated or thought about law.

In chapter 8, Irene Kull, Merike Ristikivi, and Aleksei Kelli concentrate on a period of dramatic changes to Estonian law and legal education brought about in 1991, when independence was restored after more than fifty years of Soviet rule. They explain that lawyers played a crucial role in helping the newly independent nation shed socialist laws and restructure Soviet institutions, facilitating the shift to a market economy governed by the rule of law. Given the new focus, one might have thought that the Estonian reformers would draw heavily on American models and ideas to bring about this transformation. And yet as Kull, Ristikivi, and Kelli explain, the reformers looked more to Germany, with whom they held stronger social, geographic, political, and cultural bonds. Although American law was not often used a model for law reform, American lawyers and professors provided legal training and legal education that encouraged the development of Estonian law reform along a particular track that foregrounded rule-of-law concerns and the facilitation of a market economy.

Kjell Å Modéer in chapter 9 explains that, although Swedish law professors had been curious about American ideas since the 1930s, with particularly strong interest in works on law and society and legal sociology, the end of the cold war and signing of the Maastricht Treaty in 1992 prompted a return to European legal science. In the second half of the twentieth century, law schools in Sweden experimented with American-style practice-oriented and social scientific legal education, introduced more electives and classes in the sociology of law, were influenced by aspects of legal culture (such as affirmative action programs), and were attracted to ideas from both American legal realists and critical legal scholars. And yet, since 1995, Swedish law schools have increasingly taught classes emphasizing European themes, such as European Law and European Human Rights Law, in ways that depart from the previous American approaches.

Yoshiharu Matsuura's analysis in chapter 10 concentrates on a relatively recent Japanese experiment with American practices, when in 2004 the government introduced a new system of legal education as part of a university graduate program. This new program included a shift in legal education from teaching that centered on a theoretical discussion of law toward a discussion of court cases, supported by a database that captured more than a hundred years of case law. The change led to experiments with the American-style case method that have largely failed, revealing the strong incompatibility between the culture, assumptions, and practices underpinning American legal education and the Japanese reality.

Status, Ambition, and Imagination

Despite the strong role of political and cultural factors in most explanations of why the American models did or did not take hold, some contributors point to the same factors as Kimball does when explaining why some American law schools proved resistant to the case method. These reasons include that the ambitions of foreign schools were very different to those held by the elite US institutions, as well as that the foreign schools were not inclined to recognize the superior status of either Harvard or American law schools. For example, John Harrington and Ambreena Manji suggest in chapter 5 that the aspirations of legal educators in Ghana for their students were very different compared to those of elite American law schools, including the professions they hoped their students would enter. Jean-Louis Halpérin's analysis in chapter 11 suggests that despite various points of contact between French and American jurists, the structure of French legal education, and its history, made the adoption of the Harvard model impossible. He explains how, during the time when French law professors were learning about Langdell's model, the leading French law schools were larger and more developed establishments than Harvard Law School. This disparity translated to French law professors feeling "a kind of superiority complex toward American law schools."

Other contributors suggest that another of Kimball's explanatory factors for the adoption of the case method is also relevant to the international context: the efforts of Harvard law professors to enlist and capture the imagination of influential or emerging law professors. Pnina Lahav explains in chapter 12 that, in the period following Israel's independence in 1948, Israeli law faculties changed from largely resembling European law faculties to looking more like US law schools. She suggests that key personalities in Israeli law schools contributed critically to these changes, with Americanization first gaining momentum in the 1960s when bright Israeli graduates—including Aharon Barak and Itzhak Zamir—took up opportunities to study at elite US law schools and returned with firm commitments to certain American ideas and practices. In chapter 13, David Sandomierski explores the export of Lon Fuller's ideas on the lawyer as "social architect" to one leading Canadian law faculty. He demonstrates how Fuller's gloss on the legal process ideas of the 1940s—that the lawyer should be exposed to a diversity of legal processes and that legal education should strive to emphasize legislative and adjudicative processes equally—was taken up by one Canadian acolyte, James Milner, and influenced his teaching, casebook design, and national academic leadership. Despite these efforts, however, this particular Harvard transplant was ultimately unsuccessful, owing not only to historical contingencies but also to the inertial forces of the conventional Langdellian modes and ideas about legal education.

US Triumphant?

Of all the regions studied in this collection, the Americanization of legal education seems to have been strongest in Canada, Brazil, and the Philippines, and yet even in these countries current practices do not closely mirror contemporary US models. In Canada and Brazil, economic and market forces largely explain why, despite the diminishing status of US legal education within the United States, features of US models continue to be reflected in these regions. José Garcia Ghirardi explains in chapter 14 how globalization has transformed both politics and economics, as well as legal education, in Brazil and how it has encouraged Brazilian universities to adopt American-style teaching methods such as the case method, American Legal Realist sentiment, and aspects of law and economics. He considers that the enlistment of US-style legal education as a response to dramatic social, economic, and political changes has led to a "broad reconceptualizing of legal institutions and of their social meanings."

It is perhaps no surprise that legal education in the Philippines has been strongly influenced by American ideas and practices. What is surprising, however, is that law professors have been using a Socratic method that closely resembles Langdell's original model since 1921. In chapter 15, Emily Sanchez Salcedo suggests that, despite these similarities, the way that women students in the Philippines experience and respond to the method has been materially different to the experience of women students in the United States many decades earlier. Her empirical studies suggest that, although the use of the Socratic method in the classroom often amounts to harassment and verbal abuse, women in the Philippines have not been disadvantaged in the same way as have women in the United States. She identifies factors that explain these very different experiences: broader societal culture, the nature of law practices in the Philippines, and how graduates at the most elite universities are almost guaranteed certain jobs, as well as the lesser weighting given to Socratic performance among other assessment tasks. She concludes that the continued use of the Socratic method has contributed to the failure of law schools in the Philippines to "genuinely accommodate women," forcing "them to assimilate masculine norms."

Conclusion

This collection concludes with reflections from two leading American law professors and legal historians, Susan Carle (chapter 16) and Bob Gordon (chapter 17). Each provides a further synthesis of this collection, drawing out central themes, and they add additional insight into how the experiences across these thirteen countries might inform the way we think about legal education now and into the future, both in the United States and elsewhere. They explain that US legal education is undergoing a significant period of disruption where bright students are either choosing other professions and industries, viewing them as a better means of bringing about social reform, or else are demanding (along with the profession) more streamlined law degrees that accelerate their "readiness" for practice, leaving little room for subjects that encourage critical understandings and broader reflections on law. The extent of this disruption, and the likelihood of dramatic changes to the hierarchies and operations of US law schools in the ensuing decade, suggests that their influence within the global order of legal education may soon fall into further decline.

Talk of disruption, of course, extends beyond the US context. Debates over how legal education should change in response to both student expectations as well as the way in which both legal services and legal education are delivered have reached fever pitch across North America, Europe, and Asia.[7] To meet the current challenges we need not only to come up with reforming measures but also to develop a stronger accounting of legal education that draws from a broad range of experiences, including but moving firmly beyond Western and so-called central legal cultures. If not, responses will simply serve to enforce existing hierarchies, and seemingly sound remedies will be based on a false diagnosis of the true ailments of the existing system. Further work that conceptualizes legal education as a global activity, and that is attuned to context, is therefore essential. We consider that this collection makes an important contribution to this broader endeavor.

NOTES

1 Robert Stevens, *Law School—Legal Education in America from the 1850s to the 1980s* (Chapel Hill: University of North Carolina Press, 1983).

2 Gail Hupper, "The Rise of an Academic Doctorate in Law: Origins through World War II," *American Journal of Legal History* 49, no. 1 (2007): 1–60; Gail Hupper, "The Academic Doctorate in Law: A Vehicle for Legal Transplants?," *Journal of Legal Education* 58, no. 3 (2008): 413–54; Gail Hupper, "Educational Ambivalence: The Rise of a Foreign Student Doctorate in Law," *New England Law Review* 49, no. 3 (2015): 319–447.

3 William Twining, "Rethinking Legal Education," *The Law Teacher* 52, no. 3 (2017): 241–59.

4 Here we include English models.

5 See, e.g., Bruce A. Kimball, *The Inception of Modern Professional Education: C. C. Langdell, 1826–1906* (Chapel Hill: University of North Carolina Press 2009); Daniel R. Coquillette and Bruce A. Kimball, *On the Battlefield of Merit: Harvard Law School, the First Century* (Cambridge: Harvard University Press, 2015).

6 These are two factors forming part of Kimball's explanatory framework.

7 See, e.g., B. Z. Tamanaha, *Failing Law Schools* (Chicago: University of Chicago Press, 2012); R. Susskind and D. Susskind, *How Technology Will Transform the Work of the Professions* (Oxford: Oxford University Press, 2015); Richard Susskind, *Tomorrow's Lawyers: An Introduction to your Future*, 2nd ed. (Oxford: Oxford University Press, 2017); Mitch Kowalski, *Avoiding Extinction: Reimagining Legal Services for the 21st Century* (Chicago: American Bar Association, 2012); David M. Moss, "Legal Education at the Crossroads," in *Reforming Legal Education: Law Schools at the Crossroads*, ed. David M. Moss and Debra Moss Curtis, 1–11 (Charlotte: Information Age Publishing, 2012); William M. Sullivan et al., *Educating Lawyers: Preparing for the Profession of Law*, Carnegie Foundation for the Advancement of Teaching (San Francisco: Jossey-Bass, 2007), http://archive.carnegiefoundation.org.

PART 1

Foundation Stories

1

The Proliferation and Transformation of Harvard's Case Method in the United States, 1870s–1990s

BRUCE A. KIMBALL

Beginning in the early nineteenth century in the United States, the nature of the scientific method attracted much attention from intellectuals and academics, who focused their attention on the regnant sciences of biology and botany and the associated method of "induction." In the 1870s, that interest gave rise to the practice of inductive teaching in US higher education, which generated a wave of enthusiasm throughout the emerging universities during the last quarter of the nineteenth century.

At the very start of that pedagogical movement, in 1870, the dean of Harvard Law School, Christopher C. Langdell (1870–1895), invented case method teaching, which he conceived as training in analogical inductive reasoning between particular legal decisions and legal principles.[1] This new pedagogy became a main feature in Harvard Law School's *new system* of legal education that was designed to assess students' professional merit in terms of their academic achievement.

That system included major new policies and practices that nearly all university law schools in the United States eventually adopted: the admissions requirement of a bachelor's degree, a multiyear course of study, written examinations, rigorous grading, and tiered coursework with advanced electives requiring introductory courses.[2] But the feature that attracted the most attention and controversy was the unorthodox method of teaching through Socratic questioning about the inferences that students made from studying the published reports of legal cases.[3] This was considered an "inductive" approach to teaching and constituted the first of two conceptual interpretations of case method instruction in the United States.

So contrary was case method to the established practice of didactic teaching through lectures and recitation that the vast majority of law professors, alumni, and students initially derided it, even at Harvard. At other law schools, some faculty even called it an "abomination."[4] For two decades, the case method and its associated reforms were almost entirely confined to Harvard Law School. During the subsequent twenty-five years between 1890 and 1915, a national controversy ensued as to whether case method teaching—and the concomitant academic reforms—would predominate in legal education in the United States. In this fashion, case method teaching became emblematic of the new system. Adopting case method signified that a law school had allied itself with the Harvard-led movement to emphasize academic merit in legal education.

Furthermore, the controversy and the proliferation of case method instruction were not confined to legal education. The preeminence of Harvard Law School early in the twentieth century led university schools of medicine and business to incorporate policies and practices of the new system. These university professional schools therefore increasingly adopted case method teaching during the twentieth century. But, in so doing, they transformed it by introducing a second, conceptual interpretation of case method in the United States, which sometimes became known as the "problem method." These processes of proliferation and transformation across professional schools and fields within the United States (even within Harvard University itself) therefore complicate the transplantation of the Harvard model of legal education, particularly case method teaching, to other nations during the twentieth and twenty-first centuries.

* * *

The proliferation of the emblematic case method in the United States exemplifies what social scientists have called "isomorphism": the process by which new, marginal, or reforming institutions in a social domain tend to replicate the organizational structures, policies, and practices of the dominant or preeminent institutions. This replication results in organizational homogeneity among institutions within the domain.[5]

To explain this replication, social scientists have developed the theory of "new institutionalism." The basic idea is that new or marginal institutions in a given domain need legitimacy to establish or advance themselves. To acquire that legitimacy, they adopt the features of the premier and dominant institutions, and then embrace them as their own. As a result, over time, the great majority of the institutions begin to display the same attributes, and the domain exhibits organizational homogeneity.[6]

Other explanations for the replication of structure, policies, and practices across institutions are certainly plausible. Some replicated structures and policies may have proliferated among institutions simply because they work. In other words, the structures and policies have *functioned* effectively to improve education, so other professional schools adopted them. This pedagogical functionalism has generally been rejected by sociologists studying professions and professional education since the 1960s. Instead, these scholars generally prefer some variant of the new institutionalism theory.[7] In my view, both functionalism and the drive for legitimacy or status help to explain the proliferation of case method teaching among professional schools in the United States.

Whatever the explanation, as of 1890 only Harvard Law School employed case teaching. Then, in the twenty-five years between 1890 and 1915, the controversial case method spread rapidly to forty-seven American law schools (or 40 percent), and the rest of the Harvard system advanced commensurately.[8] Consequently, legal education in the United States grew progressively isomorphic based on the Harvard template.

Table 1.1 lists the forty-seven schools that converted to case method between 1890 and 1915. Conversion began slowly during the first five years and accelerated after 1895, primarily occurring in one of three modes. University presidents encouraged their law schools to adopt case method; certain "missionaries"—Harvard LLBs hired on the faculty of other schools—encouraged those schools to convert; and other law schools chose to emulate Harvard without any direct influence by individuals associated with that law school.[9]

TABLE 1.1 Chronological Distribution of Forty-Seven Law Schools Adopting Case Method Teaching, 1890–1915

Time Period of adoption	School and date of adoption	State	Mode of Adoption**
1890–1894: 4			
	Columbia U. 1892	New York	President
	Cornell U. 1892	New York	Indirect
	*Stanford U. 1894	California	Indirect
	*Northwestern U. 1890s	Illinois	President
1895–1899: 9			
	*U. Cincinnati 1896	Ohio	Missionaries
	New York U. 1896	New York	Indirect
	U. Pennsylvania 1896	Pennsylvania	Indirect
	*U. Illinois 1897	Illinois	President
	*Western Reserve U. 1898	Ohio	President
	U. Iowa 1898	Iowa	Missionaries
	*U. Maine 1898	Maine	Indirect
	U. Denver 1899	Colorado	Indirect
	*U. North Dakota 1899	North Dakota	Missionaries
1900–1904: 10			
	Boston U. 1900	Massachusetts	Indirect
	*U. California 1900	California	President
	Hastings C. 1901	California	Indirect
	*U. Chicago 1902	Illinois	President
	*Dickinson C. 1902	Pennsylvania	Missionaries
	U. Wisconsin 1903	Wisconsin	Missionaries
	U. Nebraska 1903	Nebraska	Missionaries
	U. Missouri 1904	Missouri	Missionaries
	U. Richmond 1904	Virginia	Missionaries
	Tulane U. 1904	Louisiana	Missionaries
1905–1909: 10			
	Indiana U. 1905	Indiana	Indirect
	U. Notre Dame 1905	Indiana	Indirect
	*U. Utah 1905	Utah	Indirect
	*Duke U. 1905	North Carolina	Indirect
	New York Law School 1906	New York	Indirect
	*Fordham U. 1907	New York	Missionaries
	*U. Kentucky 1909	Kentucky	Indirect
	*U. Oklahoma 1909	Oklahoma	Indirect
	DePaul U. 1909	Illinois	Indirect
	Indiana U. Indianapolis 1909	Indiana	Indirect

TABLE 1.1 (*Cont.*)

1910–1915: 14			
	U. Louisville 1910	Kentucky	Missionaries
	U. Colorado 1910	Colorado	Indirect
	George Washington U. 1910	Washington, D.C.	Indirect
	*U. Idaho 1910	Idaho	Indirect
	*U. Montana 1911	Montana	President
	U. Minnesota 1912	Minnesota	President
	*U. Detroit 1912	Michigan	Indirect
	U. Alabama 1913	Alabama	President
	Southern California U. 1915	California	Missionaries
	*Southwestern U. 1915	California	Indirect
	*U. Arizona 1915	Arizona	Indirect
	Valparaiso U. 1915	Indiana	Indirect
	U. Oregon 1915	Oregon	Indirect
	U. West Virginia 1915	West Virginia	Indirect

*Indicates that the law school was recently established or re-opened and re-organized shortly before adopting case method. Adapted from Bruce A. Kimball, "The Proliferation of Case Method Teaching in American Law Schools: Mr. Langdell's Emblematic 'Abomination,' 1890–1915," History of Education Quarterly 46 (2006): 210–211; Bruce A. Kimball and Daniel R. Coquillette, The Intellectual Sword: Harvard Law School, The Second Century (Cambridge, MA: Harvard University Press, 2020), 49–50.

Presidential initiative was exercised primarily before 1900, followed by the direct proselytizing of Harvard LLBs between 1898 and 1904, and then indirect emulation primarily after 1904. This sequence is likely explained by the expanding network of converted institutions over time. The expansion increased the legitimacy and prestige of case teaching as an increasing number of leading law schools adopted it, and that increase made case method appear more attractive, reducing the necessity for direct personal intervention by presidents or missionaries.

In terms of geographical distribution, law schools in the southeastern states adopted case method and the concomitant Harvard system of legal education more slowly and less extensively. Only six of the forty-seven schools that converted to case method teaching between 1890 and 1915 were in the Southeast. In contrast, those in the upper Midwest were particularly receptive, numbering twenty-one of the forty-seven, likely explained by the high concentration of Harvard Law School alumni in Chicago.[10]

Law schools adopted case method instruction for a number of reasons. Two fit closely the new institutionalist explanation for the isomorphism in legal education. First, case teaching offered, in Langdell's words, a method that was suitable for "the law conceived as an inductive science." This referred to the analogical inductive reasoning in law from particular decisions to legal principles and from the principles to new cases. This kind of reasoning characterized the preeminent natural sciences of botany and biology during most of the nineteenth century.[11] Accordingly, Langdell introduced case method as part of his project to make Harvard Law School more academically respectable—that is, to legitimate legal science and legal education according to the dominant canons of knowledge of the emerging universities in the late nineteenth century.[12]

Similarly, in his 1914 report on American legal education prepared for the Carnegie Foundation for the Advancement of Teaching, Josef Redlich noted the appeal to the inductive, analogical reasoning of the academic fields of Baconian natural science, and he considered this appeal to be one of the primary reasons for the proliferation of case method in US legal education.[13] This first conceptual interpretation, expressed by both Langdell and Redlich, thus likened case teaching to the inductive method of Baconian sciences, such as biology and botany.

The second institutionalist reason was that many schools desired to elevate their status and enhance their legitimacy.[14] By the same token, graduates of Harvard Law School wished to advance the influence of their alma mater and its anomalous new system. Harvard alumni were well positioned to do so because, in 1890, the Harvard Law School Association—the most extensive alumni network of any professional school in the country at the time—comprised 1,390 alumni distributed over forty-three US states and territories, three Canadian provinces, and four foreign countries.[15] In addition, Harvard Law School dean James Barr Ames (1895–1909) and his successor Ezra R. Thayer (1910–1915) sought to arrange "missionary" appointments to the faculty of other law schools. By 1917, sixty-seven American law schools had hired Harvard LLBs on their faculty.[16]

Two pedagogically functionalist reasons also contributed to the spread of case method. Teaching inductively from cases engaged students far better than lectures or recitations. Charged with the responsibility for interpreting original sources, students became active participants, rather than passive vessels, in the classroom, observed George Kirchwey at Columbia University and Harvard University president Charles W. Eliot (1869–1909).[17] The other functionalist reason for adopting case instruction was its effectiveness in preparing for professional work in the Anglo-American case-law system.[18]

Reinforcing those four reasons, three practical developments contributed to the spread of Harvard's case method across the nation. The number of published case reporters rose dramatically, and the practice of citing precedents in legal arguments grew rapidly. These two trends made the technique of reading and analyzing cases increasingly valuable.[19]

The third related development was the publication of casebooks. A new pedagogy needed suitable instructional materials, and an increasing number of casebooks appeared after 1890.[20] Most influential were the two casebooks produced by professor James B. Thayer,[21] whose influence stemmed not from the number of his casebooks, but from his novel strategy of accommodating his readers.[22] This attention to his audience appeared in Thayer's express desire to limit the size of his casebooks to one volume and to expand the explanatory commentary in order to help the student understand the cases.[23] In addition, James Thayer drew up a list of interested or influential law professors regarding his subject and had his publisher send them free copies of his casebooks. The strategy bore fruit among law professors in England and Australia, as well as undergraduate instructors at American institutions, including Dartmouth College, Massachusetts Institute of Technology, Knox College, and the University of Kansas.[24] As a result, Thayer's casebooks became "the most successful" of those published by Harvard professors through the beginning of the twentieth century.[25]

* * *

Despite all these reasons and developments contributing to the spread of case instruction, forty-two schools—about 36 percent of the total—refused to adopt the method by 1915. These schools cited various jurisprudential and pedagogical commitments to justify their resistance. One group of four aspiring university schools ironically confirmed the salience of the new institutionalist explanation. Comprising Yale,

Virginia, Michigan, and North Carolina, this group envied Harvard's status and often attributed the leadership of that school and the proliferation of case method to other law schools' desire for legitimacy and status.[26]

Eleven local independent schools—nonprofit as well as proprietary—rejected case method because they desired neither status nor novel teaching. Rather, their interests were largely prudential, and they sought to keep their classrooms full by charging low tuition and maintaining low academic standards. Students paid little, did minimal work, and received the degree. Their faculties comprised part-time members of the local bench and bar, and their students had relatively little academic preparation, worked full-time elsewhere, and aspired to be local practitioners.[27]

The largest group of schools rejecting case method included twenty-seven university and collegiate schools that operated with the policies and norms of local proprietary schools. These institutions also filled their law faculties with part-time local members of the bench and bar, many of whom had neither an undergraduate degree nor a law degree, though they might have built up a respectable practice. Commensurately, the admissions standards were low, the term of study brief, and the academic requirements undemanding.

Among these twenty-seven university law schools with proprietary policies, the largest subgroup comprised fourteen schools in the Southeast. By the same token, James Thayer's efforts to solicit interest in his casebooks did not bear fruit throughout this region.[28] Outside of the Southeast, six university law schools following proprietary policies were clustered in Ohio, western Pennsylvania, and upstate New York.[29] Finally, seven other widely distributed university or collegiate law schools followed proprietary policies and practices.

* * *

Notwithstanding these resisters, by 1915 case method predominated among most leading law schools and began making inroads in other domains of professional education. Between 1900 and 1920 certain faculty in medical schools briefly began to borrow case method from law schools. This flirtation demonstrates both the functionalist extension of the inductive conception of case method to another professional field requiring analogical reasoning as well as the institutionalist explanation for whether and when the functionalist extension occurs.

Medicine, of course, had long had discrete cases, and one might therefore expect some kind of case method teaching to be easily and rapidly adopted in medicine. But a medical case is experiential and generally not written down or reported as were legal cases. Consequently, among the leaders of American medical education through the late nineteenth century, the inductive and progressive pedagogy was *clinical instruction*, that is, experiential practice in examining, diagnosing, and prescribing in a patient's case at the bedside in the hospital. Such clinical instruction was clearly distinguished from identifying and codifying written cases as the unit of teaching and learning, as Harvard medical professor Walter B. Cannon, an early advocate of medical case method, observed.[30]

While studying at Harvard Medical School in the late 1890s, Cannon roomed with a Harvard law student and, through him, encountered the method of teaching and studying from written legal cases. Much impressed, Cannon, who joined the Harvard medical faculty and went on to become a renowned medical scientist, published a noted article in the forerunner of the *New England Journal of Medicine* in January 1900. Cannon advocated "the case method of teaching systematic medicine" and explicitly modeled this new method upon that of law.[31]

In May 1900, the Boston Society for Medical Improvement considered Cannon's proposal at a meeting attended by president Charles Eliot, law dean Ames, and several medical professors, all of whom spoke on behalf of "the inductive method applied to medicine."[32] Not only did medicine have discrete cases; it also had an emerging consensus on the nature and forms of knowledge in the field that fit the analogical reasoning between particular cases and principles in the field. In short, medicine fit the first, conceptual interpretation of case method. Cannon's suggestion was soon put into practice by a number of medical professors at Harvard, as well as a few elsewhere, such as J. William White at the University of Pennsylvania and C. Eugene Riggs at the University of Minnesota. These scholars also published a number of medical cases in the first decade of the twentieth century.[33]

Among the notable converts was professor Richard C. Cabot, who remarked that his 1911 medical casebook followed "the method of *case-teaching* which I have used for eight years at the Harvard Medical School, applying there a method long employed at the Harvard Law School."[34] In fact, Cabot's weekly clinico-pathological exercises published in the *Boston Medical and Surgical Journal* were the direct forebears of the case records and case reports that the *New England Journal of Medicine* published weekly throughout the twentieth century and into the twenty-first.[35] By 1915, therefore, leading medical educators were borrowing case method directly from Harvard Law School.

The introduction of case method into medical education in the early 1900s demonstrates a functionalist reason for the inductive conception of case method. The medical educators believed that the legal paradigm of case teaching fit the training in analogical reasoning from particular cases to medical principles and vice versa. But the adoption of medical case method is also consistent with the new institutionalist account of case method's proliferation in the following way.

During the last quarter of the nineteenth century, as legal case method slowly gained ground in a highly public controversy, the method was ignored in medicine. That neglect may be explained, in part, by the fact that medical education had no less legitimacy than legal education at the time.[36] Thus, medical education proceeded independently, following its own didactic model of lecturing, even though medicine might have seemed a likely candidate for the inductive approach to teaching. By 1900, however, Harvard Law School was widely recognized as the national leader in professional education, whereas Harvard Medical School appeared to be somewhat retrograde in light of advances made at Johns Hopkins Medical School, which opened in 1893.[37] Consequently, the adoption of case method by medical educators in the early 1900s demonstrates the pattern of a somewhat less legitimate or lower status field borrowing pedagogy from a more legitimate field.

Then, in the 1910s, the relative wealth and legitimacy of medical education eclipsed that of legal education at Harvard and throughout the United States. This meteoric ascent of medical education resulted from several factors: the growing therapeutic effectiveness of medical science, the philanthropic funding that deluged medical schools after 1900, and the timely call for reform in the famous Flexner Report of 1910 published by the Carnegie Foundation for the Advancement of Teaching. Commensurately but conversely, the employment of case method in medical education fizzled out during the 1910s. Cannon gave up case method teaching; Cabot left the medical school to become a professor of social ethics; and no more medical casebooks were published after 1920. The extinction was so complete that later histories of medical education make no mention of case method teaching.[38]

In sum, the brief flirtation of medical education with case method teaching reveals initial neglect by a field of equal status, in which one might expect to find interest in the vociferous debate over teaching with cases during a period when higher education extolled "inductive teaching." Then, as Harvard Law School with its case method emerged preeminent in professional education, the somewhat less legitimate and lower status professional school in medicine began borrowing case method teaching from the more legitimate and higher status field. Finally, in the 1910s, the relative standing of law and medicine reversed, and the interest in and practice of case method in medicine then rapidly diminished. This sequence reveals both the functionalist extension of the inductive conception of case method to another professional field and the institutionalist explanation for whether and when the functionalist extension occurs.

* * *

Just as the replication of legal case method in medical schools was expiring, business schools, led by Harvard, began to adopt it from law schools. The background lay in the founding of degree-granting business schools by colleges and universities. In the 1890s, three such business schools were founded, followed by nine in the 1900s and nearly ninety more during the 1910s and 1920s.[39] Among these, Harvard Graduate School of Business Administration was founded in 1908, introduced the MBA, came to be the most influential, and headed the movement to borrow legal case method, as the very first course catalog announced.

The first dean of the Harvard business school, the economist Edwin F. Gay, supported this borrowing, as well as the institutionalist rationale for it, as his assistant later recalled:

> Harvard Law School . . . was by far the most serious competitor which the new Business School had to face. For some years numerous college graduates had been attending the Law School to prepare for business careers. The Law School training was highly esteemed in influential business cir-

cles, and that training was effectuated by the use of the case method of instruction. Hence, Dean Gay decided that instruction in the Business School should be patterned on the method used with such conspicuous success in the Law School.[40]

The institutionalist rationale for employing case method was also evidenced by Gay's rejection of case method for his economics classes, even as he advocated its use in the business school.[41] The explanation for this inconsistency seemed to lie in his belief that, in economics, teaching by cases would appear idiosyncratic in a field that did not need the patina of legitimacy, as did Harvard's fledgling business school.

Although the business faculty thwarted Gay's effort to establish case method at the business school, he did set the precedent. President A. Lawrence Lowell (1909–1933), a Harvard LLB, wanted to expand the practice, believing that adopting case method was the best means to legitimate the new collegiate business schools.[42] In 1919, Lowell therefore appointed as dean his former mentee and a Harvard LLB, Wallace B. Donham, who championed and established case method at the business school.

Through the 1920s, Donham explicitly tried to adopt the analogical inductive model of legal case method. In order to do so, he commissioned faculty to create business cases by writing up accounts of actual problems and decisions made by businesses and then by collecting and publishing the accounts in casebooks. Donham had these business casebooks formatted and bound to resemble legal casebooks, including a citation system modeled on legal citations.[43] While evidencing the institutionalist explanation, this resemblance also demonstrates a functionalist effort to make the cases pedagogically useful.

The adoption foundered. Some traditional faculty who preferred lectures and textbooks resisted.[44] But the fundamental problem was that business did not have codified cases or consensus on the nature and forms of knowledge in the field. Therefore, business knowledge did not resemble Anglo-American jurisprudence and did not fit the received conceptual interpretation of case method based on analogical reasoning between cases and principles.

Consequently, at the end of the 1920s, Donham and his colleagues formulated a second conceptual interpretation of case method suited to business knowledge, which continued through the end of the twentieth century. Although the philosopher Alfred N. Whitehead informed Donham's thinking in many respects, the new conceptual interpretation of case method in business education rested most directly on "the kind of thinking which has been presented by John Dewey," whose philosophy was akin to that of Whitehead.[45]

Teaching from cases in business therefore tried to effect central tenets of Dewey's philosophy of education, including: (1) that the interest of students must be stimulated in order for them to learn; (2) that experience is necessary for learning to occur; (3) that knowledge is dynamic and dependent on context; (4) that learning method is more important than learning content; (5) that learning comes through a student's purposeful reflection on problems; and (6) that the effective teacher poses problems in order to stimulate the interest of students. The aim of the teacher and student is not to arrive at a solution but to learn how to evaluate and analyze the problem.[46]

The terminology here is highly significant. Dewey maintained fundamentally and explicitly that all thought and inquiry follow from the stimulus of a "problem" arising from an experienced situation.[47] This principle led educators within the Progressive Education movement in the United States during the 1910s and 1920s to develop a pedagogy that they called the "problem method."[48] Accordingly, business case teachers employed the phrase "problem method" interchangeably with "case method," while also labeling business "cases" as business "problems."[49] As the first catalog of Harvard business school stated:

> In the courses on Commercial Law, the case-system will be used. In the other courses an analogous method, emphasizing class-room discussion in connection with lectures and frequent reports on assigned topics,—what may be called the "problem method," will be introduced as far as practicable.[50]

However, as Progressive education fell out of favor after 1930, business case educators employed the phrase "problem method" less and less. Eventually it was sloughed away in favor of "*case* method," which was associated with the prestige of Harvard Law School. But the theory and invocations of Dewey remained, providing the foundation for the second conceptual interpretation of case method. Business *cases* were treated as *problems* stimulating analysis and class discussion.

Understood in that way, business case method appeared to business schools to be functional, and many, particularly Stanford, borrowed it from Harvard, as business education boomed in the 1950s. By the early 1990s, the fraction of American college freshmen intending to study business reached nearly 30 percent, surpassing all other academic fields, and the MBA was being awarded at many European universities, which taught by case method according to its second conceptual interpretation suited to business knowledge.[51] Meanwhile, prominent business case educators—apparently believing their legitimacy and status to be secure—deemphasized the original borrowing of legal case method by business schools and proposed that business case method was a unique creation whose proliferation was solely due to its functionality in business education.[52] Nevertheless, this historical revisionism also supports the institutionalist explanation for that proliferation.

Meanwhile, in the final development during the twentieth century, medical schools—which had turned away from inductive case method in the 1910s—began to institute what they called "problem-based learning" in the 1970s. Based on the Deweyan principles identified above, problem-based learning was formally inaugurated at McMaster University's medical school in Canada in 1969, then spread throughout medical schools in the United States, including Harvard Medical School, in the 1980s and 1990s.[53]

As with the business case method, some medical educators began to argue that problem-based learning was a unique creation of McMaster University. But Harvard Medical School in the 1980s properly viewed the case method at Harvard Business School, based on the Deweyan problem method, as the actual forerunner.[54] Such conflicting interpretations demonstrate the prevalent misunderstanding of the historical proliferation and the two conceptual interpretations of Harvard Law School's case method in the United States.

Consequently, case method in the United States underwent several steps of development while yielding two conceptual interpretations. In 1870, as inductive teaching arose in US higher education, dean Langdell of Harvard Law School introduced the teaching method of questioning students about their understanding of written cases. Conceived as training in analogical reasoning between particulars and principles, this novel method was initially regarded as an abomination by the faculty at nearly every law school in the nation.

Then, amid great controversy between 1890 and 1915, 40 percent of American law schools adopted case method, and another 24 percent partially accommodated the method with the clear prospect of complete adoption on the horizon. Of the 36 percent of law schools that still rejected case method in 1915, the great majority were marginal, less influential, or rapidly losing influence in American legal education, and most of them converted in the next decade. The reasons for both the resistance and the proliferation lay in the institutionalist desire for legitimacy and the utility of training in analogical induction.

Meanwhile, between 1900 and 1910, some medical schools began adopting the new pedagogy, primarily due to the utility of training in analogical reasoning between medical principles and patient cases, but also due to the reputation and high status of Harvard Law School. Then, during the 1910s, the relative standing of legal and medical education reversed, and the interest in and practice of case method in medical schools rapidly dissipated. Just at that point, business schools began to adopt the case method from Harvard Law School, and the explicit institutionalist rationale for this adoption was to acquire esteem and thereby attract students.

But the inductive, analogical reasoning did not fit the field of business, which had no codified cases and little consensus on the nature and forms of knowledge. The Harvard business dean and faculty therefore created discrete cases and published casebooks, while they also formulated a second conceptual interpretation of case method based on the problem method of Progressive educators informed by the philosophy of John Dewey. Due to its pedagogical functionality, that problem method proliferated during the twentieth century throughout business schools, which nevertheless continued to use the name "case method," testifying to their concern for acquiring the status and legitimacy of legal case method.

Meanwhile, in 1969, the McMaster medical school inaugurated problem-based learning. This was a conceptual variation of the problem method that many medical schools in the United States and Canada adopted over the next three decades. By the end of the twentieth century, medical schools and business schools claimed that their own inductive methods of teaching were original and unique.[55] And it is true that the application of Deweyan principles to case method distinguished the problem method from the analogical conception. By this route, the inductive method of teaching through questioning students about their inferences from studying the written accounts of cases had proliferated from its origin in the case method introduced at Harvard Law School in the 1870s. That case method was also conceptually transformed as it moved across professional fields not only across North America but also within the university where it originated.

NOTES

1 Bruce A. Kimball, *The Inception of Modern Professional Education: C. C. Langdell, 1826–1906* (Chapel Hill: University of North Carolina Press, 2009), 87–88.

2 On Harvard's "new system," see Kimball, *The Inception of Modern Professional Education*, 130–232.

3 Bruce A. Kimball, "'Warn Students That I Entertain Heretical Opinions, Which They Are Not To Take as Law': The Inception of Case Method Teaching in the Classrooms of the Early C. C. Langdell, 1870–1883," *Law & History Review* 17, no. 1 (1999): 57–140.

4 Bruce A. Kimball, "Professor Langdell: The Case of an 'Abomination' in Teaching," *Thought & Action* 20 (2004): 23–38.

5 Paul W. DiMaggio and Walter W. Powell, "The Iron Cage Revisited: Institutional Isomorphism and Collective Rationality in Organizational Fields," *American Sociological Review* 48, no. 2 (1983): 147–60.

6 Quotations are from Rakesh Khurana, *From Higher Aims to Hired Hands: The Social Transformation of American Business Schools and the Unfulfilled Promise of Management as a Profession* (Princeton: Princeton University Press, 2007), 14; see esp. 12–15, 47–48; Walter W. Powell and Paul J. Dimaggio, eds., *The New Institutionalism in Organizational Analysis* (Chicago: University of Chicago Press, 1983); Mary C. Brinton and Victor Nee, *The New Institutionalism in Sociology* (Palo Alto: Stanford University Press, 2001).

7 Magali Sarfatti Larson, *The Rise of Professionalism: A Sociological Analysis* (Berkeley: University of California Press, 1977); Paul Starr, *The Social Transformation of American Medicine* (New York: Basic Books, 1982), 143–44. See Eliot Freidson, *Professional Powers: A Study of the Institutionalization of Formal Knowledge* (Chicago: University of Chicago Press, 1986), 28–29; Andrew Abbott, *The System of Professions: An Essay on the Division of Expert Labor* (Chicago: University of Chicago Press, 1988), 5.

8 Bruce A. Kimball, "The Proliferation of Case Method Teaching in American Law Schools: Mr. Langdell's Emblematic 'Abomination,' 1890–1915," *History of Education Quarterly* 46, no. 2 (2006): 190–244.

9 Quotation is from Daniel R. Ernst, *The First 125 Years: 1870–1995: An Illustrated History of the Georgetown University Law Center* (Washington, DC: Georgetown University Law Center, 1995), 85. The missionary mode has long been considered the primary, even sole, mode of dissemination of case method. See Charles Warren, *History of the Harvard Law School and of Early Legal Conditions in America* (New York: Lewis Publishing Company, 1908), 2:511–12; Steve Sheppard, "An Introductory History of Law in the Lecture Hall," in *The History of Legal Education in the United States*, ed. Steve Sheppard (Pasadena, CA: Salem Press, 1999), 31.

10 Louis D. Brandeis, *Proceedings of the Annual Meeting of the Harvard Law School Association, June 12, 1890* (Cambridge: Harvard Law School Association, 1890), 1.

11 Christopher C. Langdell, preface to *A Selection of Cases on the Law of Contracts with References and Citations . . . prepared for Use as a Text-Book in Harvard Law School* (Boston: Little, Brown, 1871); Christopher C. Langdell, Annual Report of the Dean of Harvard Law School 1873–74, 67; Christopher C. Langdell, "Address," in Harvard Law School Association, *Report of the Organization and of the First General Meeting, 1886* (Boston: Harvard Law School Association, 1887), 49–50.

12 Christopher C. Langdell, "Address," *Proceedings of the Meeting of the Harvard Law School Association, upon the 250th Anniversary of Harvard University, November 5, 1886* (Cambridge: Harvard University, 1887), 123.

13 Josef Redlich, *The Common Law and the Case Method in American University Law Schools* (New York: Carnegie Foundation for the Advancement of Teaching, 1914), 16, 35.

14 James Barr Ames to Charles W. Eliot (August 14, 1895), Harvard Law School Dean's Office Records, Papers and Presidential Records of Charles W. Eliot 1807–1945, Harvard University Archives.

15 Brandeis, *Proceedings of the Annual Meeting of the Harvard Law School Association, June 12, 1890*, 3. See James Schouler, "Cases without Treatises," *American Law Review* 23 (January 1889): 2; Warren, *History of the Harvard Law School and of the Early Legal Conditions in America*, 2:504; "Notes," *Harvard Law Review* 2, no. 3 (1888): 144; "Notes," *Harvard Law Review* 5, no. 5 (1891): 238.

16 "Memoir of James Barr Ames," in James Barr Ames, *Lectures on Legal History and Miscellaneous Legal Essays* (Cambridge: Harvard University Press, 1913), 6–7; *Centennial History of the Harvard Law School, 1817–1917* (Boston: Harvard Law School Association), 81–82, 185–86; Mary B. MacManamon, "The History of the Civil Procedure Course: A Study in Evolving Pedagogy," *Arizona State Law Journal* 30, no. 2 (1998): 412, n. 66.

17 George W. Kirchwey, "Law, Education for the," *A Cyclopedia of Education*, ed. Paul Monroe (New York: Macmillan, 1912), 3:662; Charles W. Eliot, Annual Report of the President of Harvard University 1879–80, 15–16.

18 Redlich, *The Common Law and the Case Method*, 18–25, 37, 40.

19 William P. LaPiana, "Just the Facts: The Field Code and the Case Method," *New York Law School Law Review* 36 (1991): 335, esp. 327–35. See Bruce A. Kimball,

"'The Highest Legal Ability in the Nation': Langdell on Wall Street, 1855–1870," *Law and Social Inquiry* 29, no. 1 (2004): 80–83.

20 Eugene Wambaugh to James B. Thayer (February 17, 1892), James Bradley Thayer Papers 1787–1902, Harvard Law School Library Special Collections. See Eugene Wambaugh, *The Study of Cases: A Course of Instruction in Reading and Stating Reported Cases* (Boston: Little, Brown, 1891).

21 James B. Thayer, *Select Cases on Evidence at the Common Law* (Cambridge, MA: John Wilson and Son, 1892); James B. Thayer, *Cases on Constitutional Law, with Notes* (Cambridge, MA: John Wilson and Son, 1894–1895), 2 vols.

22 Quotation is from James B. Thayer to Sophie Thayer (June 17, 1883), Memoranda Books, vol. 6, James Bradley Thayer Papers 1787–1902, Harvard Law School Library Special Collections. See Thayer, *Cases on Evidence*, iii; Thayer, *Cases on Constitutional Law*, iv.

23 See Thayer's correspondence and records in James Bradley Thayer Papers 1787–1902, Harvard Law School Library Special Collections, box 16; Thayer, *Cases on Constitutional Law*, vi. Compare John C. Gray, *Select Cases and Other Authorities on the Law of Property* (Cambridge, MA: John Wilson and Son, 1888–1892), 6 vols.

24 James B. Thayer to Charles W. Sever (August 13, 1892); Charles W. Sever to James B. Thayer (September 14, 1898); Frank Heywood Hodder to James B. Thayer (April 6, 1898); Boston Book Co. to James B. Thayer (April 18, 1901); James F. Colby to James B. Thayer (March 31, 1894); Charles F. A. Currier to James B. Thayer (March 20, 1895); Abner C. Goodell, Jr. to James B. Thayer (March 26, 1895); Robert J. Sprayal to James B. Thayer (March 22, 1901), James Bradley Thayer Papers 1787–1902, Harvard Law School Library Special Collections.

25 Samuel Williston, "James Bradley Thayer," *Harvard Law Review* 15, no. 8 (1902): 601. See Abner C. Goodell, Jr. to James B. Thayer (March 26, 1895); George E. Gardner to James B. Thayer (September 1, 1898), James Bradley Thayer Papers 1787–1902, Harvard Law School Library Special Collections.

26 Albert Coates, "The Story of the Law School at the University of North Carolina," *North Carolina Law Review* 47 (October 1968): 46. See William P. LaPiana, *Logic and Experience: the Origin of Modern American Legal Education* (New York: Oxford University Press, 1994), 144; Frederick C. Hicks, *Yale Law School: 1895–1915* (New Haven: Yale University Press, 1938), 43–45; John Ritchie, *The First Hundred Years: A Short History of the School of Law of the University of Virginia for the Period 1826–1926* (Charlottesville: University of Virginia Press, 1978), 54–56; Elizabeth Gaspar Brown, *Legal Education at Michigan: 1859–1959* (Ann Arbor: University of Michigan Press, 1959), 200, 209; Louis R. Wilson, *The University of North Carolina, 1900–1930: The Making of a Modern University* (Chapel Hill: University of North Carolina Press, 1957), 551–52.

27 See, for example, "Grant University Law Department," *The University Echo*, January 11, 1907; "Chattanooga Law College Ends Successful Year," *Chattanooga Times*, June 4, 1911; "Annual Sermon Today Starts Commencement for Graduates of Chattanooga College of Law," *Chattanooga Times*, June 5, 1927; "College of Law

Has No Freshmen," *Chattanooga Times*, September 3, 1943; Gilbert E. Govan and James W. Livingood, *The University of Chattanooga: Sixty Years* (Chattanooga: University of Chattanooga Press, 1947), 87–89.

28 Charles A. Graves to James B. Thayer (May 9, 1895); R. McPhail Smith to Charles W. Sever, (January 27 1896); C. A. [Graves] to James B. Thayer (September 3, 1900), James Bradley Thayer Papers 1787–1902, Harvard Law School Library Special Collections; J. Edwin Hendricks, *Wake Forest University School of Law: One Hundred Years of Legal Education 1894–1994* (Winston-Salem: Wake Forest University Press, 1994), 14, 21; Edwin Luther Green, *A History of the University of South Carolina* (Columbia,: The State Company, 1916), 237; Daniel Walker Hollis, *University of South Carolina* (Columbia: University of South Carolina Press, 1951), 2:117, 208–09, 239, 276–77; Orville A. Park, "History of the Mercer Law School" (June 1930) [bound typescript], Mercer University Law School Archives, 2–6; Gwen Y. Wood, *A Unique and Fortuitous Combination: An Administrative History of the University of Georgia School of Law* (Athens: University of Georgia Law School Association, 1998), 49; Robert P. Brooks, *The University of Georgia: Under Sixteen Administrations 1785–1955* (Athens: University of Georgia Press, 1956), 162–63; University of Florida College of Law, *University Record 1914–15*, 22–28; "Florida Man to be Law Dean," *Washburn Review* (August 18, 1915): 1.

29 Harry First, "Legal Education and the Law School of the Past: A Single-Firm Study" *Toledo Law Review* 8, no. 1 (1976): 135–67; Ohio Northern University Annual Catalogue 1914–1915, 99; Eugene N. Hanson, "History of the Claude W. Pettit College of Law of Ohio Northern University," *Ohio Northern University Law Review* 1 (1973): iii; H. L. Wilgus, "Founding of the College of Law of the Ohio State University," *Ohio State University Bulletin* 10 (February 1906): 19–41; Ohio State University Catalogue for 1895–96, 125–32; Ohio State University, *Catalogue of the College of Law* 1900–01, 18–19; 1910–11, 24–25; W. Edward Sell, *The Law Down: A Century Remembered—A 100 Year History of the University of Pittsburgh School of Law* (Pittsburgh: Edward W. Sell, 1995), 5–38; Jeffrey A. Unaitis, "Historical Perspective: The Syracuse University College of Law: A Ninety Year Commitment to Excellence," *Syracuse Law Review* 36, no. 3 (March 1985): 895–98; Andrew V. Clements, "Albany Law School 1851–1951," *Albany Law Review* 15, no. 2 (January 1951): 154; Elizabeth K. Allen and Diana S. Waite, *Albany Law School, 1851–2001: A Tradition of Change* (Albany: Albany Law School, 2000), 61.

30 Walter B. Cannon, "The Case Method of Teaching Systematic Medicine," *Boston Medical and Surgical Journal* 142 (January 1900): 31–36. Cannon sent his article to "William Osler [of Johns Hopkins Medical School] then dean of clinical instruction in the United States," Saul Benison et al., *Walter B. Cannon: The Life and Times of a Young Scientist* (Cambridge: Harvard University Press, 1987), 66.

31 Walter B. Cannon, "The Case Method System in Medicine," *Boston Medical and Surgical Journal* 142 (1900): 563.

32 Charles W. Eliot, "The Inductive Method applied to Medicine," *Boston Medical and Surgical Journal* 142 (1900): 557–58; Walter T. Councilman, "The Course in

Pathology at the Harvard Medical School," *Boston Medical and Surgical Journal* 142 (1900): 558–63; Herbert L. Burrell, "A Personal Experience in the Teaching of Surgery," *Boston Medical and Surgical Journal* 142 (1900): 565–67; James Barr Ames, "Discussion" in "Some Advances in Medical Instruction," *Boston Medical and Surgical Journal* 142 (1900): 568.

33 Cannon, "The Case Method of Teaching Systematic Medicine," 31–36; Cannon, "The Case System in Medicine," 563–64; Walter B. Cannon, "The Use of Clinic Records in Teaching Medicine," *Bulletin of the American Academy of Medicine* 5 (1900–02): 203–13. See, for example, J. William White and Alfred C. Wood, *Surgical Methods and Results: In Cases of Tubercular Disease, Aneurism, Ununited Fractures, Head Injuries, Neoplasms, Vesical Calculi, and Diseases of the Bones and Joints* (Philadelphia: American Journal of the Medical Sciences, 1893); C. Eugene Riggs, "A Case of Injury to the Left Angular Gyrus," *Journal of Nervous and Mental Disease* 20, no. 9 (September 1895): 560–64.

34 Emphasis in original. Richard C. Cabot, *Differential Diagnosis: Presented through an Analysis of 383 Cases* (Philadelphia: W. B. Saunders, 1911), 19. See Richard C. Cabot, *Case Teaching in Medicine*, 1st ed. (Boston: D. C. Heath, 1906); Richard C. Cabot, *Case Histories in Medicine*, 2d ed. (Boston: W. M. Leonard, 1912); Walter B. Cannon, "Dr. R. C. Cabot's 'Case Teaching in Medicine,'" *Harvard Graduates' Magazine* 14 (1906): 609–10.

35 Robert E. Scully, "Preface—Weekly Clinico-pathological Exercises Founded by Richard C. Cabot," *New England Journal of Medicine* 342, no. 2 (January 13, 2000): 115.

36 Bruce A. Kimball, *The "True Professional Ideal" in America: A History* (Oxford: Blackwell, 1992), 277–93.

37 Kenneth M. Ludmerer, "Reform at Harvard Medical School, 1869–1909," *Bulletin of the History of Medicine* 55 (1981): 343–70; Thomas N. Bonner, "The German Model of Training Physicians in the United States, 1870–1914: How Closely Was It Followed?," *Bulletin of the History of Medicine* 64 (1990): 18–34.

38 Kenneth M. Ludmerer, *Learning to Heal: The Development of American Medical Education* (New York: Basic Books, 1985); William G. Rothstein, *American Medical Schools and the Practice of Medicine: A History* (New York: Oxford University Press, 1987); Daniel C. Tosteson, S. James Adelstein, and Susan T. Carver, eds., *New Pathways to Medical Education* (Cambridge: Harvard University Press, 1994).

39 Robert Gordon and James Howell, *Higher Education for Business* (New York: Columbia University Press, 1959), 20.

40 Melvin T. Copeland, "The Genesis of the Case Method in Business Instruction," in *The Case Method at the Harvard Business School*, ed. Malcolm P. McNair (New York: McGraw-Hill, 1954), 25.

41 Copeland, "The Genesis of the Case Method in Business Instruction," 29–30. Here and below, I draw from this essay and Melvin T. Copeland, *And Mark an Era: The Story of the Harvard Business School* (Boston: Little, Brown, 1958), 254–72.

42 John C. Baker, interview with Bruce A. Kimball (October 1995), on file with the author.

43 Wallace B. Donham, "Business Teaching by the Case System," *American Economic Review* 12 (1922): 53–65.

44 Copeland, *And Mark an Era*, 254–72.

45 Quotation is from Pearson Hunt, "The Case Method of Instruction," *Harvard Education Review* 21, no. 3 (1951): 175. On Whitehead, see Wallace B. Donham, *Business Adrift* (New York: McGraw-Hill, 1931), viii.

46 See the articles in Cecil E. Fraser, ed., *The Case Method of Instruction* (New York: McGraw-Hill, 1931); McNair, ed., *The Case Method at the Harvard Business School*; C. Roland Christensen with Abby J. Hansen, *Teaching and the Case Method: Text, Cases, and Readings* (Boston: Harvard Business School, 1987), 24, 33. Note the irony that, writing during the Red Scare, McNair tried to dissociate business case method from Deweyan pragmatism but ended up endorsing Deweyan tenets. See Malcolm P. McNair, "Tough-mindedness and the Case Method," in *The Case Method at the Harvard Business School*, 15–24.

47 John Dewey, *How We Think*, 2nd ed. (New York: Henry Holt, 1933), 72–73; John Dewey, "The Nature of Inquiry," in *Logic: The Theory of Inquiry* (New York: Henry Holt, 1938), 101–19; John E. Smith, *Purpose and Thought: The Meaning of Pragmatism* (Chicago: University of Chicago Press, 1978), 88; H. S. Thayer, *Meaning and Action: A Critical History of Pragmatism*, 2nd ed. (Indianapolis: Hackett, 1981), 190–93, 424–29.

48 T. S. Henry, "The Problem Method of Teaching," *School and Home Education* 36 (1917): 162–68; A. Bess Clark, "An Experiment in Problem Teaching," *English Journal* 6, no. 8 (1917): 535–38; L. W. Mayberry, "Individualizing Problems for Pupils," *Elementary School Journal* 18, no. 2 (1917): 133–37; Herbert G. Lull, "The Problem Method of Instruction and Its Probable Correlation in Library Service," *Library Journal* 42 (1917): 683–85; C. C. More and W. L. Duckering, "The Problem Method at the Army Engineering School, Camp A. A. Humphreys," *Engineering News-Record* 83 (1919): 183–85; W. Jerold O'Neil, "The Problem Idea in Teaching History," *Normal Instructor and Primary Plans* 26 (March 1917): 50, 68; Marvin J. Stormzand, *Progressive Methods of Teaching* (New York: Houghton Mifflin, 1924); E. M. Paulu, "Classroom Activities Under the Problem Method," *Educational Administration and Supervision* 14 (1928): 217–38; Fannie J. Rayland, "Teaching Junior High School Geography through Current Problems," *High School* 4 (1927): 94–98; Mendel E. Branam, *A Teacher's Geography Emphasizing the Problem Method* (New York: Macmillan, 1929); Marietta Stephenson, "The Problem Method of Approach," *Virginia Journal of Education* 22 (1929): 422.

49 Thus, the first business casebooks were titled: Arch W. Shaw, *An Approach to Business Problems* (Cambridge: Harvard University Press, 1916); Melvin T. Copeland, *Market Problems* (Chicago: A. W. Shaw Co., 1920).

50 Copeland, "The Genesis of the Case Method in Business Instruction," 27.

51 Gordon and Howell, *Higher Education for Business*, 6, chap. 2; Frank C. Pierson, *The Education of American Businessmen: A Study of University-College Programs in Business Administration* (New York: McGraw-Hill, 1959), chap. 10; Kirsten

Gallagher, "In Europe, MBA Fever: Dramatic Growth of Programs Spurs Concern Over Quality Control," *Chronicle of Higher Education* (December 1, 1993): A41; Mary Crystal Cage, "Beyond the B.A.," *Chronicle of Higher Education* (January 29, 1994): A29.

52 James E. Howell, "Business Education: Colleges" in Lee C. Deighton, ed., *The Encyclopedia of Education* (New York: Free Press, 1971), 1:525; Christensen, *Teaching and the Case Method: Text, Cases, and Readings*, 16, 21–23; Todd Bridgman, Stephen Cummings, and Colm McLaughlin, "Restating the Case: How Revisiting the Development of the Case Method Can Help Us Think Differently about the Future of the Business School," *Academy of Management Learning and Education* 15, no. 4 (November 2016): 2–3.

53 The introduction of "problem-based learning" into medical education, beginning in the 1970s and expanding in the 1980s and 1990s, appears to evidence the same tendency to intermingle the analogical tradition, based upon formal knowledge with codified canons and rules of the game, with the problem tradition, endorsing certain Deweyan views on epistemology and pedagogy. See, for example, Howard S. Barrows and Robyn M. Tamblyn, *Problem-based Learning: An Approach to Medical Education* (New York: Springer, 1980); H. S. Barrows, "A Taxonomy of Problem-based Learning Methods," *Journal of Medical Education* 20, no. 6 (1986): 481–86; H. S. Barrows and P. J. Feltonovich, "The Clinical Reasoning Process," *Journal of Medical Education* 21, no. 2 (1987): 86–91.

54 Virginie F. C. Servant-Miklos, "The Harvard Connection: How the Case Method Spawned Problem-Based Learning at McMaster University," *Health Professions Education* (July 2018): 163–71; Tosteson et al., *New Pathways to Medical Education*, 20–29, 89, 163.

55 Bridgman et al., "Restating the Case," 2–3; Virginie F. C. Servant-Miklos, "Fifty Years On: A Retrospective on the World's First Problem-based Learning Programme at McMaster University Medical School," *Health Professions Education* 5, no. 1 (July 2018), 3–12.

2

How America Did (and Didn't) Influence English Legal Education, circa 1870–1965

DAVID SUGARMAN

The "Anglo-American Legal Community" and the Creation of Modern Law Schools and Legal Science, circa 1870–1914

The creation of modern law schools, and of liberal legal science ("classical orthodoxy"), was in important respects a transnational enterprise fashioned between approximately 1870 and 1914. A small number of full-time, elite jurists in a small number of elite institutions constituted, transmitted, and legitimated university-based legal education and scholarship for a relatively small and elite few who would become the legal establishment.[1] This informal community was essentially homogenous in terms of class, ethnicity, gender, and education. Constituted by personal relationships, members shared the conviction that the singularity of the common law tradition reflected the uniqueness of the Anglo-American character and that a common law legacy was the cornerstone of political liberty and constitutional progress—a notion that performed legal, political,[2] social, and racial functions.[3] The project created a significantly enhanced role for university law teachers at a time when most lawyers in England[4] and America[5] had no university education in law or any other subject. Establishing a competence that was both useful to the aristocracy of the profession and sufficiently scholarly to merit a place in the university sector (without being unduly threatening), the principal role carved out by the new professional law professors was the exposition, simplification, and synthesis of the leading cases of the common law, along with identifying the core principles of which the leading cases were illustrative. It sought to demonstrate that the apparent chaos of the law was in fact grounded in a few general principles akin to the axioms of geometry.

There are several important intellectual components to what has been labelled "classical legal thought."[6] First, John Austin's ideas concerning the nature of the common law—the role of force in law, the separation of law and morals and the nature of sovereignty—were enormously influential.[7] Second, the new university education focused almost exclusively on "pure law," which was defined as private law. Public law, especially administrative law, was beyond the pale. Third, it was assumed that the standpoint of law teachers was that of elite lawyers and appellate judges, that is, as insiders of the legal system. Fourth, the new legal science focused on cases, courts, and judges. Finally, while the new mode of legal education and scholarship would introduce more demanding intellectual standards for legal education, it rejected the idea of law as a policy science developed during the Scottish Enlightenment, by Jeremy Bentham and his more radical followers, and by the early American elite lawyers' conception of "lawyer statesman—science of legislation" legal education.

The classical orthodoxy also had an important social component, being a significant constitutor of identity, influencing what university law teachers did with their professional lives. Above all, perhaps, the classical orthodoxy reflected what the average student was deemed able to assimilate, what the average law professor was able and willing to teach, and what the legal profession and the judiciary were adjudged to be prepared to tolerate. As a mode of education, it had the preeminent virtue of being relatively cheap, thus enabling large numbers of students to be taught by small faculties.

None of the above should imply unanimity of thought within the Anglo-American legal community[8] or that personal relations were not competitive and strained. Moreover, it is clear that from about 1914 onward the Anglo-American legal community declined. Nonetheless, the Anglo-American special relationship survived, albeit in a less exalted form, and American law schools continued to influence English legal education and scholarship.[9]

The Anglo-American Legal Community circa 1914–1965: Discontinuity and Divergence

For all the rhetoric of the Anglo-American legal community, the reality was two seemingly divergent legal systems. The creation of the new American state, especially from the late nineteenth century onward, greatly enlarged the powers of the national judiciary. This, in turn, rendered the elites of the American bar and bench, to "a quite extraordinary extent, key actors in the battles and decisions over the design of governance"[10]—more so, and certainly more visibly, than in England. While England's lawyers did play a wide-ranging role in governance at home and abroad, they exhibited greater denial about their lawyer-statesman function. Furthermore, they tended to resist university legal education and any formal instruction in the policy bases of the common law and legislation. The principal desideratum was the maintenance of the status quo—economic, political, cultural, educational, and especially professional—that had given at least the elite of the profession significant and unprecedented autonomy, social status, monopolies, and income. Maintaining this status quo required the profession to continue preserving a considerable measure of continuity and cohesion.

Although the legal community of judges, advocates (barristers), and solicitors was neither unitary nor monolithic, it represented a form of collegial professionalism[11] within which there was a relatively clear and generally accepted pecking order reflecting a wide measure of consensus regarding basic ideas and values. In short, the institutional structure and ideology of the legal system and the legal community served to perpetuate a conservative bias, understood by those within the system to be the prototype of professionalism. Support for any other view risked stigmatization as "political" or "unprofessional."[12]

The dominant form of legal training and education in England circa 1700–1965—apprenticeship—was well suited to meet the needs of a profession so conceived.[13] Apprenticeship entailed learning on the job, emulating more experienced lawyers, and learning through repetition. As Lord Coleridge put it: "[T]he circuits [that is, associations of barristers practicing in a particular geographical area] were great schools of professional conduct and professional ethics; and the lessons learnt upon them were to receptive minds of unspeakable value."[14] In the jurisprudence of this unwritten code of homosocial behavior we see many echoes of the common law.

Apprenticeship embodied the lawyers' self-conception of law as a singular, practical craft, best learned in legal practice. "Respectability" and gentlemanly status were emphasized over technical skill and legal knowledge, thereby aligning the profession to the culture and values of the leading elites (the landed and middle classes). It was also sustained by a limited commitment to market forces: the damage that poor-performing lawyers could do was limited by "the safety mechanism of the market."

Most young men (and more recently women) of sufficient means who planned a career in the law studied Classics, Mathematics, or the Natural Sciences at university, receiving a formal legal education only from dining at the Inns of Courts (if they were barristers) and from private coaches (crammers[15]) in order to pass the intellectually undemanding examinations for aspiring barristers and solicitors. Indeed, the value of a degree of good academic quality was considered debatable:

> There is no doubt that to have gained a "blue" [that is, an award earned in the participation of sports, such as athletics and rowing, at Oxford and Cambridge] is one of the best advertisements a young barrister can have. A "blue" with only a pass degree will stand a better chance of an early start at the Bar than he would if he had sacrificed his athletics to obtain even a first class in honours.[16]

England's legal profession enjoyed a monopoly over legal education and sought to preserve it insofar as possible.[17] Under this optic, university legal education was a lower level "vocational" activity, akin to university degrees in plumbing. Therefore, in stark contrast with continental Europe and the United States, most English lawyers, and virtually all superior court judges, did not study law at university.

Moreover, academic law and academic lawyers threatened to subvert the traditional hierarchies within the profession, as well as the consensus, cohesion, and cultural capital that sustained both the legal elite and the common law. Indeed, those who practiced, especially at the Bar, regarded university law teachers as self-defined failures, unable to make it in practice. There were only a few exceptions to this condescension.[18]

It took more than fifty years for law graduates to be granted exemption from the professional examinations for lawyers.[19] Not until the late 1970s did the solicitors' profession become a graduate-entry profession and abandon five-year articles of clerkship (apprenticeship) as an alternative path to qualification. The Bar Council introduced a similar rule change in 1979.[20] Even today, some lawyers and judges claim that a university legal education is inferior to the study of nonlaw subjects and that nonlaw graduates are likely to become better and more successful lawyers.[21]

In America, the organized legal profession was weaker than its English counterparts,[22] making it easier to institutionalize academic university legal education. Being a single profession, it lacked the official ranks or specialities of lawyers that existed in England and continental Europe—distinctions that in many respects actually helped to sustain professional cohesion. The new American law schools were thus able to develop largely free of controls by the state or the organized profession.[23] They were therefore able to recruit full-time teachers rather than part-time practitioners, innovate with the curricula, and stipulate their own admissions policies, eventually requiring undergraduate degrees as a prerequisite to admission. The American Bar Association, founded in 1878, and the Association of American Law Schools, founded in 1899, increasingly argued in favor of university law schools, as both organizations wanted a postgraduate profession and an elite profession.[24] By 1945, fifteen states had abolished apprenticeships, and a three-year postgraduate law degree was well on the way to becoming a requirement in almost every jurisdiction.[25]

The opportunities for both academic–judicial–practitioner movement and collaboration, and for academic-state cooperation, were greater in the United States.[26] In England, the work of legal academics was rarely cited before the courts[27] or otherwise acknowledged, and they did not hold senior judicial appointments until the 1990s.

The experience of the New Deal and the growth of a federal bureaucracy, and the internalization of these by American law schools and lawyers, did not eclipse private law doctrinal analysis. But it did mean that administrative law was more widely recognized and that some limited policy analysis operated as an adjunct to the prevailing orthodoxy in legal education.[28]

Dissatisfaction with the classical orthodoxy, as a body of ideas and as an educational practice, had been gathering momentum from the 1890s. The advent of sociological jurisprudence and Legal Realism–which both owed more to American conditions than English forebears—were taken as challenging the classical orthodoxy of Anglo-American jurisprudence under which law is characterized as an autonomous system of rules and principles that courts apply logically in an objective fashion to reach a determinate and apolitical judicial decision.

Realists and their fellow travelers co-opted both the Socratic method of teaching and the casebook to challenge the assumptions of legal education as private law science. In both their orthodox and subversive guises, the casebook and Socratic method elevated the law teacher to center stage. The elite schools of the United States did not lack self-confidence—in striking contrast to their English counterparts, where the dogmatic textbook tradition continued to prevail and, as L. C. B. Gower complained, "English teachers of law suffer from an acute inferiority complex."[29]

One area of significant contrast between America and England during the period 1914–1965 concerned the state of higher education and support for academic research. Until the late 1960s, the university sector in England was open to a tiny proportion of the population relative to other countries in Europe, North America, and Australasia, thereby curtailing its intellectual possibilities. In the United States, there was more money for university education, research budgets, and the expansion of student numbers and academic posts and therefore greater stimulation to open thinking than in England.

In England, academic law was not held in high esteem by academics from other faculties until at least the 1980s. Brian Simpson said of Oxford in the 1950s: "The law school was treated as the appropriate home for rowing men of limited intellect."[30]

From the advent of modern legal education and science, the unenviable position of the English law school, relative to its American counterpart, increasingly became a staple of British and Commonwealth-American legal literature.[31]

> If England and America are two countries divided by a common language— . . . they were even more deeply divided by legal education. In

the 1950s, 15 times as many law students were enrolled at American universities as in English degree courses.[32] Nearly half the English students were at Oxbridge, another fifth in London, and the rest in fewer than ten provincial universities.[33] By contrast, American students were dispersed across the country in more than 200 law schools. There were fewer than 300 full-time law faculty members in England.[34] By contrast, there were several thousand American law professors. English legal education was still marginal to legal practice. Only about half of English lawyers had a university degree, and significantly fewer had a law degree, whereas all had apprenticed.[35] Because apprenticeship had effectively disappeared in the United States before World War One, virtually every lawyer graduated from law school.[36]

Legal positivism seemed to exercise a more pervasive influence in Britain than in other parts of the English-speaking world. H. L. A. Hart, England's most influential legal philosopher of the twentieth century, acknowledged that he was "terribly distrustful of sociology in general. [That distrust is] the Oxford disease."[37]

At the end of the 1970s, two successive Presidential Addresses at the annual conference of the Society of Public Teachers of Law—the principal professional association of British university law teachers at the time—reflected on the position of the contemporary law teacher; both were less than complimentary.[38] Both presidents had studied in, and been inspired by, US legal education. Harry Street observed:

> My overall view of English law teachers' periodical writing is that the standard is indefensibly low. . . . The choice of topics is often unimaginative. Article after article on the same area, normally only because there are conflicting decisions which others have also written about. Too much detailed examination of isolated decisions or tedious reanalysing of groups of decisions.[39]

While this assessment perhaps gave insufficient weight to that small body of work that was imaginative and ambitious, English legal scholarship overall fared badly. Although long debated, virtually no serious research on legal education had been undertaken in Britain. Similarly, the dearth of empirical research on law in society is striking.

While there continued to be an increase in the number of students from the new British Commonwealth (principally Africa and Asia) studying law in Britain,[40] a shift toward the United States—in terms of legal education, legal scholarship, and the preferred destination for law graduates looking to study abroad—is evident within the Old British Commonwealth, including Canada, Australia, and New Zealand, and elsewhere, especially since the 1990s.[41]

The seemingly invidious comparison between England and America was not limited to the study of law but extended to the social sciences more generally.[42] Thus, the "empirical," antitheoretical, highly vocational tendencies within English legal culture seemingly mirrored a wider bias within British cultural life.[43]

The Anglo-American Legal Community circa 1914–1965: Continuities and Convergence

The increasing gulf between American and English legal culture was more a difference of degree than kind. Moreover, in focusing on the contrasts between the two nations, commentators have tended to neglect or deemphasize important continuities, parallels, and paradoxes.

Significant contacts continued between the elite US law schools and their counterparts in Britain. Moreover, the successive challenges to the classical orthodoxy from the late nineteenth century onward was almost as much the outcome of a transatlantic network of jurists as the legal orthodoxy they sought to dethrone. A public and private transnational conversation developed that sought to change the professional identity of law professors, and contacts with the United States were further sustained by Continental scholars, émigrés, and exiles who had settled in England and were in touch with colleagues who had emigrated to the United States.[44]

The center of this Anglo-American countermovement in England was the London School of Economics (LSE); and at its heart was the British-born Harold Laski (1893–1950), LSE's professor of political science from 1926 to 1950.[45] In 1915, Laski accepted an invitation to teach history and political theory at Harvard University, largely on the recommendation of Felix Frankfurter. Laski retained strong ties with the

United States for the rest of his life. Of particular importance were his friendships with Frankfurter, later to become an adviser of President Franklin Roosevelt and a Supreme Court justice; Justice Oliver Wendell Holmes, the outstanding figure in American law; and Dean Roscoe Pound, who introduced Laski to sociological jurisprudence. Laski was a lifelong Harvard Law School enthusiast.[46] His importance to English legal education and scholarship stems from his role as a bridgehead between legal elites of American and England; as probably the person who introduced to an English audience Holmes's pragmatic attitude to law (legal pragmatism),[47] sociological jurisprudence,[48] and American Legal Realism; as a detractor of Austinian notions of sovereignty and of law as command and of the Langdell-Oxford concept of law as science; as a central figure at LSE and an important, albeit controversial, influence on the LSE faculty and students; and as a critic of English legal education who (with others) hoped to see some equivalent of Harvard Law School emerge in Britain.[49] The flagship of this movement was the *Modern Law Review*, which began publication in June 1937 by proclaiming:

> English legal periodicals have hitherto dealt almost exclusively with the technical aspects of the law. . . . [This] isolates the law too much from those contemporary social conditions in which it must always operate. . . . The *Review* deals with the law as it functions in society.[50]

The most important manifestation of this counterattack on the classical orthodoxy was in the field of public law, notably administrative law.[51] Laski, William Robson, and Ivor Jennings[52] joined forces with the American pioneers of administrative law, lawyers, and political scientists—Frank J. Goodnow (Johns Hopkins), Ernst Freund (Chicago), Felix Frankfurter, and James M. Landis (Harvard)[53]—to defend administrative justice as a legitimate mode of regulation and an academic subject. Realism was the intellectual conduit through which they recognized that judging was inherently discretionary, that judges were biased, and that, therefore, the legitimacy of judicial review was problematic.

Robson, in his pathbreaking "masterpiece"[54] of 1928, led the charge against those tenets of Austin and Albert Venn Dicey that helped to sustain the legal orthodoxy, recognizing his debt to American scholarship:

> I cannot conclude . . . without paying tribute to the work of some of the distinguished jurists and judges whose brilliant writings the United States of America is giving to the world. . . . I believe that no more brilliant literature concerning the problems of law in relation to modern life is to be found than that which is emerging from the constellation of theoretical jurists and practising lawyers who dwell across the Atlantic and whose work enriches not merely their own country but the whole civilised world. . . . I have gained much through friendly discourse on both sides of the Atlantic with friends and colleagues working in the same field.[55]

However, administrative law as an academic subject developed more slowly in England than in either the United States or Canada. Only in 1963 were the first student textbook exclusively on English administrative law and the first comprehensive study of the state of civil liberties in Britain, *Freedom, the Individual and the Law*, published.[56] One coauthor of the textbook on English administrative law, J. A. G. Griffith of the LSE faculty, was inspired by Laski, Robson, and Jennings. Griffith's coauthor, Harry Street of the University of Manchester Law Department, had also authored *Freedom, the Individual and the Law*.

Street had held a fellowship at Columbia University in 1947–1948, working with Walter Gellhorn on a comparative study of government liability. This introduced him to American legal ideas and to the role of American law professors in law reform, a role Street successfully emulated upon his return home. His research on government liability led him to advocate the reform of the civil liability of the British state,[57] his scholarship in the field of torts law stressed the interests of the plaintiff,[58] and he championed the comprehensive reform of personal injury law.[59] His views were inspired by American debates and scholarship[60] as well as by developments in continental Europe.

It was also from the 1960s onward that D. G. T. (David) Williams, a British-born, Cambridge educated scholar who won a Harkness fellowship to Berkeley and Harvard, sought to broaden further the study of civil liberties and administrative law—again stimulated in part by his American experience. Williams was an important role model for the development of civil liberties and public law within, and beyond, the Cambridge law faculty.[61]

Another legal field—corporate law—was also transformed by a transnational network presided over by L. C. B. (Jim) Gower (of LSE) and Louis Loss (Harvard). Gower was the most respected academic authority on company law that England has ever produced.[62] Loss, in turn, was the most respected academic authority on securities regulation ever to have come out of the United States. Both played significant roles in transforming corporate law/securities regulation from vocational, Cinderella-type subjects to intellectually ambitious fields fashioned for both practitioner and academic audiences. Both focused lucidly and engagingly on underlying legal principles. They also sought to understand those principles in their historical and economic contexts, emphasizing the purpose and operation of the principles pertinent to practice. Where the law could be improved, they said so. Criticism was often informed by references to developments in other jurisdictions, recognizing the value of a comparative perspective.

From 1948 to 1962, Gower was Cassel Professor of Commercial Law at LSE, and he developed the teaching of company law within the LLM, influenced by Laski, American writings, and his experience of practice. Gower and Loss corresponded regularly from the 1940s until their deaths in 1997, becoming close friends when Gower was a visiting professor at Harvard Law School in 1954. Loss's *Securities Regulation*[63] provided an important model for Gower when he was preparing his *Modern Company Law*,[64] and Loss offered detailed comments on Gower's drafts of the book. Gower's return from Harvard highlighted the significant differences in teaching load, resources, support, and time for research and collaborative work at LSE compared to Harvard. Ground down by red tape and weary of struggles with the legal profession over the reform of English legal education, Gower increasingly sought roles in Africa and elsewhere, where he felt he could make a difference, retiring early from LSE to continue his various public roles. In 1981, he was appointed as a one man commission to reform investor protection in Britain. His *Review of Investor Protection*[65] led to the adoption of a new regime of securities regulation that came as close as possible to introducing an American-style mini–Securities and Exchange Commission into Britain.

Other examples of US influence on England, frequently sustained by Anglo-American networks, include several fields: the English legal system, legal services and access to justice,[66] restitution,[67] commercial law,[68] torts,[69] constitutional and administrative law,[70] legal history and historical jurisprudence,[71] and legal education and jurisprudence.[72] American ideas and approaches were appropriated by those British scholars who subscribed to the classical legal tradition, as well as by individuals desirous of modifying or dethroning the prevailing legal orthodoxy.

There have been occasional efforts to introduce the case method and Socratic-style teaching into English legal education.

> [Harry Street] was one of the few successful English practitioners of the "case method" or Socratic method which he had observed with admiration at Columbia. . . . This rigorous method of instruction had a profound effect on his students, more fully appreciated in retrospect than at the time—an experience, one said years later, more terrifying than appearing before any High Court judge.[73]

Glanville Williams adopted the Socratic method at Cambridge for about a decade beginning around 1968. However, the experiment was not popular with students and ceased after Williams's retirement in 1978.[74] Indeed, doubts about the merits of the case method can be found in both jurisdictions.

Both the United States and England have experienced significant growth in the number of law schools, law teachers, students, as well as the range of courses on offer, thereby increasing the diversity of educational experiences, faculty, and students.[75] Another parallel between the United States and England is the ambiguous heritage of sociological jurisprudence and Legal Realism. In both countries, the critique of legal orthodoxy associated with sociological jurisprudence and Legal Realism has had a powerful impact on academic law. But in each country that impact has been contested, controversial, complex, attenuated, and paradoxical. Legal Realism has itself been subjected to caricature and ridicule.[76] Law teachers and legal scholars frequently lacked an in-depth understanding of the varieties, specifics, and ambiguities of sociological jurisprudence and American Legal Realism.

Today, most UK and US legal scholars would claim that they believe in the importance of policy, politics, context, and indeterminacy in understanding law. Nonetheless, the central tenants of legal scholarship and education in Britain and American since the 1870s continue to dominate on both sides of the Atlantic, albeit in attenuated form.[77] Making sense of, and developing strategies for addressing, the inevitable connections between law, law schools, and the outside world continue to elude legal scholars in both countries. The clash between what students want and expect, and what their teachers want to give them, remains unresolved.

The reasons for this continuity and parallelism are many and complex. Importantly, the conditions that sustain university legal education have remained constant: sufficient student demand and finance; the cost of education; and the need for legal education to be sufficiently harmonious with the status and economic interests of the legal profession, of lawyers' principal clients, and of the university and government. Innovation in legal education operates within these confines.[78]

Moreover, transcending a professional identity based on cases and the rules found in cases has proved difficult. Legal doctrinalism appears consistent and familiar, "a place where everyone knows your name."[79] Critics have yet to make substantial headway in creating the new professional identity that may be a necessary prerequisite to establishing a viable alternative to legal orthodoxy.[80]

The next section returns to the early twentieth century and considers the experience of English legal academics who studied and/or taught in American law schools circa 1914–1965.

Going to America circa 1914–1965

From the early twentieth century, formal and informal mechanisms existed at Oxford and Cambridge (known colloquially as "Oxbridge") to channel their best law graduates to US law schools to further their studies and to work as teaching assistants.[81] The elite American law schools were in good financial shape, and a variety of scholarships and fellowships enticed the brightest students. British and other foreign students were increasingly attracted to studying in US law schools after 1945, with the graduate programs' recruitment of overseas students "animated in part by a kind of missionary function: a desire to spread US legal models to other parts of the world."[82]

The preeminence of Oxbridge in sending its students to the United States reflects its hegemonic role in the production of jurists in Britain and the strength of its institutional and personal connections with the United States. The dearth of women—who only appear in any numbers from the 1980s onward–reflects the relatively small number of women in English legal education at this time. Information derived from interviews indicates that, while some English students were dissatisfied with their experience of studying law in England, the decision to study in the United States did not automatically or logically follow. Often students venturing to the United States had little idea of what they were getting into and little or no knowledge of American legal thought and education.[83] For those who were or were to become law teachers, Harvard was the most popular and important of American law schools. While an LLB/JD was the principal degree taken by English students in the United States until the 1960s, thereafter there was a significant increase in the number of British students taking masters and doctorates.[84] Those who studied in the United States had significant involvement in the broadening of legal education in England and in other jurisdictions—especially in modes that challenged the formalist orthodoxy.

The experience of those who studied in the United States should be distinguished from those who took up teaching and teaching assistant appointments shortly after graduation. Those who studied in the United States tended to praise the quality of their education and point to the significant impact on their professional development and scholarship. Similarly, those who experienced life in US law firms typically gained much from the experience.[85]

Those who taught in the United States, at least shortly after graduation, seem to have had a less satisfactory experience, largely as a consequence of the case method and Socratic method of teaching. Most subsequently rejected these approaches, reinforcing a tendency to view homegrown education and values as superior to those abroad.[86] Of the significant number of British legal scholars who taught in the United States,[87] some found the students more challenging and the law school environment more stimulating,[88] whereas others enjoyed the higher income, status, and support afforded by US law schools.

While the American law school encouraged some English students to broaden their intellectual horizons and to develop "socially orientated legal thought," this was far from universal. Only some of those who studied and taught in the United States brought back American ideas and approaches. Furthermore, English legal scholars were influenced by ideas from, or teaching in, overseas law schools other than the United States, including continental Europe and the British Commonwealth (notably, Africa).[89] Indeed, the less insular scholars engaged with both American and other foreign ideas. Criticism of misplaced reliance on American theoretical and other perspectives is occasional but recurrent.[90] It is important, therefore, not to exaggerate the impact of American ideas and experiences on the character and development of English law schools and legal scholarship.

While American law schools and legal scholarship were important, their impact existed alongside the development of legal education in Africa. During the late 1950s and 1960s, a cadre of fledgling British law teachers, inspired by Legal Realism and their experience in American legal education, elected to teach law in Africa, frequently along with American expatriates supported by the Ford Foundation. The experience of teaching, researching, writing, and institution-building, not to mention grappling with an altogether unfamiliar legal system and culture, demonstrated that law could be understood only in the light of history, culture, politics, and economic conditions. This "African moment" also fostered an interest in legal education and its politics. Upon returning to Britain, these expatriates adapted for British audiences the intellectual and pedagogical innovations fashioned for African audiences. The broadening of legal education and scholarship in England from circa 1965 onward, and the establishment of a generation of "radical" law schools in the 1970s and beyond, owe much to the American-African experience of several leading lights.[91]

Afterword

Legal education in the United Kingdom should not be viewed in isolation from the rest of the world. After all, UK lawyers and legal academics have played significant roles in the creation, development, and legitimation of international markets for goods, services, constitutions, and ideas, including the export and import of legal models. Moreover, the United Kingdom has not been immune from some aspects associated with the Americanization of legal services and education.[92] But as intellectual historians well know, "influence" is a slippery concept. American influence on English legal education was mediated by local conditions and local personalities. While some British scholars looked enviously at American law schools, others did not. For every British scholar haunted by the "invidious comparison" between America and Britain, there was probably at least an equal number who, if asked about the inferior state of English legal education, "would have protested laughingly: 'Never mind. It is *our own*—and it is greater than the sum of its defects.'"[93] Moreover, American-inspired ideas coexisted alongside antiimperialist skepticism about US-led orthodoxies. There is a sense in which people found what they wanted to find in US law schools. The United States sustained both legal orthodoxy and its critics simultaneously, more or less continuously and sometimes within the same individual.

The history of the Anglo-American relationship suggests that the American law school does not travel well.[94] Harvard Law School is so untypical; law schools vary considerably within and among countries. Reflecting on his engagement with the politics of legal education during the previous fifty years, William Twining cautioned:

> [In] advocating that American ideas should be taken seriously in the UK, I now think that I underestimated the differences in respect of funding, the higher education systems, legal culture, the organisation of legal services and the politics of legal education. A few American ideas have been borrowed and adapted, such as law school clinics and books of cases and materials, but by and large this has proved to be an indigestible transplant. However, the prestige of American law schools has provided a useful foil for critique of our own arrangements.[95]

To date, the transnational turn in legal historiography and sociolegal studies has been largely confined to the transnational promotion of legal norms, notably, the efforts to transplant American- or English-style law or lawyering to other nations and the borrowing of legal texts.[96] As the contributions in this volume demonstrate, deeply contextualized transnational histories of legal education illuminate the ways in which domestic legal institutions, movements, and ideas are a feature of international relations and the global history of ideas. The transnational history of legal education also contributes to our understanding of how, why, and when legal exports and imports can promote progressive improvements, the status quo, illiberal ideas,[97] or all of these. It is a salutary reminder that those who prescribe legal norms and institutions for another society must first consider basic issues of historical experience, institutional structure, political power, and the like.

A focus on difference as well as similarity encourages us to be self-conscious about our inevitable biases. After all, nobody can escape the peculiarities of their own place and time; even global history must come from somewhere. Similarly, the transnational history of legal education and ideas confronts us with our own conceptual and ideological frameworks, problematizing our assumptions about the fundamental character of legal systems, the fixity of its categories and institutions and the prevailing characterizations of what receives most attention, and what is suppressed or marginalized.[98] At its best, it fosters greater dialogue with historical scholarship more generally, with allied legal fields such as comparative law, sociolegal studies, and legal life-writing, as well as with cognate disciplines such as anthropology, feminism–women–gender studies, colonial/postcolonial studies, and sociology. It suggests a rebalancing while demonstrating the value of humility.

Several stimulating transnational intellectual histories of law have emerged from the comparative, transnational, and colonial/postcolonial turns in historiography. These include the examination of mutual interactions or independent but parallel developments in several jurisdictions, the influence of "foreign" thinkers, and changes in the organization and character of objects, such as legal literature, on a particular legal system. These studies give due weight to difference, refusing to treat the West, the common law, Western legal tradition, the center, or the metropolis as the unstated norm. This work explicates the distinctiveness of local and national experience, illuminating the ways in which peripheries constituted the center and vice-versa and how their experience might be quite different.[99] Moreover, it questions or qualifies the principal story lines in the historical treatment of lawyers and law schools in the English-speaking world. At its best, it recognizes the deep implication of gender,[100] race, colonialism, imperialism,[101] and power in their creation and development over time. Under this optic, the comparative history of legal education and thought adds a new and important dimension to the current reconfiguration of center periphery relations in legal history. Rather than the transplantation of particular legal institutions, models, rules, or concepts, what can perhaps be discerned is the movement of ideas, the framing of phenomena and of reactions to it. In sum, valuable though it is to focus on the transplantation of American legal education and on university legal education, to do only that is perhaps to look through the wrong end of the telescope.

NOTES

This chapter is a revised version of David Sugarman, "A Special Relationship? American Influences on English Legal Education, c. 1870–1965," *International Journal of the Legal Profession* 18, no. 1 & 2 (March–July 2011): 7–57. I would like to thank Léonie Sugarman for her helpful suggestions for improving my writing.

1 The elite character of the intended audience for academic university education is evident in the celebrated Inaugural Lectures of Blackstone (1758) and Dicey (1883).

2 Politically, it was characterized by a fear of socialism, disorder, and the consequences of majoritarianism, and in economic affairs, a commitment to classical liberalism. These concerns animated much middle-class politics and political thought during this period on both sides of the Atlantic. See, for example, George Dangerfield, *The Strange Death of Liberal England* (London: Harrison Smith, 1935); Elie Halevy, *A History of the English People in the Nineteenth Century* (London: Ernest Benn, 1952); Daniel Peck, *Faces of Degeneration: A European Disorder, c.1848–c.1918* (Cambridge: Cambridge University Press, 1989). On the connections between this conjuncture and legal thought, see, for example, Arnold M. Paul, *Conservative Crisis and the Rule of Law* (Ithaca: Cornell University Press, 1960); Charles McCurdy, "Justice Field and the Jurisprudence of Government-Business Relations," *Journal of American History* 61, no. 4 (1975): 970; P. S. Atiyah, *The Rise and Fall of Freedom of Contract* (Oxford: Clarendon Press, 1979), pt. III; David Sugarman, "'The Legal Boundaries of Liberty': Dicey, Liberalism and Legal Science," *Modern Law Review* 46, no. 1 (1983): 102, and "Bourgeois Collectivism, Professional Power and the Boundaries of the State: The Private and Public Life of the Law Society, 1825–1914," *International Journal of the Legal Profession* 3, no. 1–2 (1996): 81.

3 The Anglo-American legal community embraced the belief that England and America were linked by a joint inheritance, of which the English constitution—parent of all constitutions in the English-speaking world—was the key element. This view was frequently allied to the notion of the essential unity of "the Anglo-Saxon race." Anthony Brundage and Richard A. Cosgrove, *The Great Tradition: Constitutional History and National Identity in Britain and the United States, 1870–1960* (Stanford: Stanford University Press, 2007).

4 On the history of modern legal education in Britain, see Brian Abel-Smith and Robert Stevens, *Lawyers and the Courts* (London: Heinemann, 1967), chaps. 7 and 13; Rosemary Auchmuty, "Early Women Law Students at Cambridge and

Oxford," *Journal of Legal History* 29, no. 1 (2008): 63–97; J. H. Baker, *750 Years of Law at Cambridge* (Cambridge: Faculty of Law, University of Cambridge, 1996), and *Legal Education in London, 1250–1850* (London: Selden Society, 2007); Raymond Cocks, *Foundations of the Modern Bar* (London: Sweet and Maxwell, 1983), esp. chaps. 2 and 8; Fiona Cownie and Raymond Cocks, *"A Great and Noble Occupation!" The History of the Society of Legal Scholars* (Oxford: Hart, 2009); Neil Duxbury, *Jurists and Judges: An Essay on Influence* (Oxford: Hart, 2001); Neil Duxbury, *Frederick Pollock and the English Juristic Tradition* (Oxford: Oxford University Press, 2004); Neil Duxbury, "English Jurisprudence between Austin and Hart," *Virginia Law Review* 91, no. 1 (2005): 91; F. H. Lawson, *The Oxford Law School, 1850–1965* (Oxford: Clarendon Press, 1968); Patrick Polden, "The Education of Lawyers," in the *Oxford History of the Laws of England*, vol. 11 (Oxford: Oxford University Press), 1175–1222; David Sugarman, "Beyond Ignorance and Complacency: Robert Stevens' Journey Through Lawyers and the Courts," *International Journal of the Legal Profession* 16, no. 1 (2009): 7, David Sugarman, "Legal Theory, the Common Law Mind and the Making of the Textbook Tradition," in *Legal Theory and Common Law*, ed. William Twining (Oxford: Basil Blackwell, 1986): 26.

5 On the history of the American law school since 1850, see, for example, Alfred Z. Reed, *Training for the Public Profession of the Law* (New York: Carnegie Foundation for the Advancement of Teaching, Bulletin 15, 1921); Robert B. Stevens, *Law School: Legal Education in America from the 1850s to the 1980s* (Chapel Hill: University of North Carolina Press, 1983); Hugh C. Macgill and R. Kent Newmyer, "Legal Education and Legal Thought, 1790–1920," in *The Cambridge History of Law in America*, vol 2, ed. M. Grossberg and C. Tomlins (New York: Cambridge University Press, 2008), 36; Daniel R. Coquillette and Bruce A. Kimball, *On the Battlefield of Merit: Harvard Law School, the First Century* (Cambridge: Harvard University Press, 2015). On American legal thought and the transatlantic turn to history: David M. Rabban, *Law's History* (Cambridge: Cambridge University Press, 2014).

6 Readers will, I hope, appreciate that my model, which is based on historical materials, conveys tendencies and taken-for-granted assumptions rather than hard-and-fast extremes. One can always find counterexamples. Thus, the act of generalization—of trying to distinguish the wood from the proverbial trees—simplifies the ideas of the jurists concerned. More generally, classical legal science (like all orthodoxies, conservative or otherwise) has tended to be vulgarized by both followers and critics alike and is often more complicated than "the received view." See, for example, W. L. Morison, *John Austin* (London: Edward Arnold, 1982) chap. 5; David Sugarman, "Legal Theory, the Common Law Mind and the Making of the Textbook Tradition," 37–48 (discussing the simplification and distortion of the ideas of Bentham and Austin); Bruce A. Kimball, "Langdell on Contracts and Legal Reasoning: Correcting the Holmesian Caricature," *Law & History Review* 25, no. 2 (Summer 2007): 345.

7 Richard A. Cosgrove, *Our Lady of the Common Law: An Anglo-American Legal Community, 1870–1930* (New York: New York University Press, 1987), 110–126 and 208–210 (on Holmes and Pound, respectively); Duxbury, *Frederick Pollock*, chap. 3 (on Pollock).

8 Even in its salad days, the classical orthodoxy was the subject of countercurrents and criticism as reflected, for example, in the ideas of Maitland (England) and Holmes (United States).

9 On the influence of American case law and juristic writing on English judges: Duxbury, *Jurists and Judges* and *Pollock*.

10 William E. Forbath, "Politics, State-Building, and the Courts, 1870–1920," *The Cambridge History of Law in America*, vol. 3, ed. M. Grossberg and C. Tomlins (New York: Cambridge University Press, 2008), 644.

11 T. J. Johnson, *Professions and Power* (London: Macmillan, 1972).

12 Abel-Smith and Stevens, *Lawyers*; W. W. Pue, *Lawyers' Empire* (Vancouver: University of British Columbia Press, 2016) chaps. 4, 7, 8, 11.

13 The Inns of Court provided some formal lectures and moots for those intending to practice as barristers from the middle ages to the end of the seventeenth century. However, the teaching function of the Inns collapsed in the eighteenth century and was not revived until the mid-nineteenth century, when it operated in a limited fashion; thus we see the persistence and significance of apprenticeship in the training and education of lawyers until the late twentieth century: J. H. Baker, *The Third University of England* (London: Selden Society, 1990), and *The Law's Two Bodies* (Oxford: Oxford University Press, 2001), 73–90; Christopher W. Brooks and Michael Lobban, "Apprenticeship or Academy? The Idea of a Law University, 1830–1860," in *Learning the Law*, ed. Jonathan A. Bush and Alain A. Wijffels (London: Hambledon Press, 1999), 353–82; David Lemmings, *Professors of the Law* (Oxford: Oxford University Press, 2000), chap. 4.

14 Ernest Hartley Coleridge, *Life and Correspondence of John Duke Lord Coleridge, Lord Chief Justice of England*, vol. 1 (London: Heinemann, 1904), 177.

15 "Crammers" were so called because they were associated with that mode of legal education and testing that put a premium on memorizing ("cramming") rules and their exceptions.

16 Sir Theodore Martin, *A Life of Lord Lyndhurst* (London: John Murray, 1903), 54.

17 Cf. Brooks and Lobban, "Apprenticeship or Academy? The Idea of a Law University, 1830–1860."

18 Frederic Pollock and A. L. Goodhart enjoyed a high reputation among the judiciary and the Bar.

19 The Solicitors Act 1922 exempted law graduates from the Intermediate examination, and, following the 1934 reorganization of the Bar examinations into discrete Part I and Part II examinations, graduates were finally exempted from the whole of Part I.

20 Andrew Boon and Julian Webb, "Legal Education and Training in England and Wales," *Journal of Legal Education* 58, no. 1 (March 2008): 87.

21 Aishah Hussain, "To become a lawyer don't study law, says Supreme Court's Lord Sumption—Do History, Classics, Economics or Languages Instead," *Legal Cheek*, last modified October 10, 2018, www.legalcheek.com.

22 Michael Burrage, *Revolution and the Making of the Contemporary Legal Profession* (Oxford: Oxford University Press, 2006), 253–326, 434–61.

23 But this should be read in the light of the American Bar Association's exclusive and absolute power over the accreditation of American law schools conferred on the ABA by the US Department of Education in 1952.

24 Jerold Auerbach, *Unequal Justice* (New York: Oxford University Press, 1976); Stevens, *Law School*, chap. 6.

25 Stevens, *Law School*, chaps. 10 and 11.

26 Robert W. Gordon, "The American Legal Profession, 1870–2000," in *The Cambridge History of Law in America*, vol. 3, ed. M. Grossberg and C. Tomlins (New York: Cambridge University Press, 2008), 87–90.

27 Save for Sir Frederic Pollock: see, generally, Lord Diplock, "A.L.G.: A Judge's View," *Law Quarterly Review* 91 (1975): 458.

28 Contrast the American situation as described here with the situation in England, where the ghost of Dicey continued to temper the recognition and development of administrative law. Even passionate anglophiles, such as Frankfurter, despaired at the impoverished state of English administrative law: F. Frankfurter, Foreword to "Discussion of Current Developments in Administrative Law," *Yale Law Journal* 47 (1938): 517.

29 L. C. B. Gower, "English Legal Training. A Critical Survey," *Modern Law Review* 13, no. 2 (1950): 198.

30 A. W. Brian Simpson, *Reflections on The Concept of Law* (Oxford: Oxford University Press, 2011), 33.

31 L. C. B. Gower, "English Legal Training"; K. C. Davis, "The Future of Judge-made Public Law in England," *Columbia Law Review* 61 (1961): 201.

32 Richard L. Abel, "Comparative Sociology of Legal Professions," in *Lawyers in Society: Comparative Theories*, ed. Richard L. Abel and P. S. C. Lewis (Berkeley: University of California Press, 1989), 80–153, table 5, and *The Legal Profession in England and Wales*, table 3.2 (Oxford: Basil Blackwell, 1988).

33 Abel, *The Legal Profession in England and Wales*, 265 and table 3.2.

34 Ibid., 267.

35 In 1949, 57 percent of those called to the Bar were university graduates, and just 40 percent were law graduates; in 1956, 41 percent of admitted solicitors were university graduates, and only about a third were law graduates. Ibid., tables 1.5, 2.3.

36 Richard Abel, "Law School," *International Journal of the Legal Profession* 16, no 1 (2009): 16, 49–58, 50–51.

37 David Sugarman, "Hart Interviewed," *Journal of Law and Society* 32, no. 2 (2005): 291.

38 H. Street, "The University Law Teacher," *Journal of the Society of Public Teachers of Law* 14 (New Series) (1979): 247. W. L. Twining, "Goodbye to Lewis Eliot: The

Academic Lawyer as Scholar," *Journal of the Society of Public Teachers of Law* 15 (New Series) (1980): 2.

39 Street, "The University Law Teacher," 247.

40 On some of the contemporary linkages between African legal education and British imperialism, see John Harrington and Ambreena Manji, "'Mind with Mind and Spirit with Spirit': Lord Denning and African Legal Education, *Journal of Law and Society* 30, no. 3 (2003): 376.

41 On the American turn in Canadian legal education and thought, see, generally, *Law and Learning: Report to the Social Sciences and Humanities Research Council of Canada by the Consultative Group on Research and Education in Law* (Ottawa: Social Sciences and Humanities Research Council of Canada, 1983). On the shift within Israeli legal education toward elite American models, see Pnina Lahav's contribution to this volume (chapter 12).

42 M. Bulmer, "Pity the Poor Cousins," *Times Higher Education Supplement* 23 (January 1987): l3.

43 Contrast Perry Anderson, "The Origins of the Present Crisis," *New Left Review* 23 (1964): 26, with Stefan Collini, *Absent Minds* (Cambridge: Cambridge University Press, 2006).

44 C. Glasser, "Radicals and Refugees: The Foundation of the Modern Law Review and English Legal Scholarship," *Modern Law Review* 50, no. 6 (1987): 688; J. Beatson and R. Zimmerman, eds., *Jurists Uprooted: German-Speaking Emigré Lawyers in Twentieth Century Britain* (Oxford, Oxford University Press, 2004).

45 See, further, Kingsley Martin, *Harold Laski* (London: Gollancz, 1953); Isaac Kramnick and Barry Sheerman, *Harold Laski* (London, Hamish Hamilton, 1993); Michael Newman, *Harold Laski* (London: Macmillan, 1993).

46 However, Laski was critical of some aspects of Harvard education. He argued that the Oxbridge system of tutorials better served the goals of humanistic education relative to the American system of formal lectures.

47 Including Holmes's critique of the Anglo-American orthodoxy that judges were, or could be, wholly impartial arbiters; and Holmes's emphasis that the life of law is experience, not logic.

48 Including the ideas of Continental jurists that he had first encountered at Harvard, notably, Duguit. Cf. Carol Harlow, "The Influence of Léon Duguit on Anglo-American Legal Thought," in *Autour de Leon Duguit*, ed. F. Melleray (Brussels: Bruylant, 2011), 227.

49 Abel-Smith and Stevens, *Lawyers*, 184–85.

50 W. Robson, "Editorial Introduction," *Modern Law Review* 1 (1937): 1. The first article of the first issue was an essay by the leading American Realist Felix S. Cohen.

51 Richard Rawlings, "Distinction and Diversity: Law and the LSE," in *Law, Society, and Economy: Centenary Essays for the London School of Economics and Political Science 1895–1995*, ed. Richard Rawlings (Oxford: Clarendon Press, 1997). 7; Martin Loughlin, "Modernism in British Public Law, 1919–79," *Public Law* (2014): 56.

52 Martin Loughlin, *Public Law and Political Theory* (Oxford: Clarendon Press, 1992), chap. 6.

53 The network also included the English-born and Oxford- and Harvard-educated John Willis. Willis founded Canadian Realist–inspired administrative law.

54 Bernard Crick, "Robson, William Alexander (1895–1980)," in *Oxford Dictionary of National Biography* (Oxford: Oxford University Press, 2004).

55 Robson, *Justice and Administrative Law*, xvii–xviii (London: Macmillan first ed. 1928) (second ed., 1947). Robson, like several of his Anglo-American compatriots, was also influenced by continental European thinkers, notably François Geny.

56 J. A. G. Griffith and H. Street, *Principles of Administrative Law* (London: Pitman, 1963), and Harry Street, *Freedom, the Individual and the Law* (London: Penguin Books, 1963). On the influence of American legal culture and public law on British legal ideals, see Ian Loveland, ed., *A Special Relationship? American Influences on Public Law in the UK* (Oxford: Clarendon Press, 1995).

57 Harry Street, *Governmental Liability: A Comparative Study* (Cambridge: Cambridge University Press, 1953).

58 Harry Street, *The Law of Torts* (London: Butterworths, 1956).

59 D. W. Elliott and Harry Street, *Road Accidents* (London: Allen Lane, 1968).

60 In the case of road accidents, Street acknowledged the assistance that he had received from Michigan law professor Alfred F. Conard.

61 On D. G. T. Williams, see Bob Hepple, "Obituary: Sir David Williams," *The Guardian*, September 22, 2009.

62 The discussion of Gower and Loss derives, in part, from the author's interview with L. C. B. Gower of 1988, and David Sugarman, "In Memoriam, Jim Gower and Louis Loss: Doyens of Corporate Law and Exemplars of the Anglo-American 'Special Relationship,'" *The Company Lawyer* (March 1998): 65 and 96.

63 Louis Loss, *Securities Regulation* (Boston: Little, Brown, 1951).

64 L. C. B. Gower, *Modern Company Law* (London: Stevens, 1954).

65 Part 1, 1984; Part 2, 1985 (London: HMSO, Cmnd 9125).

66 R. M. Jackson, *The Machinery of Justice in England* (Cambridge: Cambridge University Press, 1940); Michael Zander, *Cases and Materials on the English Legal System* (London: Weidenfeld and Nicholson, 1973); Geoffrey Wilson, *Cases and Materials on the English Legal System* (London: Sweet & Maxwell, 1973); Carol Harlow and Cyril Glasser, "Legal Services and the Alternatives: The LSE Tradition," in *Law, Society, and Economy. Centenary Essays for the London School of Economics and Political Science 1895–1995*, ed. Richard Rawlings (Oxford: Clarendon Press, 1997).

67 Robert Goff and Gareth Jones, *The Law of Restitution* (London: Stevens, 1966).

68 The author's interviews with professors Roy Goode (Queen Mary College, London University, October 30, 1988) and Clive Schmitthoff (London, 1988).

69 Patrick Atiyah, *Accidents, Compensation and the Law* (London: Weidenfeld & Nicholson, 1970).

70 Ian Loveland, ed., *A Special Relationship? American Influences on Public Law in the UK* (Oxford: Clarendon Press, 1996); Martin Loughlin, "Modernism in British Pub-

lic Law, 1919–79," *Public Law* (2014): 56; P. P. Craig, *Public Law and Democracy in the United Kingdom and the United States of America* (Oxford University Press, 1990).

71 R. H. Graveson, *Status in the Common Law* (London: the Athlone Press, 1953), a work inspired by and dedicated to Roscoe Pound, who contributed an Introduction; Abel-Smith and Stevens, *Lawyers*.

72 William Twining, *Jurist in Context: A Memoir* (Cambridge: Cambridge University Press, 2019), chaps. 4 and 7.

73 J. C. Smith, "Harry Street, 1919–1984," *Proceedings of the British Academy* 72 (1987): 479.

74 The author's interview with professor Sir Bob Hepple (Cambridge, July 2011).

75 Twining, *Blackstone's Tower*.

76 Twining, "Academic Law and Legal Philosophy."

77 William W. Fisher III concluded: "A chastened version of the Harvard model still rules the waves." "Legal Theory and Legal Education, 1920–2000," in *The Cambridge History of Law in America vol III*, ed. M. Grossberg and C. Tomlins (New York: CUP, 2008), 72. See also Richard Collier, "'We're All Socio-legal Now?'" *Sydney Law Review* 26, no. 4 (2005): 503; Elizabeth Mertz, *The Language of Law School: Learning to "Think like a Lawyer"* (Oxford: Oxford University Press, 2007).

78 Robert W. Gordon, "Modes of Legal Education and the Social Conditions That Sustain Them," *SELA Papers. Paper 5* (Yale Law School Legal Scholarship Repository, 2002): 9.

79 Echoing the theme song from the television sitcom "Cheers."

80 Joseph William Singer, "Review of Laura Kalman, Legal Realism at Yale, 1927–1960," *California Law Review* 76 (1998): 467.

81 Hazeltine and Holland at Cambridge in the 1920s and 1930s, and Lawson at Oxford and Gower at LSE in the 1950s, were among the key "talent spotters" and facilitators.

82 Gail J. Hupper, "The Academic Doctorate in Law: A Vehicle for Legal Transplants?," *Journal of Legal Education* 58, no. 3 (2008): 413, 414; Bruce A. Kimball, "The Context of Graduate Degrees at Harvard Law School under Dean Erwin N. Griswold, 1946–1967," *New England Law Review* 49, no. 3 (2014–15): 449.

83 The author's interviews with professors William Twining (Oxford, April 29, 1994), Robert Stevens (Oxford, April 18, 1994), and Michael Zander (London, November 22, 1988).

84 Hupper, "The Academic Doctorate in Law: A Vehicle for Legal Transplants?,"; Kimball, "The Context of Graduate Degrees at Harvard Law School under Dean Erwin N. Griswold, 1946–1967"; Gail J. Hupper, "Educational Ambivalence: The Rise of a Foreign-Student Doctorate in Law," *New England Law Review* 49, no. 3 (2015): 319.

85 The author's interviews with professors Robert Stevens (April 18, 1994) and Michael Zander (November 22, 1988).

86 The author's interview with Peter Birks (July 13, 1994). Robert Stevens similarly did not much enjoy his experience as a teaching fellow at Northwestern, though

he enjoyed the courses he audited: the author's interview with professor Robert Stevens (April 18, 1994).

87 Some of the many British faculty who taught at US law schools during the period under review include: W. W. Buckland (Cambridge), Stanley de Smith (LSE), P. B. Carter (Oxford), J. Hackney (Oxford), G. H. Treitel (Oxford), H. W. R. Wade (Oxford), J. K. B. M. Nicholas (Oxford), J. H. C. Morris (Oxford), Kurt Lipstein (Cambridge), Clive Schmitthoff (London), G. H. Jones (Cambridge), John Tiley (Cambridge), Tony Weir (Cambridge), Sir Peter North (Oxford), L. C. B. Gower (LSE), Otto Kahn-Freund (LSE and Oxford), K. W. Wedderburn (LSE), and H. L. A. Hart (Oxford).

88 The author's interviews with professors William Twining (April 29, 1994) and Robert Stevens (April 18, 1994).

89 On which see below.

90 See, for example, Martin Loughlin, "The Importance of Elsewhere," *Public Law Review* 4 (1993): 44; Carol Harlow, "A Special Relationship? American Influences on Judicial Review in England," in *A Special Relationship? American Influences on Public Law in the UK*, ed. I. Loveland (Oxford: Clarendon Press, 1995), 79.

91 Twining, *Jurist in Context*, chaps. 5, 6, and 12; William Twining, "McAuslan in Context: Early Days in Dar and Warwick," in *Land Law and Urban Policy in Context: Essays on the Contributions of Patrick McAuslan*, ed. T. Zartaloudis (London: Birkbeck Law Press, 2017), 35; John Harrington and Ambreena Manji, "The Limits of Socio-Legal Radicalism," *Social and Legal Studies* 26, no. 2 (2017): 702–03.

92 John Flood, "Legal Education, Globalization, and the New Imperialism," in *The Law School: Global Issues, Local Questions*, ed. Fiona Cownie (Aldershot: Ashgate, 1999), 127.

93 The quotation is from Lawrence Durrell, *Mountolive* (London: Faber, 1958), 89.

94 See, for example, Jayanth K. Krishnan, "Professor Kingsfield Goes to Delhi: American Academics, the Ford Foundation, and the Development of Legal Education in India," *American Journal of Legal History* 46, no. 4 (2004): 447.

95 Twining, *Jurist in Context*, 219. For a pertinent account of how legal transplants may constitute "legal irritants," see Gunther Teubner, "Legal Irritants: Good Faith in British Law or How Unifying Law Ends up in New Divergences," *Modern Law Review* 61, no. 1 (1998): 11.

96 For an exemplary example of transnational approaches to US history, see Daniel T. Rodgers, *Atlantic Crossings: Social Politics in a Progressive Age* (Cambridge: Harvard University Press, 1998).

97 James Q. Whitman, *Hitler's American Model* (Princeton: Princeton University Press, 2017).

98 Cf. George P. Fletcher, "Comparative Law as a Subversive Discipline" *American Journal of Comparative Law* 46, no. 4 (1998): 683.

99 For example, see Assaf Likhovsky, "Czernowitz, Lincoln and Jerusalem and the Comparative History of American Legal Thought," *Theoretical Inquiries in Law* 4 (2003): 621, and "A Colonial Legal Laboratory? Jurisprudential Innovation in

the British Empire," *American Journal of Comparative Law* (forthcoming 2020); Shaunnagh Dorsett and John McLaren, eds., *Legal Histories of the British Empire* (London: Routledge, 2014); Jedidiah J. Kroncke, *The Futility of Law and Development* (Oxford: Oxford University Press, 2016); Pue, *Lawyers' Empire*; Mark Lunney, *A History of Australian Tort Law, 1901–1945: England's Obedient Servant?* (Cambridge: Cambridge University Press, 2018); R. W. Kostal, *Laying Down the Law: The American Legal Revolutions in Occupied Germany and Japan* (Cambridge: Harvard University Press, 2019). See, generally, Assaf Likovsky, "Intellectual History," in *The Oxford Handbook of Historical Legal Research*, ed. Markus D. Dubber and Christopher Tomlins (Oxford: Oxford University Press, 2018). See also the discussion of the "African moment" in English legal education above.

100 For example, see Susan Bartie, *Free Hands and Minds: Pioneering Australian Legal Scholars* (Oxford: Hart, 2019).

101 For example, see P. G. Monateri, "Black Gaius: A Quest for the Multicultural Origins of the 'Western Legal Tradition,'" *Hastings Law Journal* 51, no. 3 (2000): 479; Antony Anghie, *Imperialism, Sovereignty and the Making of International Law* (Cambridge: Cambridge University Press, 2012); Yves Dezalay and Bryant Garth, *Asian Legal Revivals: Lawyers in the Shadow of Empire* (Chicago: University of Chicago Press, 2010); John Harrington and Ambreena Manji's contribution to this volume (chapter 5).

PART 2

Americanization—Critical Histories

3

American Influences, Canadian Realities

How "American" Is Canadian Legal Education?

PHILIP GIRARD

Canada's legal profession is characterized by a hybrid heritage in which both American and English influences have played a role.[1] This chapter will focus on one particular aspect of this heritage: the influence of US-style university legal education, especially the Harvard model, on Canadian legal education. Indeed, the early adoption of the US system is one of the elements that most distinguished the Canadian legal profession from its English counterparts over the twentieth century. Statements about US influence are almost rote in accounts of Canadian legal education,[2] but few have attempted to investigate it deeply or trace it over time, and the Canadian literature remains regionally fragmented.[3] While legal education in Quebec's civil law historically followed the European model with some local variation, the influence of US legal education has not been absent there either. That complex story will not be considered here, except for the situation at McGill University's faculty of law, which sought to model itself to some extent on American Ivy League law schools in the twentieth century.[4] Consideration of the US influence on Canadian legal education provides a unifying theme that allows one to transcend the limitations of a regional perspective.

It bears emphasizing that the porous US-Canadian border has led to exchanges in both directions, in both legal education and professional organization. In a recent study of the rise and fall of the four-year, public law–oriented law degree at the University of Minnesota's law school, pioneered during the interwar years by its Canadian dean, Everett Fraser, Eric Adams questions the working assumption "that directions in legal education emanated outwards (and northwards) from an American wellspring," noting "that influential ideas about legal education . . .

travelled in both directions across the [international] border."[5] While this Canadian export did not ultimately succeed, another one did. It is seldom acknowledged that the integrated (or unified) bar, which obliges lawyers to belong to and pay fees to a statewide bar association, was a direct import from Canada. Adopted first in 1921 in North Dakota, which based itself on the Saskatchewan Legal Professions Act, it has spread to nearly two-thirds of US states.[6] Like Canadian actors in Hollywood, however, such imports are rapidly Americanized and their origins forgotten.

In one fundamental respect—the decision to maintain a unitary legal profession as opposed to two distinct professions according to the English model—it is possible to speak of a North American legal profession. Lacking Inns of Court in North America, this profession had to rely on its own resources to reproduce itself. Apprenticeship, sometimes supplemented by attendance at court, was the only viable model for educating lawyers. This was learning by doing, observing, and reading. While reading lists could cover an impressive array of law texts, the apprentice lawyer was left on his own to absorb them. Reform efforts inspired differing responses in the new American republic versus the new colony of Upper Canada, with their paths diverging for much of the nineteenth century before reconverging in the twentieth.

Market Solutions versus Collective Action in North American Legal Education

In 1784, Tapping Reeve created the Litchfield Law School, the first of the so-called proprietary law schools, which were privately owned and profit-oriented. This was a new form of legal education, promising actual instruction via lectures in the principles and details of the law by experts to a group of students, though there were no examinations or degrees. This voluntarist, market-oriented approach offered an efficient solution to the problem of professional education for a time and contained within it the seeds of the modern university-based professional law school. Indeed, some of the early university law schools, such as Yale, got their start by absorbing a proprietary law school.[7]

The proprietary law school solution was not adopted in British North America, possibly because the economies of scale did not exist there due to low population density. The creation of the Law Society of Upper Canada (LSUC) by statute in 1797 made possible another model of instruction, one taken on by the bar itself collectively. Unique in the common law world at the time, the 1797 act required that all lawyers belong to the LSUC, created a governance structure, and gave the Society the power to levy dues as well as a monopoly over legal education.[8] Apprenticeship would remain the backbone of that education, but it would be supplemented by a program of lectures, examinations, and exercises established by the Society itself and available only at its headquarters at Osgoode Hall in York, later renamed Toronto. Bar associations in the United States- tended to be city- or county-based and voluntary; in Upper Canada the LSUC was province-wide and compulsory. The ability to collect fees from lawyers everywhere in the province solved the problem of economy of scale, allowing the Society to offer a serious educational program that was fairly advanced for its day.[9]

All other British North American provinces eventually endowed their law societies with the statutory powers of the LSUC, but very gradually. Only Quebec did so prior to Confederation: in 1847 with respect to notaries and in 1849 with respect to advocates. Manitoba and British Columbia did so soon after they joined Confederation, by acts of 1871 and 1874 respectively, and the eastern and new Prairie provinces followed between 1899 (Nova Scotia) and 1907 (Alberta).[10] Thus, very different patterns of professional organization emerged between the United States and Canada in the nineteenth century. At the same time that the bar associations of the colonial period were being dismantled in the United States and apprenticeship was on the wane, British North America's two largest jurisdictions had created a statutory lawyers' guild vested with many of the regulatory powers over lawyers that had formerly been exercised by the courts, one endowed with a monopoly over the provision of legal education.

This divergence in turn profoundly affected the development of legal education, as the university law schools in the United States moved quickly into the vacuum created by the disappearance of the bar associations and the decline of proprietary law schools. It was this political circumstance, more than any other, that allowed American law schools to set their own intellectual agenda without supervision by the bar and to claim a hegemony over legal education that they have never really lost.

Consider the debate over the reintroduction of a mandatory clerkship requirement after law school, which remains one of the key distinguishing features of professional entry as between the United States and Canada. The American Bar Association (ABA) proposed this in 1910 and encouraged the Association of American Law Schools (AALS) to adopt it. In 1913, the ABA formally asked the AALS to adopt it; when it declined, the proposal was dropped, and clerkship eventually disappeared altogether.[11] From a Canadian perspective, it is inconceivable that the law societies or the Canadian Bar Association (CBA) would ever ask the law schools about the need for a clerkship requirement and nothing short of astonishing that, if sought, their opinion would be heeded.

In British North America/Canada, there was no political vacuum with regard to legal education. It was the attitude of the bar that would determine the shape of legal education, though bar leaders were not uniform in their views, and these changed over time.[12] The Canadas, with their strong bar societies, parted ways on this question. In Lower Canada (later Quebec), the grant of statutory powers to the bar assumed the establishment of university legal education. Law faculties teaching civil law were created at McGill in 1848, at Laval University in Quebec City in 1854, and at a branch of Laval at what became the University of Montreal in 1878, though a university law degree was not made a prerequisite to bar admission until much later. The LSUC, for its part, used its monopoly to undermine nascent law programs at Ontario universities in the 1850s and 1860s and to create its own law school (Osgoode Hall Law School in 1889), building on its earlier educational efforts. In this it followed the lead of the English bar, which created the Inns of Court Law School in 1852 in order to forestall demands that professional legal education be given to the universities, a move that was anathema to both barristers and solicitors.

The much weaker bar societies of the Maritime provinces did not seek to create their own law school based on the Ontario model, partly out of lassitude and partly because of the economies of scale problem again. Maritimers were well aware of developments in the US Northeast, however. Their bar societies were only too happy to partner with universities, thereby outsourcing some of their educational responsibilities to a respectable vehicle of middle-class advancement. In the later nineteenth century, many bar leaders themselves came from relatively humble backgrounds, while a few were beginning to pursue the connections between law and big business that would lead to the growth of the large law firm. The lure of a "scientific approach" to the law offered in a university, along with the prestige of a degree, became highly attractive to them, as was the idea that such preparation might better position Maritime lawyers to compete with those from Ontario and Quebec after the Dominion of Canada emerged in 1867.[13] Two generations later, the Prairie provinces followed a similar course. Thus, when Canada imported university legal education, it was largely at the behest of bar leaders, not universities, though the latter were not averse to playing host, provided that money for professorial salaries could be found somewhere.

Harvard Received: 1883–1920

Aspiring lawyers from the Maritimes had the most incentive to seek out university legal education abroad, and did so in quite impressive numbers. Looking at Harvard Law School alone, some ten Maritimers can be found there in the 1840s and 1950s, rising to thirty-seven in the 1860s and forty-three in the 1870s after Christopher Columbus Langdell had begun to work his magic.[14] While not one of these men was involved in the establishment of the law faculty at Dalhousie University in 1883, the developments at Harvard Law School were clearly known to them and to the founders of the Saint John Law School in New Brunswick. In the spring of 1883, a trio of Haligonian lawyers—John Thompson, Wallace Graham, and Robert Sedgwick—went to the United States to explore recent developments in university legal education. On April 16 they went to Harvard Law School and took four Nova Scotians studying there to see Gilbert and Sullivan's *Iolanthe* that evening. The next day, they visited the more traditional Boston University Law School, and then they were off to Columbia to see how things were done there.[15]

In fact, that very year, Harvard Law School had just begun to recover its appeal after a period of heavy resistance to the reforms instituted by Langdell.[16] His innovations are well known: the case method of teaching; a curriculum heavily weighted toward private law and divided between introductory and more advanced subjects; an emphasis on principles and analytical techniques rather than local law; rising standards of admission, eventually culminating in an arts degree or equivalent; a full-time three-year program punctuated with examinations and restricted to degree students; and the development of a career-stream professoriate not drawn primarily from the bar.[17] How far did these new Canadian law schools model themselves on Harvard? Dalhousie Law School from the outset aimed the highest in making law a genuinely university discipline. Its first dean encouraged his audience in his inaugural address "to build up in this city of Halifax a university with faculties of arts, medicine, applied science and law . . . that shall influence the intellectual life of Canada as Harvard and Yale have influenced the intellectual life of New England."[18] Dalhousie was able to contemplate such a journey only because a Nova Scotian philanthropist endowed a chair in constitutional and international law that enabled the hiring of a full-time dean, Richard Chapman Weldon, at an attractive salary. With no such benefactor in sight until much later, the Saint John Law School was for many years dependent mostly on local judges to deliver its curriculum.[19]

Dalhousie's curriculum was not a clone of Harvard's.[20] It straddled the pre- and post-Langdell versions of Harvard, offering separate courses in constitutional history and constitutional law, international law and conflict of laws, as well as private law and practice-oriented subjects, most of them taught by practitioners. It also included courses that were important to local practitioners, such as Maritime Law and Marine Insurance. In this choice one sees a vision of law as shaped by the history and values of a people, as well as a tool of social ordering. And Weldon stressed civic virtue and public service rather than wealth accumulation as proper ideals, while his second in command, Benjamin Russell, emphasized law's more utilitarian aspects and discussed the case law extensively with his students. He used Langdell's casebook on contracts as well as Anson's English text but criticized the case method as too time-consuming for legal education. Weldon, for his part, lectured in the grand manner.

The Dalhousie LLB course, from 1886, was meant to be full-time over three years, and students were discouraged from taking employment—legal or otherwise—during the school year. Dalhousie also managed to wangle a degree privilege out of the Barristers' Society, as did the Saint John Law School: those who acquired a local law degree did not have to pass the bar examination, though they had to satisfy the articling (clerkship) requirement. The admission requirements, however, were still very low by Harvard standards—little more than high school until 1914, when one year of arts at university was required, raised to two years in 1922 with effect from 1924.

Dalhousie and the Saint John Law School were also markedly different from the emerging Harvard model in that their classes were not restricted to degree candidates. Between 25 percent and 30 percent of the student body at both places to about 1925 were non-LLB students. At Dalhousie they were mostly arts students, and it was in this capacity that the first fifteen women took some law courses at Dalhousie, starting in 1899, though none proceeded to obtain the LLB; the first woman formally enrolled for the LLB in 1915, completing it in 1918.[21] Both Dalhousie and Saint John admitted a wide variety of so-called special students, demonstrating an inclusive vision of a law school that was not devoted exclusively to the preparation of future lawyers.[22]

The focus of university legal education shifted next to the Prairies, where Alberta, Saskatchewan, and Manitoba all created university law faculties in quick succession (1912, 1913, and 1914 respectively).[23] All involved cooperation between the local bar and the local university. In Manitoba, the University of Manitoba and the provincial law society created a joint board of trustees to manage the law school, but the Society really called the shots. The bar in British Columbia created its own law schools at Vancouver and Victoria in 1914 (the latter closed in 1923), but it would have been happy to partner with the University of British Columbia in the creation of a law school if the latter had been interested, which it was not until 1945.[24] In both Alberta and Saskatchewan, Maritimers were prominent in the establishment of the new law school, with one Dalhousie LLB present at the creation of each, thus indirectly carrying on the influence of Harvard.

In Manitoba one of the founders, H. A. Robson, although lacking any obvious US connections, was concerned to have the law school adopt modern methods based on American models. He was a fan of the case method and created his own casebook for a course on public corporations, while his colleague J. B. Hugg wrote one on company law. These were not terribly sophisticated casebooks, but Wesley Pue argues that they should be judged positively as a distinctive break with the textbook tradition of teaching law.[25] Robson would also have preferred to substitute a law degree for articling, though he realized this was impossible in the short term. His example shows that the influence of the Harvard model could be diffused even by those who were not graduates.

Robson had a broader platform when he was named chair of the CBA legal education committee in 1915. Founded the previous year and modeled on the ABA, the association would use its persuasive power to try to shape legal education. Much of the impetus for the CBA came from western Canada, which had already shown itself highly receptive to university legal education, and its efforts were directed there rather than shoring up the Osgoode Hall model.[26] American influences on Canadian legal education, especially those of Harvard, were well established by the end of World War I everywhere outside Ontario, but more as ideals than in reality. Starting in the 1920s, the process of implementation would begin.

Harvard Ascendant: 1920–1949

The 1920s featured a number of milestones in Canadian legal education, most of them traceable to the adoption of the Harvard model. A student at the University of Alberta Faculty of Law proudly proclaimed in 1924:

> The law school is modeled after the Harvard practice, which is the greatest law school in the English-speaking world today. The case method of study, which is used there and is recognized to be the best known system for the study of law, is also in use at the Alberta school.[27]

The emergence of a full-time career-stream professoriate and full-time studies for law students, the raising of admission standards, the adoption of the case method, and shifts in the curriculum all either date from or spread more widely during this period. All were facilitated by the growing presence of Canadians as graduate students at Harvard in the 1920s, shortly after graduate study in law was established there.

Many fewer Canadians sought the LLB degree at Harvard after the establishment of university law schools at home. Harvard's 1911 decision to offer graduate study in law to train future law professors revived the Canadian path to Cambridge, where one needed to stay only a year to obtain a doctoral degree.[28] Initially Harvard would not accept Dalhousie

LLB graduates as eligible to enter the SJD (Doctor of Juridical Science) program, but it allowed a few to enroll as special students. One was Sidney Smith (LLB 1920), who spent the next year at Harvard taking essentially undergraduate courses, including Contracts from Williston and Trusts from Scott; in these courses he was thoroughly exposed to the case method.[29] After establishing the LLM degree in 1922, Harvard permitted graduates of selected Canadian law schools to enroll. Admission to the AALS required a law school to have three full-time professors, and this seems to be the threshold that Harvard also used for graduate study eligibility. Osgoode Hall Law School, even though not a university law school, had reached it by 1925, the year before Cecil Augustus (Caesar) Wright was permitted to enroll in the SJD program. Horace Read, who helped to pioneer the advanced LLB program at Minnesota referred to earlier, did both his LLM and his doctorate at Harvard and went on to become dean at Dalhousie from 1950 to 1964.[30]

Sidney Smith became the first professor to use the case method at Dalhousie, where it was rapidly adopted by his colleagues.[31] Already in use in Manitoba in the 1910s, it spread to the other law schools in the 1920s. Other elements of the Harvard program also came into focus at the university law schools in the 1920s. The full-time three-year program spread via Dalhousie to all the Prairie schools, McGill, and the University of Toronto, although the latter offered a BA in law as opposed to an LLB; thus it was not considered by A. Z. Reed in his 1928 report on legal education for the Carnegie Foundation. Reed was particularly impressed with the Prairie law schools. He ranked the Manitoba law faculty the best in Canada and concluded that "the three prairie provinces, with their modern rules, constitute experimental laboratory stations for the rest of the Dominion."[32] The Great Depression would prevent this educational promise from being more effectively realized until after the war. On the scholarly side, however, the events of the 1930s had a more positive impact. The invalidation of New Deal–type legislative reforms by Canadian courts and the Judicial Committee of the Privy Council inspired the turn to a more critical and policy-oriented approach to existing law by some Canadian scholars, largely influenced by the emergence of Legal Realism and sociological jurisprudence in the United States.[33]

During the 1920s the stage was also set for the initial law degree to become an advanced degree on the Harvard model. Here the CBA, egged on by dean MacRae of Dalhousie, played an important role, encouraging law schools in 1922 to require at least two years of university study prior to admission. Most law schools, fearful of the impact on enrollment, opted for one year. Osgoode Hall Law School reverted to a high-school graduation requirement in the 1930s, but pressure for heightened admission standards would return in future years. Bruce Kimball has documented how Harvard was obliged to become more selective in admissions as Langdell's reforms attracted far more qualified students than could be accommodated by the faculty's physical and human resources, with graduates of Catholic colleges the main casualties of the move to restrict access.[34] Beyond Harvard, the move to higher admissions standards has been seen in the United States as an attempt to exclude the working classes and immigrant groups, but this motivation has been disputed in the Canadian context.[35] Canadian law schools had the opposite problem to Harvard: too few applicants, not too many. Before and after the gradual upward creep of admissions standards, Canadian law schools admitted practically everyone who applied.

One exception here was Jewish students at McGill: comprising 40 percent of law students in 1920, strict quotas imposed thereafter reduced their proportion to about 15 percent by 1939.[36] This was not an indirect effect of stricter admission standards but outright discrimination against a group who satisfied those standards. And, conversely, accepting all applicants does not address the fate of those who do not apply at all. Enrolment declined after the two Maritime law schools adopted the CBA admission standard of two years of arts, so severely in the case of Saint John Law School that it almost closed.[37] At Dalhousie, students from backgrounds below those of the middle class slipped from 20 percent in the 1920s to 14 percent in the 1930s.[38] Possibly, enrollments would have declined in any case even without the higher standards (the 1920s were almost as dire economically in the Maritimes as the 1930s), but clearly the new standards did not enhance access to legal education. The special students found at Dalhousie and Saint John also disappeared in the 1920s, a casualty of altered admissions standards and a different vision of legal education. While one cannot discount as a possible motive by bar leaders a desire to exclude minorities, immigrants, and the less well off, they were also concerned that higher admission standards in medicine and dentistry had left law schools with a weaker applicant pool and felt obliged to follow their lead.[39] And in one of the few detailed studies of a Canadian urban bar, that of Halifax, the interwar years witnessed the definitive breaking of the diversity barrier, with blacks, Jews, Arabs, Acadians, and women all present in small but persistent numbers in articling positions and law practice.[40]

There were two ways in which the Canadian experience in this period did not replicate Harvard—one intentional and one more or less unintentional. The intentional divergence was in curriculum. While Harvard's first-year curriculum was very largely followed in Canada—as it was at Harvard itself for 130 years—the upper-year curriculum was not. From 1886, Harvard had a purely elective upper-year curriculum, an innovation that would not appear in Canada until 1969. Before the 1960s, Canadian law schools had insufficient resources—intellectual, financial, or bibliographic—to offer a suite of electives; thus the entire curriculum, which normally featured constitutional law, constitutional history, and English legal history in upper years, was mandatory.[41] While the private law orientation of the first-year curriculum undoubtedly shaped students' ideas about law, the upper-year curriculum did provide some balance on the public law side.

The unintentional departure from Harvard was a result of Canadian regionalism. In contrast to Harvard—where the entire focus was on modes of thought and analytical techniques that were national in the sense that they were divorced from the law of any particular US state—no law school in Canada went down this route. McGill's attempt to offer a national program in both common law and civil law in the 1920s provoked opposition from both the Quebec bar and the university, and it was terminated after a few years.[42] Otherwise, each province outside Quebec had one law faculty, which attracted overwhelmingly students from that province who intended to practice there. Thus, while common law subjects might be taught using examples from various jurisdictions inside and outside Canada, in other courses knowledge of local statutory law was very much part of the curriculum. Indeed, the one law school that aimed to provide something beyond local professional preparation and to inculcate larger ideas about law was W. P. M. Kennedy's program in law at the University of Toronto, housed in the Faculty of Arts. The fact that this program was not recognized by the LSUC as qualifying a student for call to the bar liberated it from the requirements of professional law schools. Even here, however, Kennedy gradually shifted his program toward the Harvard model in the 1940s in the hope of securing LSUC recognition.[43]

Many lawyers in the United States would have preferred this Canadian model, objecting to the Harvard model precisely on the grounds of its lack of rootedness. An Illinois lawyer "had suggested in 1909 that, since between 65 and 95 percent of law students at the University of Illinois intended to practice locally after graduating, a standard curriculum based on the development of legal reasoning was less pertinent to the career goals of such students than learning the law of their particular jurisdiction."[44] And in this respect, developments in Canada were actually in accordance with Reed's recommendations in his 1928 report to the Carnegie Foundation. Reed did not believe all law schools should follow the Harvard model, because lawyers themselves were a diverse group serving different clienteles. Those motivated to provide what we might now call "storefront" legal services were not well served by the Harvard model and would be better served by improving the night schools for law study that had proliferated in the United States (though none ever emerged in Canada).[45] Reed was thinking of social rather than regional differentiation, but his message that one size does not fit all in the world of legal education would in some respects be better heard in Canada than in the United States. Canadian legal education showed that the debate need not be either-or as between the study of disembodied national theory and local state or provincial law. During this period, Canadian law faculties managed to adhere to most aspects of the Harvard model while at the same time remaining rooted in their local legal cultures.

Harvard Triumphant: 1949–1970s

The year 1949 is well known to Canadians as the moment when the "fiercest debate" over academic versus professional control of legal education in Ontario resulted in the dramatic resignation of almost the entire faculty of Osgoode Hall Law School and their migration to the University of Toronto's school of law.[46] There, dean C. A. Wright aimed to create what he always called an "honest to God law school," meaning a Harvard of the North. In fact, Wright's description of the school's mission statement in the calendar of 1950 reproduced almost verbatim that of the pre-1927 Harvard Law School. After 1957, when the LSUC finally allowed universities to open their own law faculties, Ontario had at last caught up to the rest of North America.

The 1950s and 1960s were a turning point for legal education not only in Ontario but also across Canada. The opening of three new law schools in Ontario in 1957–1959—at Queen's University, the University of Western Ontario, and the University of Ottawa—was unprecedented. But the existing law schools also benefited from the prosperity of the 1950s, with more money, better facilities, growing libraries, and more faculty members. By the time the new law schools came on stream in 1959, there were some seventy-three full-time faculty in the eleven common law faculties plus McGill. This was still not a huge number by US standards, but an average of six faculty members per law school was a quantum leap from the interwar years, when many struggled to retain half that number. The emergence of a critical mass of law professors was marked by the establishment of the Canadian Association of Law Professors/Association Canadienne des Professeur(e)s de Droit in the early 1950s, an organization that still exists today.[47]

Where would all the new law professors come from? The small cadre of professors of the early 1950s largely recommended graduate study in the United States rather than in England, and prospective legal academics heading south chose Harvard in highly disproportionate numbers over any other faculty. Of the seventy-three professors mentioned earlier, more than half (38) had US graduate degrees, and of those, nearly one-third of the entire cohort (23) were from Harvard (and included 18 LLMs and 5 doctorates). The next closest, Yale, was far behind (5 graduates, 3 LLM's, and 2 doctorates), followed by a smattering of US law faculties with one graduate degree each. Only half as many of this cohort had English graduate degrees as American degrees (19 English compared to 38 US), and of those only one was a doctorate. Of the remaining sixteen in the cohort, most had Canadian graduate degrees, a handful had European graduate degrees, and the rest had no graduate degree.[48]

Not surprisingly, these newly minted professors continued to look to Harvard for inspiration. When Daniel Soberman, with a Dalhousie LLB and Harvard LLM, was hired as one of the founding professors at Queen's, he was called on to help establish the second- and third-year curricula: he did so by turning to his Dalhousie and Harvard calendars.[49] The founding dean at Western Ontario, retired Supreme Court of Canada judge Ivan Cleveland Rand, held a Harvard LLB from 1912 but was still very much in touch with the faculty: he was invited to give the Oliver Wendell Holmes Lecture there in 1960, the only Canadian to have been so honored. Rand's biographer, moreover, argues that Harvard was the biggest intellectual influence on his subject's life.[50]

The influence of Harvard was also at its peak in the immediate postwar decades because of the strong interest in Canadian law and legal education displayed by Erwin Griswold, dean of Harvard Law School from 1946 to 1967. He and Caesar Wright overlapped as students at Harvard and were almost exact contemporaries as deans, with Wright serving at Osgoode and Toronto from 1948 to his death in 1967. Griswold carried on a correspondence with many Canadian law deans, whether Harvard graduates or not, often recommending candidates for faculty positions at the deans' request. He also commented insightfully on the scholarly work of Dean Horace Read at Dalhousie. George Curtis of the University of British Columbia was so grateful to Griswold that he arranged for an honorary degree to be bestowed upon him.[51] Griswold played an underappreciated role in the development of Canadian legal education at the time of its greatest expansion. And he was probably the only Harvard law dean ever to take such a direct and quasi-paternal interest in Canadian legal education.

By 1970–71, the number of full-time faculty in Canada expanded fourfold from 1959–1960, to 290. Of these, 152, or just over half, had US graduate degrees (116 LLMs and 36 doctorates). While the proportion of American graduate degrees remained the same from a decade earlier, the predominance of Harvard diminished somewhat, with just one-third of the LLMs and one-sixth of the doctorates. Yale (23 LLMs) closed the gap appreciably with Harvard (39), but after that some fourteen US law schools were represented, most with one or a few graduates, the next largest source after Yale being the University of Michigan with fourteen LLMs. The other noticeable trend is the revival of the United Kingdom. Oxford, London, and Cambridge accounted for fifty-four LLMs, not far behind the total of Harvard and Yale (62). As Britain recovered from a long period of wartime privation, and as transatlantic commercial flights became more affordable, it renewed its attraction for Canadians seeking graduate degrees abroad. The other noticeable trend is the presence among the Canadian professoriate of citizens of the United States, the United Kingdom, and especially Commonwealth countries such as Australia, New Zealand, and South Africa. Americans had never manifested much interest in teaching in Canadian law schools before, but sudden expansion had created a demand that could not be satisfied locally.

The arrival of the baby boomers posed novel problems relating to admissions. Just a decade earlier Canadian law deans were desperate for applicants, but soon they were overwhelmed with demand. In the United States, such issues resulted in the creation of the Law School Admission Council in 1947 and the development of the Law School Admission Test (LSAT), though various forms of triage—including outright discrimination against Jews, Catholics, and women—had emerged long before that.[52] Given that US law schools had twenty years of experience with the LSAT (an apparently scientifically based and rigorous testing tool), it is perhaps not surprising that Canadian law deans at the Anglophone schools adopted it without much analysis. It appears that Manitoba was the first to employ it in 1968, and all Canadian law deans were encouraged to use it starting with the 1970–1971 admission year.[53] Francophone law schools in Canada do not use the test, but all Anglophone law schools except McGill require it, in conjunction with undergraduate grade point average.[54]

In contrast to the AALS, which ultimately decided not to allow any non-US law schools to join, Canadian law schools were welcomed at LSAC, and Canadian representatives participate in all aspects of its work.[55] The price of admission is a certain homogenization: LSAC assumes that Canadian and US law schools are essentially fungible and has traditionally included data from Canadian law schools in some of its studies. There have been numerous concerns expressed about the fairness of using the LSAT in both the United States and Canada for a long time, but these tend to focus on the impact on disadvantaged groups; the suitability of the test for the Canadian context in general has seldom been addressed.[56] The LSAT stresses problem-solving skills that are useful in private practice but not the abilities required to deploy law as a tool of social ordering. If Canadian legal education has tended to stress the latter more than its US counterpart, the use of the LSAT is arguably problematic in the Canadian context.

The appeal of the Harvard model during this period did not persuade Canadians to give up the precall articling requirement, and occasional challenges to it were easily rebuffed. In the wake of World War II, the glut of veterans seeking to qualify as lawyers led the LSUC to suspend its normal requirement of prearranged articles, but after the bulge had passed it reverted to its traditional position.[57] After 1957, when legal education was opened up to universities, the articling period was set ultimately at one year, and the LSUC also created a six-month bar admission course. This left the normal period for qualifying for the bar post–high school at 7.5 years, though it could vary between 6.5 and 8.5 years. In the early 1970s, a special committee of the LSUC (the MacKinnon Committee) recommended various measures to shorten this period and also recommended the abolition of the articling requirement, but the first were watered down and the second was rejected outright by the LSUC's governing body.[58] Not until 2012 was the abolition of articling again debated seriously in Ontario, as discussed below.

Beyond Harvard: 1980s and After

From the 1980s onward, a variety of crosscurrents rippled through Canadian legal education. The influence of Harvard in particular declined even as American influence in general increased in some respects while diminishing in others.[59] Significantly, Canadian legal academics no longer assumed that the US model would provide all the answers, and they began at last to adapt legal education to Canadian realities. Two significant restraints disappeared. The infusion of resources in the 1960s and 1970s meant that Canadian law faculties no longer struggled merely to survive; and the opening up of the upper-year curriculum after 1969 meant that a greater diversity of topics and perspectives could find a home in the law school.

The most obvious changes responding to Canadian conditions related to Indigenous peoples, the trans-systemic study of law, and bilingualism (i.e., English–French). If Indigenous persons were (and are) overrepresented in prison populations, they were sorely underrepresented in the legal profession, a fact the Native Law Centre at the University of Saskatchewan set out to change after its foundation in 1975. The Centre runs a Head Start–type summer program that aims to facilitate access to legal education for Indigenous persons; its 1,000 alumni constitute three-quarters of the hundreds of Indigenous lawyers in Canada today.[60] The Centre's other goals are sponsoring and diffusing academic scholarship on a wide variety of legal issues affecting Indigenous peoples, in addition to encouraging research into Indigenous legal orders. The latter mandate has also been taken up elsewhere, with the University of Victoria in British Columbia admitting the first entrants into its joint degree in Canadian common law and Indigenous legal orders in September 2018. But it is the 2016 *Report of the Truth and Reconciliation Commission of Canada*, which investigated the history and legacy of the residential school system for Indigenous youth, that is likely to have the greatest impact on Canadian legal education. Its Call to Action No. 28, which implored Canadian law schools to require all students to take a course on Aboriginal peoples and the law, has already generated changes going beyond this particular recommendation. Many Canadian law faculties have at least one Indigenous faculty member, and steps to decolonize and/or indigenize the law schools are also being taken.[61] New scholarship on the reinvigoration of Indigenous legal orders nourishes these curricular and institutional changes.

Trans-systemic legal education grew out of the cohabitation of the civil law and common law in the mixed jurisdiction of Quebec, but it need not remain so confined in today's globalized world. McGill's National Programme, created in 1968, saw both legal traditions taught side by side; in 1999 the faculty went further, instituting a trans-systemic approach in which "[b]asic private law courses are no longer taught in function of a single legal system but in function of overarching categories of law such as contracts and civil responsibility."[62] Other law faculties have been reluctant to follow McGill's lead, but in classic Canadian fashion it may require uptake abroad before this innovation will spread within Canada itself. Interestingly, McGill's approach has been hailed as a possible "new Langdellian moment" by Columbia law professor Peter Strauss.[63]

In 1978, the Université de Moncton began offering a common law degree in French—the first anywhere in the world. The faculty of common law at the University of Ottawa followed suit, while a number of Canadian law faculties offer some common law courses in French, and some Francophone law schools in Quebec offer common law degree programs in English. Given that the federal jurisdiction and three provinces are required to publish their laws in English and French (while Ontario does so of its own volition), the development of such programs was long overdue. Meanwhile, scholarly study of legal bilingualism has emerged from the shadows.[64]

Two other trends in Canadian legal education also deserve notice. The first relates to the nature of its scholarly mission. Here, the 1984 *Law and Learning* report commissioned by the Social Sciences and Humanities Council of Canada (widely known as the Arthurs Report after its main author, Harry Arthurs) marked a turning point, making a number of recommendations for improving the quality of Canadian legal scholarship and legal education.[65] Shortly before this, in 1982, the Canadian Law and Society Association was established, providing an intellectual home for all scholars working on law-related scholarship. A significant improvement in the quality and reputation of graduate legal education accompanied these developments.[66] Indeed, the emphasis on strengthening graduate programs and on the acquisition of doctoral degrees (usually but not necessarily in law) for new hires has emerged as one of the most salient differences between US and Canadian legal education.[67] Graduate legal education is far more respected in Canada than in the United States, where, aside from a very few specialized programs, it is provided mainly for foreign candidates and is not seen as a career path to the legal academy.

The second trend relates to the increasing racial diversity of the Canadian legal professoriate, beyond those of Indigenous origin already noted. While the influx of Commonwealth and American legal academics in the 1960s and 1970s provided some intellectual diversity, nonwhite professors were extremely rare in Canadian legal academe prior to 1990. Since then, the so-called Commonwealth contingent has continued, but the countries of origin are more likely to be those of sub-Saharan Africa than Australia or New Zealand. Most Canadian law schools have at least one such faculty member, often from Nigeria, although other countries are also represented. Professors from Canada's own Black population born locally are few, mainly because that population was historically small, but this cohort will likely increase over time. South Asia is also well represented in the Canadian legal academy, although its members were mostly born in Canada and received their initial law degree locally; professors of African origin tend to have obtained at least their first law degree in their home country. Professors of East Asian origin are rare as yet, but their number may be expected to increase in coming years.

However, against these Canadianizing developments must be set new types of US influence on Canadian legal academe. These relate mainly to financing and prestige. Even though all Canadian law schools are located at public universities, their tuition fees rose dramatically in the late 1990s, as did a more overt concern with marketing, reputation, and ranking.[68] Many Canadian law schools followed the University of Toronto's lead in changing the name of the degree from LLB to JD in an effort to make their graduates more marketable in the prestigious US market, New York in particular. Some US law firms now recruit on Canadian campuses. Having begun to carve out new intellectual frontiers responsive to Canadian realities, Canadian law schools now paradoxically find themselves under pressure from their students and outside constituencies to mimic the trappings and ethos of elite American law schools.[69]

Meanwhile, the main feature distinguishing Canadian from US legal education—the articling requirement—is under severe pressure in Canada's largest province as large numbers of foreign-trained lawyers (both Canadians and non-Canadians) seek to enter the Canadian market via Toronto.[70] This development is not a result of American influence, though the lack of an articling requirement in the United States presents a ready precedent for those opposing its continuance in Canada. After experimenting with an optional alternative to articling (the Law Practice Program), offered at a university but exposing students to the practice environment via placements, the Law Society of Ontario recently made the program permanent. The replacement of articling by such a program might be a desirable goal in the long term, but it has been accompanied by a North America–wide move to push more and more practical or experiential training into the law schools. The Law Society of Ontario has approved the programs of two new law schools in the province as sufficiently "practice-oriented" that their graduates do not need to fulfill the articling requirement or the Law Practice Program.[71] It remains to be seen what kind of pressure these developments will exert on existing law schools, both in Ontario and elsewhere in Canada.

Conclusion

Canada's turn to American-style university legal education in the nineteenth century signaled a major departure from English professional traditions. The fact that the Ontario bar, long the most Anglophile of any in Canada, resisted this trend until the mid-twentieth century should not obscure its adoption and success everywhere else. Perhaps the most important feature of the Canadian experience with American legal education is that, unlike some other jurisdictions, it was imported voluntarily and never imposed. The embrace of the American model—essentially the Harvard model—was measured at first, and for quite some time it existed more as an ideal than in reality. When self-conscious modeling of Harvard—especially with regard to the adoption of the case method and the restriction of legal education to degree candidates—became more obvious in the interwar period, inadequate resources and the local pull of the provincial law schools inhibited the full adoption of the Harvard model. It is only in the postwar period, as American values and practices took on global significance, that the hegemony of the US model, and particularly the Harvard model, became entrenched in Canadian legal education. Since the 1980s, however, the model has become a base upon which various additions responsive to Canadian needs and conditions have been erected.

The legacy of this model is mixed. The idea of recruiting university involvement in legal education was undoubtedly positive, as outside Ontario and Quebec provincial bars did not have the critical mass or the resources to mount effective educational efforts. The creation of a cadre of full-time legal academics meant that Canadian legal scholarship could in due course evolve beyond the efforts of practitioners and judges, whose contributions diminished considerably over time, and could address different issues. But the larger questions—for whom legal education existed and what it was for—remain more troubling aspects of the American model. That legal education should be reserved for an intellectual elite, and that the elite of that elite could expect to serve corporate America (or Canada), have been powerful ideas in North America. No amount of affirmative action or legal clinics or social justice programming seems to be able to overcome this basic postulate, while dramatic increases in Canadian tuition fees over the past quarter-century have served only to entrench it.

Thus, if the content of legal education north of the 49th Parallel looks increasingly Canadian, the institutional context, student body, and general ethos look more and more like their counterparts to the south. Whether other countries—less integrated culturally and economically with the United States than Canada is—can import only those aspects of American legal education they desire, without the entire package, is an open question.

NOTES

*I thank Bobby Mackenzie and David Sworn for research assistance in the preparation of this paper. It is dedicated to the memory of G. Blaine Baker (1952–2018), whose work on the history of legal education in Canada has exerted a great influence on later scholarship.

1 Philip Girard, "The Making of the Canadian Legal Profession: A Hybrid Heritage," *International Journal of the Legal Profession* 21, no. 2 (2014): 145. The profession of notary, which exists only in Quebec, has been strongly influenced by the French tradition, but it is not treated in this study.

2 The most intensive study is that of J. E. Bickenbach and C. Ian Kyer, "The Harvardization of Caesar Wright," *University of Toronto Law Journal* 33, no.2 (1983): 162, which is largely devoted to Ontario.

3 John McLaren, "The History of Legal Education in Common Law Canada," in *Legal Education in Canada: Report and Background Papers of a National Conference on Legal Education . . . 1985*, ed. Roy J. Matas and Deborah J. McCawley (Montreal: Federation of Law Societies of Canada, 1987).

4 John E. C. Brierley, "Quebec Legal Education since 1945: Cultural Paradoxes and Traditional Ambiguities," *Dalhousie Law Journal* 10, no.1 (June 1986): 5; Roderick Macdonald, "The National Law Programme at McGill: Origins, Establishment, Prospects," *Dalhousie Law Journal* 13, no. 1 (May 1990): 211.

5 Eric Adams, "The Dean Who Went to Law School: Crossing Borders and Searching for Purpose in North American Legal Education, 1930–1950," *Alberta Law Review* 54, no. 1 (2016): 38.

6 D. D. McKean, *The Integrated Bar* (Boston: Houghton Mifflin 1963); The Progressive Era background to these developments is analyzed in Girard, "Hybrid Heritage," 151–52.

7 John Langbein, "Blackstone, Litchfield, and Yale: The Founding of the Yale Law School," in *The History of Yale Law School: The Tercentennial Lectures*, ed. Anthony T. Kronman (New Haven: Yale University Press, 2004). Yale absorbed the New Haven law school.

8 Christopher Moore, *The Law Society of Upper Canada and Ontario's Lawyers, 1797–1997* (Toronto: University of Toronto Press, 1997).

9 G. Blaine Baker, "Legal Education in Upper Canada: The Law Society as Educator, 1785–1889," in *Essays in the History of Canadian Law*, vol. 2, ed. David H. Flaherty (Toronto: University of Toronto Press for the Osgoode Society, 1983).

10 Philip Girard, *Lawyers and Legal Culture in British North America: Beamish Murdoch of Halifax* (Toronto: University of Toronto Press for the Osgoode Society, 2011), 71–73.

11 Robert Stevens, *Law School: Legal Education in America from the 1850s to the 1980s* (Chapel Hill: University of North Carolina Press, 1983), 120.

12 Harry Arthurs, "The Political Economy of Canadian Legal Education," *Journal of Law and Society* 25, no. 1 (March 1998): 14.

13 Philip Girard, "The Roots of a Professional Renaissance: Lawyers in Nova Scotia, 1850–1910," *Manitoba Law Journal* 20, no. 1 (1991): 148.

14 Girard, "Professional Renaissance," 165. This was in marked contrast to aspiring lawyers from Ontario and Quebec, almost none of whom went to the United States to seek an LLB.

15 P. B. Waite, *The Man from Halifax: Sir John Thompson, Prime Minister* (Toronto: University of Toronto Press, 1985), 123.

16 Bruce A. Kimball, *The Inception of Modern Professional Education: C. C. Langdell, 1826–1906* (Chapel Hill: University of North Carolina Press, 2009), 265.

17 See, generally, Kimball, *Modern Professional Education.*

18 A. G. Archibald and R. C. Weldon, *The inaugural addresses, &c., delivered at the opening of the Law School [at] Dalhousie . . .* (Halifax: Nova Scotia Printing, 1884), 51.

19 D. G. Bell, *Legal Education in New Brunswick, A History* (Fredericton: University of New Brunswick, 1992), chap. 3. Weldon held an MA in economics and a PhD in political economy from Yale, where he studied under Richard Henry Dana and Theodore Dwight Woolsey, followed by postgraduate work at Heidelberg. He never practiced law, and his vision of legal education was rather broader than Langdell's; Philip Girard, "Weldon, Richard Chapman," Dictionary of Canadian Biography, www.biographi.ca.

20 John Willis, *A History of Dalhousie Law School* (Toronto: University of Toronto Press, 1979).

21 Women were not allowed to enroll at Harvard Law School, although this was at the insistence of the university, not the law faculty itself.

22 D. G. Bell, "Slamming the Door on Brains: Two Early Twentieth-Century Law Schools and the Narrowing of Educational Opportunity," in *The Promise and Perils of Law: Lawyers in Canadian History*, ed. Constance Backhouse and W. Wesley Pue (Toronto: Irwin Law, 2009), 37.

23 W. Wesley Pue, "Common Law Legal Education in Canada's Age of Light, Soap and Water," *Manitoba Law Journal* 23 (1995): 654.

24 W. Wesley Pue, *Law School: The Story of Legal Education in British Columbia* (Vancouver: University of British Columbia Faculty of Law, 1995).

25 W. Wesley Pue, "'The Disquisitions of Learned Judges': Making Manitoba Lawyers, 1885–1931," in *Essays in the History of Canadian Law, vol. VIII, in Honour of R. C. B. Risk*, ed. G. Blaine Baker and Jim Phillips (Toronto: University of Toronto Press for the Osgoode Society, 1999): 525.

26 Pue, "Common Law Legal Education."

27 "First Class in Law to Graduate," *The Gateway*, May 14, 1924, cited in Adams, "Dean Who Went to Law School," 8.

28 Arthur E. Sutherland, *The Law at Harvard: A History of Ideas and Men, 1817–1967* (Cambridge: Harvard University Press, 1967), 233–35. Curiously, after the first generation of US law professors had obtained graduate degrees in law, they were largely abandoned as part of the career path to legal academe in the United States; Gail J. Hupper, "The Academic Doctorate in Law: A Vehicle for Legal Transplants," *Journal of Legal Education* 58, no. 3 (2008): 413.

29 On Smith's later role in supporting university legal education against the wishes of the LSUC, see C. Ian Kyer and Jerome E. Bickenbach, *The Fiercest Debate: Cecil A. Wright, the Benchers, and the Legal Education in Ontario, 1923–1957* (Toronto: Osgoode Society, 1987).

30 His doctoral thesis was published by Harvard University Press in 1938 as *Recognition and Enforcement of Foreign Judgments in the Common Law Units of the British Commonwealth*.

31 Bickenbach and Kyer, "Harvardization of Caesar Wright," 164–65.

32 Alfred Z. Reed, *Present-Day Law Schools in the United States and Canada* (New York: Carnegie Foundation, 1928), 348.

33 R. C. B. Risk, "Canadian Law Teachers in the 1930s: 'When the World Was Turned Upside Down,'" *Dalhousie Law Journal* 27, no. 1 (2004): 1; Philip Girard, "Harvard," chap. 4 in *Bora Laskin: Bringing Law to Life* (Toronto: University of Toronto Press for the Osgoode Society, 2005).

34 Bruce A. Kimball, "Triumph and Betrayal, 1886–1890s," chap. 8 in *The Inception of Modern Professional Education: C. C. Langdell, 1826–1906* (Chapel Hill: University of North Carolina Press, 2009).

35 H. W. Arthurs, review of Jerold Auerbach, *Unequal Justice: Lawyers and Social Change in Modern America*, in *University of Toronto Law Journal* 27, no. 4 (October 1977): 513.

36 Gerald Tulchinsky, *Canada's Jews: A People's Journey* (Toronto: University of Toronto Press, 2008), 132, 318.

37 Bell, "Slamming the Door on Brains," 43–44.

38 Mélanie Pascale Brunet, "Becoming Lawyers: Gender, Legal Education and Professional Identity Formation in Canada, 1920–1980" (PhD diss., University of Toronto, 2005), 85.

39 Bell, "Slamming the Door on Brains," 44.

40 Philip Girard and Jeffrey Haylock, "Stratification, Economic Adversity, and Diversity in an Urban Bar: Halifax, Nova Scotia, 1900–1950," in *Promise and Perils of Law: Lawyers in Canadian History*, ed. Constance Backhouse and W. Wesley Pue (Toronto: Irwin Law, 2009).

41 Philip Girard, "Who's Afraid of Canadian Legal History," *University of Toronto Law Journal* 57, no. 4 (September 2007): 727.

42 Macdonald, "National Law Programme at McGill"; A. J. Hobbins, "'A couple generations ahead of popular demand': The First National Law Program at McGill University, 1918–1924," *Dalhousie Law Journal* 31, no. 1 (2008): 181.
43 Girard, *Bora Laskin*, 145.
44 Stevens, *Law School*, 41.
45 Reed, *Present-Day Law Schools*, chap. 22.
46 Kyer and Bickenbach, *Fiercest Debate*. On what follows, see Girard, *Bora Laskin*, chap. 8.
47 Girard, *Bora Laskin*, 184–89.
48 Figures from *Canadian Association of Law Teachers Directory*, various years.
49 Mark D. Walters, "'Let Right Be Done': A History of the Faculty of Law at Queen's University," *Queen's Law Journal* 32, no. 2 (2007): 328.
50 William Kaplan, *Canadian Maverick: The Life and Times of Ivan C. Rand* (Toronto: University of Toronto Press for the Osgoode Society, 2009).
51 Girard, "Who's Afraid," 740.
52 William LaPiana, "Merit and Diversity: The Origins of the Law School Admissions Test," *St. Louis University Law Journal* 48, no. 3 (2004): 961, 965.
53 Annette Demers, "A History of the University of Windsor Faculty of Law . . . 1968–2008" (University of Windsor, 2010), 21.
54 McGill does not require the LSAT but will consider the score if it is written, which is in effect an invitation to write it.
55 McGill joined the AALS in 1921 but was obliged to leave in 1933 when it could not satisfy some of the basic requirements. In the late 1950s, the AALS decided that no law school outside the United States, other than Puerto Rico's, could join; Carole Silver, "Globalization and the Monopoly of ABA-Approved Law Schools: Missed Opportunities or Dodged Bullets?," *Fordham Law Review* 82, no. 6 (May 2014): 2869.
56 See, however, Dawna Tong and W. Wesley Pue, "The Best and the Brightest? Canadian Law School Admissions," *Osgoode Hall Law Journal* 37, no. 4 (1999): 852–57.
57 Girard, *Bora Laskin*, 177.
58 *Report of the Special Committee on Legal Education* (Toronto: Law Society of Upper Canada 1972).
59 On the continuing popularity of US graduate legal education for Canadian law professors, see Edward Veitch and R. A. Macdonald, "Law Teachers and Their Jurisdiction," *Canadian Bar Review* 56, no. 4 (December 1978): 710, 717–19.
60 See the report of the University of Saskatchewan College of Law at https://ccld-cdfdc.ca.
61 Jeffery G. Hewitt, "Decolonizing and Indigenizing: Some Considerations for Law Schools," *Windsor Yearbook of Access to Justice* 33, no. 1 (2016): 65.
62 Helge Dedek and Armand de Mestral, "Born to be Wild: The 'Trans-systemic' Programme at McGill and the De-Nationalization of Legal Education," *German Law Journal* 10, no. 6/7 (June/July 2009): 905.

63 "Transsystemia: Are We Approaching a New Langdellian Moment? Is McGill Leading the Way?," *Journal of Legal Education* 56 (2006): 161.

64 Roderick A. Macdonald, "Legal Bilingualism," *McGill Law Journal* 42, no. 1 (February 1997): 119; Pierre-André Côté, "Bilingual Interpretation of Enactments in Canada: Principles v. Practice," *Brooklyn Journal of International Law* 29, no. 3 (2004): 1067.

65 Consultative Group on Research and Education in Law, *Law and Learning: Report to the Social Sciences and Humanities Research Council of Canada* (Ottawa: Minister of Supply and Services, 1983).

66 For a twenty-year retrospective on the Arthurs Report, see the contributions to volume 18 of the *Canadian Journal of Law & Society* (2003).

67 Sanjeev S. Anand, "Canadian Graduate Legal Education: Past, Present and Future," *Dalhousie Law Journal* 27, no. 1 (2004): 55.

68 Craig Jones, "The Rating Game: Thoughts on *Canadian Lawyer*'s Thoughts on UBC's Law School," *The Advocate* (BC) 63, no. 3 (2009): 373; Harry Arthurs, "Poor Canadian Legal Education: So Near to Wall Street, So Far From God," *Osgoode Hall Law Journal* 38, no. 3 (2000): 381; Susan B. Boyd, "Corporatism and Legal Education in Canada," *Social and Legal Studies* 14, no. 2 (June 2005): 287.

69 Roderick A. Macdonald and Thomas McMorrow, "Decolonizing Law School," *Alberta Law Review* 51, no. 4 (June 2014): 717.

70 "Options for Lawyer Licensing: A Consultation Paper," Law Society of Ontario, last modified May 24, 2018, https://lsodialogue.ca. The Law Society of Upper Canada changed its name to the Law Society of Ontario with effect from January 1, 2018.

71 Lakehead University, Thunder Bay, Ontario (approved 2013); Ryerson University, Toronto (approved 2019).; *The Lawyer's Daily*, April 26, 2019.

4

Functionalism, Legal Process, and the Transformation (and Subordination) of Australian Law Schools

SUSAN BARTIE

The 1950s and 1960s were crucial transformative decades in the history of Australian legal education. For the first time, Australian law schools had both the means and mass to advance agendas that placed Australian legal thought and Australian law at the heart of the curriculum and a new band of career legal academics to lay down the foundations for modern Australian legal education. Changes to law schools came about largely through government funding, which enabled more students to study law. The funding also accommodated the ambitions of some law school deans to expand the size of the full-time legal academy and to reduce the number of legal practitioners teaching on a part-time basis. As a result, the number of full-time legal academics across Australia soon moved into double digits. While there were some notable exceptions, most of the new recruits were Australian citizens who had studied undergraduate law in Australia and had some foreign (usually English, but increasingly US) postgraduate qualifications, although a bachelor degree in law was in many cases sufficient for entry into the academy. This first Australian legal academic community (the "first community") produced textbooks and articles to assist both their students and the profession to reference Australian, rather than purely English, materials. Their literature had the potential to create models and traditions that would define Australia's discipline of law.

Concentrating on the role that US legal educational models played during this transformative period, this chapter advances four core claims, each intended to provide a nuanced account of the role of progressive liberal legal thought during the founding of modern Australian legal education. First, this chapter suggests that the way Australian legal scholars took an interest in US ideas and critiqued English practices refutes some common myths about this generation of scholars. Perhaps the most striking myth is the idea that most members of the first community, apart from Julius Stone, subscribed to "expository," "positivist,"[1] or "legalist"[2] approaches to the study and conceptualization of law.[3] The myths place earlier Australian legal scholars in a narrow light, supporting a linear account of the discipline whereby from the 1970s onward legal scholars freed themselves from an expository tradition by engaging in critiques of law and institutions and drawing from bodies of thought beyond law.

In contrast, this chapter explains how members of the first community were keen to depart from English practices, believing that US models and ideas that rejected formalism demonstrated there were viable alternatives. This small community of just over thirty full-time legal academics considered and debated whether to adopt a functionalist approach to textbook writing and whether to embrace the case method, Langdell's brainchild that was subsequently adapted to embody the functionalist conception of law of the American Legal Realists.[4] Sometimes a handful of these scholars are drawn out and treated as exceptions by later commentators.[5] What my studies suggest, however, is that the number of these scholars was greater and their role in founding the discipline was more important than is commonly acknowledged. While these agitators also had considerable and lamentable blind spots, and their ambitions did not always, or even often, translate to vibrant educational models, criticisms of this generation should not begin with the premise that they were narrow "legalists" who viewed the discipline in wholly insular terms. Instead, studies should critically examine the role that progressive liberal legal thought, both from the United States and from within Australia itself, including its racist and sexist tendencies, contributed to the founding of the modern Australian discipline of law.

The second, possibly surprising, claim of this chapter is that another American school of legal thought, the Legal Process School, in fact played a key role in the creation of Australia's textbook tradition—perhaps more so than did functionalism. In the first community's debates about the incorporation of US ideas and methods, the leading theory at Harvard at the time, the Legal Process School, was not mentioned. And yet, of all of the twentieth-century US legal theories, it appears to have been the one that best reflects some of the central features of Australia's textbook tradition, at least when it comes to doctrinal analysis.

Third, this chapter suggests that there are several reasons—including the relationship between the academy and the profession—that explain why Australia's legal academy, in the end, did not wholly embrace a functionalist approach when writing textbooks. Finally, this chapter suggests that, although American ideas and models served as vehicles of liberation and permitted deviation from English traditions, they were also a source of subordination. Part of the subordination came from American professors, most notably Harvard dean Erwin Griswold, who suggested that Australian law schools were in a parlous state and in desperate need of reform. Part of the subordination has also come from subsequent Australian commentary suggesting that, whenever Australian law schools and scholars adopt US ideas and practices, they are acting in progressive and innovative ways. This has created a false dichotomy, suggesting all English pedagogical practices are bad and all US practices are good. The possibility that Australian legal scholars created novel concepts and methods of their own—including hybrids of the foreign models—is largely ignored. Rather than progressive and liberating, it is possible to view the US influence and the use of US labels to describe Australian practices as distracting Australian legal scholars from tailoring legal education to the unique concerns of Australian society and reforming Australia's legal profession. Further, the tendency to associate progress with US ideas has also spread from the academy to the judiciary. This, too, has had the effect of subordinating Australian legal thought and has fed criticisms of the judiciary.

A Strong Band of Liberal Progressives

I have previously examined the book reviews of Australia's first community of legal scholars published from 1948 to 1968.[6] Reading these reviews (all 357 of them) convinced me that they provided some of the best evidence of the ambitions and inclinations of the founders of modern Australian law schools.[7] The book reviews were not simply devices to evaluate and promote books; they were conversations "about the materials, methods and values" of the discipline.[8] At a time when Australian legal scholars were only just beginning to publish a body of scholarship and create an Australian textbook tradition based on Australian law, as opposed to English law, the book reviews identified models, bodies of knowledge, and lines of investigation that would inspire this new literature. Not only did they provide the best evidence of this community's aspirations; they also starkly revealed the existence of a strong band of liberal progressives who wanted Australia's legal academy to deviate from the practices of their English counterparts.[9] The book reviews indicated that at least half of this community (which comprised just over thirty full-time academics) strongly rejected the notion of following English conceptions of law or English approaches to textbooks. While the highest number of books reviewed were English (46 percent followed by 36 percent Australian and 13 percent American[10]), it is important to look beyond the numbers and appreciate that many of the reviews were highly critical of those books.

The Australian reviewers leveled several criticisms at the insularity they perceived in English law books. They expressed strong dismay when English authors referred largely, or even exclusively, to English law and developments, ignoring leading authorities from the Commonwealth.[11] They were frustrated that Australians had to pay such close attention to English law while their English counterparts made so few attempts to familiarize themselves with developments beyond their own borders.[12] The reviewers' critiques suggest they held firm ambitions to place Australian legal developments on a global stage and intended to draw heavily on Australian law within the curriculum. They perceived that the English insularity stood in the way of those ambitions.

The Australian reviewers also frequently criticized the growing English practice of creating new editions of textbooks by long-dead authors. This, according to the Australians, was a sign of English conservatism (even "sterility"[13]) and complacency.[14] They believed the new editions diminished, rather than improved or retained, the quality of the earlier works.[15] Australian tort law scholar John Fleming, for example, spoke critically of Philip Landon's "repeated emphasis on the self-sufficiency of 'rules' created by 'just men of past generations' (the older the better)" and his contempt for "the fluid and ephemeral morality and sociology, which in some circles, especially in America, are nowadays set up as the sole objective of modern law," which Fleming concluded "reveal a mind fundamentally out of sympathy with contemporary law and legal thought."[16]

Perhaps more important (and controversial), the Australian reviewers were frustrated by the English authors' unwillingness to issue a strong critique of England's law and legal institutions. For example, Colin Howard criticized one English book on the basis that it "perpetuates the insularity and self-congratulation universally regarded as the hallmark of the English Law."[17] They were dismayed by the English scholars' unwillingness to take risks and their apparent desire to appease the conservative members of England's legal profession through conventional and unremarkable scholarship. They also criticized their English counterparts' hostility toward American legal thought and suggested they ought to pay greater attention to American ideas.[18] The criticisms point to their desire to create an Australian legal academy that would possess a strong degree of autonomy and would freely critique professional (including judicial) practices.

These strong criticisms sat alongside reviews of American books. The Australian reviews suggests that the first community found the American books both novel and intellectually exciting. The reviewers adopted the catchphrases of key American Legal Realists, and throughout the reviews we find endorsements of the proposition that law should be thought of as a social science, an instrument of social policy, and that it ought to be studied as such.[19] The Australians praised the collaborative projects some American scholars had arranged with social scientists and found the way they incorporated the social and political dynamics of law worthwhile.[20]

These early scholars were not, however, critical of all English scholars. For example, they lavished praise on English law professor Glanville Williams, whose work, in their view, displayed an innovative approach to criminal law, torts, and jurisprudence.[21] The very positive reviews of Williams's works suggest that the first community preferred books that incorporated learning beyond law while also explaining how that broader thought might assist with law reform.[22] They favored ambitious books that delved into leading thought from the humanities and social sciences but that retained obvious and direct utility.

It is important to think carefully about what US ideas and models meant to this generation of Australian law teachers. The book reviews reveal that a relatively large number of the first community—more than a third—were attracted to the spirit of American Legal Realism. This attraction did not, however, mean that these Australian legal scholars were creating an Australian community of functionalists or that most members of this generation were legal theorists. As with many of the experiences detailed in this volume, the US models they spoke of and applied strategically were often more imagined than real. Their mere familiarity with aspects of legal theory did not make them jurisprudes. Instead, functionalism served as a device that granted them permission to pursue some of their central ambitions for the discipline. Functionalist commitments allowed the progressive Australian legal scholars to challenge some of the rhetoric, pretension, and conservatism that accompanied how many members of Australia's legal profession, including several judges, perceived the judicial function. It also provided a legitimating force for this generation's departure from an English tradition of textbook writing that remained insular and was stagnating. The English model did little to embolden or encourage this generation's ambitions to create scholarship that inspired law reform. It worked against Australian legal scholars' desire to grow the academy and to play a greater role in shaping the way that Australia's legal profession thought about law. In contrast, the US books and scholarship, particularly those grounded in functionalist commitments, legitimated such critiques of the English textbooks as well as the bold law reform ambitions of several key scholars.

Legal Process and Australia's Textbook Tradition

The early legal scholars' interest in functionalism and their critique of English practices did not lead to the creation of an Australian textbook tradition in a largely functionalist mold. In keeping with the American enthusiasms, members of the first community adopted some features typically associated with US legal education, such as versions of the student-run law reviews and moot court exercises.[23] Some professors experimented with various versions of the Socratic method. At the same time, only one Australian textbook followed wholly a US model, and this model was *not* American Legal Realism. Instead, it followed closely within the Legal Process School and was inspired by its founders. It is therefore important to distinguish between the aspirations, the strong support for functionalism outlined in the book reviews, and the reality of the "making" of Australia's textbook tradition.[24]

The only Australian textbook of the period to wholly embrace an American model, beyond Julius Stone's jurisprudence books,[25] was Peter Brett and Louis Waller's *Cases and Materials in Criminal Law*, first published in 1962.[26] It represented the best opportunity for one of the major US legal theories to influence the curriculum of Australian law schools. The textbook was inspired by and based on the "problem method" devised by Henry Hart and Al Sacks. As a mature student in his thirties, Brett obtained an SJD (Doctor of Juridical Science) with distinction in 1958–1959, under the guidance of Henry Hart, his greatest mentor and source of inspiration, as well as Lon Fuller.[27] Brett wrote to Henry Hart for permission to use the Hart and Sacks format in his criminal law textbook, and such permission is acknowledged in the preface to the book.[28]

I have explained elsewhere how Brett and Waller's textbook, along with Brett's first monograph,[29] followed closely within the Legal Process tradition and was underpinned by its associated moral philosophy, which Charles Barzun has expertly explained.[30] Most notably, the book encouraged students and practitioners to believe that lawyers and judges had choices when applying the law and that principle ought to be elevated over precedent. Each substantive chapter began with a hypothetical problem followed by an array of case extracts, legislation, and commentary from Australia, the United States, England, and Canada, and the reader was prompted to evaluate the reasoning in each to determine the best underlying principles. In this way, Brett and Waller followed the Legal Process concept of reasoned elaboration, an approach that Hart and Sacks believed would, by permitting reevaluations and changes over time, assist the law to remain in touch with its social context and policy underpinnings.[31] As Barzun explains in answering criticisms that the school was largely instrumentalist, Legal Process embraced aspects of William James's philosophy, in particular his theory that people hold obligations to respect one another's feelings and desires (including their ideals) merely by virtue of them coming into existence.[32] According to Barzun, the Legal Process School adopted James's position that "over time, as individuals were faced with dilemmas requiring action of one sort or another, the ethical truth would come out."[33] In this same vein, Brett and Waller's casebook, through the hypotheticals and extracts, presents the development of sound legal principles as a work in progress. The book also, consistent with Barzun's thesis, contained quotes and exercises that prompted students to think critically about utilitarianism.[34]

The success of *Cases and Materials in Criminal Law*—demonstrated by the volume of sales, glowing reviews, and its longevity—suggests that it was an influential work that contributed to Australia's textbook tradition and the concept of law that underpinned some aspects of university legal education.[35] Throughout the second half of the twentieth century, several other Australian legal scholars created legal textbooks that adopted several features from Brett and Waller's casebook. Rather than pronouncing or presenting the central authorities, they grouped together extracts from cases, legislation, and commentary that spoke to particular legal issues in various ways and prompted students to critically appraise principles and reasoning. It is doubtful that the authors of these books were well acquainted with the tenets of the Legal Process School. That approach is barely mentioned in Australian scholarship across the second half of the twentieth century (including jurisprudence textbooks), and when it is mentioned it does not receive a strong endorsement.[36] This mode of delivery—and perhaps also some aspects of the concept of legal reasoning that underpinned it—no doubt simply made sense to the textbook writers, and they likely appreciated the popularity of Brett and Waller's casebook. This suggests that some Australian legal scholars beyond Brett and Waller followed the Legal Process School largely unwittingly.

Functionalism and Australia's Textbook Tradition

The idea that Australia's textbook tradition was founded partly on the Legal Process School, more so than functionalism, may seem strange. However, there are reasons beyond the success of Brett and Waller's *Cases and Materials in Criminal Law* that help explain why the Functionalist School did not take a stronger hold within Australia's textbook tradition. In 1956, the Melbourne Law School journal *Res Judicatae* published an article by Harold Ford, a law professor at the school, titled "The Evolution of the American Casebook."[37] Ford, who specialized in corporate law, had spent a year at Harvard in 1954, completing a thesis on nonprofit associations. Upon his return to Australia, his thesis was accepted for publication by Clarendon Press at Oxford. He went on to publish several textbooks in the field of commercial law. The article is a well-considered and insightful analysis of the case method that points to Ford's careful study of this American practice.

Ford appreciated that the case method was underpinned by a particular concept of law and that this concept had changed over time. He understood that, when Australians created their own casebooks, their choices about what cases to include and how to organize them would determine whether Australian textbooks followed a formalist, functionalist, or other tradition. The article also suggests that Ford accepted, in line with American thinking, that the textbooks Australians created would influence the way that students conceived of law. The article therefore helped increase awareness among this generation of Australian legal scholars that the choices they made about the content and organization of their casebooks made a statement about how they wanted Australian lawyers to perceive law, as well as Australia's relationship with England.

Ford's analysis of the US casebooks suggests that Australian casebook compilers who chose to include older English cases and cases that minimized the impression of variation among jurisdictions, and who did not include legislation[38] and commentary, were taking a largely formalist approach. He explained that in formalist texts the "ubiquitous character of common law principle was emphasized and local variations were minimized."[39] Emphasizing coherence, consistency, and endurance among common law principles and deemphasizing variations in reasoning and principles, brought about by differences in people and social context, helped to promote Langdell's idea of law as a science.[40]

Ford's analysis of casebooks suggested that Australian scholars who chose cases that highlighted the inconsistency, variability, and illogical nature of reasoning fell within the Functionalist School.[41] He also explained that including modern cases in casebooks to enable consideration of the role of social practices and customs in law was a hallmark of a functionalist approach. He suggested that some earlier cases should be included to make "the point that social change was reflected in changes in the law, but the proportion of these cases appearing in new casebooks would be smaller than heretofore."[42] He also considered that functionalist casebooks should include supplementary material from outside of law to better determine the social purpose of law and that they ought to be forward-looking, suggesting that the lawyer's role was to shape the future development of law.[43] Further, a functionalist book would organize cases in accordance with social facts rather than abstract legal concepts.[44]

Assessing the extent to which Australia's early legal textbooks followed the functionalist model is complicated by a number of factors. Irrespective of their views on functionalism, formalism, and American approaches, most Australian legal scholars realized that law schools needed more books that compiled case law. As Australia's law libraries were vastly inadequate, with insufficient copies of law reports, casebooks were the only way that law schools could provide all of their students with access to published judgments and opinions. A law professor's decision to create casebooks therefore did not necessarily signal a desire to follow the American tradition, and several casebooks created during that period appear to have been assembled with some haste and without a clear conceptual underpinning.[45]

Further, even where Australian legal scholars wanted to follow a functionalist approach and incorporate more recent Australian case law, they could not ignore the fact that Australian citizens had the right to appeal to the Privy Council and that Australian courts drew heavily from English authorities. The Privy Council was, until 1986, the highest appellate court in Australia's court hierarchy. A book that left out or minimized English cases would mislead students about the role and relevance of English law in Australia. Several Australian textbook writers included English cases out of a sense of responsibility rather than a preference for formalism or legalism. The book reviews suggest that Australian legal scholars wanted more casebooks and textbooks that emphasized the decisions in Australian cases but that there were limits to how much they could include.

For example, at first glance William Morison (Sydney), Norval Morris (Melbourne), and Robin Sharwood's (Melbourne) torts casebook,[46] published in 1962, appears to sit within either a formalist or a legalist mold, containing "little text matter, few references to text books and articles, and no extracts from State statutes."[47] However, this view ignores the authors' explanation that these materials were omitted simply to keep the size of the book manageable.[48] It also ignores other functionalist components of the textbook and the fact that the three scholars in their introduction expressed a commitment to some functionalist ideals. Consistent with functionalist sentiment, the authors emphasized their efforts to include Australian over English cases, explaining:

> This policy has the deliberate aim of directing the attention of Australian law students to the abundance of tort case law arising in an environment familiar to them and colored by the local characteristics of the land and its people.[49]

Further, they explained their expectation that the book would be used alongside John Fleming's book *The Law of Torts*,[50] Fleming being a known functionalist sympathizer.

Fleming, a tort law scholar who began his career at King's College London in 1946, moved to Australia in 1949 to become a lecturer at Canberra University College, and in 1961 he took up a permanent post at Berkeley, California, after a short time serving as first Chair of Law and then dean of the Faculty of Law at Australian National University. The Australian legal historian Mark Lunney suggests that there are clear signs that Fleming was attracted to the thinking of another member of Australia's legal academy, Julius Stone, who followed in the US sociological tradition, and that he also admired Karl Renner, an Austrian social philosopher.[51] Over time Fleming's interest in American legal ideas grew, and in 1954 he spent six months in the United States, thanks to a Carnegie Corporation fellowship.[52] Lunney explains that Fleming took a moderate stance toward American Legal Realism.[53] Fleming's torts textbook did not adopt a functionalist organizational structure,[54] and he did not use the casebook method when teaching.[55] Nonetheless, his textbook did possess functionalist characteristics: "[T]he juxtaposition between function and doctrine in which the court was to cooperate formed the basis of Fleming's claim that he was writing a '*modern* text on the Law of Torts with reference to the Australian context.'"[56]

Despite the early enthusiasm and some experiments with aspects of the functionalist model, none of the early Australian textbooks adopted a functionalist organization. Legal concepts, not social facts, formed the basis of chapter headings and dictated their structure. There are several reasons that help to explain why Australians did not wholly embrace a functionalist model. First, Lunney argues that a fully functionalist approach to textbook organization would have drawn a negative reception from the profession and would not have been commercially viable.[57] Some reactions to Fleming's work suggest that he was right to take this tentative approach. One practitioner wrote a long and scathing review of the book's reformist and American qualities, the work taking its structure from the American Law Institute's *Restatement of the Law of Torts* (1934).[58] In New South Wales, the profession's negative reception to the appointment of Julius Stone, just over a decade earlier, provided further evidence that there was a strong conservative strain among Australia's lawyers that rejected US approaches that might challenge prevailing conceptions of the judicial role.[59]

Second, Australian student culture was resistant to highly interactive teaching methods. In contrast to the US postgraduate legal education model, Australian law students were undergraduates, commencing their studies in their late teens.[60] At Melbourne Law School students made their disapproval of the case method clear,[61] avoiding lectures that expected them to speak up in class.[62] In one instance they removed the numbers placed on chairs in a lecture to sabotage the lecturer's intentions to teach through a Socratic method.[63] Finally, there is also a sense that the Australians believed that US models were far from perfect and that, while they were attracted to some aspects of the casebook innovations, they also considered that it was not an ideal teaching method. While from the early 1900s Australians had toured American law schools and marveled at their richly resourced buildings and libraries and their dynamic classrooms, they had also identified what they perceived as significant limitations to the American methods.[64] Similar criticisms were made by a number of Australian legal scholars who toured US law schools in the late 1940s and 1950s.[65] It is also worth noting that there were several signs that Australians were skeptical of the value of constraining teaching to a particular legal theory or jurisprudential school.[66]

Subordinating Australian Law Schools

It is important to recognize that some members of the first community, especially those at Melbourne Law School, believed that Australian law schools would not only equal the sophisticated educational projects led by the US law schools but also one day surpass them. They wanted their libraries and buildings to be as grand as those of the elite US schools, and they wanted to command the respect of both the legal profession and their own students. However, they were not wholly sold on the case and Socratic methods, and there were intellectual, social, and practical reasons (noted earlier) that meant Australian law schools would never become mini-Harvards.

Griswold's Project

The independent spirit and the scope of ambitions of some of these scholars were, it appears, lost on the American legal missionaries, most notably Harvard Law School dean Erwin Griswold. Griswold visited Australia on a number of occasions and developed close connections with several members of the first community of Australian legal scholars.[67] He arranged funding and positions for Australian scholars to visit the United States and also arranged for American scholars to teach in Australia.[68] As the Harvard Law School historian Gail Hupper explains, Griswold believed that Harvard Law School should be at the "center of advanced legal thinking" and believed that its SJD program, which attracted many foreign students, helped "the School to meet this part of its responsibility to the community."[69]

For Griswold's plan to succeed, it was essential that Harvard Law School in particular, and American law schools more generally, were viewed as the greatest law schools in the common law world. His words and deeds in the context of Australian legal education suggest that he was highly sensitive to the suggestion that Harvard provided anything other than the best legal education on offer. They also suggest that he believed that, in order to transplant the US model to countries like Australia, it was necessary to imply that their law schools were vastly inferior to US law schools and in desperate need of reform. Perhaps the best example of this attitude occurred when Geoffrey Sawer published an article that reported on his tours of US law schools.[70] In the article, he stated his belief that Harvard was not the best American law school and suggested that none of the US models provided an ideal form of university legal education.[71]

Griswold retaliated with an article of his own that heavily criticized law schools in Australia, with a section devoted to a strong critique of Sawer's Department of Law at the Research School of Social Sciences at ANU.[72] His views of Australian legal education were also adopted uncritically in an article written by professor Willard Pedrick, from Northwestern University near Chicago, who spent time teaching the case and Socratic methods in 1956–1957 at the University of Western Australia.[73] Several of Griswold's criticisms were unfounded, and he mischaracterized the nature of legal education at several Australian law schools, basing his critique largely on how well Australian law schools matched US models.[74]

Griswold's assessment of Australian law schools had the desired effect. In subsequent accounts of the state of Australian legal education and scholarship, it is Griswold's views that have had the most traction, with commentators ignoring Sawer's responses.[75] The idea that Australian law schools in the 1950s were vastly inadequate and would be much improved by American models and ideas persisted throughout the second half of the twentieth century. In these ways, Griswold's attempt to transplant US models, and the preparedness of subsequent generations to accept his account, both contributed to the subordination of Australian law schools.

All Dynamism Leads to American Legal Realism?

In the United States, despite Griswold's protests and his campaign for Harvard domination, legal education at Harvard and other elite law schools in the 1950s and 1960s is often depicted by former students in negative and conservative terms. Even Peter Brett, who profited greatly from his time as a student at Harvard, detected a lack of collegiality among his law professors and considered that most of them were unexceptional and did not live up to Harvard's reputation.[76] Similarly, Australian scholars who visited US law schools always came back with both praise and criticisms, and (as noted earlier) several believed

Australia could do better. American ideas encouraged Australians to strike out from England, but with the exception of Brett there are few signs that Australians wanted law schools to wholly follow any of the American models. The more cautious assessments regarding the United States, however, sit at odds with some more recent accounts of Australian legal education suggesting that many of the progressive, dynamic, and meritorious aspects now found in Australian law schools were of American origin.[77] Such accounts rarely speak of Australian legal scholars devising new and novel practices of their own, drawing from a range of intellectual influences that responded to local conditions. This association of new and better methodology with US practices, as well as the use of American labels when describing Australian initiatives, perpetuate the idea that Australian law teachers contributed little to legal pedagogy and conceived of law largely in accordance with either their English or American counterparts.

The idea that Australian legal thought and practices, if they were to be progressive or dynamic, should follow US models appears to be part of a larger trend and can be detected in accounts of Australian judicial practices. The slippage from the classroom to the judiciary is not surprising given law schools' preoccupation with the judiciary across the second half of the twentieth century. For example, the label "American Legal Realism" has been used to describe or explain changes in the High Court of Australia's approach to legal reasoning, most notably apparent during Sir Anthony Mason's tenure as chief justice from 1987 to 1995. In his highly publicized book on shifting judicial perceptions of the High Court's legal reasoning, Jason Pierce relied on American labels to describe the changes that have taken place in Australian judging:

> If one described in a single sentence the changes that the Mason Court brought to legal reasoning it would be this: Legal realism secured a footing in a judicial culture where formalism long dominated.[78]

It is unsurprising that Pierce, an American political scientist, adopts language that is most familiar to him to categorize a judicial approach. He makes no distinction between a legal theory associated with certain American legal theorists during the 1920s to 1940s and the judicial method adopted by Australian judges. He uses the "legal realist" or "realist" label loosely and without a close examination of leading judicial writing, characterizing all judges who do not perceive the judicial function as mechanistic in the same manner.

Conflating judicial attitudes with academic legal theories is problematic for many reasons.[79] It is made even more problematic where theories emerge in a very different context—in the United States rather than Australia—and consist of a range of different theories that speak to phenomena beyond judicial reasoning.[80] Australian commentators have also drawn connections between American Legal Realism and the Mason Court, although they have generally avoided Pierce's conflation of American legal theory and Australian judicial method. Some have suggested that Sir Anthony and other members of the High Court were influenced by their jurisprudence teacher at Sydney Law School, Julius Stone, who sat within the sociological jurisprudential mold of Harvard law professor Roscoe Pound.[81] It is interesting that Pierce does not draw these connections, and neither, it appears, did any of the judges he interviewed about their perception of the Mason Court's jurisprudence.

There are also strong grounds to question whether American Legal Realism is the best or even the closest American descriptor of "the new rhetoric, if not a new judicial ethic" of the "judicial role transformation" created by the Mason Court.[82] If one were to find merit in using American labels to describe these changes, it could be argued that the Mason Court's new ethic—where judges place emphasis on principle over precedent and furnish developments in the law with an extensive set of reasons that acknowledge the choices involved—seems more closely aligned with the Legal Process School and its concept of reasoned elaboration. Had Brett lived during Mason's tenure, I suspect he would have considered the High Court to be fulfilling the Legal Process expectations he had placed on it in the 1960s and that it was in line with the concept of judicial reasoning contained in Brett and Waller's criminal law textbook.

My sense is that the label "Realist" (or "American Legal Realist") has become an easy descriptor that perpetuates myths about the role of US legal thought in Australia. It is used because the studies required to better understand and conceptualize the range of ideas, relationships, and political circumstances that have historically influenced Australian judges, lawyers, and scholars throughout the twentieth century have not yet been performed. Extrapolating from the legal historian Tanya Josev's intellectual and social history on the topic, the analogies often drawn between Australian judicial reasoning and the US judiciary may have also encouraged Australian journalists and politicians to adopt the same pejorative "activist" label to the Mason Court that American journalists and politicians applied to the United States Supreme Court under Chief Justice Earl Warren.[83] In short, the US analogies and labels have had a tendency to subordinate Australian legal thought and practices, thereby ignoring important distinctions, and ought to play a more limited role in future understandings of judges and lawyers.

Conclusion

This chapter has concentrated on the way that Australia's legal academy, during a formative period, looked to American ideas and practices to free themselves from some English legal traditions. It suggests that Australian law schools did not adopt wholly or substantially any of the elite American models. This chapter also suggests that subsequent tendencies to attribute progressive, innovative, or otherwise desirable changes and practices in legal education to American influences has, in some ways, served to subordinate Australian legal education and legal thought. In the third quarter of the twentieth century, Australian legal scholars had an appetite to create distinctively Australian materials that placed emphasis on Australian legal developments and that were created by Australian scholars. There were some, particularly in New South Wales, who favored the English traditions, and the attention given to Anglo-American questions meant that deviating from norms and common concerns risked alienation from the legal profession. However, as I have argued here, there were many legal scholars in Australia with strong progressive inclinations who were critical of both US and English traditions and wished to forge their own paths. And they had the freedom—perhaps more so than present-day scholars—to do so. As law schools were largely valued by outsiders as educational rather than research institutions, they remained insulated from the universities' broader research agendas, with legal academics being left largely free to set their own scholarly agendas.[84]

Why, then, over the second half of the twentieth century, did Australian legal scholars not develop more distinctively Australian educational theories and practices? While there is not a single explanation, this chapter suggests that the later failure to recognize earlier attempts to be innovative and to concentrate on the Australian environment has, at least in part, encouraged Australians to think of their traditions as impoverished and inferior and allowed Anglo-American legal thought to remain at the center of Australian legal education.[85] That later failure to readapt has also discouraged historical studies that would otherwise bring to light interesting and distinctive contributions by Australian legal scholars across the second half of the twentieth century. Placing innovative and/or progressive practices under the label "American Legal Realism" has buried and possibly stunted local innovations.

The absence of such studies has meant that Australian legal academics cannot draw from a rich body of evidence that shows how various intellects and personalities have approached the responsibilities that sit at the heart of running any law school: how to advance knowledge and teaching that will improve the functioning of law and lawyering within society to serve the greater good. And it prevents Australians from seeing themselves as part of a much larger, long-running, and distinctive endeavor that transcends local fads and fashions, global trends, and institutional imperatives constructed from prevailing political and economic pressures. It discourages Australians from investigating the unique needs and concerns of their environment, permitting, for example, the perpetuation of a core curriculum that most often engages only very lightly with the thinking, practices, and experiences of Aboriginal and Torres Strait Islander communities. In addressing the realities confronting the first community of Australian legal scholars, this chapter encourages legal scholars to think more critically about common perceptions of the discipline's history as well as the role they play in its present and future.

NOTES

[*] I would like to thank participants at the University of Melbourne's Legal Theory Group for commenting on a draft of this chapter and particularly professor Julian Webb for providing a robust commentary. I would also like to thank the contributors to this collection for their engagement at symposiums and conferences.

1 In this sense "positivist" appears to be divorced from any thinker and is instead used synonymously with expository approaches to teaching and legalist, or perhaps even mechanical, conceptions of legal reasoning.

2 In this sense, "legalist" is used to either suggest an approach aligned with Sir Owen Dixon's complete and strict legalism or else a form of mechanical jurisprudence. See Owen Dixon, "Concerning Judicial Method," speech, Howland Memorial Prize Ceremony, Yale University, New Haven, CT, September 9, 1955.

3 I have provided examples of this tendency in several places. See Susan Bartie, "Towards a History of Law as an Academic Discipline," *Melbourne University Law Review* 444, no. 38 (2014): 452; Susan Bartie, *Free Hands and Mind—Pioneering Australian Legal Scholars* (Oxford: Hart Publishing, 2019), 2–3.

4 Throughout this chapter "American Legal Realism" and "functionalism" are used interchangeably to refer to the body of thought that emerged from attempts by some American law professors in the first half of the twentieth century to "redefine the concept of abstract thought as constructs, or functions, or complexes, or patterns, or arrangements, of the things that we actually see or do" in "an attempt to understand law in terms of its factual context and economic and social consequences." See Karl Llewellyn, "Some Realism about Realism," *Harvard Law Review* 44, (1931): 1234, quoted in Laura Kalman, *Legal Realism at Yale, 1927—1960* (North Carolina: University of North Carolina Press, 1986), 2. As William Twining points out, "Concerns about the realities of the law in action was never an American exclusive." Twining, *Jurist in Context*, 166.

5 For example, see Dennis Pearce, Enid Campbell, and Don Harding, *Australian Law Schools: A Discipline Assessment for the Commonwealth Tertiary Education Commission*, vol. 1 (Canberra: Australian Publishing Service, 1987), para. 1.20.

6 Several of the results from this study were published in Susan Bartie, "A Full Day's Work—A Study of Australia's First Legal Scholarly Community," *University of Queensland Law Journal* 29, no. 1 (2010): 67–99.

7 Angela Fernandez and Markus Dubber take a similarly meta approach in their collection, which examines legal treatise. See Angela Fernandez and Markus Dubber, *Law Books in Action: Essays on the Anglo-American Legal Treatise* (Oxford: Hart Publishing, 2012).

8 Michael Adams, "In the Profession: Re-Viewing the Academic Book Review," *Journal of English Linguistics* 202, no. 36(2) (2007): 202.

9 See Bartie, "A Full Day's Work," 68–69.

10 The remaining 5 percent were from Austria, Canada, France, Germany, India, the Netherlands, New Zealand, Scotland, Singapore, and South Africa.

11 Bartie, "A Full Day's Work," 77.

12 Ibid.

13 A criticism issued in John Fleming, review of *Pollock's Law of Torts*, 15th ed., edited by Philip Landon, *Sydney Law Review* 282, no. 1 (1954): 283.

14 For example, see Colin Howard, review of *Kenny's Outlines of Criminal Law*, revised by J. W. Cecil Turner, *Adelaide Law Review* 137, no. 2 (1963): 137. See also Bartie, "A Full Day's Work," 90–91.

15 Bartie, "A Full Day's Work," 90–91.

16 Fleming, review of *Pollock's Law of Torts*, 283.

17 Colin Howard, review of *English Courts of Law* by H. G. Hanbury, and *Elements of English Law*, revised by William Holdsworth and H. G. Hanbury, *Adelaide Law Review* 233, no. 1 (1960–1962): 233; Bartie, "A Full Day's Work," 90–91.

18 Bartie, "A Full Day's Work," 89–90.

19 Ibid., 84.

20 Ibid., 86.

21 Ibid., 94.

22 Ibid.

23 Both English and American models influenced the university law reviews that were created in Australian law schools from the middle of the twentieth century. For example, see Leonie Star, *Julius Stone—An Intellectual Life* (Sydney: Sydney University Press, 1992), 118–19; Michael Blakeney, "The University of Western Australia Law Review: The First Seventy Years," *University of Western Australia Law Review* 43, no. 1 (2018): 5–6; George Syrota, "The University of Western Australia Law Review: Past, Present and Future," *University of Western Australia Law Review* 114, no. 32 (2004): 119–20. Australian law schools also introduced mooting competitions.

24 In the opening of E. P. Thompson's 1963 classic *The Making of the English Working Class*. As Thompson he explains, he used the word "making" in his title "because it is a study of an active process, which owes as much to agency as to conditioning." Similarly, Sugarman uses this word in the title of his seminal work on the English legal academy and argues that the textbook tradition in England, and I would add Australia, is also a product of both agency and conditioning. See David Sugarman, "Legal Theory, the Common Law Mind and the Making of the Textbook Tradition," in *Legal Theory and Common Law*, ed. William Twining (Oxford, Basil Blackwell, 1986), 26; Edward Thompson, *The Making of the English Working Class* (London: Penguin Books, 1991), 8.

25 As Stone's books were designed largely for classes in international law and jurisprudence, the approach to studying law they embodied was less likely to influence the format of common law textbooks. Fleur Johns's writing on the reception of the American legal realist strands of Julius Stone's work suggests we should be cautious in assuming his presence within Australia's legal academy promoted strong functionalist agendas. See Fleur Johns, "The Gift of Realism: Julius Stone and the International Legal Academy in Australia," in *Julius Stone a Study in Influence*, ed. Helen Irving, Jaqueline Mowbray, and Kevin Walton (Sydney: Federation Press, 2010), 21–37.

26 Peter Brett and Louis Waller, *Cases and Materials in Criminal Law* (Sydney: Butterworths, 1962).

27 See Peter Brett to Henry Hart, May 2, 1961, Henry Melvin Hart Papers, HOLLIS 601611, Harvard Law School Library, Historical and Special Collections.

28 Peter Brett to Henry Hart, May 2, 1961; Brett and Waller, *Cases and Materials*, vii.

29 Peter Brett, *An Essay on a Contemporary Jurisprudence* (Sydney: Butterworths, 1975).

30 Bartie, *Free Hands and Minds*, 57–61; Charles Barzun, "The Forgotten Foundations of Hart and Sacks," *Virginia Law Review* 99, no. 1 (2013): 1–61.
31 See William Eskridge Jr. and Philip Frickey, "The Making of the Legal Process," *Harvard Law Review* 107, no. 8 (1994): 2043.
32 Barzun, "The Forgotten Foundations," 23.
33 Ibid., 25.
34 For example, see Peter Brett and Louis Waller, *Cases and Materials*, 713.
35 Bartie, *Free Hands and Minds*, 76–78.
36 For example, see Julius Stone, *Legal System and Lawyers' Reasonings* (Sydney: Maitland Publications, 1964), 317–319.
37 Harold Ford, "The Evolution of the American Casebook," *Res Judicatae* 7 (1956): 256–275.
38 Ibid., 260.
39 Ibid., 263.
40 Ibid., 264. Although Bruce Kimball, in his biography of Langdell, suggests that Langdell appealed to science for largely strategic reasons: to align law with the president of Harvard's mission. It was not, perhaps, a reflection of his academic convictions. See Bruce Kimball, *The Inception of Modern Professional Education—C. C. Langdell, 1826–1906* (Chapel Hill: University of North Carolina Press, 2009), 351.
41 Ford, "American Casebook," 264.
42 Ibid.
43 Ibid.
44 Ibid., 271.
45 Somewhat surprisingly, Ford's first casebook appears to lack a clear conceptual underpinning. See Harold Ford, *Cases on Trusts* (Sydney: Law Book Company, 1959).
46 William Morison, Norval Morris, and Robin Sharwood, *Cases on Torts* (Sydney: Law Book Company, 1962).
47 Ibid., 3.
48 Ibid.
49 Ibid.
50 Ibid.
51 Mark Lunney, "Legal Émigrés and the Development of Australian Tort Law," *Melbourne University Law Review* 36, no. 2 (2012): 512.
52 Ibid., 512, 516.
53 Ibid., 514–15.
54 Ibid., 517–18.
55 Hyman Tarlo, "Law Schools and Law Teachers in Australia: 1946–1974," *University of Queensland Law Journal* 9, no. 1 (1975): 28, quoting John Fleming.
56 Lunney, *Legal Émigrés*, 517518.
57 Ibid.
58 Ibid., 517.

59 Ibid., 500. Stone biographer Leonie Star suggests that opposition to Stone's appointment was fueled both by the rejection of his American brand of legal theory, in favor of English approaches, as well as anti-Semitism. See Star, *Julius Stone*, 59–60, 62–63.

60 While university legal education remains largely an undergraduate education, there are now some exceptions, most notably Melbourne Law School's JD (Juris Doctor).

61 John Waugh, *First Principles—The Melbourne Law School, 1857–2007* (Melbourne: Miegunyah Press, 2007), 178–180.

62 Bartie, *Free Hands and Minds*, 83–84.

63 Waugh, *First Principles*, 180.

64 See Jethro Brown, "The American Law School," *Law Quarterly Review* 21, no. 1 (1905); Jethro Brown, "Law Schools and the Legal Profession," *Commonwealth Law Review* 6, no. 1 (1908); Harrison Moore, "Legal Education in the United States," *Journal of the Society of Comparative Legislation* 13, no. 2 (1913).

65 This is reflected in the study-leave reports of several Australian legal scholars of the period. See also Geoffrey Sawer, "Legal Education in the United States," *University of Western Australia Annual Law Review* 1 (1950): 398–403.

66 Bartie, *Free Hands and Minds*, 211.

67 He was in regular contact with the dean of Melbourne Law School and kept in touch with Australians who spent time at US law schools during the 1950s and 1960s.

68 Zelman Cowen, *The Public Life of Zelman Cowen* (Melbourne: Miegunyah Press, 2006), 180–90.

69 Erwin N. Griswold, "Graduate Study in Law," *Journal of Legal Education* 2, no. 3 (1950), quoted in Gail J. Hupper, "Educational Ambivalence: The Rise of Foreign-Student Doctorate in Law," *New England Law Review* 49, no. 3 (2015): 335.

70 Sawer, "Legal Education". Bartie, *Free Hands and Minds*, 45.

71 Sawer, "Legal Education," 400–02.

72 Erwin Griswold, "Observations on Legal Education in Australia," *University of Western Australia Law Review* 5, no. 2 (1953): 197–214.

73 Willard Pedrick, "A Case Study in Case Method Teaching," *University of Western Australia Law Review* 4, no. 1 (1957–1959): 76.

74 Geoffrey Sawer, "An Australian National School of Law," *University of Western Australia Law Review* 483, no. 2 (1953).

75 For example, see Syrota, "Western Australia Law Review," 116–17.

76 See handwritten letter from Peter Brett to Harold Ford, October 26, 1958, Harold Arthur Ford Papers, 1984.0033.0000.0014, University of Melbourne Archives.

77 For example, Barker speaks of how Hal Wootten, the founding dean of the University of New South Wales (UNSW) Law School, drew from his experiences in the United States and encouraged a more interactive teaching style. Barker suggests that this challenged existing Australian law teaching norms. He describes the launch of the *University of New South Wales Law Review*, following in the

US style of student-edited publications, as one of the initiatives that "epitomise the early radical approach of the UNSW law school." See David Barker, "The Swinging Sixties and Beyond—The Influence of the Second Wave University Law Schools in the Development of Australian Legal Education," *Journal of the Australasian Law Teachers Association* 9 (2016): 14, 16.

78 Jason Pierce, *Inside the Mason Court Revolution—The High Court of Australia Transformed* (Durham: North Carolina Academic Press, 2006), 147.

79 Most obviously because suggesting that a judge can adhere to a particular theory devised outside of the judicial realm ignores the distinctive role, culture, and perspective of judges, as well as the history and ideologies of the common law.

80 See footnote 86.

81 Adrienne Stone, "Julius Stone—A Reflection," in *Julius Stone a Study in Influence*, ed. Helen Irving, Jacqueline Mowbray, and Kevin Walton (Sydney: Federation Press, 2010), 38–48; Tony Blackshield, George Williams, and B. Fitzgerald, eds., *Australian Constitutional Law and Theory: Commentary and Materials* (Sydney: Federation Press, 1996), 838; Anthony Blackshield, "The Legacy of Julius Stone," *University of New South Wales Law Journal* 215, no. 20 (1997): 225. See also the summary by historian Tanya Josev, who suggests that Stone's influence may be an explanatory factor, rather than *the* explanatory factor, for the changes in the High Court of Australia's approach: Tanya Josev, *Campaign against the Courts* (Sydney: Federation Press, 2017), 103–04.

82 Pierce, *Inside the Mason Court*, 147.

83 Josev, *Campaign against the Courts*, 114–36.

84 In this I consider that law may have had greater autonomy for a longer period of time than arts. For the position of arts, see Hannah Forsyth, *A History of the Modern Australian University* (Sydney: NewSouth, 2014), 28. I hold doubts over whether modernizing trends rolled the academic agendas of legal scholars into that of government in the way that some studies suggest. See, for example, Judith Lancaster, *The Modernisation of Legal Education: A Critique of the Martin, Bowen and Pearce Reports* (Sydney: Centre for Legal Education, 1993).

85 On the need to consider carefully the extent that Australian judges and academic lawyers have been innovative, see Mark Lunney, *A History of Australian Tort Law, 1901–1945: England's Obedient Servant?* (Cambridge: Cambridge University Press, 2018), 7.

5

Conservatives, Nationalists, and American Romantics Debating Legal Education in Kwame Nkrumah's Ghana

JOHN HARRINGTON AND AMBREENA MANJI

In many African nations during the immediate postindependence period starting in the late 1950s, the establishment of university law schools for the first time often led to bitter battles over the purpose of legal education.[1] The stakes in these struggles were high. Leaders such as Tanzania's Julius Nyerere and Zambia's Kenneth Kaunda gave landmark speeches lauding new law faculties at national universities during this period.[2] The same is true of Ghana, whose first prime minister (later president), Kwame Nkrumah, had a personal interest in legal education. The early years of independence from 1957 were marked by considerable disagreements about the Constitution and functions of the Law Department at the University of Ghana. These pitted academics (often though not exclusively expatriates) against Nkrumah and his advisers. Tensions came to a head between 1962 and 1964 when the Law Department was at the center of "a whole circle of institutional convulsions . . . that went to the very heart of the Ghanaian political system."[3] These events added impetus to the conspiracy of senior military and political conservatives that overthrew Nkrumah in a coup d'état on February 24, 1966.

The purpose of this chapter is to document these complex struggles, to identify the broader political stakes within them, to pick out the major competing philosophies of legal education that animated them, and to relate all of these to the broader historical context of decolonization. Drawing on relevant primary and secondary sources as well as interviews,[4] we aim to show that debates over legal education had a significance going beyond the confines of the law faculty, engaging questions of African nationalism, development, and social progress, the ambivalent legacy of British colonial rule, and the growing influence of the United States in these territories.

This study builds on the long-standing work looking at the tensions between academic autonomy and state-building in many postcolonial states in Africa.[5] If universities were "born out of nationalist aspirations for freedom," how did they fare as the states to which they were responsible encountered fiscal constraints and political challenges from disillusioned groups in the population?[6] How did they avoid the impression that their autonomy merely functioned as "a figleaf for anti-national expatriate dominance"?[7]

After setting the background to the establishment of the University College of the Gold Coast (later, the University of Ghana) after World War II, we focus on the early history of its Law Department, founded in 1958. We locate this analysis in the context of the struggles between Kwame Nkrumah's government and the opposition. We start by describing the government's attempts to influence appointments and teaching at the university, which would lead to the deportation of the American dean. We demonstrate that these conflicts were animated by three main conceptions of legal education: an *instrumentalist model*, associated with the government, which sought ways to bypass the university and to train the large number of lawyers needed for development; a *humanistic American model*, which emphasized interactive teaching methods over lecturing and would give the university a monopoly of training; and a *traditionalist model*, which sought continuity with British forms of legal professionalism and teaching practices. We note in particular how each model resonated with specific local and international political tendencies. And finally,, we consider the important and growing role currently played by Ghanaian political and educational actors in these struggles.

Founding the University College of the Gold Coast

British policy on education in its African colonies went through two significant phases in the period following the end of World War I in 1918. The first, aimed at supporting the general policy of exercising control through local chiefs exercising customary powers or "indirect rule,"[8] limited education to primary schooling in vernacular languages rather than English. Nationalist thinkers in the Gold Coast, such as J. E. Casely Hayford, argued that this policy effectively confined Africans to subordinate roles in administration and the economy.[9] The second phase, after the end of World War II in 1945, saw a shift from indirect rule to "modernization" and a concern with bringing on board sympathetic local elites who would eventually rule after the departure of Britain.[10] As part of this empire-wide process, and as a result of strong campaigning within the colony, the University College of the Gold Coast was opened near Accra in 1948.[11]

The manner in which the new college—and its equivalents elsewhere—was to be run was addressed by a body known as the Asquith Commission (named for its chair, Cyril Asquith, who was at the time a justice of the English High Court).[12] At the heart of the so-called Asquith Doctrine was a concern that African institutions should be held to an academic "gold standard" that would allow their graduates "to enter the world community of intellect" on equal terms.[13] This aim was realized through the creation of a "special relationship" between the new colleges and the University of London.[14] The latter approved syllabi, scrutinized examination processes, and participated in staff appointments and the installation of expatriates at those institutions. Though funded by the state, the new colleges would be self-governing, their autonomy a precondition of entry into any relationship with the University of London.[15] Finally, the Asquith doctrine favored residential universities, with students of diverse geographic and ethnic backgrounds studying and living together on the Oxford-Cambridge model.[16]

The college's first principal was David Mowbray Balme, a former classics lecturer at Cambridge University. Under his guidance, the college closely followed the Cambridge standard and adopted British forms, rituals, and organizational models for university life. Though popular with early students and the small but growing number of African staff, this approach was criticized not least by Sir Eric Ashby, a senior British educationalist, as "a vivid expression of British cultural parochialism" married to imperial self-interest.[17] At least during the early years, this view was not shared by Kwame Nkrumah, who declared in his party's 1954 manifesto an "ambition to make the university among the finest places of learning on earth."[18] This attitude was to change as issues of higher education standards, financing, staffing, and autonomy became a key focus for contestation among political factions in the Gold Coast. The tensions between these ambitions were evident particularly in relation to legal education both at the university and beyond. Before examining these tensions in detail, it is worth reflecting on the evolving role of the legal profession in the politics of pre- and postindependence Ghana, which provides important background for the academic struggles during the early 1960s.

Politics and the Legal Profession in the Gold Coast

Due to the lack of facilities for training lawyers locally, young men from the Gold Coast were sent to London to attend the Inns of Court. This group of aspiring practitioners, given their class background, created a cultural and professional bond with England and reflected a notable brand of political and social conservatism.[19] These ties were sustained by their very mode of practicing law, which centered predominantly on litigation, as well as by the exclusive focus at the Inns on English law.[20] British caution regarding the creation of a "babu class" hostile to colonial power was particularly acute in the case of lawyers. As a result, no widening of their legal education beyond the bar was contemplated until 1950, when a number of scholarships were provided to enable Gold Coast students to read law at British universities.[21]

The campaign for self-government in the Gold Coast had been initiated after World War II by the United Gold Coast Convention (UGCC). This was, in effect, a coalition of chiefs and an educated class, mostly made up of the English-trained lawyers.[22] They had invited Kwame Nkrumah, who had studied at Lincoln University in the United States before moving to England in 1945, to take up the position of general secretary of the UGCC in 1947. However, the relationship soon deteriorated, and in June 1949 Nkrumah broke away to form the Convention People's Party (CPP), which was more insistent and urgent in demanding independence compared to the gradualist UGCC.[23] The latter, as Dennis Austin wrote,

> had a liberal view of society—a lawyer's view perhaps; they were never quite able to understand the appeal or techniques of mass organisation; and they had a lawyer's caution too, against rash precipitate action.[24]

Nkrumah's success in the elections of 1951, 1954, and 1956 led to his accession to power as prime minister of the Gold Coast under British rule, then as prime minister of independent Ghana in 1957 and its president from 1960. This caused an enduring enmity between Nkrumah and his former colonial employers, led by a group of "lawyer-merchants," who articulated their disdain in class terms, dismissing Nkrumah and his followers as undereducated "verandah boys."[25] Resistance to increasing centralization under the CPP led to the creation in 1954 of the National Liberation Movement (NLM), which mobilized traditional opponents and disaffected former supporters of Nkrumah.[26] Embracing first constitutional and then "extra-constitutional" methods,[27] the opposition was alleged to have fomented a coup plot in 1958, a series of bomb attacks on CPP meetings, and two assassination attempts on Nkrumah himself in 1958 and 1964. In response, the government had recourse to its own extraconstitutional measures, most notably the Preventive Detention Act of 1958, which allowed internment without trial and was largely used against political opponents. By the time of Nkrumah's overthrow in 1966, over 1,000 people were detained under its provisions.

Nkrumah's steady accumulation of executive powers culminated in the declaration of a one-party state after a rigged plebiscite in 1964.[28] Expatriate critics were deported, and opposition leaders went into exile. The drift to authoritarianism was particularly evident in relations with the judiciary. Measures in response to a wave of strikes in 1961 included declaring a state of emergency and the creation of a Special Court of three judges to try security-related cases arising under it, with no appeal permitted.[29] When the Supreme Court of Ghana acquitted three politicians charged with involvement in the 1962 assassination attempt, the constitution was amended to allow the president to dismiss any judge of the superior courts.

The Wider Cold War Context

These struggles had a wider resonance. As the first African state to win independence, Ghana was the object of considerable attention from the United States, the Soviet Union, and the former colonial powers in Europe, as well as from anticolonial and black liberation movements in Africa and North America. The president continued the engagement with socialist activists and pan-Africanist thinkers that had marked his years abroad. Thus, British left-wingers and antiapartheid activists were invited to join the teaching staff at the University of Ghana's main campus at Legon.[30] Ghana's attempt to steer a course between the cold war superpowers was a central concern of Geffrey Bing, Nkrumah's Attorney General. Formerly a London barrister and Labour Member of Parliament, Bing had long been active in the influential Movement for Colonial Freedom, which campaigned for more or less immediate British decolonization in the 1940s and 1950s.[31] His considerable influence over Nkrumah in this regard was sometimes attributed to his alleged membership of the Communist Party of Great Britain or fellow traveler inclinations, though this has never been proven.[32]

Nkrumah was also accused of pro-Soviet sympathies by critics throughout his career, but in fact the early period of his rule was marked by considerable openness to the United States. The latter indeed made much of its own anticolonial origins in its engagement with Africa in the late 1950s. Nkrumah's turn toward the USSR and its allies came relatively late and was motivated less by ideology and more by disillusionment with the West in the aftermath of the Congo crisis of 1960–1961 and the realization that US involvement in his flagship industrialization project on the Upper Volta River had proved more disadvantageous than expected.[33]

Independent Ghana was consistent in its leading role in the movement of nonaligned states.[34] The most tangible manifestation of this commitment was the contribution of around 2,000 troops to the United Nations (UN) mission in the Congo and a diplomatic push in support of the beleaguered President Patrice Lumumba.[35] It was out of that context that Bing recruited the Irish diplomat Conor Cruise O'Brien as vice chancellor of the University of Ghana in September 1962. Having resigned in protest for the UN's own failure to block these neocolonial ambitions, and given his record as a scholar and author, Cruise O'Brien was considered by Nkrumah to be an ideal leader for the national university of a former British colony such as Ghana.[36] However, the relationship between Cruise O'Brien, on the one hand, and Nkrumah and Bing on the other deteriorated due to conflicts over academic freedom in the university generally and in its law faculty in particular as we discuss in the following sections.

Conflicts over Academic Freedom at Legon

The Legon campus of the University of Ghana became a site of struggle between Nkrumah's government and an array of opposition forces, including Ghanaian and expatriate academics, in the early 1960s for four main reasons.[37] First, the deteriorating economic situation meant that the government grew more aware of the cost of running the university under its then-current format. Of the 13 percent of the 1960 national budget dedicated to education, a full 40 percent of the total was absorbed by the university.[38] Second, the government's growing disaffection with the United States and its allies, including the United Kingdom, registered locally in an atmosphere of suspicion and accusation. Expatriate staff members were accused of spying and of promoting neocolonialist and racist attitudes. Third, some Ghanaian staff members were openly associated with and involved in the opposition movement. And fourth, the student body was growing increasingly disaffected with the CPP.

Tensions came to the fore when the University College, as it had been know to that point, abandoned its formal link with the University of London in 1961 and became the University of Ghana, with Kwame Nkrumah as its chancellor. Controversy immediately followed as the government formally dismissed all academic staff members, ostensibly on the grounds that their employer had changed.[39] Although in the event only six lost their jobs, claims of a dire threat to academic freedom found an echo with political and educational commentators internationally, adding to Nkrumah's growing reputation as an autocrat.[40]

These conflicts also played out in and around the Law Department, founded in 1958, with dedicated funding from the government, and admitting its first students (a total of thirty) in 1959.[41] J. H. A. Lang was recruited from the United Kingdom as its first dean by Bing, having been forced to resign his post as legal counsel at Imperial Chemical Industries for political reasons. He recruited three young Ghanaian law lecturers, along with two from the United Kingdom. Supplementary teaching was provided by eminent legal practitioners. However, Lang's tenure came to a controversial end when he resigned in January 1962 in protest of Nkrumah's insistence, without further consultation, that one of the Ghanaian staff members, Alex Kuma, widely seen as a CPP loyalist, be promoted to a presidential chair.[42] The new dean, William Burnett Harvey, took over in October 1962 with the support of the Ford Foundation on a two-year secondment.[43] Ford had just launched a dedicated program, Staffing of African Institutions of Legal Education and Research, which was to contribute to developing law schools across the continent over the next decade. A contract lawyer and legal theorist, Harvey was a professor of law at the University of Michigan. With him came Robert Seidman, a Harvard graduate, who took up a senior lectureship (also with Ford support). From the start, Harvey pursued a vigorous program of reform and expansion in law at Legon. He achieved faculty status for the department, helped found a university law journal, and began the move to dedicated premises. He also had clear ideas about the ideal scope and form of legal education, informed above all by his career in the United States, which we will explore in detail below.[44]

Ironically, while Harvey's innovations were seen as revolutionary by local practitioners associated with the opposition, his American origins also made him suspect in the eyes of government ministers and CPP activists, especially as he took Vice Chancellor Cruise O'Brien's side in defending university self-government.[45] In a sign of the government's growing insecurity, Harvey was accused by party newspapers of being involved in the assassination attempt of January 1963. Reports claimed that "the so-called Michigan professor from Legon," had been inexplicably standing behind Nkrumah when there was an attempt on his life by a bodyguard, leading many to infer complicity on his part.[46] He was also charged with supporting the racist government of South Africa on the basis of his inaugural professorial lecture in May 1963. His dry and fairly brief discussion of the peculiarities of the Roman-Dutch legal system was interpreted by CPP supporters in the press as endorsement of apartheid.[47]

Cruise O'Brien was unsuccessful in his attempts to reassure Nkrumah personally that the accusations against Harvey were unfounded. On the contrary, government outlets went on the offensive, emphasizing the need for the law faculty (and, indeed, the legal profession) to align themselves with national objectives as defined by the party.[48] The president himself sanctioned this line of attack in a speech at the opening of the university's Institute of African Studies in October 1963, in which he affirmed that "the Law Faculty should be staffed by Africans."[49] Some months later, demonstrators loyal to the government marched on campus, taunting students and demanding the Africanization of the staff and teaching methods.[50] The crisis culminated in the deportation of Harvey and Seidman, along with a further five expatriate teachers from other faculties, on February 8, 1964. The contest between academic freedom, on the one hand, and promotion of social relevance on the other cannot simply be attributed to the differences between expatriate versus African staff. In fact, many Ghanaian academics were critical of government interference in the running of the university.[51] Equally, many expatriates—including Harvey and Seidman—acknowledged the importance of law and other disciplines in contributing to national development, as well as the need to Africanize the cohort of lecturers and professors.[52]

Comparing the Modes of Legal Training in Ghana

It is most likely that all of the charges alleged against Harvey were conjured up by party activists. But there were substantive issues in dispute, too.[53] These concerned the appropriate institutions for training legal professionals in Ghana, the relations among them, and the style of teaching that each would adopt. Thus, in 1957, at the instigation of Geoffrey Bing, the government moved to establish a center for training lawyers that would eliminate the necessity for Ghanaians to travel to London to study at the Inns of Court.[54] The Ghana Law School (GLS) opened in 1958 and was located in the heart of the commercial district of central Accra, near the main courts, a setting that contrasted with that of the university's Law Department, which was located in a then-rural setting on Legon Hill. Though both were founded in the same year, there was no formal connection between them. The GLS was subject to the direct control of the General Legal Council, which regulated admission to the legal profession.

Under the initial plan, the GLS would offer a one-year practical course for law graduates. But its main task was to prepare students for the English bar examination through evening classes. Students would be eligible to practice law in Ghana after completing a compressed syllabus over the course of a three-year diploma program. By contrast, the university law degree required four years of full-time study in traditional common law subjects, as well as African customary law and one non-law elective. Entry requirements were similarly divergent. The university demanded passes in the national school-leaving examinations, while the GLS accepted a range of qualifications, from bachelor's degrees to commercial courses in accounting. Poor student completion rates in the school seemed to reflect this generous admissions policy.

In July 1959, the unclear relationship between the GLS and the university's Law Department was considered by the International Advisory Board on Legal Education; its members included Arthur Sutherland (United States), Zelman Cowen (Australia), and L. C. B. Gower (United Kingdom). The advisory board recommended that Ghana's bifurcated system of legal training come to an end: The GLS should be absorbed into the university, the part-time diploma should be phased out, and efforts should be focused on postgraduate training for legal practice.[55] These recommendations had not yet been implemented when William Burnett Harvey took up the deanship at Legon. In October 1962, only a month after his arrival, he addressed the issue of the GLS in a memorandum submitted to the Academic Board of the university and the General Legal Council.[56] Going one step further than the advisory board, he proposed that the GLS be abolished completely and recommended the provision of separate vocational training in legal practice. The latter, he argued, could be delivered more efficiently by the university's Law Department, as was the case in the United States. To achieve this, students would take a three-year BA course, followed by two years of LLB studies to entitle them to practice. This would have the benefit of improving the quality of teaching and, thus, of graduates and practitioners. It would also concentrate national research capacity in law. Although accepted by the General Legal Council, Harvey's proposals did not survive his deportation in 1964. Moreover, they provoked significant opposition, as we discuss below. Before addressing that, however, we investigate the rival conceptions of legal education that underpinned the different positions in this debate.

Nkrumah, Bing, and the Instrumentalist Approach

Geoffrey Bing's memoir, published after his expulsion in 1966, include a chapter of historically and theoretically well informed reflections on education in Ghana. Examining this, along with views expressed by Nkrumah himself, will provide insight into the distinctive aims and values that each felt should shape legal training in a postcolonial state. Bing adopted Sir Eric Ashby's critique of the Asquith Doctrine but gave it a more political, even anticolonial edge. Asquith's elite (or "Platonic") model of university education, he argued, was rooted in imperial strategies of domination, exemplified, for example, in the criteria laid down by Cecil Rhodes for scholarships awarded in his name to students attending Oxford.[57] That model, by privileging classicists and historians as candidates for administrative and political leadership in Britain and the colonies, aimed to teach "men how to rule men," not "how the world might be improved."[58]

For his part, Bing took a more instrumental and democratic view, one rooted in the ethos of the natural sciences prevalent at midcentury. Education, he wrote,

> consists of passing on and augmenting the knowledge which enables man to conquer his environment. The student's mind must be so trained that he will for ever after question, in accordance with scientific principles, the world in which he lives.[59]

This generalized instrumentalism was given concrete substance in independent Ghana by the government's developmental ambitions, and it was in these specific terms that Bing recounted and evaluated the relationship between Nkrumah's government and the university at Legon. He dismissed the sequence of on-campus demonstrations and deportations as no more than the "sordid brawling between 'town' and 'gown'" typical of medieval Cambridge. Rather, the true "crime of the University was its passivity in face of the crying economic and social needs of the country" and its failure "to provide the skilled personnel necessary for development."[60] The banner of academic freedom, raised against Nkrumah by Conor Cruise O'Brien and his colleagues, as well as by international critics, in reality served to protect the corporate and material interests of disproportionately well paid expatriates and the entrenched class position of established Ghanaian elites.[61]

A better, more development-focused model for Ghana and other African states, according to Bing, lay in the land-grant colleges and universities established in the United States during the second half of the nineteenth century.[62] Governed by a committee drawn from the surrounding community, rather than by academics themselves, these institutions were founded explicitly to promote economic and social progress in their own regions.[63] Courses of varying length therefore focused on practical training, oriented to the needs of local industries, including agriculture. This approach was widely discussed elsewhere in Africa during the period of decolonization, most notably by Dr. Nnamdi Azikiwe in Nigeria, who adopted it as the model for the University of Nigeria at Nsukka, founded in 1955. More democratic and more oriented toward social problems, according to Ashby, the land-grant institution was concerned "with the making of citizens, not just leaders . . . its campus [was] the whole state."[64]

Nkrumah's and Bing's interventions on legal education were also marked by a steady focus on the collective, articulated in instrumentalist terms. Bing argued that through its "inefficiency, slowness and uncertainty," colonial legislation was "a clog on industrialization and an invisible surcharge on every commercial transaction."[65] According to the president, practitioners had concentrated on conducting litigation "between wealthy individuals," neglecting less lucrative disputes and effectively promoting "colonial economic interests."[66] This group understood law in absolute terms—as an end in itself—operating above all in defense of private property and the established order. By contrast, in an independent Ghana law would be deployed dynamically for transformation and growth. For Nkrumah, "law must represent the will of the people and be so designed and administered as to forward the social purpose of the state," a view warranted by the essential communitarianism of historic African societies.[67]

Legal education in the new Ghana would be reshaped to serve this end. Not litigators but "legally trained administrators and legal technicians" were required for development through socialist planning.[68] The reorientation of practice toward external goals meant that the curriculum should include nonlaw subjects such as economics, social and political science, and even science and technology. This vision of the new lawyer as technocrat was complemented by a more populist concern with the needs of "the ordinary man and woman" in small towns and villages whose "everyday legal problems" had been neglected by elite litigators.[69] Through the GLS, civil servants, the police, and army personnel, for example, would be able to gain the legal knowledge necessary for the more effective discharge of their public duties. Equally, its lower cost would attract into the profession "those whose families lacked the money to send them to London to read law."[70] So-called legal letter writers operating as informal advisers in the countryside would be offered instruction "in the rudiments of law" as a condition for being formally licensed. Significantly, these initiatives were resisted in the name of maintaining standards. The GLS curriculum, as we have seen, was pegged to the bar course in London, and its quest for the authority to train lawyers from scratch was thwarted. The letter-writers proposal was also rejected by the General Legal Council, as a "colonialist suggestion" that Ghanaians could not aspire to the same quality of legal education as that prevailing in England.

Harvey, Seidman, and the Humanistic Approach

In taking steps to ensure a widening of legal education suited to Ghanaian conditions, Bing and Nkrumah were opposed by W. B. Harvey. Admittedly, he acknowledged, like them, that the Law Department faced the challenge of promoting Ghanaian staff, and he shared their concern that the university's law faculty should not isolate itself from the wider society.[71] In form and substance, however, his vision differed from theirs quite sharply. Harvey arrived at Legon "carrying the torch for American legal enlightenment."[72] Like Bing, he started with a critical view of the legal profession as it then existed: numerically small, overconcentrated geographically, and skewed toward advocacy. He also argued that the new curriculum should include nonlaw courses to alert the lawyer to "the pressures and needs felt at the growing edge of . . . society."[73] But these concessions did not amount to an acceptance of Bing's assumption that law was merely a tool of national development subject to government direction. On the contrary, Harvey emphasized first and foremost that

> law is a learned profession [and the lawyer] who is faithful to the highest standards of his profession is not merely a skilled craftsman manipulating a technique for social ordering.[74]

Lawyers required a "broad and liberal education" rendering them sensitive to "the values of the cultural tradition of which they are a part" through "substantial exposure to the learning of the humanities and the social sciences."[75] Acquiring familiarity with "the body of positive legal norms" was not enough.[76] Echoing the Asquith Report, he invoked the "gold standard." Ghana should concentrate on producing "soundly and liberally educated" lawyers entitled "to full acceptance in the international community."[77]

Harvey robustly defended the inherent academic value of the academic law degree. In its core subjects, as much as through nonlaw electives, it offered a "rich storehouse of data of general humanistic and social significance."[78] Law was a worthy subject of study even by those who would not go on to practice. The law of contracts provided an insight into the workings of the market economy, tort law into the costs of industrialization, and so on. This potential was sold short by the abbreviated training offered at institutions like the GLS, which he dismissed as "'crash programs' for the training of minimally qualified legal technicians."[79] If national resources were scarce, then they should be devoted to providing law degrees to a high standard, rather than to supplementary and inevitably mediocre law teaching aimed at public servants and the like. The practical corollary of this view for Harvey, as we have seen, was that legal education should be solely delivered by the university, as in the United States.

This humanistic, as opposed to purely instrumentalist, conception of legal education was also evident in how Harvey and his colleague Robert Seidman represented their teaching practice. Trained at the University of Michigan and Yale law schools, respectively, both followed the Socratic (or dialogic) method of teaching. Famously, this inducted students into the practice of common law reasoning by a rigorous and open-ended questioning on the details of important cases, through which they were expected to grasp the principles of a given legal area. The function of the law teacher in this mode was "to organize an apt body of working materials, to stimulate the student to consider them in such a way as to sharpen his own analytical skills and insights, and by his questions and criticisms to light the student's path toward discovery, but not to carry him along it."[80] In regard to teaching materials, this approach privileges casebooks containing extracts from primary legal sources, rather than straightforwardly descriptive textbooks; American staff members at Legon were active producing such casebooks for their courses, containing specifically Ghanaian and other African materials.[81] Historically associated with Harvard Law School, the Socratic method was much different than the magisterial style common in British law faculties and among Ghanaian colleagues who had studied there. In the latter model, according to Harvey, legal information was imparted in unidirectional fashion through lectures that students attended "without prior preparation on the materials to be considered . . . quietly taking their notes."[82] This ultimately rested on a view of the law not as an activity but as a body of rules and principles in the first instance.

This difference in teaching methods had a clear political valency for Seidman. While American professors' role was "to guide students to discover for themselves underlying patterns of law," their European counterparts used "a heavily didactic, authoritarian instructional method."[83] Thus, it is small wonder that the president, himself seen as an incipient autocrat, "objected to the way Americans taught 'Western law'" or that proponents of the traditional lecturing style in the university had also sought to introduce compulsory courses for students in the party doctrine of "Nkrumahism."[84] The popularity and inherent democratic potential in the Socratic method was borne out for Seidman during the same week of his expulsion in January 1964. He recalled with pride a criminal law class from that period that saw students tease out the implications of the common law doctrine of provocation with reference to a Ghanaian defendant poised between "rational understanding" and "traditional beliefs." His own departure from Accra's airport was attended by most staff from the law faculty and a large body of obviously distressed but supportive students. Even in his absence, he was sure that their acquired skill in Socratic techniques would allow them to run their own classes for a number of weeks.[85] Harvey, too, expected that students who had been "encouraged to question, to criticize and to attempt to defend their own analyses [would] never again be content with passive note-taking on lectures."[86]

English Conservatism and Ghanaian Nationalism

Legal conservatism, in teaching and practice, was attacked in the name of Ghanaian development by Bing, as well as by Harvey and Seidman. In both cases, the British origin of these traditions was explicitly disparaged. Harvey traced the tendency toward rote learning and regurgitation among his students to the imposition of the British school system in Ghana, one of the most the "most regrettable aspects" of the colonial legacy.[87] Against this legacy he hoped that "even after the direct American involvement in law teaching has ended, the American insistence that rule-learning through neat lectures is not legal education will still influence the Faculty of Law."[88]

Nonetheless, the British connection continued to be highly valued by many Ghanaian scholars and legal practitioners. Thus, in 1960, addressing the University of Hull, Mr. Justice N. A. Ollennu, then a judge of the Ghanaian High Court and occasional lecturer at Legon, affirmed:

> [N]ot only are we indebted to England for that part of our law which we have received from England, but also, and much more significantly, we are indebted to you for giving us the heritage of your own methods of creating, declaring, and developing the law.[89]

Indeed, lawyers' resistance to Nkrumah was represented at the time by S. K. B. Asante as the result of "solid attitudes instilled by a hundred years of contact [which meant that] the essential ingredients of the English concept of the rule of law were sufficiently rooted in Ghanaian public life to generate a revulsion against wanton totalitarianism."[90] And in the university (even though the formal link to the University of London was abandoned in 1960), a more informal shadowing of the gold standard was achieved through the appointment of British or British-trained external examiners for its law programs.[91] Even the Ghana Law School, which was founded to outflank the conservative, Anglophile legal profession, was concerned to show it would maintain parity with English standards, at least in its early years, by using the same examination papers as the Council of Legal Education in England.[92] This affinity formed part of a broader pattern among the educated elite that emerged in the Gold Coast during the postwar period. The memoir of Alex Kwapong, who succeeded Cruise O'Brien as vice chancellor at Legon, makes this clear.[93] Trained as a classicist at Cambridge, he expressed a determination in the aftermath of the 1966 coup that the university at Legon should endure as a "microcosm of the national freedom of Ghana."[94]

The defense of legal Englishness was not limited to established professionals and political conservatives, however. W. C. Ekow Daniels, who had joined the faculty after returning from doctoral studies at University College London, was strongly identified with President Nkrumah. Like Bing, he was accused of offstage plotting to subvert the autonomy of the university in the name of Africanizing the lecturing staff. Indeed, Cruise O'Brien, Harvey, and Seidman all asserted privately that he was instrumental in having the latter two deported in order to secure a chair in law for himself.[95] Ekow Daniels strenuously denied this at the time and ever since.[96] What is indisputable, however, is that he openly challenged Harvey's proposed reforms to the organization and format of teaching law in Ghana with a memorandum of his own to faculty staff in late 1962.[97] This was made clear in terms of a defense of the English form of legal education that he had experienced as an undergraduate (i.e., as a separation of academic study, to be delivered at the university, versus vocational instruction, to be provided through a separate institution such as the GLS). He argued that Harvey's typically American proposal to deliver the entirety of legal education through a university degree program confounded theory and practice. Casting Harvey's ambition to overcome British traditions as a kind of legal educational "imperialism," he proposed instead that students take a diet of solely legal subjects, with no room for extra coursework in economics, social studies, and so on.[98] Contextual and critical perspectives on law were therefore more likely to be offered to students by American staff rather than by British-trained Ghanaian colleagues, no matter how radical their politics.[99]

A further irony is evident when we consider the views of L. C. B. Gower, who at the time was chair of law at the London School of Economics and the founder of academic company law in England, and who was highly active in law reform and the development of law faculties across West Africa in this period.[100] Gower had served on the International Advisory Committee on Legal Education in Ghana, but he was no missionary for the traditional English model. He had long-established contacts with leading US scholars of corporate law.[101] Like many British academics who made the journey to the United States at the time, he was greatly impressed by the breadth and vigor of American legal scholarship and equally convinced of the inferiority of its counterpart at home.[102] He brought this awareness with him to his work in and on Ghana, arguing repeatedly for the value of a university law degree as a prerequisite for professional practice.

Gower dedicated his Oliver Wendell Holmes Lectures at Harvard in 1966 to the theme of "Independent Africa," starting from the assumption that well-trained lawyers were essential to political order and economic development.[103] He reviewed the "colonial inheritance" in this regard. Positives included the rule of law, policing, an apolitical military, and the common law itself. Foremost among the negatives was the education system, which was elitist at the highest level and simply insufficient at lower levels.[104] While recommending that Britain and the United States should address these deficiencies "in combination" rather than in competition, Gower clearly cast his American peers as the agents of progress.[105] He counseled due modesty, warning against "dollar imperialism," over zealousness and the naïve assumption that Africans saw the United States as a "loveable" ally with a shared anticolonial past. What was required above all was for "more for more African lawyers to be exposed to American methods at American law schools, and more American teachers to practise American methods at African law schools."[106] African lawyers and their British counterparts needed to be shaken "out of complacency."[107] Recalling a friendly comment from his year at Harvard to the effect that he "wasn't a typical Englishman," he added that "I wouldn't know about that. But I think too many African lawyers are."[108]

Conclusion

Legal education, which had been neglected and discouraged under colonial rule, received much attention after independence, but there were often conflicting outlooks on its aims and how it should be provided. In this chapter, we have shown that starting in 1957 debates about the roles of the Law Department at the University of Ghana and the Ghana Law School must be understood as part of wider, complex struggles. At stake were the political positions of the main protagonists and competing philosophies of legal education, while the broader historical context was one of decolonization. Struggles over legal education had a significance far beyond the law faculty. They were also about African nationalism, development, and social progress, the impact of British rule on legal education, and the growing involvement of the United States in this domain. There was no straight alignment of perspective with national origin, however.

As to the shape of legal education in Ghana, it must be admitted that in the medium and longer terms Harvey and Bing failed in their ambitions. The bid to create a university monopoly of legal training was thwarted by Harvey's deportation in 1964. The bid to bypass the university by allowing nongraduates to practice after studying at Ghana Law School was frustrated by Bing's own expulsion after the coup against Nkrumah in 1966. Our discussion shows that neither proposal was supported by a sufficiently numerous and influential domestic constituency.[109] Ultimately, the mixed English model, as supported by the International Advisory Committee, was retained. In the aftermath of the 1966 coup, the university council declared its intention to return Ghana "to the academic gold standard," and this development was a noted ambition of the conspirators themselves.[110]

We have already noted the irony in all of this. Britain was exhausted as a world power by the early 1960s. The ruling class had lost an empire, and its ruling ideas had lost purchase, most of all with the ambitious children of its own working and middle classes. The veneration of tradition, complemented by an empiricist anti-intellectualism, which marked both the common law and the wider culture, was being challenged by imported Continental and American models of thought and pedagogy.[111] In some former colonies, by contrast, the "peculiarities of the English" retained a certain purchase in debates over the future of law and legal education. The metaphor of the gold standard, repeatedly invoked, suggests a certain nostalgia for the days when money and qualifications had an intrinsic worth underwritten by the imperial metropole. Dollar convertability had fewer attractions. National money threatened inflation and a loss of value. It would be erroneous, however, to see this as mere imitation or simple neocolonial deference. Well-founded strategic concerns (about US intentions in Africa, for example), as well as the tactical demands of the political moment within Ghana, meant that the English model had value even for radical nationalists. We need to remind ourselves that the Anglophile lawyer-elites in Accra, like their conservative peers in other former colonies, were no less committed to independence and development than their radical rivals, albeit with more caution. Finally, it is worth noting that many teachers and students positively embraced the plurality of teaching styles and scholarly orientations on offer at Legon during this period. They rallied in support of deported US lecturers and in protest against Nkrumah's constraints on the judiciary. British and American methods were appropriated, adapted, and partly rejected across different disciplinary contexts by distinguished Ghanaian scholars and judges over the ensuing decades.[112]

NOTES

1 See, for example, William Twining, "Legal Education in East Africa," *International and Comparative Law Quarterly Supplementary Publication* 12 (1966): 115–52; Yash Ghai, "Law, Development and African Scholarship," *Modern Law Review* 50, no. 6 (October 1987): 750–76; Issa G. Shivji, *Intellectuals at the Hill: Essays and Talks, 1968–1993* (Dar es Salaam: Dar es Salaam University Press, 1993).

2 Julius Kambarage Nyerere, "Inaugural Speech at Opening Ceremony of University College Dar es Salaam," October 25, 1961 (copy on file with authors); Kenneth D. Kaunda, "The Functions of the Lawyer in Zambia Today," *Zambia Law Journal* 3, no. 1–2 (1971–1972): 1–4.

3 Donald Harman Akenson, *Conor: A Biography of Conor Cruise O'Brien* (Ithaca: Cornell University Press, 1994), 223.

4 Professors S. K. B. Asante and W. C. Ekow Daniels allowed us to consult their papers. We also studied relevant papers of Conor Cruise O'Brien, held in the Archives of University College Dublin (referenced here as "UCD Archives"), and those of William Burnett Harvey (referenced here as "Indiana Archives"), which are held in the online collection of the Maurer School of Law, Indiana University, at www.repository.law.indiana.edu.

5 See most recently Mahmood Mamdani, "The African University," *London Review of Books* 40, no. 14 (July 2018): 29–32.

6 George P. Hagan, "Academic Freedom and National Responsibility in an African State: Ghana," in *Academic Freedom in Africa*, ed. Mamadou Diouf and Mahmood Mamdani (Dakar: Codesria, 1994), 39–58, 39.

7 Mahmood Mamdani, "Introduction: The Quest for Academic Freedom," in *Academic Freedom in Africa*, ed. Mamadou Diouf and Mahmood Mamdani (Dakar: Codesria, 1994), 1–16, 2.

8 See Clive Whitehead, "Education Policy in British Tropical Africa: The 1925 White Paper in Retrospect," *History of Education* 10, no. 3 (1981): 195–203.

9 See Sybille Küster, "'Book Learning' versus 'Adapted Education': The Impact of Phelps-Stokesism on Colonial Education Systems in Central Africa in the Interwar Period," *Paedagogica Historica* 43, no. 1 (February 2007): 79–97.

10 Alan Cousins, "Governing Africa: The Imperial Mind in British Colonies, 1938–1947, in the Light of Indian Experience," *Social Scientist* 27, no. 7/8 (July/August 1999): 140–67, 160.

11 Charles P. Emudong, "The Gold Coast Nationalist Reaction to the Controversy over Higher Education in Anglophone West Africa and Its Impact on Decision Making in the Colonial Office, 1945–47," *Journal of Negro Education* 66, no. 2 (Spring 1997): 137–46.
12 Report of the Commission on Higher Education in the Colonies, 1944–45, Cmd. 6647.
13 ICM Maxwell, *Universities in Partnership: The Inter-University Council and the Growth of Higher Education in Developing Countries, 1946–70* (Edinburgh: Scottish Academic Press, 1980), 13.
14 See Eric Ashby and Mary Anderson, *Universities: British, Indian, African: A Study in the Ecology of Higher Education* (London: Weidenfeld and Nicolson, 1966), 233.
15 Maxwell, *Universities in Partnership*, 33.
16 Ibid., 17.
17 Eric Ashby, *African Universities and Western Tradition* (London: Oxford University Press, 1964), 19.
18 Maxwell, *Universities in Partnership*, 145.
19 See further Robin Luckham, "The Ghana Legal Profession: The Natural History of a Research Project," *Journal of Legal Pluralism and Unofficial Law* 8, no. 13 (1976): 106–44.
20 Samuel O. Manteaw, "Legal Education in Africa: What Type of Lawyer Does Africa Need?," *McGeorge Law Review* 39, no. 4 (2008): 903–76, 916.
21 S. K. B. Asante, "Recollection of the History of the Law Faculty at Legon: The Turbulent Early Years," in University of Ghana Faculty of Law, *50th Anniversary Celebrations—Grand Durbar*, April 20, 2009 (copy on file with authors).
22 David Birmingham, *Kwame Nkrumah: The Father of African Nationalism* (Athens: Ohio University Press, 1998), 11.
23 Dennis Austin, *Politics in Ghana, 1946–1960* (Oxford: Oxford University Press, 1964), 85.
24 Dennis Austin, *Ghana Observed: Essays on the Politics of a West African Republic* (Manchester: Manchester University Press, 1976), 12–13.
25 Austin, *Politics in Ghana*, 181.
26 Report of the International Advisory Committee on Legal Education, Accra (n.d.), 235ff (copy on file with authors).
27 Austin, *Ghana Observed*, 99.
28 Austin, *Politics in Ghana*, 414–15.
29 The case is discussed in Obed Y. Asamoah, *The Political History of Ghana (1950–2013): The Experience of a Non-Conformist* (Bloomington, IN: AuthorHouse, 2014), 53–55.
30 Rohit De, "The Flying QC: The Postcolonial Career of DN Pritt and the Jurisprudence of Decolonization" (forthcoming).
31 See Stephen Howe, *Anti-colonialism in British Politics: The Left and the End of Empire, 1918–1964* (Oxford: Oxford University Press, 1993), 250.

32 A document in the British National Archives from 1956 refers to Bing as having been a member of the CPGB's "secret legal group" before the Second World War and a "fellow traveller" after it: TNA V 2/3819.
33 Ebere Nwaubani, *The United States and Decolonization in West Africa, 1950–1960* (Rochester, NY: University of Rochester Press, 2001), 162.
34 Nwaubani, *The United States and Decolonization*, 136–39.
35 Ibid., 146.
36 Basil Davidson, *Black Star: A View of the Life and Times of Kwame Nkrumah* (London: Allen Lane, 1973), 56.
37 For a firsthand account by the then–vice chancellor and professor of classics, see Alexander A. Kwapong, *A Life in Education: A Memoir* (Legon-Accra: Sub-Saharan Publishers, 2016), 183–85.
38 Akenson, *Conor*, 227.
39 Asante, "Recollection of the History of the Law Faculty at Legon."
40 See Ashby, *Universities: British, Indian, African*, 329.
41 Francis Agbodeka, *A History of the University of Ghana: Half a Century of Higher Education, 1948–1998* (Accra: Noeli Publishing Services, 1998), 210.
42 Akenson, *Conor*, 234.
43 See Jayanth K. Krishnan, "Academic SAILERS: The Ford Foundation and the Efforts to Shape Legal Education in Africa, 1957–1977," *American Journal of Legal History* 52, no 3 (July 2012): 261–324, 301–03.
44 Akenson, *Conor*, 234.
45 The union of radical and conservative opponents is noted in C. Cruise O'Brien, Letter to WB Harvey, July 1, 1965, P82/99, UCD Archives.
46 Akenson, *Conor*, 236.
47 W. B. Harvey, "Legal Education in Ghana. A Report to the SAILER Programme of the Institute of International Education and the Ford Foundation" (n.d.), Indiana Archives, 313.
48 Quoted in Akenson, *Conor*, 235.
49 Quoted in ibid., 238.
50 Harvey, "Legal Education in Ghana," 333.
51 Akenson, *Conor*, 219, 231.
52 W. B. Harvey, *Law and Social Change in Ghana* (Princeton: Princeton University Press, 1966), 371; R Seidman, Letter from a Deportee (n.d.), P82/121, UCD Archives.
53 See Akenson, *Conor*, 234.
54 The discussion in this and the following paragraph draws on Harvey's memorandum "Legal Education in Ghana" presented on behalf of the Faculty of Law to the Academic Board of the University of Ghana in November 1962 and reprinted in Harvey, *Law and Social Change*, 369–89.
55 Report of the International Advisory Committee on Legal Education, 6–7.
56 An Integrated Programme for Legal Education in Ghana, Accra, 1962, reprinted in Harvey, *Law and Social Change*, 369–89.

57 Geoffrey Bing, *Reap the Whirlwind: An Account of Kwame Nkrumah's Ghana from 1950–1966* (London: MacGibbon & Kee, 1968), 345.
58 Ibid., 341. This was also Nkrumah's view; see Davidson, *Black Star*, 163.
59 Bing, *Reap the Whirlwind*, 340.
60 Ibid., 364.
61 Regarding the former, he mentions the defense, in terms of intellectual autonomy, of holiday leave allowances including first-class airfares. The latter accounted for one-ninth of the annual university budget. Ibid., 360.
62 Ibid., 340. See also Earle D. Ross, "On Writing the History of Land Grant Colleges and Universities" *Journal of Higher Education* 24, no. 8 (1953): 411–14, 451–52.
63 See Ashby and Anderson, *Universities*, 276–81.
64 See ibid., 279.
65 Bing, *Reap the Whirlwind*, 330.
66 Kwame Nkrumah, "Law in Africa," *Journal of African Law* 6, no. 2 (July 1962): 103–12, 107.
67 Ibid., 103.
68 Ibid., 103, 107.
69 Bing, *Reap the Whirlwind*, 316.
70 Ibid., 318.
71 Harvey, *Law and Social Change*, 178.
72 S. K. B. Asante, interview with John Harrington, Accra, October 8, 2018.
73 Harvey, *Law and Social Change*, 369.
74 Ibid., 369.
75 Ibid.
76 Ibid..
77 Ibid., 370.
78 Ibid.
79 Ibid.
80 Harvey, "Legal Education in Ghana," 286.
81 The fruits of this effort are recorded in ibid., 281.
82 Ibid., 285.
83 R Seidman, Letter from a Deportee (n.d.), P82/121, UCD Archives.
84 Ibid.
85 Ibid.
86 Harvey, "Legal Education in Ghana," 287.
87 Ibid., 284.
88 Ibid., 287.
89 N. A. Ollennu, "The Influence of English Law on West Africa," *Journal of African Law* 5, no. 1 (April 1961): 21–35.
90 S. K. B. Asante, "Law and Society in Ghana," *Wisconsin Law Review* 1966, no. 4 (1966): 1113–24.
91 Asante, "Recollection of the History of the Law Faculty at Legon."
92 "Law School Opens," *New Ghana*, November 19, 1958.

93 Kwapong, *A Life in Education*.

94 See "The Vice-Chancellor's Address to Congregation, 26th March 1966," reproduced in Kwapong, *A Life in Education*, 326–42, 341.

95 C. Cruise O'Brien, Letter to Alan Nunn May, February 24, 1964, P82/99, UCD Archives; Harvey, "Legal Education in Ghana," 289, 306; R. Seidman, Letter of a Deportee (n.d.), P82/121, UCD Archives.

96 Libel proceedings arising out of a piece that Cruise O'Brien had written to this effect were settled in 1969 with an apology. See, respectively, C .Cruise O'Brien, "Return to Ghana," *The Observer*, April 24, 1966, and relevant litigation papers (on file with professor W. C. Ekow Daniels).

97 W. C. Ekow Daniels, "Some Comments on Professor Harvey's Memorandum on the Future of Legal Education in Ghana" (n.d.) (copy on file with authors).

98 W. C. Ekow Daniels, interview with John Harrington, Accra, October 10, 2018.

99 Even Asante, who was considerably more critical of Nkrumah and supportive of Harvey and Seidman than was Ekow Daniels, felt that the Americans were "over-confident" in seeking to impose a "romanticized" US conception of legal education "against English tradition" in Ghana. Asante interview, October 8, 2018.

100 Most notable in Ghana was Gower's work on company law reform; see Final Report of the Commission of Enquiry into the Working and Administration of the Present Company Law of Ghana (Accra: Government of Ghana, 1961), 2.

101 Gower's American connections are carefully mapped in David Sugarman, "A Special Relationship? American Influences on English Legal Education, c. 1870–1965," *International Journal of the Legal Profession* 18, no. 1–2 (March–July 2011): 7–57, 23–25.

102 For an early statement, see L. C. B. Gower, "English Legal Training a Critical Survey," *Modern Law Review* 13, no 2 (April 1950): 137–205.

103 L. C. B. Gower, *Independent Africa: The Challenge to the Legal Profession* (Cambridge: Harvard University Press, 1967), 144, 107.

104 Ibid., 34, 13.

105 Ibid., 134.

106 Ibid., 144.

107 Ibid., 145.

108 Ibid.

109 Asante interview, October 8, 2018.

110 Austin, *Ghana Observed*, 176.

111 See generally Perry Anderson, "Components of the National Culture," *New Left Review* 1, no. 50 (July/August 1968): 3–57; and, on law, A. W. B. Simpson, "The Common Law and Legal Theory," in *Legal Theory and Legal History: Essays on the Common Law* (London: Hambledon Press, 1987), 359–82.

112 Asante interview with John Harrington, Accra, October 8, 2018; S. Date-Bah, telephone interview with John Harrington, October 10, 2018.

6

Transplantation and Domestication of American Models of Legal Education in Nigeria

J. JARPA DAWUNI AND REBECCA EMIENE BADEJOGBIN

Among the many debates on higher education—including law schools—is the need for internationalization, an amorphous term that means different things to different users.[1] The two main schools of thought include, on the one hand, those who argue that law schools produce lawyers who deal with domestic issues and therefore should be trained to address domestic matters. Adherents of this view are not very welcoming to the introduction of legal models from other places. On the other hand are those who argue that global changes have occasioned the development of transnational laws and practices that require lawyers to be trained in domestic as well as international law.[2] Proponents of this view are more open to the process of internationalization and transplanting models of teaching and learning.

Nigeria, like many other African nations, has been at the center of global experiments to internationalize higher education, including those promoted by the United States. This chapter evaluates the impact of American influences on the types and forms of legal education adopted in Nigeria beginning in 1962 up to the present. In 1962, Nigeria established its system of legal education by founding the Council of Legal Education and the Nigerian Law School following recommendations from the Unsworth Committee which concluded that "Nigeria should establish [its] own system of legal education."[3] The year 1962 was about a century after British rule in the colony of Lagos was formalized and during which a British-style legal profession was practiced.[4] Transplanting the British legal system into Nigeria was in the interest of the British colony; the increase in both internal and transborder commercial activities necessitated the establishment of a legal profession similar to what prevailed in the metropole. Legal education in Nigeria, established in this context, was driven by economic incentives and had to meet the needs of the emerging nation and its attendant socioeconomic and political development, considering the crucial role that education played in advancing the goals of economic development.[5]

While the Nigerian legal education system was based largely on the British legal education model in the early years, ideas on the curriculum and form of legal education in Nigeria have also been influenced by the United States. In this chapter, we focus on two main sources of US influence on Nigerian legal education: funding provided by US-based philanthropic organizations, and engagement with elite US law schools.

This chapter explores whether and how these legal transplants were achieved, particularly with respect to American educational pedagogies in legal education and the extent of the influence of funding on teaching practices and curriculum design. We also evaluate the tensions between internationalization and the desirability of providing a "domesticated" legal education that meets the needs of the Nigerian state and its citizens. The chapter proceeds by first contextualizing the idea of legal transplants and internationalization. It then traces the historical development of legal education in Nigeria. It then explores the two main forms of Americanization of legal education through funding and elite school engagement and discusses the challenges of transplantation. The final section synthesizes and concludes the chapter, where we find that, while funding regimes from the United States and institutional exchange programs have had an impact on the Americanization of the Nigerian legal education system, consistent attempts have been made to domesticate these impacts in order to meet the local context of legal education and legal practice in Nigeria.

Framing Legal Transplants

"Legal transplants," words coined by Alan Watson,[6] have gained prominence in contemporary legal scholarship. This chapter does not dwell on the distinctions among—or appropriateness of—common terms such as "transplant," "diffusion," and "borrowing," all used by scholars to depict the adoption of teaching pedagogies in legal education in other jurisdictions. Rather, our discussion draws on the constitution of legal transplants, the motivations behind them, and their effectiveness.[7]

This chapter uses the term "legal transplant" to denote the adoption of foreign laws, norms, and institutions into a different legal system. The quest here is to determine whether aspects of American legal theories and legal education were transplanted into Nigerian legal education and to assess the outcomes of such transplantation.

If the effectiveness of the transplant is measured against the backdrop of the prevalent debates on the subject, it will fit strictly into neither Watson's position of easy adaptability of legal transplant, where legal transplants adapt to the prevailing context,[8] nor Legrand's position of impossibility of effective legal transplant, a misfit between transplanted norms and preexisting contexts.[9] Rather, it will find a place between the extreme positions of adaptability and impossibility, accommodating contextual circumstances determined by socioeconomic and political factors, organizations and the prevailing local conditions. It is in this middle ground that pragmatism—which this chapter identifies as the main determining factor of Nigeria's legal education system and its evolving pedagogy—fits in. We argue that pragmatism cannot be divorced from the needs of an emerging nation and that Nigeria's legal plurality distinguishes its legal traditions from European and American legal traditions,[10] which have largely been imported and domesticated in the current system of legal education.

American idealism has taken many forms, one of which is the spreading of American ideals through educational encounters with the rest of the world. The response among some scholarly circles has been less than favorable, with some scholars arguing that the global educational reach of the United States is another manifestation of imperialism—in this case, academic imperialism.[11] In particular, critiques of legal transplantation have characterized the export of US rule of law programs as being underpinned by a policy of "legal imperialism," embedded in the 1960s and 1970s Law and Development movement and viewed as attempts to export American teaching models around the world.[12]

The response from the United States, in the works of philanthropic organizations and foundations, has been to frame these academic engagements and funding schemes as activities separate from the US government, with the goal of helping emerging postcolonial states achieve rapid development. In rebutting the charges of American chauvinism and imperialism, one of the architects of the Ford Foundation's Staffing of African Institutions of Legal Education and Research (SAILER) project, Francis Sutton, an American social scientist with a PhD from Harvard and a Ford official, is said to have "rejected the charge that he was anti-British, anti-European, or that he promoted a purely American type of law school model in Africa."[13]

What were the means through which transplantation of the American legal system took place in Nigeria? As will be discussed below, the SAILER project provides some insights into the form and content of US legal transplantation. Legal transplants are a natural offshoot of colonial linkages, but in recent times they have occurred due to the desirability of internationalization, funding schemes, and the building of intellectual community.[14]

Colonial administrations across Africa may have resisted establishing law schools out of the fear that lawyers would push for political change. The push to establish law faculties and law schools in the early postindependence era by the newly independent states was consequently met with a lack of financial and human resources to staff such faculties and schools. The natural response was to turn to former colonial powers and the United States to seek funding and human resources.[15] The outcome of seeking external funding has been to open the gates for the transplanting of foreign legal norms, teaching pedagogies, and institutional design, often to the detriment of the receiving country, whose existing customary legal systems were not always incorporated.[16]

Development of Legal Education in Nigeria

Prior to colonial rule, Nigeria had its own systems of law regulated by customary norms and principles.[17] Resolution of disputes was performed by traditional rulers and elders.[18] Functions of advocacy akin to that being carried out by advocates or barristers were performed by male relations and friends of parties to a dispute, and this tradition was passed down the generations through informal and formal learning.[19] The Western model of legal practice commenced in the territories that eventually became part of Nigeria through trade, religion, and colonial exploits that brought about interactions between the citizens of Nigeria and European traders and administrators, mainly for commercial and colonial interests.[20] These interactions required the application of some form of regulation, for which the Europeans brought in their own laws. The formal establishment of British colonial rule fostered the enactment of laws that regulated such activities and interactions.

Nigeria, like other African countries colonized by Great Britain, adopted the English legal system and consequently its legal education model after British law became applicable in Nigeria in 1863,[21] following the commencement of formal British rule in 1861.[22] Subsequent laws drafted during colonial times would reflect the legal systems and theories prevalent and applicable to the English legal system, education models, and practice of law.

By virtue of the Supreme Court Ordinance of 1876, two categories of persons practiced law: those with formal legal education, on the one hand, and locally licensed persons who acquired legal skills informally by association with practicing lawyers on the other.[23] The early preindependence lawyers were trained mainly in England, Ireland, and Scotland under the English legal system and therefore carried the perspective of European legal theories and concepts. Later Supreme Court ordinances and rules[24] modified the categories of those who could practice law regarding the extent of the practical experiences acquired by practitioners, but the source of legal training and legal philosophy remained largely British.

Training lawyers outside Nigeria resulted in a number of challenges. First, lawyers trained in England, Ireland, and Scotland possessed deficient knowledge and skills, partly because they were trained either as barristers or solicitors but practiced as both in Nigeria.[25] They studied English texts, the laws of England, and the British system of government,[26] but they did not study Nigerian laws, legal theories, and indigenous jurisprudence with its customary norms.[27] Second, there was the challenge of inadequate training, as legal education was not formally institutionalized and did not require students to attend lectures. Some students did not attend classes but paid for compressed private tutoring or merely read for bar exams.[28] Third, some newly trained lawyers also avoided the necessary pupillage in law firms after they were called to the English bar and therefore lacked the practical experience necessary for law practice at the outset of their legal career. These three factors resulted in gaps in training for those who practiced as lawyers in Nigeria, thereby affecting their potential contributions toward the development of the colony.[29]

Responding to the challenges posed by training domestic lawyers abroad led to efforts to domesticate the training of lawyers within Nigeria. The need to provide legal education within the country was intensified by the anticipation of the independence of the colony from British rule, which required an acceleration in training lawyers to meet the legal, economic, social, and political needs of the newly independent nation.[30] Domestication of legal training also gave rise to the need to enact new laws that would reflect, regulate, and accommodate the distinctiveness of the new nation.[31] Together, these factors necessitated the establishment of a Nigerian system of legal education that would provide satisfactory legal training for practice within the new polity.[32] The Nigerian bar also exerted pressure for a standardized formal regulation of its affairs at about the same time.[33] The bar's effectiveness depended on the quality of legal education, according to Odita:

> The role of a lawyer in a fledgling democracy goes beyond the traditional role of catering for the professional needs of the citizens, administering justice and manning the various legal institution of the state, to include involvement in social change through a commitment to law reform to ensure the harmonisation of the law with the culture of the people and entrenchment of the rule of law.[34]

In 1959, the Unsworth Committee was established by the Nigerian government. The committee, chaired by the then–Attorney General of the Colony E. I. G. Unsworth and composed of eminent legal practitioners,[35] had the responsibility to "*inter alia* look into the future of the legal profession in Nigeria with particular reference to legal education, admission to practice and the right of audience before the courts."[36] Based on the recommendations of the committee, which worked extensively and visited a number of countries for observation and consultations, Nigeria established its own system of legal education. It became a two-tiered system consisting of training at university faculties of law for the LLB program, and the Nigerian Law School established in 1962 for vocational training.[37]

The appointments by the federal government of professor L. C. B. Gower, "a renowned English Solicitor and jurist"[38] who was the dean of the faculty of law at the University of Lagos and an adviser to the law school in 1962, and G. R. Studd, an English barrister as the first director of the institution, must have aided the adoption of the common law legal tradition. This was vital to the foundation of legal education in Nigeria, as the University of Lagos was the first faculty of law at a federal university, preceded only by the University of Nigeria at Nsukka, which was a regional university. At that time, the University of Lagos and the law school were the pioneer institutions of legal education run by the federal government and were integral to the foundation of legal education in Nigeria.

The early attempts at establishing a legal educational system led to competing interests, perhaps unconsciously, between Great Britain and the United States in the institutional design, pedagogical content, and training of prospective lawyers in Africa, including Nigeria.[39] Thus, at the birth of Nigeria's legal education there were competing external interests and systems. The prevailing inclination was to toe the line of its colonial forebears. The renewed interest of the United States in the legal educational system would later lead to the transplantation of the prevalent American system, ideologies, and methodologies into the Nigerian system. The Ford Foundation supported this through the SAILER project in the 1960s and 1970s. This was based on its policy to provide sponsorship in order to aid emerging independent African nations in establishing suitable institutions and governance models.[40] The Ford Foundation believed it was necessary to provide aid in the form of monetary and other assistance to establish legal educational institutions in Africa.

The US influence began in the form of funding assistance for institutional design and was later extended to providing teachers from US law schools and training Nigerian lawyers and teachers in US law schools. It is vital to clarify that, while "law school" in the United States refers to law faculties in the universities, in Nigeria it refers to a separate institution outside of the university system that offers vocational legal training leading to the call to the bar.

Strategies Employed in Americanizing and Internationalizing Legal Education in Nigeria

In the early 1800s, American legal education was based on its colonial forebears and was mainly English in form,[41] as was the case in Nigeria. Christopher Columbus Langdell, a legal formalist and the dean of Harvard Law School in the late 1800s, restructured legal education based on his conception of law.[42] He introduced the case method, which required students to read cases prior to class and to question the reasoning behind the decisions to understand the law.[43] The teacher would test the student's knowledge through content-relevant questions designed to unravel knowledge[44] in a process called the Socratic method of questioning.[45] Over the years, the Langdell method developed to include a functional approach to legal education that considers social contexts,[46] the utilization of additional materials such as texts, statutes, and other interdisciplinary subjects into legal education, and culminating in the adoption of clinical legal education to enhance practical skills and ethics.[47] These methods and pedagogies have over the years been steadily gaining application in Nigeria's legal education.

Moving away from Britain, Nigeria adopted the fused system of legal practice also applicable in the United States, where a lawyer is both a solicitor and an advocate, as a pragmatic solution to the challenge of inadequate number of lawyers to meet the needs of the emerging nation.[48] In England, a law degree was not a requirement for being called to the bar, and lecture attendance in law schools was not compulsory until 1967. From the outset of the establishment of Nigeria's system of legal education in 1962, it was institutionalized and lectures were compulsory, a feature that one may argue was adopted from the US system. Nigeria, however, differed from the United States in that attendance of lectures for vocational training was not compulsory.[49]

The Nigerian legal educational system, like those in other African countries, has constantly been at the mercy of global efforts in pushing forward the internationalization of higher education. The following discussion provides a critical overview of two main strategies through which American legal education was transplanted to Nigeria: funding schemes, and engagement with elite schools.

Funding

The persistent challenges of funding higher education in Nigeria by the federal government from the postcolonial era led to a reliance on external sources of funding. One such foreign funding program was the Ford Foundation's SAILER program. Framed within the law and development paradigm of the 1970s–1980s, SAILER was a spinoff from the Ford-India project[50] and advanced US influence through educational diplomacy. The underlying motivation for both projects was to equip new and emerging democracies by training law professionals to engage in democratic development. Nigeria was one of three countries (the others being Ethiopia and Ghana) where the SAILER project was piloted. The major objective of SAILER was to "financially support law schools in African countries" and to aid those governments that made "an express request for assistance . . . [and] to assist only those institutions where SAILER teachers would be welcome and where their teaching and research would add special dimensions or fill vital needs."[51]

As part of the initiatives under this program, the SAILER project in Nigeria included programs at the University of Lagos such as "shoring up its library, establishing the *Nigerian Law Journal*, creating a think-tank called the Institute of Advanced Legal Studies, and hiring erudite Nigerian teachers to bring a scholarly milieu to the university."[52] However, the primary areas of investment in legal education were directed at recruiting and appointing legal scholars from the United States to teach in the law faculties, as well as the transfer of knowledge through collaborative research and workshops; these contributed to advancing American philosophy, concepts, and pedagogy into the teaching models adopted in Nigerian schools. The benefits derived from research grants undoubtedly influenced the content of scholarship produced by Nigerian professors, with a heavy reliance on citing US scholars.[53]

FACULTY EXCHANGES

The invitation by Nigerian legal academics to the Ford Foundation to help fund legal education, which was supported by the government of Nigeria, was crucial to the development of legal education and no doubt advanced US influence. The need for external help lay not only in the quality of education but also in the lack of human capital in the form of legal academics who could meet the growing need for legal education in the early postcolonial state.

Nigeria became a recipient of American-trained lawyers under the SAILER project sent to teach in Nigeria.[54] From 1962 to 1968, SAILER brought nine or so law lecturers who had trained in the United States to teach at three universities in Nigeria: Ahmadu Bello University, Zaria, University of Ife, Ile-Ife, and University of Lagos.[55] Academics from Syracuse and MIT were also carrying out notable research in the country's institutions,[56] which subsequently contributed to this influence through association and impact.

The ambition of sending American legal scholars to Nigeria to teach and engage in the development of pedagogies that invariably extended US influence was short-lived, as successive military coups broke out and ethnic tensions flared up and degenerated into a civil war.[57] These developments led to a change in the direction of the legal transplant agenda, and the mid-1970s saw a turnaround. Rather than send Americans to teach in Nigeria, Nigerian scholars were sent to the United States to acquire the necessary skills through research, access to resources, and the opportunity to further their education by enrolling in master's (LLM) and doctoral (SJD) programs, after which they could return home to teach.[58] This change in strategy was based on the two-way process of promoting legal education promoted by the Ford Foundation. According to J. K. Krishnan, the interest and presence of American education and administration in Nigeria exceeded that of Britain,[59] but the civil war in Nigeria disrupted the Americanization exercise.[60]

COLLABORATIVE RESEARCH, CONFERENCES, AND WORKSHOPS

US influence was also advanced through conferences funded by US organizations either solely or in collaboration with the Nigerian government. Conferences and also workshops featured aspects of US educational pedagogies through alliances and networks forged for legal research.[61] However, under the second phase of the SAILER project, African scholars who went to the United States to receive training and conduct research also brought with them a lot that enriched US universities. By providing contextually rich background on issues framed within the law and development paradigms, these scholars were in many ways internationalizing the US law school curriculum as well.[62] While these scholar exchanges saw the growth of law networks that allowed for collaborative work and research on a diverse array of topics, it is imperative to note that the theoretical frameworks used for these research agendas were undoubtedly Western.

At that time, legal education in Nigeria was in its formative years and was saddled with the legacy of British colonial policy, and the effect was to sideline the development of traditional customary laws and to promote the universality of Western norms and theoretical frameworks, which were the only sources available to scholars. The development of postcolonial and critical frameworks of inquiry that grew in the late 1970s shifted the focus to grounding African scholarly work in African theoretical frameworks and schools of thought. The later works of scholars like T. O. Elias were to play critical roles in establishing the ground for an Africa-relevant epistemology, even if the funding for such projects was still coming from the United States and England.

Notwithstanding the impact of funding on research agendas, SAILER refuted any claims of deliberately exporting American education and teaching methods. It insisted that its motives were simply to provide aid in development programs where needed by supporting legal education. Krishnan's assertion that SAILER "was not a single, monolithic program, nor was its mission to advance some grand Cold War, American foreign policy objective"[63] confirms this position. John Howard, who was the director of Ford's International Training and Research program, expressed that "one fact about this program—and this is true of all our activities—is of central importance. . . . We are not trying to export the United States system of laws to another country."[64] Despite these statements, the impact of the American legal system and American legal education was still felt by recipients of the funding programs through the pedagogies used in the workshops and the knowledge production and dissemination through conferences.

Engagement with Elite Law Schools

Engagement with elite law schools largely occurred through travel undertaken by staff members of the Nigerian Law School who were searching for improvements to their teaching models.[65] The overseas tours of legal institutions that took place from 1965 to 1976 included trips to the English Council of Legal Education in Great Britain, to

Osgoode University in Toronto, Canada, and to Australia for a law teachers' conference.[66] Furthermore, relying on sponsorship by the Ford foundation, both the director of the Nigerian Law School and the secretary to the Council of Legal Education made numerous visits to American law faculties such as Harvard, Yale, Howard, and several others, as well as to the national and state bar associations to study their course content, methods, and pedagogies.[67] Although some of these visits were made to assess whether the law graduates of American universities were qualified to be admitted into the Nigerian Law School, the acceptance and subsequent training of these law graduates launched them into Nigerian society as practitioners. Some of these graduates became academics, and their scholarship bore the impact of their training in the United States, with its pragmatic approach based on the theory of American realism.[68] During these tours, the pragmatism of American universities and the theory of American Realism was acknowledged by the leadership of the Nigerian Law School.[69]

Study of the institutions, courses, and teaching methods was thorough and included attendance of classes, meetings, and discussions with students, in addition to other in-depth participation in and scrutiny of academic programs, subjects, and administrative operations, which included attendance at Board of Examiners and Board of Studies meetings to compare notes for best practices for Nigeria.[70] Visits were also made to courts, chambers, and law firms to engage with lawyers, judges, and court staff.[71]

Adapting and Adopting Teaching Methods and Pedagogies

Paolo Freire's highly acclaimed critique of the "banking education" model of teaching, which views the learner as an empty container that ought to be filled with knowledge in the same way a coin bank is filled, has been the foundation upon which African educational systems,[72] including legal education in Nigeria, were built. Realizing the shortcomings of the banking education model, attempts to move away from the lecture-based format that explored legal philosophies, principles, and rules from texts, cases, and statutes have seen the adoption of American pedagogies and philosophies such as caselaw on constitutional review.

From its inception to the present, legal education in Nigeria has been two-tiered, comprising a four- to five-year university degree in law and one year of vocational training at the law school. A university degree in law is a prerequisite for admission into the Nigerian Law School and subsequently to the bar. This current model differs from the structure of legal education in England,[73] but it is similar in form to that of the United States in that it is two-tiered. One difference however is that vocational legal training has always been centrally controlled by federal institutions and governing bodies such as the Council of Legal Education in Nigeria,[74] with limited input from the bar; admission to the bar entitles one to practice in all the states of the federation. In the United States, by contrast, each state has an independent regulatory body with strong bar influence, and admission to practice is restricted to each particular state; such practice is not used in Nigeria, as every lawyer is licensed under the federal system and can practice in all thirty-six states and the Federal Capital Territory.[75]

In recent times, efforts from the Carnegie Foundation to provide funding for academic programs have also contributed to the Americanization of legal education. Carnegie has had engagements with universities such as the Ahmadu Bello University in Zaria, University of Jos, Obafemi Awolowo University, Ile Ife, and the University of Lagos. For the University of Jos, for instance, preconditions for funding included the training of lecturers to acquire skills on effective mentoring of students and the establishment of law clinics as a teaching model.[76] Further actions have included an emphasis on the need to train African lawyers with the clinical and experiential models, which are a central feature of the US teaching models.[77] Training for academic staff sponsored by Carnegie took place in locations within Nigeria, other parts of Africa, the United Kingdom, and the United States.[78] Training in clinical legal education was conducted within and outside Nigeria, sometimes in the United States, sponsored by individual law teachers and institutions. The ongoing Americanization of legal education in Nigeria, especially at the law school, has been accelerated by a plethora of rigorous training and workshops[79] with the goal of impacting teaching methods that enhance students' acquisition of the skills, knowledge, and values necessary for the domestic and global practice of law. Examples include moot court competitions students participate in on the African continent and in the United States, where students learn new skills and are exposed to American ways of arguing court cases.

There has also been a growing adoption of skills-based legal education within the law faculties and at the law school.[80] This is achieved through the diverse methods of teaching adopted at the law school, such as the "integration of learning in the modules with values, ethics and skills."[81] Teaching in this context involves "discussions, simulation clinics and activities, role plays, video demonstrations, mock trials and drafting exercises."[82] At the university level, the trend toward interdisciplinarity[83] may have been partly informed by global trends associated with the influence of American Realism, which promoted interdisciplinary engagement in legal education.[84] The prescription for the LLB program recommended under the National University Commission's Draft Benchmark for the LLB program in Nigerian universities[85] includes the compulsory inclusion of other subjects not directly related to law for the development of a broader interdisciplinary perspective; some of these courses focused on gender issues, the environment, and disability studies. The Nigerian Law School has also undertaken extensive capacity-building projects such as teacher skills training and curriculum development workshops funded and supported by the World Bank/International Development Fund, which has influenced new curriculum development and adaptation fostering the acquisition of lawyering skills.[86]

The US influence stretches beyond teaching methods and pedagogies and includes the adoption of US constitutional theories in the context of government design. For instance, the impact of the US legal system on the Nigerian legal system is seen in Nigeria's adoption of the presidential system of government in its 1979 constitution over the unitary parliamentary system inherited from Great Britain in the 1960 independence constitution. Thus, the presidential system of government is taught in constitutional law at the universities, with a heavy reliance on the theories and scholarship developed in US jurisprudence.

Challenges of Transplantation

Despite the seeming advancement and integration of the US model of legal education, the adoption and domestication of these teaching methods resulted in challenges that are worth addressing here. First, the implementation of US educational models could have been done at a faster pace but for the major institutional challenges confronting legal education in Nigeria and Africa more broadly, including limited availability of books and library resources and the increasing student-to-teacher ratio, which does not allow for the application of Socratic teaching methods. Applying the Socratic teaching method also meant a drastic departure from teaching methods that students were accustomed to from primary school and in some cases to the law degree program. The heavy workloads within an academic year created tensions for students, who were suddenly required to adopt new learning methods. Other challenges included the dearth of teaching facilities, inadequate numbers of teaching staff, and the lack of well-equipped libraries,[87] especially because students would need to access relevant texts for assignments and studies. Despite attempts to address these, some of the challenges have remained to the present, thereby undercutting the extent to which American teaching models have impacted the Nigerian Law School and faculties.

A second challenge has been balancing internationalization with pragmatism, that is, the desire to domesticate contemporary models of legal education in Nigeria. At its inception, the Nigerian Law School was open to new ideas that would help legal education in Nigeria meet the needs of the young nation and Nigerian society. The Unsworth Committee's recommendation to train lawyers locally grew out of a vision to develop a legal educational system that would adapt to the country's needs.[88] In other words, it sought best practices that would suit the specific situation irrespective of substance and origin; this pragmatic consideration heightened the need to domesticate imported forms of teaching to make them relevant to the local context. The necessity of striking a balance between transplantation and domestication had earlier been the basis for the Nigerian Law School's staff concern about the suitability of courses offered at the Inner Temple in the United Kingdom.[89] Mamman succinctly states that "legal education should fashion programmes that are relevant to the varied social, economic and constitutional needs of its society,"[90] particularly for developing countries[91] and, in this context, Nigeria.

A third challenge was the influence of globalization on local economies. The desirability of internationalizing law school curricula brought about a push to develop curricula with global relevance.[92] There was also the inevitable effect of globalization of education on emerging fields of scholarship.[93] Law schools everywhere, including in Nigeria, needed to provide students with skills and knowledge that were relevant to transnational treaties and new frontiers of rights. The push for global relevance is also reflected in the "Philosophy and Fundamental Principles" of the above-mentioned Draft Benchmark for LLB degree programs in Nigerian universities, which aims to "produce graduates who can compete actively in legal, social, economic and political developments on a global scale."[94]

Fourth, transplanting teaching methodologies from jurisdictions with functional institutional resources into a place lacking such resources produced many challenges that affected students and faculty members. The effectiveness of such transplantation, and attempts at domestication, were further exacerbated by the dwindling funding by philanthropic organizations of programs such as the SAILER project. Nigeria, as with other African countries, faces many challenges due to the negative effects of globalization[95] and inadequate resources, resulting in the inability to sustain and retain competent staff members to meet the needs of higher education.[96] The effect has been an overreliance on external funding assistance, which often comes with strings attached. The challenge has been how to ensure that conditions imposed by funders are streamlined to fit with the objectives of the developmental needs of the country.

Fifth, there is a desire to balance needs in the local context against the pressure to internationalize, which derives from the need to remain relevant during the ongoing process of globalization, which itself is viewed as the "growth of links and interdependence between countries, marked by an increasingly integrated global economy, free trade, capital flow and tapping of cheaper foreign labour markets."[97] Internationalization has been viewed as an offshoot of the trend toward the "Americanisation of legal education" around the world in areas of "functions, philosophy, curriculum, pedagogy, legal professional ideals, . . . and . . . the increasing facilitative engineering role of legal education in socio-economic development."[98] Despite efforts to internationalize Nigeria's legal education, the abiding consideration for the country has been to adopt pedagogical methods that suit its developmental needs. Nigeria, as one of the earliest African states to establish a separate institution for the vocational training of lawyers,[99] could not establish its legal education without foreign influence—in this case US influence—and it did so as a pragmatic step toward growing a new population of lawyers who understood the connections between the law and the lived realities on the ground. Balancing domestic needs against international assistance and influence required a delicate dance between the desire to meet international standards and the desire to meet domestic needs.

Conclusion

The internationalization and transformation of legal education in Nigeria and much of Africa is the combined result of historical and current trends. These inevitable results have been spurred by globalization and the demand for, and the desirability of, internationalization in higher education. Continued cooperation between Nigeria and the United States has shifted from institutional-level assistance to individual-level engagement as more students seek postgraduate degrees in American universities. Philanthropic foundations such as the Ford Foundation, as well as the US government through the United States Agency for International Development, have had varying impacts on Nigeria's legal education landscape.

This chapter has demonstrated the historical linkages and the impacts of the American model on the Nigerian legal education system. Law is changing globally, and global trends point to a divergence and multiplicity of teaching methods, techniques, and foci. In this chapter, we have shown that, notwithstanding the colonial links between Nigeria and Great Britain, the funding regimes employed by the Ford Foundation's SAILER project played a crucial role in transplanting US education models to Nigeria at the genesis of its legal education system. The global influence of internationalization in legal education has opened the way for more American influence going forward.

NOTES

The authors acknowledge with gratitude insightful comments made at the presentation of this chapter at the symposium "Beyond Harvard: Transplanting Legal Education (National and Foreign Tensions and Hybrids)" held by the Law Society of Upper Canada at Osgoode Hall, Toronto, June 5–6, 2018, and by the Law and Society Association Annual Conference held at Sheraton Centre, Toronto, June 9–10, 2018.

1 For discussions on internationalization of legal education, see generally Jan Klabbers and Mortimer Sellers, eds., *The Internationalization of Law and Legal Education* (Berlin: Springer, 2008).

2 Claudio Grossman, "Building the World Community through Legal Education," in *The Internationalization of Law and Legal Education*, ed. Jan Klabbers and Mortimer Sellers (Berlin: Springer, 2008), 21–36.

3 Niki Tobi, "Meeting the Needs of the Profession and the Nation: A View from the Bench," in Council of Legal Education, *Nigerian Law School: Four Decades of Service to the Legal Profession* (Abuja: Council of Legal Education, 2003), 74. See also Oluremi Adegoke, Rebecca Badejogbin, and Emetejife Onoriode, *Law in Practice: Professional Responsibilities and Lawyering Skills in Nigeria* (Jos: Jos University Press Limited, 2014), 24.

4 Taslim Elias, *The Nigerian Legal System*, 2nd ed. (London: Routledge & Kegan Paul Limited, 1963) 41.

5 Afeisimi Badaiki, "Devising Strategies for Legal Education as Tool for Development," in Council of Legal Education, *Fifty Years of Legal Education in Nigeria-Challenges and Next Steps Nigerian Law School 1963–2013* (Lagos: Council of Legal Education CSS, Sterling Printing Ltd, 2015), 206–10.

6 Alan Watson, *Legal Transplants: An Approach to Comparative Law*, 2nd ed. (Georgia: University of Georgia Press, 1993).

7 James Gardner, "Legal Imperialism: American Lawyers and Foreign Aid in Latin America," *Journal of Latin American Studies* 14, no. 1 (1982): 43–50 and 211–12; John Cairns, "Watson, Walton, and the History of Legal Transplants," *Georgia Journal of International and Comparative Law* 41, no. 637 (2014): 638–86.

8 Ibid., 683.

9 Ibid., 684.

10 Sylvester Shikyil, "Legal Education in the Context of a Mixed Jurisdiction: The Nigerian Experience," in Council of Legal Education, *Fifty Years of Legal Education*, 246.

11 Robert Listenbee, "Close-out Evaluation of the Sailer Project, Ford Foundation Memorandum" 1, 319 (August 27, 1975), referred to in Jayanth Krishnan, "Ácademic Sailers: The Ford Foundation and the Efforts to Shape Legal Education in Africa," *American Journal of Legal History* 52 (2012): 261. See generally Gardner, "Legal Imperialism," 211–12.

12 David Trubek and Marc Galanter, "Scholars in Self-Estrangement: Some Reflections of the Crisis of Law and Development Studies in the United States,"

Wyoming Law Review 4, no. 1 (1974): 1062–103. See also David Trubek and Alvaro Santos, eds., *The New Law and Economic Development: A Critical Appraisal* (Cambridge: Cambridge University Press, 2006); See also Cairns, "Watson, Walton".

13 Francis Sutton, "Strengthening of African Legal Education," *Institute of International Education* (August 29, 1977) (on file with author), as quoted in Krishnan, *Academic Sailers*, 320.

14 Watson, *Legal Transplants.*

15 Thomas Geraghty and Emmanuel K Quansah, "African Legal Education: A Missed Opportunity and Suggestions for Change: A Call for Renewed Attention to a Neglected Means of Securing Human Rights and Legal Predictability," *Loyola University Chicago International Law Review* 5, no. 1 (2007): 88–93.

16 Charles Fombad, "Africanisation of Legal Education Programmes: The Need for Comparative African Legal Studies," *Journal of Asian and African Studies* 49, no. 4 (2014): 383–98.

17 Omoniyi Adewoye, *The Legal Profession in Nigeria, 1865–1962* (Nigeria: Longman Nigeria Limited, 1977), 1–6. See also Adegoke, Badejogbin, and Onoriode, *Law in Practice.*

18 Ibid.

19 Ibid.

20 Tahir Mamman, *The Law and Policy of Constitution Making in Nigeria, 1862–1989: Issues, Interests and Compromises* (Maiduguri: Ed-Iform Services, 1998), 47–48.

21 By virtue of Supreme Court Ordinance No. 3 1863.

22 Akintunde Obilade, *The Nigerian Legal System* (London: Sweet and Maxwell, 1979), 4.

23 Olakunle Orojo, *Conduct and Etiquette for Legal Practitioners* (London: Sweet & Maxwell, 1979), 7–8. See also Adewoye, *The Legal Profession in Nigeria*, 14–35, and Adegoke, Badejogbin, and Onoriode, *Law in Practice*, 14. Section 74 of Supreme Court Ordinance No. 4 (1876) empowered the chief justice to issue such license on the fulfilment of certain conditions related to the applicant's experience and moral conduct.

24 Such as Supreme Court Ordinance 1943 and rule 1, order 6 of the Supreme Court Civil Procedure Rules 1945.

25 John Adams and Roger Brownsword, *Understanding Law* (London: Sweet and Maxwell, 2003), 244. See also Peter Smith, Stephen Bailey, and Michael Gunn, *Modern English System*, 4th ed. (London: Sweet and Maxwell, 2002), 143–46.

26 Smith, Bailey and Gunn, Modern English System, 1.

27 Elias, *The Nigerian Legal System*, 6; Adewoye, *The Legal Profession in Nigeria*, 42–43; and Adegoke, Badejogbin, and Onoriode, *Law in Practice.*

28 Babatunde Ibironke, "Mission Statement as Director-General of the Nigerian Law School December 1979 to December, 1993," in Council of Legal Education, *Nigerian Law School*, 60.

29 James Paul, "Legal Education in English-Speaking Africa," *Journal of Legal Education* 15, (1962–1963): 189–204.

30 Olakunle Orojo, *Legal Education and the Socio-Political Future of Nigeria*, (Lagos: NADL, 2003), 5.

31 Ibid. See also Adegoke, Badejogbin, and Onoriode, *Law in Practice*, 22.

32 Tobi, "Meeting the Needs of the Profession," 74; Adegoke, Badejogbin, and Onoriode, *Law in Practice*, 22.

33 John Jegede, "A Historical Perspective of the Nigerian Law School," in Council of Legal Education, *Nigerian Law School*, 7.

34 Fidelis Odita, "Legal Education and the Challenge of National Development in 21st Century Nigeria" (40th Anniversary Lecture Lagos Campus, Nigerian Law School, May 6, 2004). See also Adegoke, Badejogbin, and Onoriode, *Law in Practice*, 22.

35 The Attorneys General of the Western and Eastern Regions, Solicitor General of the Federation, Solicitor General of the Northern Region, and Legal Secretary of the Southern Cameroon, and six lawyers.

36 Nigeria, "Report of the Committee on the Future of the Nigerian Legal Profession" (Lagos: 1959), 1–2 in Adewoye, *The Legal Profession*, 107.

37 This was by virtue of the Legal Education Act and the Legal Practitioners Act, both passed into law in 1962. See also Adegoke, Badejogbin, and Onoriode, *Law in Practice.*

38 Olakunle Orojo, "Forty Years of Service to the Nation," in Council of Legal Education, *Fifty Years of Legal Education in Nigeria*, 49.

39 Krishnan, *Ácademic Sailers*, 263.

40 Ibid., 264.

41 Charles McManis, "The History of First Century American Legal Education: A Revisionist Perspective," *Washington University Law Review* 59, no. 3 (1981): 609.

42 William Schofield, "Christopher Columbus Langdell," *The American Law Register* no. 5 (May 1907): 273.

43 Ibid.

44 Kathryn Harden-Thew and Bonnie Dean, "Focusing in Six First Year Firsts: A Professional Development Framework Supporting Teachers of First Year Subjects," *University of Wollongong Research online paper* (2015): 2–3, http://ro.uow.edu.au.

45 Orin Kerr, "The Decline of the Socratic Method at Harvard," *Nebraska Law Review* 78 (1999): 117.

46 Ibid., 118–20.

47 Ibid., 119–20.

48 Ernest Ojukwu, *Legal Education in Nigeria: A Chronicle of Reforms and Transformation under Tahir Mamman* (Abuja: Council of Legal Education, 2013), 137.

49 Ibid., 138.

50 Krishnan *Ácademic Sailers*, 265.

51 John Bainbridge, "The Sailer Project 1962–1967," Ford Foundation Document 7 (July 1967) as quoted in Krishnan, *Ácademic Sailers*, 264.

52 Krishnan, *Ácademic Sailers*, 308.

53 Dakas Dakas, "Towards Enhancing the Quality of Legal Education and Research in Nigeria through the Instrumentality of Research Grants: Practical Insights," in Council of Legal Education, *Fifty Years of Legal Education*, 182–84. The benefits that accrue from grants are extensively listed here. These benefits directly or indirectly impact the content of scholarship.
54 Ibid., 267, 312, and 273.
55 Ibid., 284–85.
56 Ibid., 285–86.
57 The Biafra War, between 1967 and 1970.
58 Krishnan, *Ácademic Sailers*.
59 Ibid., 283.
60 Ibid., 311.
61 For instance, the conferences in 1961 in Lagos and at Yale, where the advancement of human rights was clearly featured. See Krishnan *Ácademic Sailers*, 288.
62 Ibid.
63 Ibid., 262.
64 Ibid., 312.
65 Jacob Sofolahan, "Reflections and Reminiscences on my Days at the Nigerian Law School," in Council of Legal Education, *Fifty Years of Legal Education*, 42–45.
66 Ibid.
67 Ibid., 47.
68 Ibid.
69 Sofolahan, "Reflections and Reminiscences," 73.
70 Ibid., 43.
71 Ibid., 42–44.
72 Paulo Freire, *Pedagogy of the Oppressed* (New York: Herder and Herder, 1972). See also Mahbubul Alam, "Banking Model of Education in Teacher-Centered Class: A Critical Assessment," *Research on Humanities and Social Sciences* 3, no. 15 (2013): 27. The banking model of education, as espoused by Paulo Freire, features a learning environment where the teacher produces the knowledge through one-dimensional lecturing and the students receive the knowledge with little to no interaction and critical engagement on the part of the student.
73 Oko Okechukwu, "Legal Education and Training in Nigeria," *African Journal of International & Comparative Law* 6 (1994): 271–92. The LLB became a compulsory requirement for the bar in Britain in 1967 five years after this was adopted for Nigeria.
74 There are more than forty faculties of law in Nigerian universities comprising federal, state, and private universities uniformly regulated by the National Universities Commission and the Council of Legal Education, which prescribed minimum standards covering core course contents, staffing, and facilities.
75 Jegede, "A Historical Perspective," in Council of Legal Education, *Nigerian Law School*. He was the director-general of the law school from 1993 to 2004.

76 Conversation with professor Jemila Nasir, who was then the dean of law.

77 Samuel Manteaw, "Legal Education in Africa: What Type of Lawyer Does Africa Need?," *McGeorge Law Review* 39 (2016): 903–76. As Adewumi and Bamgbose's recent study shows, the introduction of the Clinical Learning Education (CLE) model of teaching at the University of Ibadan has been well received by students. Afolasade Adewumi and Oluyemisi Bamgbose, "Attitude of Students to Clinical Legal Education: A Case Study of Faculty of Law, University of Ibadan," *Asian Journal of Legal Education* 3, no. 1 (2015): 106–16.

78 Petricia Lar, Kieran Ekpeyong, Sarah Lwahas, Amos Lungu, and Mark Kparmark, eds., *Trasformation through Partnership: The Jos Carnegie Story* (Jos: University of Jos and Carnegie Corporation of New York, n.d.), 30.

79 Such as: the Workshops on Legal Education Capacity Building Project (World Bank Assisted) Curriculum Development Workshop, January 24–26, 2008; Nigerian Law School Curriculum Development Workshop, Abuja, September 17–18, 2007; Nigerian Law School Skills and Clinical Legal Education Teacher Training Workshop, Abuja, May 14–25 2007; and Workshop on Model Standards for Clinics, Abuja, February 21, 2007.

80 See Draft National University Commission Benchmark LL.B Programme in Nigerian Universities (2018), 3.

81 Gbemi Odusote, Rebecca Badejogbin, Mercy Onoriode, Obi Okoye, and Ibrahim Mohammed, eds., *Property Law Practice: Practice Handbook* (Abuja: Council of Legal Education Nigerian Law School, 2019), 2.

82 Ibid., 2.

83 In natural sciences, social sciences, commercial faculty, humanities, and the arts. Draft National University Commission Benchmark, 138.

84 Luis Aldaco, "What Can Mexican Law Schools Learn from the American Legal Realists?," *Mexican Law Review* 7, no. 1 (2014).

85 Ibid., 138.

86 Ojukwu, *Legal Education in Nigeria*, 114, 177, and 195. See also Rebecca Badejogbin, "Reforming Legal Education in Nigeria: The Nigerian Law School Experience," in *Topical Issues in Nigerian Law: Essays in Honour of Hon Justice S K*, ed. Otta Oluremi Adegoke and Samuel Osamolu (Abuja: Vintage Law Publishers, 2011), 208.

87 Badejogbin, "Reforming Legal Education in Nigeria," 216–17.

88 Tahir Mamman, "A Review of the Framework of Legal Education in Nigerian Universities," Justice M. M Akanbi Annual Lecture, University of Ilorin, Nigeria, November 8, 2010.

89 Ojukwu, *Legal Education in Nigeria*, 109.

90 Ibid., 7–8. (Professor Tahir Mamman was the director general of the Nigerian Law School from 2005 to 2013.)

91 Shiv Dayal, "Dynamics of Development in Legal Education and Developing Countries," in *Law in Zambia*, ed. Muna Ndulo (Nairobi: East African Publishing House, 1984).

92 Osaro Eghobamien, "Emergence of the Global Lawyer and the Nigerian Legal Education," in Council of Legal Education, *Fifty Years of Legal Education in Nigeria*, 138.

93 Muna Ndulo, "Legal Education in an Era of Globalisation and the Challenge of Development," *Journal of Comparative Law in Africa* 1, no. 1 (2014): 1–2.

94 Draft National University Commission Benchmark, 2. The Law School Vision has a similar aim: "[T]he objectives of accreditation of academic programmes in Nigerian universities are to ensure that at least the provision of Minimum Academic Standards . . . are attained, maintained and enhanced. Employers and other members of the community are assured that Nigerian graduates of all academic programmes have attained an acceptable level of competency in their areas of specialization. International communities are assured that the programmes offered in Nigerian universities are of high standards and their graduates are adequate for employment and for further studies." Oliver T. U. Onwudinjo et al., "Council of Legal Education Standards for Law Report Collection in Nigerian Universities," *International Journal of African and Asian Studies* 13 (2015): 182. https://iiste.org.

95 Muna Ndulo, "Legal Education in an Era of Globalisation," 1–2.

96 Muna Ndulo, "Legal Education, Internationalisation and African Law Schools," *Journal of Commonwealth Law and Legal Education* 2, no. 2 (2008): 23–47.

97 Eghobamien, "Emergence of the Global Lawyer."

98 Badaiki, "Devising Strategies for Legal Education," 221.

99 Sofolahan, "Reflections and Reminiscences," 55.

7

Model, System, or Node?

Understanding Legal Education Reform in Twentieth-century China and Beyond

JEDIDIAH J. KRONCKE

In examining the role played by American law and legal institutions abroad from the late nineteenth to the early twentieth century, evaluations often struggle to differentiate between *influence* and *impact*. While the fact that American law has impacted global patterns of legal reform is undeniable, the record of foreign emulation of American legal institutions is murky at best.[1] Moreover, while foreign and American lawyers alike assert that such potential impact is driven by the particular intentional influence of American lawyers, their expressions on the issue frequently comprise tangled thickets of idealism and cynicism.[2]

Demonstrating impact is, in an empirical sense, easier than demonstrating influence, as it primarily involves descriptive accounts. Did a new law reflect American doctrines, or did the reorganization of a legal institution borrow from American examples? Influence, by comparison, generally implies some conscious intentionality, either by adopter or exporter. And these intentions carry with them (as often explicit as implicit) causal arguments about the consequences of such impact.

Part of the struggle to clearly distinguish between evaluations of impact and influence is that they are commonly embedded in the ideologically charged and contested cultural politics of lawyering common to almost every modern nation-state.[3] Arguments about the impact of American legal education abroad involve exercises such as counting the hypothetical number of classrooms in which the Socratic method is deployed and then tying the resulting number to either normatively desirable or undesirable consequences for future lawyers. Rarely are such arguments limited to evaluating the impact of American legal education practices on the internal operation of the legal profession. Instead, such arguments further evaluate, often in the broadest economic and political terms, what these consequences for lawyers mean for society.[4] Such causal chains are common, if not endemic, in debates about legal transplantation writ large and have a historical pedigree going back to the earliest encounters between legal systems.[5]

It is no surprise, then, that as the rapid (sometimes revolutionary) changes in China's legal system have unfurled over the previous hundred-plus years, the reform of legal education has inspired debates both domestically and abroad at this level of systemic social consequence. While few informed histories continue to assert the false image of traditional China as a society without law or lawyers,[6] the sweeping changes that accompanied the collapse of the dynastic system in 1911 undoubtedly led to struggles over the nature and role of lawyers debates that are, in full measure, still unresolved today.[7] As a state of active legal reform became the norm in China for most of the twentieth century, a wide variety of legal ideals and practices emerged across the country, often implicating very different basic concepts of what a "lawyer" was.

As with any domestic legal history, no coherent, singular, and progressive narrative emerges about modern Chinese lawyering. Instead, regular contest and contingency constitute the norm. As classically noted by Eric Wolf, during the colonial era non-Western legal histories were commonly removed of indigenous agency and regarded as containing timeless "cultural" traits and dispositions.[8] Paul Cohen traced the ways in which long-standing arguments about foreign influence in China exhibited similar characteristics; in particular, the attribution of primary causal importance to the actions of Western nations spoke more to the priorities of the observer than the observed.[9] Exploring the role of American legal education, and American lawyers, in Chinese legal reform requires an understanding of the contest over lawyering within China, where domestic political rivalries and interests sought to control how modern Chinese lawyers would be educated and regulated. This exploration also requires prioritizing an understanding of American perceptions of Chinese legal reform. Specifically, Americans continually presumed that their impact in China was consequential in this process, when in practice, prior to the reopening of China in 1978, this was rarely, if ever, the case.

From the onset of what might be called "modern" Sino-American legal relations at the beginning of the twentieth century, American and Chinese lawyers engaged on quite uneven terrains of financial and political capital, including terrains strewn with powerful symbols of both American and Chinese modernity. The necessary optimism of the domestic or foreign legal entrepreneur required some willful disregard of structural drivers of legal reform and cross-national engagement. The psychological resources that sustained individual reformers' ambitions to shape the future of Chinese lawyers also led these reformers to suffuse influence with individual merit—both moral and technical—rather than with economics or geopolitics.[10] The sum force of this entrepreneurial optimism, written from the perspective of such reformers and with conscious attention to interested audiences, has consisted of misplaced attributions of both impact and influence.[11]

As a result, much less energy has been devoted to establishing the descriptive *realities* of what constituted "Chinese legal education" in various eras. New histories make clear that American legal education as an ideal was widely discussed, invoked, and promoted in China. Yet these historical and contemporary discussions rarely, if ever, had the systemic empirical import to support claims of impact, much less influence. Such claims of impact nonetheless persist, perhaps for two reasons. First, no system of legal education became so globally wedded to ideals of modern law as American legal education. And second, this symbolic international ideal was equally important to domestic American contests over lawyering—more important within the American context itself than has been recognized in domestic histories of American legal education. Thus, at the same time as claims were being made about the import of modern American legal education for China throughout the twentieth century, similar claims about the new "Harvard model" were being advanced in the United States, accompanied by the rapid transformation and reconfiguration of the American legal profession.[12] And such claims were, moreover, made alongside similarly ambitious claims about the meaning of changes in American legal education not only for law but also for American politics and economics. One tangible outcome of this focus on the social meaning and import of legal education reform in both countries has been reference to ideal models of legal education, even when these models were often poor, if not obscuring, indicators of dominant practices on the ground.[13]

Teasing out the full contours of the intertwined history of the United States and China is a task beyond the scope of this chapter, but it is illuminating to explore the role of American legal education at two key points in China's twentieth-century struggles over legal reform: those being the postrevolutionary eras after 1911 and 1978. In both of these eras the impact (in descriptive terms) and influence (in causal terms) of American legal education were minor. Yet such minority status did little to dampen consistent claims by Americans that American legal education helped to produce a new generation of Chinese lawyers who would be specifically equipped to facilitate the emulation of American economic and political institutions within China.

Understanding Patterns of Legal Education Reform

The difficulties involved in supporting claims of influence and impact for American legal education abroad prompt the need for a conceptual framework for better differentiating between descriptive and ideal arguments regarding the influence of American legal education in China from the late nineteenth century onward.

Modeling Empirical Realities

The simple analytic scheme advanced here involves distinguishing between a particular country's *system* of legal education, its ideal *model* of a law school, and discrete *nodes* for integrating elite domestic and international forms of legal, economic, and political capital. This schematic helps to demonstrate that a large gap between the descriptive and the ideal here raises serious questions about common causal arguments that underpin more normatively charged claims about the meaning/consequence of legal education reform.

In this context, *system* refers to the dominant descriptive reality of how lawyers are trained in a particular country. A system can have mono- or polycentric pathways for lawyer certification; a wide variety of areas of professional practice classified as "legal" (addressing, for example, concerns about the unauthorized practice of law); rules regarding the specialization of lawyers (such as the traditional barrister/solicitor divide in the Commonwealth countries); and a unified or nonunified profession of public and private lawyering (including judging).[14] Systems of legal education are primarily determined by often path-dependent state choices about certification and respond to other institutional design choices that shape the market for lawyers. In some rare instances, such as in the United States, states can devolve some of these powers to the profession itself, though this is globally rather exceptional today.[15]

A *model* under this scheme can have two potential meanings. In the primary sense, a model refers to the ideal form of the law school as defined by state regulation and by the terms of status competition in the public and private markets for legal services. Competing models can exist in a secondary sense, with the potential aspiration that a new model could be replicated to serve as a baseline for a different, or significantly reshaped, system of legal education. The trajectory of the model pioneered during the late nineteenth century at Harvard Law School in the United States by Christopher Langdell is a prime example of a model that was both new and that would eventually become the baseline for a new system of legal education.[16]

A *node*, then, is more of a conclusory descriptor. To call a law school a "node" is to mark its importance as a site for training lawyers whose professional trajectories are not solely bound to domestic or local markets. These nodes have existed throughout the nineteenth and twentieth centuries in locations where there was the need to train lawyers who could engage in public and private networking by drawing on different forms of nonlocal professional capital. Such nodes have grown in importance following a new upswing in globalization and the concurrent need for integrating domestic elites across national boundaries. The need for such integration implicates not only the role of lawyers in specifically transnational spaces but also their domestic competition with other professional elites for domestic legitimacy and influence.[17] However, such nodes are inherently nonreplicable. For financial or other reasons attached to the narrowness of the market that nodes allow access to, nodes cannot become models for new systems of legal education. The conclusory nature of the descriptor allows for the possibility of such a role, but only following very substantial social changes beyond the law itself as a new "model."

This tripartite division is useful for thinking about legal education reform in general, but it is also surgically instructive when claims are made about the impact of American legal education abroad, as such claims often extrapolate from nongeneralizable nodes of legal education reform. Thus, a new elite law school may in fact draw on some aspects of American legal pedagogy, but only to feed the limited demand for a niche market of internationally oriented public and private lawyers in a resource-intensive manner that could never be sustained across the nation in question. In parallel fashion, outside visitors commonly affiliate the pedagogical ideas or practices of domestic agents (especially entrepreneurial actors) at such nodes with the general conditions/perspectives of legal education in the country as a whole, or they advance these ideas or practices as serious contenders to serve as a new model for future systemic change.

In the context of Sino-American relations, almost all discussion about the influence and impact of American legal education has descriptively overprivileged unrepresentative nodes in this manner, arguing that nodal practices have systemic status or potential. Such overprivileging has been especially acute in warping understanding of the development of Chinese legal education and the domestic interests involved: American pedagogical practices (let alone the specific institutional nature of the Harvard model) have rarely, if ever, impacted the ideal model of the Chinese law school, much less shifted the basic logic of its larger system of legal education.

While the modern American law school had virtually no impact on China's legal education *system* at any meaningful empirical level, it was often advanced as a *model* for reform. Furthermore, while it was never implemented as such by the state, it nevertheless served, in certain limited instances, as the basis for some *nodes*—either in full, in the post-1911 era, or partially so, in the post-1978 era.

Legal Education as Vector of Contested Modernities

The distinctions of *system*, *model*, and *node* are clarifying not simply as a matter of empirical description but also because they help ground the often highly general chains of causality that are invoked when identifying the meaning and consequence of changes in each category. Such chains generally comprise the following three components: (1) Changes in legal education lead to changes in the lawyers that emerge from law schools; (2) these "changed" lawyers hold new, normatively desirable qualities and can engage in superior forms of legal practice; and (3) these new forms of practice and qualities in lawyers lead to social changes, both political and economic. Such arguments are most often made by lawyers, but in recent history these claims have also been advanced by nonlawyer reformers and governments alike.

The power of this chain of causality is that the dual social and moral nature of lawyering lends an air of plausibility to such claims that would be harder to sustain for other purely scientific practices.[18] For more than a century, changes in lawyers' public and private roles—primarily, but no longer exclusively, in democratic nations[19]—have allowed lawyers to assert, in turn and in tandem, the broad political and economic significance of lawyering. While some legal systems segregate public and private lawyering, in most countries even fully private lawyers are engaged in both the routine resolution of private disputes and the growing regulatory functions of the state. Claims that a more efficient contracting system would improve economic growth, or that a more robust regime of civil liberties would improve democratic accountability, thus have intuitive appeal even to those outside the profession.[20]

For lawyers themselves, contests over the regulation and image of lawyering make battles over legal education an attractive point from which to advance arguments about the quality of lawyering and broader social change.[21] In a more immediate and pragmatic sense, attempts to argue that lawyers are central to the production of both public and private goods impact lawyers' authority to act in four nonprofessional capacities: (1) as proponents for social reform; (2) as agents for regime change; (3) as actors staffing regulatory institutions; and (4) as the primary ruling professional class. The legitimacy of lawyers across this spectrum of roles finds natural roots in claims about lawyers' education and self-regulation, with an internal professional preference for claims that emphasize their technical expertise and moral virtue, rather than social reproduction or subservience to other economic or political elites. As a result, competition between ideal models of lawyering, whether open or implicit, articulates *in nuce* contested notions of what an ideal modern national state should look like.[22]

Such issues of legitimacy and power lie at the heart of a whole genre of modern historical and sociological studies of legal professions around the world.[23] In cross-national contexts, or ones with strong transnational elements, these battles are affected by a number of powerful distorting issues relating to transcultural understanding and entrepreneurialism.[24] If we take as our premise the influence of a foreign model of legal education (as we do here), then we have to disaggregate the causal chains advanced by naturally self-interested insiders/locals and self-promotional foreigners. Assertions by local actors that nodal practices are general or generalizable are rarely interrogated by outsiders, especially when asymmetries of capital and status flow in the favor of outside entrepreneurs, and when such claims of generalizability reinforce the professional self-identity of the foreign actors.[25]

Recent historical research has explored such mismatches of insider/outsider perspectives in the Sino-American context. The often orthogonal relationship between intra-regime reform politics and external geopolitical aims frequently leaves domestic reformers and foreign actors alike with difficulty devising effective reform strategies that satisfy both domestic and foreign supporters. The category of the node is especially important here: while the legal actors trained at nodes can become important for international diplomatic and market coordination, they do so while prominently deemphasizing any conflict between the public good and personal enrichment.[26] Following this pattern, American legal education was often advanced as a potential stimulus for China's economic and political liberalization by invoking the same causal chains as are averred about American lawyers' role in energizing twentieth-century American liberalism.[27] The high-mindedness of such arguments thus rarely engaged the existing mainstream structure or pedagogical orientation of China's system of legal education. Moreover, arguments about ideal types and potential long-term outcomes left American observers blind to the role that modern American forms of private and public lawyering (as carried out by Chinese and overseas American lawyers) had played in facilitating the economic and diplomatic objectives of what have been almost exclusively nonliberal regimes in China. This focus on hypothetical extrapolations with weak contemporary empirical groundings could serve only to restate or reaffirm idealizations of American lawyering, rather than lead toward their critical interrogation. The fact that authoritarian rulers continued to tolerate nodal schools and their pedagogical practices suggests that these rulers view nodal lawyers' market integrative roles as being more dominant, in practice, than their putatively liberalizing public roles.

This incongruence between insider and outsider viewpoints has been widely understood domestically in China, where invocations of American legal education have been deployed strategically by a range of actors, some with little to no attachment to liberal values.[28] Such misperceptions also exist with respect to the relationship between the ideal model of American legal education and the actual legal education system in place. Until the early twenty-first century, many domestic Chinese reformers were exposed only to the ideal type of American lawyering and legal education. They rarely confronted the reality that the ideal model of modern American legal education itself seldom fully reflected American legal education in practice or substantiated broader claims about the social implications of its transition from model to system.[29]

Two Eras of Postrevolutionary Chinese Legal Education

The revolutionary moments of 1911 and 1978 in China were characterized by quite different social contexts and ideological motivations. The Republican Revolution of 1911 involved an explicit rejection of dynastic feudalism and carried out regime change under the formal banner of establishing a new democracy. The year 1978 witnessed no formal change in governing ideology but nonetheless ushered in sweeping changes in the relationship of the Chinese state to political and economic regulation, with perhaps even more immediate repercussions compared to 1911. And as with any revolutionary change in the structure of political rule and economic regulation, new imaginations of the future role of lawyers in the private and public spheres also reflected novel visions of Chinese modernity.[30]

In each period, lawyers and reformers in China made public claims about the modern American model's potential to reshape Chinese legal education. These claims were joined by excited assertions in American discourse about the foreign impact of American legal education in China. Again, though, at the level of systemic change, the American model would have little to no influence on how Chinese legal education would develop during either era.[31] In different ways, legal education in China consistently reflected the larger subordination of university education to the Chinese state.[32] Each period also initially developed a quite limited market for private legal services, at least those provided by professional lawyers. The larger logic of the emergent systems of legal education during both these periods followed path-dependent influences from the preexisting dynastic system, as well as civil law and Soviet influences indigenized by Chinese actors.[33]

The relative pragmatism of Chinese regimes during both the post-1911 and post-1978 eras allowed for some pedagogical experimentation drawing on aspects of the American model. Yet this experimentation was undertaken with the common understanding that it was meant to serve diplomatic and commercial interests by creating nodes of engagement to assist integration with the global world, rather than by generating new baselines for more systemic changes.

Even as both eras evolved toward greater authoritarianism and control over private lawyers, these nodal institutions and experiments were allowed to persist to the extent that they served these integrative purposes.[34] The post-1911 era witnessed a relative decline in such experimentation, while the post-1978 era was, until the late 2010s, one of relatively increasing experimentation.

The continued vibrancy of causal claims about the impact of American legal education has been sustained by characteristics of this nodal reality in China—including the promotion of the American model abroad as a proxy war in the cultural politics of American lawyering—and by the use of foreign examples in internal American domestic debates about legal education.[35] The very nature of these nodes created warped feedback loops between local entrepreneurs and self-styled foreign reformers who were implicated in the self-interested circulation of international legal capital. Both American and Chinese lawyers continued to see American legal education through the lenses of their respective domestic agendas. The circumscribed set of legal elites with whom these lawyers engaged, and the nodal legal educational spaces in which they socialized, erected significant barriers to reliable feedback about both the current and future influence of American legal ideas in China.

Nodal Lawyers after China's 1911 Republican Revolution

The ideological motivations of the actors behind the 1911 movement, which brought an end to the Qing Dynasty, were far more diverse than is still popularly assumed. The series of events and social developments that led to the collapse of the Qing were multiple, with some of long and some of short gestation.[36] The instability of the national government of China over the ensuing four decades would speak to stark divides in perspective and motivation, leading to the ultimate rise to power of the Chinese Communist Party (CCP) in 1949.[37] Yet, for foreign observers, especially those in the United States, the idea of China becoming a republic generated excited proclamations of inspiration and predictions that the young republic would emulate American institutions.[38] At the same time, there was an ongoing conflict in the United States itself with respect to basic questions of economic and political governance—questions posed by the ascendance of the United States as a global and industrial power.[39]

Thus, both in China and the United States during this era, new arguments were advanced about the role of future lawyers and about how to educate them to serve the nation in the building, or rebuilding, projects that were under way on both sides of the Pacific. The destabilization of the traditional modes of regulating legal practice and knowledge under the Qing was accompanied by a far more cosmopolitan search for reform possibilities than was then taking place in the United States, where national confidence turned to reshaping other nations rather than learning from their experiences.[40] The republican rhetoric in China persuaded Americans to see China as a site for potential emulation, while the citation of foreign ideas was key to Chinese reimaginations of the Chinese state. The symbolic force of the American legal example was championed (even if not in terms Americans clearly understood) by the early Republican leaders. Such advocacy created a sense of anticipation and possibility for American lawyers that had never existed before.

Legal ideas from the United States would be of rare practical influence in China compared to those from Europe or Japan. Yet, ironically, in the realm of elite education, the United States did, in fact, have an impact due to the preexisting systemic investments of the US missionary movement.[41] For a century prior to 1911, foreign educational missionaries had been active in China. After the American Civil War (1861-1865), missionaries traveling abroad from the United States became the prime movers in the Chinese missionary movement and helped turn educational efforts toward the law. Many Chinese reformers of pre- and post-

1911 had educational experiences in this system and often converted publicly to Christianity.[42]

While there were earlier American missionaries who pushed for legal education reform in China,[43] it was not until the 1890s that the model of American legal education that would be held up as its modern ideal began to emerge at Harvard under the deanship of Christopher Langdell.[44] The complexity of the rise of the so-called Harvard model has been explored with increasing depth in recent historical scholarship. Yet, its specific contours as an ideal model of legal education had both clear pedagogical aspects—focused on the use of the Socratic case method of instruction—and institutional aspects—concentrating all forms of legal education into a three-year postgraduate degree, the eventually termed juris doctorate. The contested nature of the Harvard model's rise to truly systematic status in the United States was most often hidden from foreign perception, where it was often taken to be systemic long before this was descriptively accurate.[45] Nonetheless, one less appreciated aspect of the rise of the Harvard model was that its development in the United States had transnational elements in China from the outset.

Prior to 1911, there had already been a generation of American lawyers educated through the Harvard model who had attempted to promote its qualities in China. Edgar Allen taught the first Chinese students American law in 1902 and worked to motivate the American Bar Association (ABA) to sponsor Chinese citizens to study law at Harvard.[46] Allen was followed by the future legal luminary and Harvard law professor Warren Seavey, a recent Harvard Law School graduate who brought his casebooks to Tianjin straight from Cambridge in 1906.[47] And Judson Crane, who later became dean of the University of Pittsburgh School of Law, similarly taught in China after his graduation from Harvard Law School in 1909.[48] This generation held a generally dim view of Chinese law but also an optimistic view of the potential to transform China by transforming Chinese legal education.

The vast majority of legal practice and legal institutional reform after 1911 was based on an amalgam of adapting Qing law to European influences, especially if we consider law outside of China's southern urban centers.[49] Additionally, while interest in American legal education was limited domestically, excitement about China was undiminished in America. As such, a variety of American legal projects were undertaken in China at this time; the institutional exemplar of this was Soochow Law School, founded in 1915 as an explicit emulation of the Harvard model.[50] Many elite Chinese lawyers and diplomats would pass through Soochow's halls, including some truly remarkable pioneers of China's new public and private legal elite.[51] With faculty drawn from the United States and the local American bar, Soochow attempted to replicate the pedagogical and institutional qualities of Harvard. Casebook instruction was promoted, and attempts were made to introduce prior undergraduate studies as an admission requirement. Smaller details, such as American-style, student-led law reviews and a modern law library, were also championed internally and externally as indicia of Soochow's status as an emulation of modern American legal education.

Claims that Soochow's graduates would help facilitate—through public and private legal practice—China's political and economic liberalization were rarely made with restraint.[52] However, they were consonant with the very same claims that were concurrently being invoked to justify the spread of the Harvard model beyond the American Northeast—a process that would not be complete until the mid-1950s. The penetration of Soochow's graduates into elite urban practice, primarily in Shanghai, was often advanced as evidence of Soochow's success.[53] This was not surprising, as the initial success of modern Harvard law graduates in piercing elite urban corporate law practice served as a prime motivation for inducing the adoption of the Harvard model in US universities.[54] The symbolic power and allure of the American model also drew on the American presumption that lawyers so educated could simultaneously pursue not only elite practice but also public virtue through professional activities, even when those activities were in service of private interests.

However, while the Harvard model would eventually become the basis for the American system of legal education, Soochow would exist only as a site-specific node, producing just a small subset of China's new elite, whose employment prospects were never wider than the market for their particular form of transnational capital allowed. Thus, while rhetoric about the consequence of Soochow as a model for Chinese legal education was grandiose, it remained, in reality, wholly nodal in nature. Even more telling in this regard was that Soochow was, in practice, quite far removed from the Harvard model. Tellingly, during this same period, Soochow engaged in many of the same practical compromises in teaching and institutional organization as American law schools that had also claimed to adopt the Harvard model.[55] Most Soochow instructors were not trained at Harvard and could not easily replicate its pedagogical elements. More critically, the financial realities in China made a solely postgraduate education infeasible—a barrier that also was not alleviated fully in the United States until massive investments in public universities started being made in the mid-twentieth century. Over time, Soochow relaxed most every element of the Harvard model, especially as the Republican (or Guomindang) Party engaged in progressively greater oversight of Chinese university education.[56]

By contrast, other elite Chinese law schools, representatively Chaoyang Law School in Beijing, were oriented toward domestic legal and political careers, without parallels in the American system.[57] While it might be difficult to say that there was any single coherent "system" of legal education in China during these decades of political strife, schools like Chaoyang, which were embedded in Chinese universities and followed the predominantly undergraduate model from Europe, were far more standard. The myriad of backgrounds and educations possessed by Chinese legal actors during this time has been the subject of renewed interest.

The success of Soochow as an international node allowed those involved as instructors and students to form a mutualistic but obscuring set of circumscribed feedback loops that warped American perceptions of Chinese legal education specifically and of Chinese legal development more generally. Even as the limited practical impact of American legal education waned over time, American faith in the influence of American law in China was sustained by networks of elite circulation (partially centered on Soochow) and, increasingly, by Chinese graduates of elite American law schools themselves.[58] While the abstract invocation of American legal ideas, both negatively and positively, became a consistent part of domestic reform stratagems between 1911 and 1949, most of the small number of internationalized Chinese legal elites who needed to engage with the United States diplomatically (such as those involved in extraterritorial negotiations or serving in new public international law institutions) or economically (such as those working with US international firms and investors) were in fact shifted to American law schools themselves. Over time, Soochow's track record as an emulation of Harvard or as an instigator of social change was hard to justify as the individual careers of its graduates (even those who publicly praised liberal virtues) ended up, in the statistical super-majority, facilitating more often than not, authoritarian economic interests.

There are many other stories that could be told about the intertwined nature of legal education in China and the United States during this era.[59] Despite the failure of these other reform efforts during this time, their symbolic command was sustained by similar warped feedback loops of elite interaction. These loops kept alive continued interest in reforming China in the American legal image even when there was no evidence that such reform was happening at any level of empirical generality. The symbolic power of the American model thus persisted, and the intermixed entrepreneurial agendas of local and foreign actors was part and parcel of the ungrounded discourse that led up to the national shock in the United States after the Chinese Communist Party's victory in 1949, couched as America's "loss of China."[60]

Producing Lawyers for What Future in the Post-1978 Era?

China became largely closed to the United States after the end of the Chinese Civil War in 1949.[61] In fact, the Chinese Communist Party used the Guomindang's association with American law to stigmatize it by tying issues of economic and racial inequality to American lawyering.[62] However, the reopening of China in 1978 to a global economic and political order increasingly dominated by the United States led to a resurgent interest in American lawyering as one aspect of reinstitutionalizing Chinese legal practice. In turn, American interest in influencing Chinese legal development restarted anew, with the initiation of ABA and diplomatic exchanges extolling the liberalizing effect that American law would have in China.[63] For all the same reasons, American legal education was often cited as an ideal beginning to this causal chain of influence.[64]

Moreover, in the intervening decades, the nodal reality of the Harvard model in the United States had (still with some significant caveats) transitioned to systemic status. The grant to the ABA of sole accreditation power for law schools (even if still formally regulated at the state level) in 1952 constituted the culmination of a dual domestic and foreign strategy to represent modern American lawyers, their practice, and the meaning/value of their practice to American society.[65] The pre-1949 era of the American lawyer in China had largely been forgotten.[66] And while faith in the transformative effect of American legal transplants abroad had become deeply embedded in popular and professional culture alike, law schools now served as sites for coordinating public and private overseas promotion efforts.[67]

In contrast to the pre-1949 era, the volume of economic interaction between China and the United States quickly became central to both national economies. Trade exploded, and over time the flow of goods, capital, and debt would make each country its largest respective trading partner. The demand for agents who could manage the public and private aspects of this interface generated a much larger cross-national market for legal services than ever existed previously. The form of market liberalization undertaken in China after 1978 involved massively reshaping the domestic economy and making the largest modern national investment in legal infrastructure building to date.[68]

Still, as common as strategic deployment of American *legal ideals* in intra-elite competition within and without Chinese universities came to be, there was still little impact in *legal education*.[69] The majority of Chinese law graduates would never aspire to become private lawyers, and the undergraduate model of civil law—taken from Europe—would still predominate as it had in the pre-1949 era. Law instructors pursued traditional doctoral degrees, and patterns of studying abroad for future lawyers and officials still favored non-US trajectories. More critically, legal practice in all spheres of Chinese life was thoroughly state-dominated.[70] Presumptions about the causal chains of change that legal education reform could achieve were invariably short-circuited by the CCP's unflinching commitment to suppress professional self-regulation and independence among even formally private legal associations.

Despite the limited impact of American legal ideals within Chinese legal education, both the increased diplomatic profile of China post-1978 and the logistical demands of global economic integration meant that change in Chinese lawyering was nonetheless unavoidable. Real educational reform did happen, the number of private lawyers produced by Chinese universities skyrocketed, the formal legal training of Chinese judges began to slowly standardize, and the leadership of the CCP itself became staffed increasingly by those with both domestic and foreign legal training.[71] There was no real political rival to the CCP at this time, and while the symbolic politics of Sino-American relations would never find completely stable ground, there was less need to roundly reject American legal examples, especially when it came to issues of economic governance.[72] As a result, the CCP allowed a wider range of experiments in Chinese legal education, and it would invest directly in developing domestic capacities for participation in both public and private international legal forums. Foreign agencies and foundations would (initially, at least) be allowed to promote aspects of American legal education,[73] conferences at law schools would serve as open and welcoming discursive spaces for American legal ideas, and opportunities for American law professors and students to engage with Chinese counterparts were established. In contrast to the still quite limited place of comparative legal expertise in US law schools, Chinese law schools became important sites for growing domestic comparative legal expertise.

What can be seen is that, although the American model of legal education was perhaps even more widely discussed as a model in the post-1978 era than in the pre-1949 era, a very different system of legal education was actually entrenched. With one exception—the Transnational School of Law, addressed below—there was no single school that could be classified as a discrete node like Soochow, which had operated, at least in theory, to train Chinese students as American lawyers. In contrast, in the post-1978 era discrete nodal elements were allowed to develop at elite Chinese law schools that were premised on the traditional Chinese model.[74] The state-driven nature of legal reform allowed for strategic investments in adapting American legal training methods for targeted state-perceived needs—including, most recently, Chinese participation in international forums of dispute resolution.[75] These investments, however, rarely took hold on the systemic level (again with a single exception—the introduction of the JM degree discussed below). Additionally, the primary avenue for educating China's internationalized legal elite was still outsourced to foreign law schools, in the United States as well as Europe, and to regional hubs in Japan and Hong Kong.

While there was no single law school to point to, this space for experimentation—coupled with an intentional strategy to allow for circumscribed bubbles of freer discourse involving foreigners—was often lavished with the same grandiose language of emulation and liberalization that Soochow had enjoyed.[76] Perhaps the best example was the promotion of various legal clinics at Chinese law schools, the experiential focus of which is still very much an American novelty. Clinical legal education had never been a core aspect of the Harvard model and was, in truth, part of an ongoing, sometimes bitter struggle over pedagogy in American law schools.[77] Part of the argument for developing legal clinics in the United States, especially by early proponents, was that they would imbue American law graduates with a sense of social mission and service that many felt was lacking among the long-standing corporate orientation of elite American practice.[78] Such debate was often completely absent from discussion or promotion efforts in China, and, as in other areas of the world, clinicians often found more welcoming Chinese interlocutors abroad than they could at home.[79] American status brought with it access for those with little to no expertise in China, and thus the promotion of idealizations was more appealing than honest discussion of marginality at home. The stateside circulation of evaluations and prognostications about the impact of these projects (often made possible by large grants from ostensibly nonlegal private foundations) operated much as they had in the Soochow era.[80] While some might have contested this conclusion during the heyday in the 1990s and 2000s, the actions of the CCP to curtail almost all such activities reveal that they were always contingent experiments rather than true brewing grounds for greater change—similarly elusive in the United States.

Similarly, the expansion of American graduate legal degrees among elite Chinese academics was itself taken as an indicator of American influence.[81] However, the interests of Chinese legal academics with foreign law degrees often operated more to exacerbate than to rework the same warped feedback loops for American interlocutors. Many Americans still folded China into their own domestic reform agendas, and they were eager to grant broad legitimacy and accuracy to any individual anecdote provided by Chinese interlocutors who affirmed claims about the impact of American legal ideas and education in China. Openness to engaging with American legal ideas was rarely critically evaluated in consideration of issues such as intense ranking systems, the need for English-language publications for Chinese academics, or highly asymmetrical access to financial resources. Sources of aversion to American legal ideas—such as the controversial place of interdisciplinary legal study in Chinese law departments seeking academic differentiation from other academic disciplines—were similarly overlooked in the search for affirmation.

Thus, while the study of American law is still active in China (perhaps now more than ever regarding economic regulation), the influence of American lawyers and the impact of American legal education are almost purely limited to these disaggregated nodal elements at elite schools.

The two most significant exceptions to this overall pattern serve to prove the general rule. In 2008, the first real inheritor of Soochow's model was founded in Shenzhen under the aegis of Beijing University (though it was of American impetus); this was generally referred to as the "Transnational School of Law."[82] The founding of the school represented perhaps a high point in the post-1978 optimism about the future of American legal education in China, as the school was initially staffed by American lawyers teaching solely American law. The school aspired not only to reproduce the Harvard model in China but also to have its graduates sit for admission to American bars. Such aspirations badly misjudged both the domestic market for legal services in China as well as the priorities of the ABA. Application to have its graduates' degrees recognized by the ABA failed, and to its credit the school has had to completely rework and indigenize its curriculum in order to provide reasonable employment prospects for its students in a market where even the private legal profession is ever more embedded in the state.[83]

The other exception to the generally limited impact of American lawyering and legal education arose in the context of public experimentation. One enabling aspect of the Transnational School of Law experiment was the attempt by the CCP to establish a postgraduate degree in law akin to the American juris doctorate: the juris master, or JM.[84] In the mid-1990s, the official promotion of the JM began with the general presumption that the degree would help produce a new genre of lawyers who could help replicate the type of economic success that American lawyers had achieved in the international legal services market and facilitate the type of causal chains related to economic growth that American lawyers had long proclaimed for themselves. The CCP has not been alone in this view, as Japan and Korea have made similar moves with the aspiration of transforming at least a segment of their legal professions.[85]

However, as of today, the JM experiment has yet to live up to its original aspirations (in many ways akin to the modern Japanese experience). Like Soochow, spinning a new system of legal instruction from whole cloth faces many problems inherent in educational innovation. The most prominent problem is finding instructors capable of teaching a new system in which they themselves have not been trained. More directly, the original market for JM graduates was quite limited.[86] Recent changes to requirements to sit for the Chinese bar have led to an explosion (in tuition if not in student opportunity) of JM programs while simultaneously becoming less and less like the JD model, with the JM emphasizing lectures and part-time instruction.[87] As a more honest evaluation of the Harvard model's own rise in the United States would reveal, the idea that legal pedagogy itself can lead to downstream legal change, or even produce an objectively "better" lawyer, is highly contingent on other institutional factors, often found outside of the law. What the JM experiment does reveal is that, whatever causal chains some in the CCP came to believe about American lawyering and economic gain, such beliefs were matched by an equally solid faith that the JM would not lead to liberalizing political change. Without the latter convictions, the experiment would never have been allowed to proceed.

As with the Soochow experience, the lack of concrete influence of American legal education in China beyond these nodal experiments should not give rise to laments about their forsaken value. Instead, this limited influence should inspire a critical evaluation of the validity of the same causal chains for American lawyering at home—especially those tied to democratic vitality.

Conclusion

This chapter has aimed to provide a general analytic scheme to frame discussions of legal education reform—one that is especially useful in cross-national contexts, where clarity about the empirical state and normative consequences of such reform is often beset by misperception and entrepreneurial optimism. For some, claiming that American legal education has had little influence in China over the past hundred-plus years is taken as a conclusion that implicates personal failure or the rejection of the legitimacy of cherished aspects of American lawyering. On some level this is correct, as the project of exerting individual efforts, or even well-funded collective efforts, to reshape any aspect of Chinese legal reform requires ignoring fundamental structural issues in China's political and economic systems and the role of lawyers therein. And perhaps it is jarring to consider that what is assumed to be true and demonstrated in a domestic setting is revealed to be less coherent, even contraindicated, abroad. But such should be the beneficial outcome, more often than not, expected from comparative legal experience.

The fusion of public and private virtue at the heart of American lawyering's legitimacy was near its relative historical high point when China reopened in 1978, in the same way that these virtues were first being asserted with vigor during the era of China's 1911 revolution. In 1978, the relative status and prestige of American law schools was only beginning to reach its peak—a trend that continued through the 1990s. Yet, as recent historical work on American legal education increasingly reveals, the true narratives about the how and why of the Harvard model's ascendance are far different than what is traditionally presumed within the profession, and the actual content of the model, especially its pedagogical elements, has a far more obscured relationship to the causal chains of liberalization than is typically asserted at home and abroad. The pragmatic engagement of even authoritarian regimes with aspects of American lawyering and legal education should invite the type of critical self-reevaluation that can enable effective reform at home, rather than holding tight to a dream of foreign influence.

The less-sanguine current moment for Chinese lawyers (at least those committed to more liberal visions of China's future) has led many to feel justified pessimism and cynicism. The explicit crackdown of the CCP on almost all forms of public-interest lawyering not wholly controlled by the state is in many ways similar to the dashed dreams of Republican-era reformers who found themselves caught between two authoritarian regimes that saw law only as a tool to institutionalize their symbolic or material power.[88] American lawyers today face their own domestic challenges to liberal norms in the private and public spheres, though at least with the opportunity to think through past mistakes so as to enable a more transformative future.

Certainly, there are vibrant democracies with systems of legal education far afield from the American system, as well as nonliberal systems that are actively adopting some of its institutional and pedagogical aspects. If, as seems descriptively uncontestable, American private law has had great impact abroad, then Americans should not balk from seeing ourselves more clearly through the eyes of others, especially those we claim to normatively reject.

In the end, the specific fate of American legal education in China demonstrates that the social context and implications of lawyering are often driven by concerns orthogonal to the pedagogical practices of law schools. The people whom lawyers serve—even *whom* lawyers can serve—is most often be determinative of the social consequences of lawyering.[89] If, for example, we are concerned about the democratic distribution of legal knowledge among a populace, or about whether dominant modes of public and private lawyering support or degrade democracy, then the internal aspects of legal education are far less important than the structure of employment markets, barriers to access into the profession, or broader trends in postsecondary education funding. Certainly, the modern crisis in American legal education has reinforced the salience of these very questions.[90]

The confident expression by American lawyers that they are simultaneously agents of private and public goods still finds traction in increasingly fraught global debates over the role of markets in modern democracies.[91] The ability to effectively serve public and private ends without the trade-off of personal sacrifice is alluring on many levels, but such is historically rare for most any profession.

The attractiveness of invoking the American model in China and elsewhere is in large part driven by the very basic fact that its ideal form represents a radical break from domestic traditions. Moreover, such a break offers hope and leverage for negotiating political uncertainties and opportunities.

In a world increasingly turning away from faith in democracy, whatever merit this symbolic example still has is put at risk by complacency, and not by being defended by closed minds.

NOTES

1 Compare, e.g., George Athan Billias, *American Constitutionalism Heard Round the World, 1776–1898* (New York: New York University Press, 2009), and David Law and Mila Versteeg, "The Declining Influence of the United States Constitution," *New York University Law Review* 87, no. 3 (2012): 762–858.

2 For a general overview, see Jedidiah Kroncke, *The Futility of Law and Development: China and the Dangers of Exporting American Law* (New York: Oxford University Press, 2016).

3 See generally Yves Dezalay and David Sugarman, eds., *Professional Competition and Professional Power: Lawyers, Accountants and the Social Construction of Markets* (London: Routledge, 1995).

4 John Ohnesorge, "Developing Development Theory: Law and Development Orthodoxies and the Northeast Asian Experience," *University of Pennsylvania Journal of International Economic Law* 28, no. 2 (2007): 219–308.

5 Alan Watson, *Legal Transplants: An Approach to Comparative Law* (Athens: University of Georgia Press, 1993), and Daniel Berkowitz, Katharina Pistor, and Jean-Francois Richard, "The Transplant Effect," *American Journal of Comparative Law* 51, no. 1 (2003): 163–203.

6 Teemu Ruskola, *Legal Orientalism: China, the United States, and Modern Law* (Cambridge: Harvard University Press, 2013).

7 Xiaoqun Xu, *Trial of Modernity: Judicial Reform in Early Twentieth-Century China: 1901–1937* (Stanford: Stanford University Press, 2001), and Michael Ng, *Legal Transplantation in Early Twentieth-century China: Practicing Law in Republican Beijing* (London: Routledge, 2016).

8 Eric Wolf, *Europe and the People Without History* (Berkeley: University of California Press, 1982).

9 Paul Cohen, *Discovering History in China* (New York: Columbia University Press, 1984).

10 Jonathan Spence, *To Change China: Western Advisers in China* (London: Penguin Books, 1969).

11 The cross-cultural politics of representing China abroad goes back to some of the earliest Jesuit writings on China for Europe. See Hung Ho-Fung, "Orientalist Knowledge and Social Theories: China and the European Conceptions of East-West Differences from 1600 to 1900," *Sociological Theory* 21, no. 3 (2003): 254–80.

12 Bruce Kimball, *The Inception of Professional Legal Education: C. C. Langdell, 1826–1906* (Chapel Hill: University of North Carolina Press, 2009).

13 The classic counter-representation is Morton Horwitz, *The Transformation of American Law: 1870–1960*, vol. 1 (New York: Oxford University Press, 1979).

14 Richard Abel, "Comparative Sociology of Legal Professions: An Exploratory Essay," *American Bar Foundation Research Journal* 10, no. 1 (1985): 5–79.

15 Andrew Boon, "Professionalism under the Legal Services Act," *International Journal of the Legal Profession* 17, no. 3 (2010): 195–232.

16 Daniel R. Coquillette and Bruce A. Kimball, *On the Battlefield of Merit: Harvard Law School, the First Century* (Cambridge: Harvard University Press, 2015).
17 Yves Dezalay and Bryant Garth, *The Internationalization of Palace Wars: Lawyers, Economists, and the Contest to Transform Latin American States* (Chicago: University of Chicago Press, 2002).
18 See, e.g., Robert Lawry, "The Central Moral Tradition of Lawyering," *Hofstra Law Review* 19, no. 2 (1990): 311–63.
19 Fu Hualing, "Challenging Authoritarianism through Law: Potentials and Limit," *National Taiwan University Law Review* 6, no. 1 (2011): 339–66.
20 David Trubek, "Max Weber on Law and the Rise of Capitalism," *Wisconsin Law Review* 72, no. 3 (1972): 720–53.
21 Lucien Karpik and Terence Halliday, "The Legal Complex," *Annual Review of Law and Social Science* 7, no. 1 (2011): 217–36.
22 Yanic Roznai, "Revolutionary Lawyering: On Lawyers' Social Responsibilities and Roles during a Democratic Revolution," *Southern California Interdisciplinary Law Journal* 22, no. 2 (2013): 353–84.
23 Wesley Pue and David Sugarman, eds., *Lawyers and Vampires: Cultural Histories of Legal Professions* (Oxford: Hart Publishing, 2004).
24 Jedidiah Kroncke, "Law and Development as Anti-Comparative Law," *Vanderbilt Journal of Transnational Law* 45, no. 2 (2012): 477–556.
25 Victor Li, *Law without Lawyers: A Comparative View of Law in the United States and China* (Boulder: Westview Press, 1978).
26 Jamie Horsley, "Doing Business with the People's Republic of China: The Role of Foreign Lawyers," *Michigan Journal of International Law* 7, no. 1 (1985): 63–79.
27 Philip Selznick, "American Society and the Rule of Law," *Syracuse Journal of International Law and Commerce* 33, no. 1 (2006): 29–39.
28 Ju-Ao Mei, "China and the Rule of Law," *Pacific Affairs* 5, no. 10 (1932): 863–72.
29 Benjamin Schwartz, *In Search of Wealth and Power: Yen Fu and the West* (Cambridge: Harvard University Press, 1964), and Weili Ye, *Seeking Modernity in China's Name: Chinese Students in the United States, 1900–1927* (Stanford: Stanford University Press, 2001).
30 Xu, *Trial of Modernity.*
31 Han Depei and Stephen Kanter, "Legal Education in China," *American Journal of Comparative Law* 32, no. 3 (1984): 543–82.
32 Xiaoqing Lin, *Peking University: Chinese Scholarship and Intellectuals, 1898–1937* (Albany: State University of New York Press, 2005).
33 Harold Berman, "Soviet Perspectives on Chinese Law," in *Contemporary Chinese Law: Research Problems and Perspectives*, ed. Jerome Cohen (Cambridge: Harvard University Press, 1970), 318–27.
34 Dooeum Chung, *Elitist Fascism: Chiang Kaishek's Blueshirts in 1930s China* (Aldershot: Ashgate, 2000).
35 Aziz Rana, "Statesman or Scribe? Legal Independence and the Problem of Democratic Citizenship," *Fordham Law Review* 77, no. 4 (2009): 1665–1730.

36 Stephen MacKinnon, *Power and Politics in Late Imperial China: Yuan Shi-kai in Beijing and Tianjin, 1901–1908* (Berkeley: University of California Press, 1980).

37 Lucien Bianco, *Origins of the Chinese Revolution, 1915–1949*, trans. Muriel Bell (Stanford: Stanford University Press, 1971).

38 Joseph Goodrich, *The Coming China* (Chicago: A. C. McClurg, 1911), and Walter Briggs, *From Swatow to Chungking* (Chungking: China Information Committee, 1941).

39 Robert Gordon, "The Role of Lawyers in Producing the Rule of Law: Some Critical Reflections," *Theoretical Inquiries in Law* 11, no. 1 (2010): 441–68.

40 Kroncke, *The Futility of Law and Development*.

41 Robert Bryan, "The Legal Profession," in *American University Men in China*, ed. American University Group of Shanghai (Shanghai: Comacrib Press, 1936), 89–95.

42 Jay Taylor, *The Generalissimo: Chiang Kai-shek and the Struggle for Modern China* (Cambridge: Harvard University Press, 2009).

43 The first notable American legal instructor in China was William Martin. Ralph Covell, *W. A. P. Martin, Pioneer of Progress in China* (Washington, DC: Christian University Press, 1978).

44 Anthony Chase, "The Birth of the Modern Law School," *American Journal of Legal History* 23, no. 4 (1979): 329–48.

45 Robert Stevens, *Law School: Legal Education in America from the 1850s to the 1980s* (Chapel Hill: University of North Carolina Press, 1983).

46 Edgar Allen, "Legal Education in China," *ABA* 39th *Conference Annual Report* (1916): 671–77.

47 Donald King, *A Harvard Law School Professor* (Buffalo: W. S. Hein, 2005).

48 J. W. Madden, "In Memoriam: Judson Adams Crane," *Hastings Law Journal* 16, no. 2 (1965): 151–53.

49 Ng, *Legal Transplantation in Early Twentieth-Century China*.

50 Alison Conner, "Anglo-American Law at Soochow," in *China's Christian Colleges: Cross-Cultural Connections, 1900–1950*, ed. Daniel H. Bays and Ellen Widmer (Stanford: Stanford University Press, 2009), 147–72.

51 Alison Conner, "Training China's Early Modern Lawyers," *Journal of Chinese Law* 8 (1994): 1–34.

52 Charles Lobingier, "Legal Education in Twentieth Century China," *Lawyers Guild Review* 4, no. 4 (1944): 1–5.

53 Xiaoqun Xu, "Between State and Society, Between Professionalism and Politics: The Shanghai Bar Association in Republican China, 1912–1937," *Twentieth Century China* 24, no. 1 (1998): 1–29.

54 See Frank Ellsworth, *Law on the Midway: The Founding of the University of Chicago Law School* (Chicago: University of Chicago Press, 1977).

55 Nianyi Xu, *Rise and Demise of the Comparative Law School of China* (2012) (paper on file with author).

56 Alison Conner, "Soochow in the South," *Soochow Law Journal* 2, no. 1 (2005): 1–23.

57 Ng, *Legal Transplantation in Early Twentieth-Century China.*

58 Stephen Craft, *V. K. Wellington Koo and the Emergence of Modern China* (Lexington: University Press of Kentucky, 2004).

59 Jedidiah Kroncke, "An Early Tragedy of Comparative Constitutionalism: Frank Goodnow and the Chinese Republic," *Washington International Law Journal* 21, no. 3 (2012): 553–90; Ching-Sze Wang, *John Dewey in China: To Teach and to Learn* (Albany: State University of New York Press, 2007); and Jedidiah Kroncke, "Roscoe Pound in China: A Lost Precedent for the Liabilities of American Legal Exceptionalism," *Brooklyn Journal of International Law* 37, no. 1 (2012): 77–143.

60 Harold Isaacs, *The Tragedy of the Chinese Revolution* (London: Secker & Warburg, 1951).

61 Jerome Cohen, "The Chinese Communist Party and 'Judicial Independence': 1949–1959," *Harvard Law Review* 82, no. 5 (1969): 967–1006.

62 Xilao Li, "'I Know Why the Caged Bird Sings!': Dunbar in China," *African American Review* 41, no. 2 (2007): 387–93.

63 See, e.g., Ruth Ginsburg, "American Bar Association Delegation Visits the People's Republic of China," *ABA Journal* 64, no. 10 (1978): 1516–25.

64 Matthew Stephenson, "A Trojan Horse Behind Chinese Walls? Problems and Prospectus of US-Sponsored Rule of Law Reform Projects in the People's Republic of China," *UCLA Pacific Basin Law Journal* 18, no. 1 (2000): 64–97.

65 Robert Storey, "Under God and the Law," *ABA Journal* 39, no. 9 (1953): 787–90.

66 Philip Beidler, "China Magic: America's Great Reality Hiatus, 1948–73," *Michigan Quarterly Review* 47, no. 2 (2008), http://hdl.handle.net.

67 Thomas Carothers, *Promoting the Rule of Law Abroad: In Search of Knowledge* (Washington, DC: Carnegie Endowment for International Peace, 2006).

68 Randall Peerenboom, *China's Long March toward Rule of Law* (Cambridge: Cambridge University Press, 2002).

69 Matthew Erie, "Legal Education Reform in China Through U.S.-Inspired Transplants," *Journal of Legal Education* 59, no. 1 (2009): 60–96.

70 Ethan Michelson, "Lawyers, Political Embeddedness and Institutional Continuity," *American Journal of Sociology* 113, no. 2 (2007): 352–414.

71 Cheng Li, "The Rise of the Legal Profession in the Chinese Leadership," *China Leadership Monitor* 42 (7 October, 2013): 1–26.

72 Shiping Hua, "The U.S. Impact on China's Legal System during the Reform Era," *International Journal of China Studies* 5, no. 3 (2014): 681–703.

73 Cecily Baskir, "Crossing Borders: Creating an American Law Clinic in China," *Clinical Law Review* 19, no. 1 (2012): 163–206.

74 Wenhua Shan, "Legal Education in China: The New 'Outstanding Legal Personnel Education Scheme' and Its Implications," *Legal Information Management* 13, no. 1 (2013): 10–24, and Wang Zhizhou, Liu Sida, and Li Xueyao, "Internationalizing Chinese Legal Education in the Early Twenty-First Century," *Journal of Legal Education* 66, no. 2 (2017): 237–66.

75 Gregory Shaffer and Henry Gao, "China's Rise: How It Took on the US at the WTO," 2018 *University of Illinois Law Review* 115 (2018): 115–84.
76 Carl Minzner, "The Rise and Fall of Chinese Legal Education," *Fordham International Law Journal* 36, no. 2 (2013): 334–95.
77 Jerome Frank, "Why Not a Clinical Lawyers-School?," *University of Pennsylvania Law Review* 81, no. 8 (1933): 907–23.
78 Stephen Wizner, "The Law School Clinic: Legal Education in the Interests of Justice," *Fordham Law Review* 70, no. 5 (2002): 1929–38.
79 Michael Dowdle, "Preserving Indigenous Paradigms in an Age of Globalization: Pragmatic Strategies for the Development of Clinical Legal Aid in China," *Fordham International Law Journal* 24, no. 6 (2002): 56–82.
80 Jay Pottenger, "The Role of [Clinical] Legal Education in Legal Reform in the People's Republic of China: Chicken, Egg–or Fox?" *International Journal of Clinical Legal Education* 4 (2004): 65–80.
81 Wang, Liu, and Li, "Internationalizing Chinese Legal Education."
82 Philip McConnaughay and Colleen Toomey, "China and the Globalization of Legal Education: A Look into the Future," Peking University School of Transnational Law Research Paper No. 17-10 (2017).
83 Weidong Ji, "Legal Education in China: Reforms and Requirements," *Asian Journal of Law and Society* 3, no. 2 (2016): 237–46.
84 Hou Xiandan, "Legal Education and the Transformation of the Legal Profession," in *China's Journey Toward the Rule of Law*, ed. Cai Dingjian and Chenguang Wang (Leiden: Brill, 2010), 251–99.
85 Thomas Chih-hsiung Chen, "Legal Education Reform in Taiwan: Are Japan and Korea the Models?," *Journal of Legal Education* 62, no. 1 (2012): 32–65.
86 Jerome Cohen, "China's Lawyers and Their Training," in *Legal Reforms in China and Vietnam: A Comparison of Asian Communist Regimes*, ed. John Gillespie and Albert Chen, 271–75 (Milton Park: Routledge, 2010).
87 Xu Bingxuan and Zhuang Zhiguo, "Problems and Suggestions for Improvement on Juris Master (JM) (Non-Law) Education in Contemporary China," *US-China Education Review* 7, no. 4 (2017): 200–8.
88 Carl Minzner, *End of an Era: How China's Authoritarian Revival Is Undermining Its Rise* (New York: Oxford University Press, 2018).
89 Richard Abel, *American Lawyers* (New York: Oxford University Press, 1992).
90 Brian Tamanaha, *Failing Law Schools* (Chicago: University of Chicago Press, 2012).
91 Trevor Farrow, "Ethical Lawyering in a Global Community," *Manitoba Law Journal* 37, no. 1 (2013): 61–84.

8

Transplants in Estonian Legal Education

Influences from the US Legal System

IRENE KULL, MERIKE RISTIKIVI, AND ALEKSEI KELLI

The history of Estonian law and legal education is in many respects the history of interruptions. After establishing one system of legal education, a generation of academic lawyers had to give up and start teaching new law in a new way when sociopolitical formation swept away everything that had previously been achieved. The purpose of this chapter is to show how much of this process was influenced by US legal doctrine and methods. Training lawyers was one of the main requirements for moving from socialist principles and a socialist legal system to a society based on a market economy and the rule of law. The aim of changing the university system was to provide legal education according to Western standards and to meet the specific needs of a country in transition. However, legal training during the transformation period was chaotic and inconsistent. Having transplanted legislation and doctrines in all fields of law, the method of comparative law became a crucial component of legal research and legal studies. Here, we can see the contribution from visiting lecturers from the United States, starting from the beginning of educational reforms in Estonia and continuing today. In this chapter, we give a historical overview of legal education in the country before 1940 and describe the main challenges of transformation society in building up a legal system. We also outline how teaching the law evolved due to changes in the legal system, transplanting methods and systems of teaching, transplanting legal methods,[1] and using comparative law in training and applying the law in practice.

Legal Education and Legal Languages in Estonia before 1940

Straddling the frontier between East and West, the geographical location of Estonia has influenced the country's legal science, legal culture, and legal language. The faculty of law is one of the oldest faculties at the University of Tartu. Lawyers have been educated there since 1632, when the university was founded by the King Gustavus Adolphus of Sweden. Over the centuries, Estonia was governed by rulers from Germany, Denmark, Sweden, Poland, and Russia. Such developments meant that extensive reforms were made in legal education. Also, the very language in which law was studied and taught changed repeatedly, from Latin to German to Russian.

At the beginning of the twentieth century, Estonia was part of the Russian empire. Before that, until the end of the nineteenth century, the Baltic German nobility constituted the highest class in society, and German was the language used for business, administrative matters, and in universities as the language of instruction. During the 1880s, however, Estonia faced an intensive Russification policy, which brought about significant changes in the cultural and educational fields and in the composition of educated people. Russian replaced German as the official language. Simultaneously during the second half of the nineteenth century, the process of national awakening began, and Estonians came to acknowledge themselves as a separate nation-state. This growing national sentiment was expressed by zealous efforts to educate people and to spread the printed word using the Estonian language. During those first decades of the twentieth century, the level of education of Estonian men and women increased significantly. As a result, educated Estonians formed a social class of national intelligentsia. Such cultural, educational, and social developments helped to form a basis for the new Republic of Estonia, founded in 1918. Estonian[2] became the official language in administrative matters, legislation, courts, and education. Since 1920, the constitution of the Republic of Estonia provided for Estonian as the state language.

In 1919, the University of Tartu became a national university with Estonian as the language of instruction, ousting the Russian and German languages, which had previously been used for legal purposes. Estonian thus became a component of national identity as well as a political object and resource, particularly during the early years of independence, as draft legislation was prepared by lawyers and politicians of Estonian origin. The interwar period laid the foundation for a consciously Western-oriented legal education, including the enrollment of female students[3] on an equal basis with male students.

With the imposition of Communist rule and the violent incorporation of Estonia into the Soviet Union in 1940, the natural development of the faculty of law at the University of Tartu toward the Western tradition ceased. The Soviet era (1940–1941, 1944–1991) brought along with it the USSR's legal system and wider use of Russian as the official language. During the Soviet occupation, use of Estonian became one of the most powerful forms of national identity opposing Soviet ideology. After restoring the independence of the Republic of Estonia in 1991, Estonian became the only official language in local government and state institutions. It is also the official language of legislation, the court system, and legal studies.[4]

Social Transformation–Challenges for Law Faculties

During the Communist-led regime, Estonia had no independent judiciary, court system, law libraries, independent bar associations, or organized law firms. A new stage in the history of the faculty of law[5] of the University of Tartu began when Estonia regained its independence in 1991.

Changes in Society and the Legal System

This new situation posed a challenge to the law faculty as the only one of its in the country at the beginning of the 1990s. Radical economic reforms were implemented, with a considerable body of new laws supporting a shift toward private ownership and economic freedom.[6] As a country in transition, the most crucial objective of legal reforms was to change society through laws (e.g., to restore traditional, pre-Soviet Estonian values and traditions such as the rule of law, religious tolerance, civility, etc.).[7]

Due to Estonia's small population (1.3 million inhabitants), changes in society and legislation happened within a relatively short time frame.

Creating a new private law system had already started in 1988, when legislation necessary for legal reforms was passed. After regaining independence, the most important decisions and choices for future legislation were made in 1992 and 1993. Between 1994 and 2002, the majority of private law legislation was drafted and went into force.[8]

It is important to mention that the United States offered help in drafting new laws immediately after Estonia regained independence. Some programs were created to support legislative processes and to advise lawyers and judges. For example, Georgetown Law School, through the US Department of Commerce's Commercial Law Development Program, gave support by advising on a range of economic law reform issues in Estonia.[9] In the fall of 1990, the American Bar Association introduced the Central and East European Law Initiative (CEELI) to facilitate law reform in the newly independent countries of the former Soviet bloc.[10] This initiative was immediately accepted by the Estonian government and the University of Tartu because Estonia needed the experience of US experts to build up legal structures and to implement reform. CEELI[11] offered legal training to law professors, students, practicing lawyers, and judges.[12] The project also sponsored visits by US private and government lawyers specializing in commercial law and provided assistance with drafting commercial legislation in areas such as bankruptcy, intellectual property (IP), secured transactions, competition, privatization of public enterprises, and so forth.[13] It is important to mention that advice provided by CEELI representatives and specialists from other nonprofit US organizations included at least as much Western European law as American law because Estonia declared itself to stand within the civil law tradition and devoted itself to being a member of the European Union in the future.[14] Therefore, CEELI brought together American professors with comparative law experience.[15] From the beginning of the 1990s, the European tradition, especially German law, was followed rather than American models due to the historic relationship between Germany and Estonia.[16]

Maintaining historical continuity was also the main reason why the Estonian Parliament decided, after the adoption of the Constitution in 1992, that new laws would follow the laws that were in force before 1940. For private law, the relevant law was the 1939 Draft Civil Code,[17] which was based on a pandect system and consisted of five books similar to the

German Civil Code (BGB).[18] The 1939 draft was used only as a model, not as a direct source for the new civil code. During the preparatory phase it was decided not to copy the laws of any particular country but rather to follow the German legal system as the primary model.[19] However, in the law reform process, US law was often used as a source for understanding a field of law (though not as a source of drafting).[20]

By choosing the 1939 Draft Civil Code as a basis for the new civil code, a particular private law system was also chosen. The most important field influenced by Parliament's decision was property law.[21] Property law rules in the 1939 Draft Civil Code were based on the German Civil Code, and the final version of the Property Law Act of 1993 was based on the BGB as well.[22] Second, important legislation, the General Part of the Civil Code Act (GPCCA), was passed and entered into force in 1994. The 1994 GPCCA was replaced by a new version in 2002.[23] The Family Law Act was passed on October 12, 1994, and entered into force on January 1, 1995.[24] The adaption of the Law of Succession Act followed in 1997.[25] The Law of Obligations Act (LOA), adopted on September 26, 2001, and entered into force on July 1, 2002, was the last of the five laws of the new civil code.[26] As can be seen from this timeline of the primary private law legislation, the reform was very intensive, carried out during a five-year time frame from 1992 to 1997.[27] From the beginning, Estonian law students participated with professors in drafting the new laws, which meant they had to study law, court practices, scholarly literature, and commentary on other legal systems and to analyze these materials comparatively.[28]

The process of drafting of private law legislation and finding models for transplantation will not be described in detail, as our main purpose is to focus on the influence of US legal doctrine and methods. One of the best examples is the preparation of the LOA, the most substantial part of the new civil code, which started in 1994, immediately after the GPCCA was brought in, the Georgetown group started drafting a sales law as early as 1992. It was quickly understood that the US commercial code would not be a suitable model for Estonian law, as it is too flexible and requires too active of a role for the judiciary to be suitable for a country with a strong Continental tradition.[29] So, the United Nations Convention on Contracts for the International Sale of Goods (CISG)[30] and the Swedish and Finnish Sales of Goods Acts[31] were the primary sources for the draft proposed by the Georgetown group working with Estonian experts.[32] Even though there is very little that was used from this draft sales law in the final version of the LOA, the role of US professors and practitioners—who explained the basic principles of sales law and the role of contract law in a liberal market economy—cannot be underestimated.

Another example of the influence of US law is intellectual property law, which belongs to the European tradition yet has several connections to the US system for protecting those rights. The US system is focused on the protection and the enhancement of IP-based entrepreneurship. This is manifested in the adoption of legal instruments such as the Agreement on Trade-Related Aspects of Intellectual Property Rights[33] (TRIPS Agreement) and other policy initiatives. The TRIPS Agreement, a foundation of the modern IP framework, is part of the Estonian IP system as well. US policy initiatives also impacted the Estonia IP system through the improvement of IP enforcement[34] and expert assistance (e.g., analysis of the Estonian legislative initiatives).[35]

Yet another aspect of US influence was the reorganization of the court system. Pursuant to the Estonian Constitution, everyone whose rights and freedoms are potentially violated has the right of recourse to the courts, as well as the right, while his or her case is pending before the court, to petition for any relevant legislation or procedure to be declared unconstitutional. The Estonian court system was reorganized in accordance with the principle of the rule of law,[36] which meant that the *courts* must be separate from both the executive and legislative branches of government in the performance of its duties.[37] Because the primary source of law in Estonia is written (i.e., statutory) law, case law promulgated by the courts in their decision-making process has limited precedential value insofar as the judgments of the Estonian Supreme Court are used as a subsidiary source of law in interpreting and founding the general principles of law. However, the decisions of the Estonian Supreme Court are used as a subsidiary source of law in interpreting and founding the general principles of law.[38] One can see that, incrementally over time, the judgments of the Estonian Supreme Court have gained more and more importance in shaping the legal system and the legal order in the country.[39] This is due mainly to the tradition that has been developing since the first decade of the 2000s to write very long judgments, often with *obiter dicta* and theoretical explanations on how to interpret and apply the law. This process was unavoidable because of the lack of textbooks, academic publishing, and legal scholars at the beginning of the 1990s. In addition, most Estonian law professors and high-level lawyers participated in the process of drafting legislation and had little time and opportunity to publish thorough theoretical works during this period.[40] All of these processes lead to the importance of educating judges.

In June 1993, professor Tom Krattenmaker, from Georgetown Law School, and Keith Callow, former chief justice of the Washington Supreme Court, conducted a weeklong seminar by the invitation of Rait Maruste. The topic of the seminar was constitutional adjudication, and it was organized for members of the new Estonian Supreme Court.[41] The great success of the seminar, the personal rapport of Krattenmaker and Maruste, and the strong support from Georgetown led to the foundation of a permanent Estonian judicial training center in Tartu.[42] An important aim of the center is to educate judges and other legal professionals, provide lectures on legal principles underlying Western law and the judicial function, and to promote the role of judges in a democratic society.[43]

Teaching Students, Practitioners, and Professors a New Legal System and New Legal Principles: Transplanting Methods and Systems

Training lawyers was one of the main prerequisites if Estonia was to move from a socialist legal system reflecting socialist principles to a society based on a market economy and the rule of law. To this end, changing the university system meant providing legal education according to Western standards to meet the specific needs of a country in transition.

One of the bases for a well-functioning liberal market economy and a democratic state is freedom in scientific education within the universities.[44] The legislative basis for free scientific education can be found in the Constitution of the Republic of Estonia (section 38),[45] which declares the freedom of science and autonomy of universities and research institutions within limits prescribed by law. The primary purpose of this provision is to promote high-level research, academic traditions, and modern standards of higher education.[46]

The Education Act of 1992,[47] the Universities Act of 1995,[48] and the University of Tartu Act of 1995[49] constitute the legal basis for university education. This legislation decentralized the system of higher education, moving away from the so-called German university model to establish a three-level system of higher education (bachelor's, master's, and doctoral degree programs). After Estonia regained independence, the University of Tartu was the only one offering legal education at all three levels. Soon, several private and public law schools were established. However, while the size of the higher education sector has changed since then, the current number of law schools is comparable to that of 1993;[50] Tartu is still the only law school offering degrees at all three levels.

The University of Tartu Faculty of Law adopted a new curriculum in 1992–1993, immediately after the restoration of independence. The curriculum was first evaluated at the international level by professor J. P. Grant, dean of the Faculty of Law at the University of Glasgow, followed by an evaluation made at the request of the EuroFaculty by professor W. Schlüter from the University of Münster.[51] For the new curriculum, the socioeconomic and political changes in Estonian society, as well as the need to integrate the Estonian legal system with that of continental Europe, had to be taken into consideration.[52] The main goal was to provide broad, science-based education, which meant that comparative law and legal research would be part of the law faculty's curriculum following independence. A number of visiting lecturers made important contributions to the exchange of ideas, the amendment and development of courses, and the application of new teaching methods.[53] This was a significant change; in the Soviet Union and countries of the Eastern bloc, higher education was substantially practice-oriented, with the main emphasis being on public law. Private law courses constituted only a third of the curriculum. The task, therefore, was to change the balance between public and private law disciplines so that about two-thirds of disciplines belonged to the sphere of private law.

Since the 1990s, the curriculum of the law faculty has been regularly reassessed and amended in cooperation with representatives from various legal professions (e.g., attorneys, notaries, judges, prosecutors, and business lawyers). As a result, the share of private law courses is significantly higher today in comparison to the early years of independence; also, the importance of public law courses has changed over the years.

After adopting the so-called Bologna model in 2002/2003, significant changes were made, such as grading on the basis of three years for BA studies plus two years for MA studies, replacing the bachelor's thesis with an exam and reducing the number of master's students.[54]

The reform of the curriculum and the legal system required that mainly traditional teaching methods were used. In a situation where contemporary textbooks and legal literature were not yet available to students, and there was no case law, the extent of study in the classroom (obligatory participation in lectures, seminars, workshops, and colloquia) was relatively high. One of the aims was and still is to teach students to work independently and to develop their writing and analytical skills. For example, students were required to prepare research papers on different legal topics each academic year, and theses required for a master's degree were part of the curricula from the beginning of the 1990s. Every year more attention has been paid to seminars, workshops, and colloquia, together with the introduction of new teaching methods and new technologies.[55] The faculty set itself the goal of holding seminars in every subject or carrying out practical tasks in some other form as part of its teaching. For example, students in all fields of civil law must attend compulsory seminars. They are required to consider solutions to all of the key cases, read all the relevant literature, and understand the case law of the Supreme Court of Estonia. Responses are discussed, and professors draw attention to errors and irregularities. Cases are addressed mainly from the perspective of the judge. Many different forms of oral presentations are used in combination with resolving practical cases. Each student must prepare one research paper during the first three years of study on a topical legal problem, which is assessed by a committee of at least two faculty members during an oral defense procedure.

Changes in the content of the teaching process and curricula were made, to a great extent, with the contribution of visiting lecturers.[56] Law professors and practitioners from the United States came to Estonia through several programs such as EuroFaculty,[57] the Civic Education Project,[58] Fulbright Fellowships, and the special CEELI program. Also, the Georgetown project for Estonia moved quickly from very general legislative drafting to the specifics of training lawyers, judges, and legal professionals after the Estonian Parliament's decision to follow the Germanic civil law system.[59] Aid provided by the United States was important in establishing the Estonian Law Centre Foundation,[60] where judges are taught the legal principles underlying Western democratic legal systems and the role of the judiciary. World Bank and the United States Agency for International Department supported professional educational programs for practicing lawyers and police department chiefs .[61] A special twinning program for training lawyers was introduced in 1999 in cooperation between the Estonian Ministry of Justice, Germany, and the European Union.[62]

Since 1991, teaching law was based mainly on the comparative legal method, which continues in the current curricula.[63] The main reason for the comparative approach is that Estonian legislation consists of rules adopted and transplanted from other legal systems.[64] A number of private law concepts based on legal transplants caused confusion for a long time, which was reflected in practice as well as in teaching.[65] For example, the concepts of separation and abstraction of real rights agreements and obligational contracts in private law were already adopted as general principles of the Estonian civil law system in 1992 in the Property Law Act and later in the General Part of the Civil Code Act in 1994. The principle of separation (e.g., differentiation between the obligation to transfer ownership and agreement on the disposition of real rights) was accepted without any difficulties, whereas the principle of abstraction (e.g., that the validity of a real right agreement or disposition and that of the causal agreement do not depend on each other and have to be contested separately) was not fully understood and applied until nearly twelve years after the adaption of the rule.[66]

The strong influence of the German legal system on Estonian private law was first and foremost evident in legislation, which in turn led to the transposition or adaptation of German legal theory and methods used in teaching. The influence of German law was supported by the translation of German textbooks, starting in 1998 with a textbook on the General Part of the Civil Code Act. For a long time, this was the only book used for teaching private law.[67] The German analytical style of writing and reasoning was adopted gradually, with Estonian adaptions based on substantive law and judicial lawmaking. Today, the elaborated methods of resolving cases are used widely in all private and public law subjects.[68]

Finally, Estonian lawyers are trained as German lawyers, who always think in terms of "general" and "special" and "rule" and "exception."

Similarly, the distinction between contractual and legal obligations is as clear as the distinction between obligations and rights in rem. In this respect, it must be acknowledged that, without proper knowledge of German law, the implementation and development of Estonia's adopted system of law is complicated, especially if rules have been transposed only partially or inaccurately and do not comply with the whole system. However, there are areas where the influence of US legal doctrine is stronger (e.g., in the fields of intellectual property and business law). There are a number of reasons for this, among them the fact that the United States leads the world when it comes to innovative entrepreneurship, the United States promulgates extensive and relevant case law, and there are significant professional and scientific relations between professors at the University of Tartu, Estonian practitioners, and US intellectual property law experts.

Teaching during this transformation period was chaotic; studying occurred mainly during lectures, as teachers and students could not rely on textbooks and case law. Teaching methods and materials were largely transplanted from guest lecturers. Importantly, visiting US lecturers were the first to offer expertise to help Estonian lawyers and officials understand principles of Western law, the judicial function, and the legislative process. From the beginning, Estonian law students cooperated with professors in drafting new legislation. Often, the draft (as opposed to the finally enacted) legislation was taught in the classroom, with foreign-court practices used as examples. The ability of the younger generation to follow foreign experts was specially mentioned by members of the Georgetown group and other foreign experts visiting Estonia with different projects.[69] The teaching staff of Tartu's law faculty changed considerably, with the younger generation of professors (trained in Western legal thinking) taking over teaching positions. Those professors who decided to leave the law faculty of the University of Tartu at the beginning of the 1990s found teaching positions in some private law schools opened at the end of that decade.[70] Today, students are introduced to foreign legal sources, and Estonian legal scholarship is based mainly on the comparison of Estonian court practice and doctrine versus practices and doctrines in the countries from which legal transplants were accepted. Though foreign practices and doctrines are not followed in all fields of the law, use of the comparative law method became an obligatory part of lawyers' daily work as a consequence of the historical process of building up the Estonian legal system.

Conclusion

Estonian private law is an excellent example of borrowing from foreign legal systems, successful use of transplants, and the implementation of different regulatory models. From the beginning of the 1990s, the European tradition—and especially German law—was followed due to the historical relationship between Estonia and Germany. Even though little was used from US laws in drafting Estonian private laws, the role of American professors and practitioners—who taught the basic principles of law and the importance of judicial independence in a liberal market economy—is difficult to overstate. The first foreign experts who taught Estonians how to draft legislation in the Western tradition were Georgetown University professors, scholars, and students.[71]

Lawyers' freedom is based on nothing other than command of legal argumentation.[72] The main aim of the law faculty at the University of Tartu since the 1990s has been to prepare lawyers who understand the new legislation and are trained to skillfully apply the legal method corresponding to the legal system, which in turn leads to the correct resolution of cases—the very purpose of studying law and following the rules wherever they lead. Changes to the teaching process and to curricula were made thanks to important contributions from visiting lecturers from the United States and other countries. Also, a number of educational programs were introduced with the help of American universities as well as US government and professional organizations. Comparative law and comparative jurisprudence were part of the law faculty's curriculum from the beginning of independence.

Estonian lawyers, in many ways, are trained as German lawyers. However, there are areas of law in which the influence of US legal doctrine is clearly stronger, as seen in the fields of intellectual property and business law. There are intertwined factors affecting this analysis. First, the United States leads the field in innovative entrepreneurship. Second, the United States maintains centuries of applicable case law. Finally, culture—especially legal culture—is not rationally designed, and rules of conduct passed down through cultural transmission is a process that is not always consciously planned. Foreign textbooks were translated into Estonian, and the substance of legislation was taught by foreign professors. The concept of transplants—cultural as well as legal—became a daily reality.[73] It was clear from the beginning that successful use of transplants and the implementation of different regulatory models could be achieved only through a deep understanding of which solution would fit best within the Estonian legal culture.

NOTES

1 Today, in civil law systems, "legal method" is used in the meaning of a method of thinking, which leads to the correct resolution of cases, the way of studying law and finding the rules. As Estonian law is based mainly on German legal method; see more about the legal method in German law in J. Rückert, Friedrich Carl von Savigny, "The Legal Method and the Modernity of Law," *Juridica International* 11 (2006): 55–67.

2 The Estonian language belongs to the Finno-Ugric language family and is closely related to the Finnish language. Today, Estonian is spoken by about 1.1 million people throughout the world. About 950,000 of them live in Estonia.

3 For more about women's opportunities for higher education in Estonia before World War II, see M. Ristikivi, "Establishing New Traditions for Legal Profession: First Women Law Students in University of Tartu," in *First Women Lawyers in Great Britain and the Empire Record*, ed. J. Bourne (St Mary's University, Twickenham, London 2016), 31–43.

4 Specifically, 68.5 percent of the population speak Estonian as their native language, while Russian is the native language for 29.6 percent of the population (data from 2018). See "PHC 2011: 157 Native Languages Spoken in Estonia," Population and Housing Census, last modified 30, 2012,www.stat.ee. Estonian as an official language is established by §6 of the Constitution and §3 of the Language Act (2011). In government agencies and local authorities the official language is Estonian (§52 of the Constitution). Proceedings before the courts and clerical business in the courts are conducted in the Estonian language under the §32(1) of the Code of Civil Procedure. Hearings and evidence may be in foreign language if, for example, the other participants in the proceedings do not object to accepting the evidence in another language. Participants without representatives are granted translations if they have been granted procedural assistance for bearing translation costs (§33 (4) of the Code of Civil Procedure).

5 The School of Law (previously Faculty of Law, *õigusteaduskond*) has been a part of the Faculty of Social Sciences of the University of Tartu since January 1, 2016, along with the Institute of Social Studies, the School of Economics and Business Administration, the Institute of Education, the Institute of Psychology, the Johan Skytte Institute of Political Studies, the Narva and the Pärnu College. In Estonia, two schools (the School of Law and the School of Economics and Business

Administration) kept their previous name "Faculty." For clarity we use the name "Faculty of Law" throughout the text.

6 See also N. Reich, "Law and Civil Justice in the New EU Countries," in *The Institutional Framework of European Private Law*, ed. F. Cafaggi (Oxford: Oxford University Press, 2006), 271–302, and N. Reich, "Transformation of Contract Law and Civil Justice In new EU Member Countries—The Example of the Baltic States, Hungary and Poland," *Pennylvania State International Law Review* 23, no. 3 (2005): 587–623.

7 M. Luts, "Textbook of Pandects or New Style of Legislation in Estonia?," *Juridica International* 6 (2001): 158.

8 See also P. Varul, "Legal Policy Decisions and Choices in the Creation of New Private Law in Estonia," *Juridica International* 5 (2000): 104–118.

9 J. deLisle, "Lex Americana? United States Legal Assistance, American Legal Models, and Legal Change in the Post-Communist World and Beyond," *University of Pennsylvania Journal of International Law* 20, no. 2 (1990): 196. See also J. P. Byrne and P. G. Schrag, "Law Reform in Estonia: The Role of Georgetown University Law Center," *Law and Policy in International Business* 25, no. 2 (1994): 449. Byrne and Schrag are describing in this article the Georgetown project, supported through the Commercial Law Development Program.

10 R. Margolis, "The Role of Law: American Rule of Law Reform Abroad and the Central and East European Law Initiative," *Yale Review of International Studies* (2016), http://yris.yira.org.

11 Central and East European Law Initiative, established in 1990 by the American Bar Association. Subsequently changed its title to the Central European and Eurasian Law Initiative (CEELI) and became a freestanding, independent institution in 2004.

12 See J. Key, "Old Countries, New Rights," *ABA Journal* 80, no. 5 (1994): 68–67.

13 deLisle, "Lex Americana?," 231–232. For example, G. Myers as representative of CEELI commented on the Copyright Law of Estonia in 1992.

14 Byrne and Schrag, "Law Reform in Estonia," 452.

15 M. Ellis, Valerie J. Pellegrini, and Michael C. Diedring, *Country Strategies for the Rule of Law Program for Albania, Bulgaria, Croatia, Czech Republic, Estonia, Hungary, Latvia, Lithuania, Macedonia, Poland, Romania, and Slovakia* (Washington, DC: American Bar Association, 1993), 73, http://pdf.usaid.gov.

16 Ibid., 69.

17 See more about the drafting of the 1939 Civil Code in H. Siimets-Gross, M. Luts-Sootak, and K. Kiirend-Pruuli, "The Private Law Codification as an Instrument for the Consolidation of a Nation from Inside—Estonia and Latvia between Two World Wars," in *Modernisation, National Identity and Legal Instrumentalism*, ed. A. Klimaszewska and M. Gladek, vol. 1, *Private Law* (Gdansk: Brill Academic Publishers, 2019), 285–310.

18 Bürgerliches Gesetzbuch, 18.08.1896. Bürgerliches Gesetzbuch in der Fassung der Bekanntmachung vom 2. Januar 2002 (BGBl. I S. 42, 2909; 2003 I S. 738),

das zuletzt durch Artikel 1 des Gesetzes vom 21. Dezember 2019 (BGBl. I S. 2911) geändert worden ist, www.gesetze-im-internet.de.

19 The preliminary decision to follow German legal system as a model in building up the private law system was made by an expert committee for civil law consisting of jurists set up in 1990 and continued from 1992 as the chief committee for the civil code and the commercial code. In 1992, the Supreme Council of the Republic of Estonia passed the decision that the preparation of the legal system had to be guided by the principles applicable in Estonia before the year 1940. For private law, this implied guidance mainly by the principles characteristic to the Germanic family of law. See more about the models used in drafting private law acts in Varul, "Legal Policy Decisions," 104–18.

20 For example, the decision not to follow US bankruptcy law was formulated as follows: "In choosing a model for the act, the examples of the USA and France were discarded, as the time was not ripe in Estonia to protect the interests of the debtor to the extent that is done in these countries." See more about the American Bar Association Central and East European Law Initiative (CEELI), "Analysis of the Draft Bankruptcy Act of the Republic of Estonia" (1994), in P. Varul, "On The Development of the Bankruptcy Law in Estonia," *Juridica International* 4 (1999): 172.

21 The Law of Property Act (1993) reformed ownership law and restored private ownership of land.

22 Property Law Act (1993) (*asjaõigusseadus*). Available in English at "Law of Property Act," Riigi Teataja, www.riigiteataja.ee. See also J. Paju, "Basic Features of Estonian Property Law," *ZeuP* 4 (2000): 878; P. Pärna, "The Law of Property Act: Cornerstone of the Civil Law Reform," *Juridica International* 6 (2001): 89, 90.

23 General Part of Civil Law Act (2002) (*tsiviilseadustiku üldosa seadus*). Available in English at "General Part of the Civil Code Act," Riigi Teataja, www.riigiteataja.ee. Choices in drafting new version of the act have been greatly influenced by model laws (the Principles of International Commercial Contracts, 1994, and the Principles of Europen Contract Law, 1995), as well as the civil codes of other countries, like the civil code of the Netherlands; German and Swiss civil codes, civil code of the province of Quebec, the state of Louisiana, Italy, Austria, and Russia, were analyzed for comparison. See Varul, "Legal Policy Decisions," 110–13.

24 Family Law Act (FLA, 1994) (*perekonnaõigus*). The Family Law Act from 1994 was largely based on the Soviet Marriage and Family Code, although substantial amendments and corrections were made to it. The main change concerned the regulation of the proprietary relations of spouses. The new FLA was passed in 2009 and in force from 2010. New version of the Family Law Act is based mainly on German family law. Available in English at "Family Law Act," Riigi Teataja, www.riigiteataja.ee.

25 Law of Succession Act (1996) (*pärimisseadus*). Law of Succession Act from 1996 was largely based on the German BGB, but also on the Swiss, Austrian, and Italian civil codes and also the civil code of the Netherlands. The new Succession Law

Act was passed in 2008 and entered into force in 2009. Changes in the new version of the act were made mainly on the bases of German succession law. Available in English at "Law of Succession Act," Riigi Teataja, www.riigiteataja.ee.

26 Law of Obligations Act (2001) (*võlaõigusseadus*). Available in English at "Law of Obligations Act," Riigi Teataja, www.riigiteataja.ee. There is no Estonian Civil Code, but the five laws—General Part of Civil Code Act, Property Law Act, Law of Succession Act, Family Law Act, and Law of Obligations Act—are applied as parts of the internally coherent Civil Code.

27 See M. Käerdi, "Estonia and the New Civil Law," in *Regional Private Laws and Codification in Europe*, ed. Hector L. MacQueen, Antoni Vaquer, and Santiago Espiau (Cambridge: Cambridge University Press, 2003), 250, 251; M. Luts and J. Sootak, "Rechtsreform in Estland als Rezeptions- und Bildungsaufgabe," *Juristenzeitung* 53, no. 8 (1998): 401–03; I. Kull, "Codification of Private Law in Estonia," in *The Scope and Structure of Civil Codes*, ed. J. C. Rivera (Dordrecht: Springer Netherlands, 2013), 133–53.

28 See Byrne and Schrag, "Law Reform in Estonia," 454.

29 Ibid., 457.

30 United Nations Commission on International Trade, "United Nations Convention on Contracts for the International Sale of Goods," (New York, 2010), www.uncitral.org.

31 Finnish Sale of Goods Act, 355/1987; Swedish Sales of Goods Act, SFS 1990:931.

32 From the Estonian side, R. Paron, a young lawyer at that time, was a member of the sales law group. See more in Byrne and Schrag, "Law Reform in Estonia," 456. In addition, valuable comments on the first draft of the Estonian sales law were received from professors Barry Nicholas of Oxford University (who represented the United Kingdom in work on the CISG) and Richard Hyland of Rutgers Law School. See more in ibid., 458. Finally, CISG became the main source of the regulation of sales contracts in the Law of Obligations Act. See, about the CISG as source of the LOA, P. Varul, "CISG: A Source of Inspiration for the Estonian Law of Obligations," *Uniform Law Review* 8, no. 1–2 (2003): 209.

33 The Agreement on Trade-Related Aspects of Intellectual Property Rights (as amended on January 23, 2017). Available at "TRIPS Agreement," World Trade Organization, www.wto.org.

34 For the discussion on the early development of the Estonian IP system, see A. Kalvi, "The Impact of Copyright Industries on Copyright Law," *Juridica International* 10 (2005): 95–104.

35 A. Kelli, "The Conceptual Bases for Codifying Estonia's IP Law and the Main Legislative Changes: From the Comparative Approach to Embedding Drafted Law into the Socio-Economic Context," *International Comparative Jurisprudence* 1 (2015): 44–54.

36 On the Estonian court system, see J. Laffranque, "The Judicial System of Estonia and European Union Law," *International Journal of Legal Information* 33, no. 2 (2005): 224–239.

37 On judicial independence, see T. Ligi, "Judicial Independence in Estonia," in *Judicial Independence in Transition*, ed. A. Seibert-Fohr, vol. 233, *Beiträge zum ausländischen öffentlichen Recht und Völkerrecht* (Berlin: Springer, 2012).

38 See also M. Sillaots, "Supreme Court Judgments as Source of Estonian Criminal Procedural Law," *Juridica International* 5 (2000): 94–103.

39 See I. Kull, "Principle of Good Faith and Constitutional Values in Contract Law," *Juridica International* 7 (2002): 142–49.

40 Law drafting processes during the first period of independence from 1918 to 1940 were quite similar to the processes starting in 1991. See M. Luts, "Scientific Legal Education and the Faculty of Law of the University of Tartu," *Juridica International* 1 (1996): 129–139.

41 At this seminar, Estonian judges were introduced to the Socratic method of US legal education for the first time. As a method of teaching, the Socratic method was unknown to Soviet professors, who mainly used lectures. However, in the Faculty of Law of Tartu State University before 1991, some elements of the case method were used in the form of seminars. Also the case method was used sporadically and its importance to teaching was minimal.

42 Byrne and Schrag, "Law Reform in Estonia," 457. It functioned as an independent legal entity until 2009. After reorganization, professional training of judges was taken over by the Estonian Supreme Court. It has to be mentioned that Estonian Supreme Court is situated in Tartu.

43 Byrne and Schrag note that Estonian lawyers who drafted private law rules were very wary of the possibility that the rules should be interpreted by judges. See Byrne and Schrag, "Law Reform in Estonia," 455.

44 Luts-Sootak, "Scientific Legal Education," 129–139.

45 Constitution of the Republic of Estonia (1992) (*Eesti Vabariigi põhiseadus*). Available in English at "The Constitution of the Republic of Estonia," Riigi Teataja, www.riigiteataja.ee.

46 R. Narits, "Legal Foundations of University Education in Estonia," *Juridica International* 1 (1996): 125–129.

47 Republic of Estonia Education Act (1992) (*Eesti Vabariigi haridusseadus*). Available in English at "Republic of Estonia Education Act," Riigi Teataja, /www.riigiteataja.ee.

48 Universities Act (1995) (*Ülikooliseadus*). Available in English at "Universities Act," Riigi Teataja, www.riigiteataja.ee.

49 University of Tartu Act (1995) (*Tartu Ülikooli seadus*). Available in English at "University of Tartu Act," Riigi Teataja, www.riigiteataja.ee.

50 E. Saar and T. Roosalu, "Inverted U-shape of Estonian Higher Education: Post-Socialist Liberalism and Postpostsocialist Consolidation," in *25 Years of Transformations of Higher Education Systems in Post-Soviet Countries: Reform and Continuity*, ed. J. Hulsman, A. Smolentseva and I. Froumin (London: Palgrave Macmillan, 2018), 166. In Estonia, private law schools merged with public universities. For example, the private university Tallinn Law Institute joined the Univer-

sity of Tartu in 2001. University Nord, established in 1991, merged with University of Tallinn in 2010. Concordia International University Estonia (CIUE), founded in 1996, merged with Audentes University in 2003, and the law school continued its English-language law programs within International University Concordia Audentes (IUCA). In 2008, IUCA merged with Tallinn University of Technology.

51 See Narits, "Legal Foundation," 125–29. EuroFaculty was an educational institution in Estonia, Latvia, and Lithuania, established in 1992 to reform higher education in economics, law, public administration, and business administration. See G. N. Kristensen, *Born into a Dream: EuroFaculty and the Council of the Baltic Sea States* (Berlin: Berliner Wissenschafts-Verlag, 2010).

52 Agreement between the European Economic Community and the Republic of Estonia on trade and commercial and economic cooperation, signed on May 11, 1992, in Brussels, entered into force on February 1, 1993. Riigi Teataja II, 1993, 3, 2, The Free Trade Agreement with the European Union was signed on July 18, 1994, and entered into force on January 1, 1995. Riigi Teataja II 1994, 34, 146. The Association Agreement between the European Communities and their Member States and the Republic of Estonia was signed on June 12, 1995.

53 For example, from 1994 to 1996 a number of lecturers from the United States visited the University of Tartu Faculty of Law: Michael Listgarten (US, EC Law, Private International Law), Richard C. Visek (US, International Law, Comparative Legal Systems, EC Law), Michael Gallagher (US, Legal Writing), Charles Lipton (US, International Arbitration, International Business Agreements).

54 "The Bologna Declaration of 19 June 1999," the European Higher Education Arena, www.ehea.info. All graduates of bachelor's programs are eligible to continue their studies at the masters level if they qualify on the basis of their final examination results. All graduates with master's-level qualification can be considered for admission to the PhD level. To become a judge, notary, prosecutor, or attorney, a master's degree is required. See also Saar and Roosalu, "Inverted U-shape of Estonian Higher Education," 149–75.

55 For example, using interactive classrooms. See "School of Law opened Smart Classrooms in Tartu and in Tallinn," University of Tartu School of Law, https://oigus.ut.ee.

56 This change began with the first seminar on international human rights law conducted by professors from Georgetown University and organized under the auspices of the Estonian Human Rights Institute, founded by President Lennart Meri. See more in Byrne and Schrag, "Law Reform in Estonia," 457.

57 Founded in the University of Tartu in 1993, the first director was the Estonian Canadian professor Toivo Miljan.

58 CEP was established in 1991 to enhance the development of higher and professional education in societies engaged in political and economic transition.

59 See more in deLisle, "Lex Americana?," 252.

60 The Estonian Law Center Foundation was founded in 1995 and was responsible for judicial training until 2009.

61 For example, international seminars on "Issues of Improvement and Application of Labour Legislation," "Continental European Legal System (Public Law and Private Law)," and "Intellectual Property (Copyright)" were organized between 1995 and 1996.

62 Twinning is a European Union instrument for institutional cooperation between Public Administrations of EU Member States and of beneficiary or partner countries; its aim is to bring together public-sector expertise from EU Member States and beneficiary countries to achieve concrete mandatory operational results through peer-to-peer activities. See more at "Twinning," European Neighbourhood Policy and Enlargement Negotiations, European Commission, https://ec.europa.eu.

About Financing Memoranda and Project Fiches for all National, Multi-Beneficiary, Cross-Border, and other Programs, see at "PHARE Financing Memoranda & Project Fiches," European Neighborhood Policy and Enlargement Negotiations, European Commission, https://ec.europa.eu.

63 P. Pruks, "Academic Legal Education in Estonia: Current State and Perspectives (Faculty of Law of the University of Tartu)," *Juridica International* 1 (1996): 147.

64 For example, the German, Swiss, Dutch, Austrian, Italian, and Russian Civil Codes, legal acts of the state of Louisiana, the province of Quebec in Canada, and the sales laws of Scandinavian countries (Sweden, Finland and Denmark), the Czech Commercial Code, and the Japanese Civil Code. See Varul, "Legal Policy Decisions," 114. The Estonian Supreme Court stated in a 2004 judgment that if a provision of Estonian law has never been applied, and an analogous provision exists and has been applied in other states with a similar legal system, the Court may take into account the decisions of these states. In 2011, the Supreme Court of Estonia stated that analogous laws and practices of other countries may, at least in the case of private law, be taken as reference material in identifying the purpose of Estonian law. Judgment of the Estonian Supreme Court in civil case no. 3-2-1-145-04, 2004, 39, available in Estonian at www.riigikohus.ee. See also judgments of the Estonian Supreme Court in civil case no. 3-2-1-103-08, 2008, 20, available in Estonian at www.riigikohus.ee; in civil case no. 3-2-1-23-11, 2011, 15, available in Estonian at www.riigikohus.ee; and in civil case no. 3-2-1-89-14, 2014, 26, available in Estonian at www.riigikohus.ee. Comments of Estonian private law acts (and comments of legal acts from other legal fields) also consist of references to the sources or similar provisions in soft law instruments.

65 Kull, "Principle of Good Faith," 142–49.

66 Judgment of the Estonian Supreme Court in civil case no. 3-2-1-140-07, 2008.

67 In 2008, the textbook on the general part of civil law was translated from German: H. Köhler, *BGB Allgemeiner Teil* (München: Beck, 1996). The first Estonian textbook on civil law was published in 2012.

68 It has to be mentioned that students are not typically exposed to the Socratic method where teachers actively question and challenge students. However, stu-

dents can express their argumentation skills in seminars where solving cases is a widely used teaching method.

69 Byrne and Schrag, "Law Reform in Estonia," 454.

70 After regaining independence, the main private schools teaching law were Academy Nord (1991–2010), Concordia International University Estonia (1992–2003), Private School of Social Sciences Veritas (1997–2003), International University Audentes (1999), Higher School I Studium (2003), Institute of Humanities and Social Sciences (2003–2011), and Institute of Law (1994–2006).

71 See more in the very precise description of the drafting process by Byrne and Schrag in "Law Reform in Estonia," 451–53.

72 Luts-Sootak, "Scientific Legal Education," 129–39.

73 I. Kull, "Legal Integration and Reforms—Innovation and Traditions," *Juridica International* 5 (2000): 120.

9

"The Turn to the West"

American Legal Education and Educational Reforms in the Swedish Welfare State, 1950–2000

KJELL Å MODÉER

This article addresses the modernization of Swedish legal education and how related reforms were influenced by the American model. Generally, American influences became more frequent in the Scandinavian countries during the interwar period. The development of legal education in Sweden has to be put into the larger context of the process of modernization of the Swedish welfare state, the *Folkhome*. It became a model for the New Deal liberals in the United States. Marquis Childs's *Sweden—The Middle Way* (1936) was a widely read book on corporativism in a Swedish society dominated by its social-democratic government.[1] And in 1941, the Swedish social scientists Alva and Gunnar Myrdal published a parallel to Childs's book titled *Kontakt med Amerika—Contact with America*, in which they described the culture they had encountered during their long stay in the United States. They noted that for Swedes, the actual spirit in American social life was inspiring, "dynamic, bold and experimental in its methods but conservative in its principles, to some extent juvenile and idealistic."[2] First of all, the America they encountered was democratic. "We never can afford not to be our friends' friend," they wrote, "[l]east of all now, in a fateful time of tribulation in the Nordic countries."[3] Their statement opened up an important interaction between legal scholars in Sweden and the United States after World War II. Gunnar Myrdal, a Swedish lawyer and professor of economics, was to American readers best known for his 1944 book regarding race problems in the American South, *An American Dilemma: The Negro Problem and Modern Democracy*,[4] a scholarly work of great importance analyzing discourses on civil rights in postwar America.[5]

Duncan Kennedy has observed the overall (global) transition within law from the social into the human rights paradigm when World War II ended in 1945.[6] In Scandinavia, the Norwegian and Danish judiciaries, as well as law professors in those countries, had been suppressed by the totalitarian German occupation.[7] In neutral Sweden, jurists had been divided between those who remained German-influenced and those who supported the Western legal tradition. Before World War II, the jurists in all four countries (Finland included) to a great extent were affiliated with what can be described as a "Germanic" legal culture. Legal education was a part of this culture.

Since the creation of the Second Empire in Germany in 1870, Swedish law professors, as well as ambitious law students, attended German universities for further studies. German legal culture in scholarly work, as well as in education, became the archetype for elite legal studies for more than a half-century.[8] To a great extent, teachers at the law faculties transplanted the German model of scientific lectures and seminars into the Swedish educational system. They, too, traveled to Berlin, Heidelberg, and Munich to listen to and learn from those who developed legal science and introduced within legal education the concept of combining professorial law with legal practice. Rudolf von Jhering's legendary lecture "The Struggle for Law" ("Der Kampf ums Recht"), presented in Vienna in 1872, on the lawyers' relation between legal theory and praxis, influenced greatly the reformation of modern Scandinavian legal education, beginning in Sweden in 1904.[9] This state of legal education in the early 1900s was still the dominant tradition in Sweden when the World War II ended.

The Turn from South to West

In their book, the Myrdals argued for more extensive contacts with the United States during the era of Franklin D. Roosevelt's New Deal. They were impressed by the modern American culture reflected in the New Deal.[10] "All literature in the United States which claims literary value has also got social value," they wrote.[11] Their book sparked a discourse in 1942 regarding legal education in Sweden.[12] In their book, they included a chapter on education in the United States titled "Upbringing in the Middle of the Society." Gainful employment in the United States resulted in the broader recruitment of students from a range of economic classes. Law students in particular either earned their money for their tuition through work or through the economic sacrifice of their parents. What this discourse also emphasized was the disproportion in the law schools between the representation of the working class (5.6 percent) and farmers (7 percent), in contrast to the vast majority of students from the bourgeoisie.[13] It was more an economic recruitment than an intellectual one, they argued. This argument dominated the reforms of higher education in Sweden during the postwar years.

Gunnar Myrdal had close contact with the law faculties at Uppsala University and Stockholm University (*Stockholms högskola*), and in an article in a Swedish law journal he argued that Swedish legal education had to be reformed.[14] He pointed out that Swedish legal education was traditional and old-fashioned. Law students were offered theory-based and scholarly lectures by professors, and to gain relevant information for their examinations they had to pay for courses at private proprietary colleges (*kollegier*) given by the law professors. Criticism of this educational system was harsh, and after World War II this critique was again articulated and led to the abolition of private colleges in 1957. Myrdal contributed to this discourse by pointing to the educational reforms in the United States as an important role model.

After World War II, Scandinavian jurists' source of inspiration shifted toward the West. The major legal influences turned from the German-speaking countries south of the Baltic Sea to those from the Western tradition, especially the United States and Great Britain. In Norway, this cultural transition even has been a metaphor: "The Turn to the West," or *Vestvendingen*.[15] "It demands a wiser humility than most of humanity possesses for a victorious nation to study the institutions of defeated ones," the then-dean of the University of Texas School of Law stated at the time.[16]

One example of the influence of American legal education includes the honorary degrees given to American law professors at the Scandinavian law faculties. They demonstrate the interaction between American legal academic society and the Nordic one during the postwar period. Some examples: Oslo gave an honorary degree after the war (1946) to Philip Caryl Jessup, a professor of international law at Columbia Law School; two German law émigrés and professors of comparative law,

Max Rheinstein at the University of Chicago and Hessel E. Yntema at the University of Michigan, received honorary degrees from Stockholm in 1958; some ten years later, in 1969, Ruth Bader Ginsburg, who became a justice of the United States Supreme Court, received an honorary degree from Lund.[17]

American influence on Swedish legal education was brought about as a result of Swedish legal academics' travels to the United States. During the war, academic jurists in Sweden had been incarcerated within Swedish borders, but as soon as the German army capitulated in May 1945, they were liberated and began preparing for studies abroad. Professor Folke Schmidt (professor of Private law) at Lund immediately prepared for a yearlong journey to American universities. During the 1945–1946 academic year, he spent time at three private law schools (Harvard, Yale, and Chicago). He learned that the primary purpose of the school was not to become a law teacher or a judge but "to prepare [the student] for the practice of legal profession where the common law prevails."[18]

Inspired, professor Schmidt came back to Sweden and pushed for education reform. "Time must be ripe for a reform of the Swedish legal education. The degree ordonnance, to a great extent going back unchanged since 1904, is now obsolete," Schmidt argued,[19] and he suggested that the American legal education system could be a model. It was, for example, much more efficient from the student's perspective to replace the current system with a much more "school like" (*skolmässig*) study plan. He also argued that the attempt to cover the whole legal system should be replaced with freedom of choice to study particular areas of law. He wrote that "[i]t's more valuable that the students learn to master legal technique than to have a superficial knowledge regarding a wide breadth of legal material." There were also similarities between the Swedish and the American systems. The law curricula in Sweden as well as in the United States needed a basic orientation of social science research.[20]

The American professional law school, entered after obtaining an undergraduate degree, was unlike anything within the Scandinavian educational system. Schmidt related to the current discourses in the United States regarding the implementation of social sciences within the law curriculum. He quoted the dean at the University of Chicago's law school, Wilber G. Katz, who in a law journal had emphasized the rapid changes being made to the American legal system through regulations and legislation. The law school had to teach students the driving forces in the development of law. The law curricula had to "illustrate the nature and the function of the law and the importance of the law as a social-political instrument. It's also essential, that the lawyer has thorough insights in the economic structure of the society."[21]

With Schmidt's article, he introduced to his Swedish readers the field of comparative legal education, which since the end of the 1930s had garnered attention from several contributors in Europe as well as in the United States. In the United States, German law émigrés had observed the differences between the legal educational systems in Europe and the United States. Max Rheinstein at Chicago compared the German educational system with the American,[22] and Stefan Riesenfeld, at the University of California, Berkeley, since 1935, compared the American system with the continental European system.[23] Schmidt referred as well to the work of the Austria-born lawyer Erich Fritz Schweinburg on continental European legal education, published in 1945.[24]

A PhD student from Uppsala, jur.lic. Björn Ahlander prepared his dissertation in jurisprudence during a yearlong visit (1948–1949) to what was regarded as the most modern American law school, Yale Law School. He also reported to the *Swedish Law Journal* on the independent character of American legal education. For example, he noted that some of the best students were offered work in the law reviews. There were moot-court classes, as well as legal clinics where students, under supervision from their teachers, gave legal aid to the public. At Yale, moot courts also were complemented by pretend settlement negotiations.

Ahlander emphasized the pragmatism of American legal education. With astonishment, he noticed that law students to a great extent constructed the composition of their curriculum. The free choice of courses and the importance of political science and other topics within the social sciences were modern trends within the study of law. He noted that even if there were conservative law professors, the majority of them, including the most influential, emphasized the need for knowledge of economic, political, and social structures and about the different institutions in society and their functions and activities.[25]

Swedish legal education had to be much more functional and "real life-oriented," Ahlander argued. It was a modern trend that had also been discussed within the reformation of Swedish legal education.[26] In the United States, a more functional legal education had been introduced in labor, commercial, administrative, and criminal law. Students had to solve legal problems related to the areas of law they studied. Ahlander wrote that "[s]tudents who in this way learn to construct a correct contract for different situations, will acquire legal knowledge and above all a legal judgment that a systematic and organized education hardly would have given."[27] Most important, Ahlander emphasized the need for Swedish jurists to include the social sciences in legal education.

The scholarly part of the teacher's work in the law school was not represented in US law schools. And even if the concept of legal science in the United States had been extended to include elements of sociology, psychology, social psychology, history, social science, economics, anthropology, and other subjects, there was no university institution just for scholarly legal work in the United States.[28]

Immediately after the war, however, a university proposal urged the formation of a committee to study the apparent need for reforms in Swedish legal education.[29] From inside the law faculties, the critique described the current education system as "intellectually frugal."[30] Too few teachers taught too many students with too few textbooks. In 1949, a public inquiry, led by members of the law faculties and different parts of the legal profession, was established by the minister of education. It resulted in a reform-oriented official report by the Swedish government in 1953. Even if the reforms were intended to be national, the inquiry also used international comparisons and commented on legal education in the United States. Information on American law schools was given by Ahlander and a member of the Swedish Bar Association, Bertil Ahrnborg.[31] In a special opinion, Ahrnborg emphasized the importance of the practical aspects of education. The very abstract Swedish education had to be supplemented with practical elements by members of the legal profession. He wrote that "[t]he education at the American law schools has got its efficiency and its ability to train lawyers to practical professions largely due to the interplay between theoretically and practically schooled teachers."[32]

The postwar interaction between Swedish legal scholars and their American colleagues demonstrated the necessity of comparison, and comparative law became a common legal field during the postwar years. Comparative law had—to a great extent due to German émigrés—

established a place within the curriculum at some of the top law schools in the United States. Max Rheinstein is a good example. After the war, he traveled to Europe on a regular basis and visited law faculties in the Nordic countries. In September 1951, he attended the second German Congress in Comparative Law in Cologne and combined it with a tour of Scandinavia. After visiting Copenhagen and Lund, he lectured at the law faculties in Uppsala and Stockholm, where the professors Åke Malmström and Folke Schmidt were his hosts. Folke Schmidt and Max Rheinstein met during Schmidt's visit to Chicago in 1946 and became close colleagues. When Schmidt was invited to visit Chicago in 1963, Rheinstein wrote the dean and introduced him as "one of the outstanding legal scholars of Scandinavia. . . . Schmidt also plays an influential role in Scandinavia, both in the Academic world and in politics."[33] Malmström was a pioneer in the establishment of comparative law in Sweden.[34] At Uppsala, Malmström founded the Institute of International and Comparative Law and was the host of the VIIth International Congress of Comparative Law in Uppsala in 1966. Rheinstein returned to Scandinavia several times, and (as mentioned) when the law faculty in Stockholm celebrated its first fifty years, in 1958, Rheinstein received an honorary degree.

The extensive networks of contacts among the transatlantic representatives of comparative law were a significant element in the reform efforts within legal education during this period.

Legal Education Reform after 1958

The 1953 report of the formal inquiry resulted in a royal ordinance in 1958.[35] The discourse during the preparation of the reform had been national. The chapter on comparing Swedish legal education to some "foreign countries" was dense and concentrated on Nordic and European countries. However, there was also important information regarding American law schools in the report, highlighting the students' opportunity to take optional courses in social sciences.[36] Even if Swedish legislators regarded this option as an effect of the American university exam, which (unlike the Swedish exam) didn't require competence in practical professional work (such as an American bar exam),[37] they accepted the concept of specialized optional courses. The report also offered a possibility to deepen legal education by writing an essay during the last semester of the 4.5-year-long curriculum.

There is another example of contemporary influence from American law schools, represented by the field of Law and Society. In the United States, the sociology of law (from the German *Rechtsoziologie*) had become an important part of the implementation of a socially oriented curriculum. Roscoe Pound had already introduced this field at Harvard Law School at the beginning of the twentieth century, but it was when Lloyd K. Garrison served as dean at the University of Wisconsin School of Law in the late 1930s that he, together with the legal historian Willard Hurst, introduced classes in law and society.[38] And after Max Rheinstein at Chicago translated Max Weber's posthumous work *Law in Economy and Society* into English in 1954, interest in this field increased dramatically.[39]

Swedish legal scholars found this field to be of great interest. It resonated with the new relationship between state and society fostered by the social democratic government in its modernization of legislative regulation in the Swedish welfare state. Already in the 1950s, Per Stjernquist, a professor of civil law at Lund, had observed new trends within the legal sciences.[40] He belonged to the "modern" law professors of his generation who pleaded for a functional legal science that studied "the interaction of the legal rules with other social and economic factors in social life." From the beginning of the 1960s, he introduced classes in legal sociology, influenced by American standards at his university. He also wrote a monograph titled *Laws in the Forests* in 1973, a parallel to Willard Hurst's classic work on the historical development of the lumber industry in Wisconsin.[41] Similarly, Per Olof Bolding, a professor of legal procedure at Lund University, offered classes in fields open to the social sciences and interdisciplinary studies. Bolding and Stjernquist, however, were the exceptional liberal and open-minded representatives in the more tradition-oriented Swedish legal environment.

There were great difficulties facing the Swedish jurists—who were trained in a positivistic concept of the law and in Scandinavian Legal Realism—when they had to translate this modern discipline taken from the social sciences into their scholarly legal system.[42]

The 1953 report's proposal regarding "Applied studies" (one semester) were made compulsory in this reform of 1957. In this class, which ended the educational program, students had to write an essay in any of the areas they studied during their education. There was, however, an alternative. Instead of writing the essay, law students could take introductory classes in nonlegal fields. The class in legal sociology presented by the faculty of social sciences was the class most frequently taken by law students who chose this alternative. It soon gained a reputation an easy pass, so this option was increasingly misused. In the early 1970s, about 40 percent of students chose to write the essay and 60 percent chose to take nonlegal classes. These introductory classes didn't live up to the qualification standards intended by the government.[43] Of the 433 law students who in 1972 chose the option to take nonlegal classes, 202 took the class in sociology of law. This option was openly described by the students as a course that "with fair diligence could be accomplished in a month or so instead of the five months it normally should take for the field of Applied studies."[44]

Legal Education Post-1968

In the wake of the student revolts of 1968, a more general and radical university reform was drafted by an educational inquiry (the U 68 Commission). The old professorial faculties were abolished, and a new modern and democratic structure was established in which the students, the labor unions, and the staff were represented. This inquiry presented not only a new organization for Swedish universities; it also included a new concept of legal education. The results were presented in 1973,[45] and after being discussed and labored over by representatives from the three Swedish law faculties, the reform was adopted in 1977 and implemented on January 1, 1978.[46] This new reform was highlighted in one Swedish law journal as "A New Legal Education at a New University."[47]

The aim of this reform was to introduce practice oriented and social scientific perspectives into legal education.[48] The modern jurists had to observe the connection between legal regulation and other social conditions, as well as legal phenomena from perspectives other than solely legal ones.[49] The most significant reform was the introduction of alternative and optional courses, called "special courses." They allowed for a deeper and broader legal education for the individual student—as with longtime practices in American legal education. There were also requests for more practically oriented elements within legal education. This request, however, was met with reluctance by the commission. It could be met by case-based education.[50]

Another important change made it compulsory for law students to write a substantial essay (*examensarbete*) at the end of their education. Students could no longer choose between an essay and alternative courses. The reform resulted in a reduction of time for some of the compulsory classes (e.g., in criminal law and procedural law and some parts of private law) in the still 4.5-year-long education.

The U 68 Commission also introduced a class in sociology of law in the new law curriculum. Even if this field was still immature at Swedish universities—the first professor (Per Stjernquist) was appointed in 1972—the commission suggested a class to promote the study of the "function of laws, contracts and forms of organizations in societal life."[51] The commission suggested three ways that the sociology of law should be implemented in the curriculum. First, law students should pay attention to the existence of this field at the beginning of their studies and to the possibilities regarding the legal system in its social context. Second, the sociology of law could be studied continuously within legal education more generally. And third, it would be valuable during students' education to get "a more collected picture of what an approach of sociology of law will mean."[52]

When the drafts were adopted, the fields of legal history and sociology of law were combined into a basic course at the beginning of curriculum.[53] There was another element in the basic course that could also be traced to American legal education: a short course titled "Law and Society" (*Rätt och samhälle*). It introduced students to the practical side of the law. This class was intended to be "thematic and project oriented" and was strongly pushed for by the Ministry of Education despite great reservations among representatives of the law faculties.[54] In this class, students would work in small groups on a current interdisciplinary theme of the law. The unpredictability of how this class was to be implemented increased the criticism from the conservative law faculties. This class was abolished in the revision of the law curriculum in 1988; in Stockholm, however, it was kept as a basic course in the sociology of law.[55]

Clinical work was also introduced in the class on procedural law, where students had the opportunity to actually practice law during a few weeks in court or in a law firm. This part of the curriculum ran into practical problems, as members of the labor unions at the courts objected to the increased inconveniences required to implement this reform.

Human Rights and the Moot Courts, 1988

Jacob Sundberg, professor of jurisprudence at Stockholm University, spent time at New York University School of Law from 1956 to 1957. He served as professor at Stockholm University (1970–1993) but also as a guest professor at University of Akron School of Law in Ohio from 1986 to 1987. During that academic year, he organized a symposium titled "Human Rights as Comparative Constitutional Law."[56]

As a pioneer in human rights law, he became a foreign honorary member of the American Academy of Arts and Sciences in October 2002. He was nominated to this membership by Justice Ruth Bader Ginsburg, who met Sundberg during his time as a student at New York University and later when she was a teacher at Columbia.[57]

Sundberg's class titled "Practical European Procedure" at Stockholm University was also presented by other law faculties in Scandinavia (and continues today). He also initiated the Scandinavian Sporrong-Lönnroth Moot Court Competition (today the Nordic Moot Court Competition on Human Rights). In this competition, students participate with teams from all the Nordic countries in a human rights case law competition. It has been of great importance to the "dissemination of knowledge and practice concerning the ECHR" since the beginning of the 1980s.[58] This Nordic competition has also been noticed in the United States.[59]

Swedish Missionaries in US Law and Legal Education

US influence on Swedish legal education can be traced to American financial support in the form of grants from the American Council of Learned Societies (ACLS). From 1961 to 1992, the ACLS American Studies Program aided overseas communities of scholars specializing in the study of the United States. This council, along with other members of the Associated Board of Research Councils, founded the Council for International Exchange of Scholars, the agency that administers the Senior Fulbright Program. With the help of those programs, Swedish legal scholars not only became inspired by the legal educational reform in the 1970s but also inspired others to create important transatlantic networks within the law. Several younger Swedish scholars during this period had the opportunity to spend an academic year at an American law school, and the new ways of thinking they encountered contributed to the implementation of US legal education methodologies into the Swedish legal environment.

Swedish legal education in 1950 lacked didactic perspectives. Students went to law schools just to take their exams. An increasingly didactically based legal education was successively introduced during the post–World War II period. During the postwar period, reforms within Swedish legal education were inspired by young Swedish scholars who had spent a year abroad studying at a US law school.

Conclusion

When intellectual interest after World War II turned from southward (Europe) to westward (the United States and Great Britain) within Nordic legal culture, American influence became increasingly strong. Beginning in the 1970s, affirmative action programs, as well as American legal concepts such as class actions and leasing and franchising, were adopted into Swedish legal practice and legislation.

Swedish law professors who visited US law schools after the war met pedagogical instruments related not only to American Legal Realism (a parallel to Scandinavian Legal Realism)[60] but also to new directions within legal science, alternative jurisprudence, and critical legal studies.[61] The American post–World War II concept of "law ands . . ."—especially law and economics, law and religion, and law and literature—has in the twenty-first century developed proponents at Swedish law schools as well.

Five elements of US legal education have been translated into the Swedish educational system: (1) comparative law in the law curriculum; (2) a functional approach to education; (3) sociology of law as an alternative approach to the law; (4) the moot court competitions; and (5) the creation of the Swedish practice-oriented law journal *Juridisk Tidskrift*, founded in 1989–1990 and affiliated with the Stockholm University Faculty of Law.[62]

However, if there was a turn from south to west regarding influences within Scandinavian legal cultures during the period 1945–1990, the end of the cold war and signing of Maastricht Treaty in 1992 created a new turn back to the importance of European legal science, and classes in European law and European human rights law became increasingly popular. The Erasmus student exchange program, which started in 1987, resulted in an increase in classes related to European integration. Pierre Legrand has predicted that there will not be a common European legal culture as long as the member states uphold their national systems with different legal educational systems and different career systems.[63] The curricula at the European—and Swedish—law faculties have, since 1995, developed classes that emphasize European themes, such as European legal history and European contract law. Even if this trend has contributed to a decline of direct influences from American legal education, the internationalization of the modern law curriculum demonstrates important global influences.

NOTES

1 Marquis Childs, *Sweden—The Middle Way* (New Haven: Yale University Press 1936).

2 Alva & Gunnar Myrdal, *Kontakt med Amerika* (Stockholm: Bonniers Förlag 1941), 30.

3 Ibid., 30.

4 Gunnar Myrdal, *An American Dilemma: The Negro Problem and Modern Democracy* (New York: Harper and Row, Publishers 1944).

5 David W. Southern, *Gunnar Myrdal and Black-White Relations: The Use and Abuse of an American Dilemma, 1944—1969* (Baton Rouge: Louisiana State University Press 1987).

6 Duncan Kennedy, "Three Globalizations of Law and Legal Thought: 1850–2000," in *The New Law and Economic Development: A Critical Appraisal*, ed. David M Trubek & Alvaro Santos (Cambridge: Cambridge University Press 2006), 19–73.

7 Hans Petter Graver, *Okkupasjonstidens Høyesterett, Høyesterett i Norge 1940* (Oslo: Pax Forlag 2019).

8 David M. Rabban, *Law's History: American Legal Thought and the Transatlantic Turn to History* (Cambridge Historical Studies in American Law and Society) (Cambridge: Cambridge University Press, 2014).

9 Kjell Å Modéer, "Jherings Rechtsdenken als Herausforderung für die skandinavische Jurisprudenz," in Juristische Theoriebildung und Rechtliche Einheit, ed. Claes Peterson, Beiträge zu einem rechtshistorischen Seminar in Stockholm im

September 1992, in *Rättshistoriska studier [Studies in Legal History]*, vol. 19 (Lund: Olin Foundation for Legal History, 1993), 9.

10 Alva & Gunnar Myrdal, *Kontakt med Amerika.*

11 Ibid., 172.

12 G. Danielson, "Demokratin och juristutbildningen [Democracy and the Legal Education]," *Svensk Juristtidning* (1942): 46.

13 Statens offentliga utredningar [The Government's Official Investigations] (SOU) 1935:52 [Ministry of Education and Religion] and SOU 1936:34 [Ministry of Education and Religion].

14 Gunnar Myrdal, "Den juridiska vetenskapens ställning och de juridiska studiernas anordning i Sverige [The Position of Legal Science and the Arrangements Regarding the Legal Studies in Sweden]," *Svensk Juristtidning* (1945): 357.

15 Fredrik W Thue, "In Quest of a Democratic Social Order: The Americanization of Norwegian Social Scholarship" (PhD diss., University of Oslo, 2006).

16 Charles T. McCormick, "[Review] Law Training in Continental Europe (Eric F Schweinburg)," *Louisiana Law Review* 7, no. 1 (1946): 260.

17 Kjell Å Modéer, "Young Men Go West! Nordiska jurister, deras studieresor till efterkrigstidens U.S.A. och den rättskultur de mötte," in *Vänbok till Axel Adlercreutz*, ed. Boel Flodgren et al. (Lund: Juristförlaget i Lund, 2007), 309.

18 Folke Schmidt, "Amerikansk juristutbildning [American Legal Education]," *Svensk Juristtidning* (1947): 410.

19 Ibid., 417.

20 Ibid.

21 Wilber G. Katz, "What Changes Are Practical in the Legal Education?," *ABA Journal* 27, no. 12 (December 1941): 759–62.

22 Max Rheinstein, "Law Faculties and Law Schools: A Comparison of Legal Education in the United States and Germany," *Wisconsin Law Review* 1938, no. 1 (January 1938): 5–42.

23 Stefan Riesenfeld, "A Comparison of Continental and American Legal Education," *Michigan Law Review* 36, no. 1 (1937): 31–55.

24 Erich Fritz Schweinburg, *Law Training in Continental Europe, Its Principles and Public Function* (New York: Russell Sage Foundation, 1945).

25 Björn Ahlander, "Moderna tendenser i amerikansk juristutbildning [Modern Trends within American Legal Education]," *Svensk Juristtidning* (1949): 578–585.

26 The government's official investigation regarding the university reform discussed this issue. 1945 års universitetsberedning, SOU 1946 [The Advisory Committee of 1945 on Universities; Ministry of Education and Religion]: 81, 47.

27 Ahlander, "[Modern Trends]," 582.

28 Ahlander, "[Modern Trends]," 585.

29 Christian Häthén, "Legal Educational Reform in the Emerging Swedish Welfare-State," in *Juristische Fakultäten und Juristenausbildung im Ostseeraum*, ed. Jörn Eckert and Kjell Å Modéer (Stockholm: Rättshistoriska skrifter 6, 2004), 432.

30 Ragnar Bergendal, Reformförslag angående den juridiska utbildningen. [Proposals Regarding Reforms in the Swedish Legal Education], *Svensk Juristtidning* 38 (1953): 737. See also Häthén, "Legal Educational Reform," 437.
31 Partner in the Stockholm law firm Bertil Ahrnborg, Nils Öhman & Björn Bygge.
32 Bertil Ahrnborg, special opinion, in the government's inquiry regarding the education in law and social sciences, [Juridisk och samhällsvetenskaplig utbildning], SOU 1953:15, 547.
33 Max Rheinstein to Dean Neal, January 1, 1964, Max Rheinstein's Papers, Joseph Regenstein Library at University of Chicago.
34 Stig Strömholm, "Åke Malmström in memoriam," *Svensk Juristtidning* (1985): 616.
35 Swedish Statutebook 1958: SFS 1958:435. K.M:t stadga ang. juridiska och samhällsvetenskapliga examina [Governmental Charter Regarding Exams in Law and Social Sciences].
36 Kap. 6. Juristutbildningen i vissa främmande länder, SOU 1953:15, 69–74.
37 SOU 1953:15, 73.
38 Kjell Å Modéer, "Finalisten som katalysator: En jurist i Franklin D. Roosevelts New Deal: Lloyd K Garrison från New York, [The Runner Up: A Lawyer in Franklin D. Roosevelt's New Deal: Lloyd K. Garrison from New York]," in *Festskrift till Per Olof Bolding*, ed. Lars Heuman (Stockholm: Juristförlaget, 1992): 347.
39 Max Weber, *Max Weber on Law in Economy and Society*, ed. and trans. Edward A. Shils and Max Rheinstein (Cambridge: Harvard University Press 1954).
40 Per Stjernquist, "Samhällsutvecklingen och rättsvetenskapens arbetsfält," *Statsvetenskaplig tidskrift* 55, no. 2 (1952): 198.
41 Willard Hurst, *Law and Economic Growth: The Legal History of the Lumber Industry in Wisconsin, 1836–1915* (Cambridge: Belknap Press of Harvard University Press, 1964).
42 Staffan Rylander, "Strömholm och rättssociologin," *Svensk Juristtidning* (1970): 484.
43 Stig Strömholm, "En ny juristutbildning vid ett nytt universitet," [A New Legal Education at a New University], *Svensk Juristtidning* (1977): 499.
44 Stig Strömholm, "En ny juristutbildning," 499.
45 Högskoleutbildning: Juristlinje—Förvaltningslinje—Sociallinje. Betänkande av 1968 års utbildningsutredning (U 68), [College and University Education: Legal Education—Administrative Education—Social Education], SOU 1973:59.[Ministry of Education]
46 Prop. 1976/77:59, [Governmental bill 1976/77: 59]
47 Stig Strömholm, "En ny juristutbildning," 497–513.
48 Kjell Å Modéer, "Åt helvete med harmonin!," in *1968 och därefter: de kritiska rättsteoriernas betydelse för nordisk rättsvetenskap*, ed. Kjell Å Modéer and Martin Sunnqvist (Copenhagen: Museum Tusculanum Förlag, 2010): 23.
49 SOU 1973:8 [Commission report on Legal Education; Ministry of Education]: 59, 79.
50 Ibid., 106.

51 Ibid., 146.
52 Ibid., 149.
53 Stig Strömholm, "En ny juristutbildning," 508.
54 Stig Strömholm, "En ny juristutbildning," 511.
55 Ulf Bernitz, "Nyheter I juristutbildningen," *Svensk Juristtidning* (1988): 71.
56 Jacob W. F. Sundberg, "Preface (Human Rights as Comparative Constitutional Law)," *Akron Law Review* 20, no. 4 (1987): 593–609.
57 Jacob W. F. Sundberg, "Om doktrinen, Avskedsföreläsning," 29.9.1993 [Sundberg's farewell lecture; Stockholm University Law Faculty]. Jacob W. F. Sundberg, *Minnen från landet där den offentliga lögnen fått en svindlande omfattning*, 42, www.ioir.se.
58 Helen Keller and Alec Stone Sweet, eds., *A Europe of Rights: The Impact of the ECHR on National Legal Systems* (Oxford: Oxford University Press, 2008): 219.
59 Jacob W. F. Sundberg, "[Comparative Note] Moot Court: An American Idea in a Nordic Setting," *Justice System Journal* 19, no. 2 (November 1997): 229–233.
60 Heikki Pihlajamäki, "Against Metaphysics in Law: The Historical Background of American and Scandinavian Legal Realism Compared," *American Journal of Comparative Law* 52, no. 2 (2004): 469.
61 Kjell Å Modéer, "Comparative Critical Legal Studies: U.S. and the Nordic Countries," review of *A Menace to Society: Radicalism and Legal Scholarship in the United States, Scandinavia, and Finland*, by Juhana Mikael Salojärvi, *Retfaerd* 37 (2014): 117–30.
62 *Juridisk Tidskrift vid Stockholms universitet*. Since 2008 another law journal, *Juridisk Publikation*, run by the law students at Stockholm, Uppsala, Lund, and Gothenburg, has been published.
63 Pierre Legrand, "European Legal Systems are not Converging," *International and Comparative Law Quarterly* 45, no. 1 (January 1996): 52–81.

10

The American Case Method and New Japanese Legal Education

YOSHIHARU MATSUURA

Professional legal education is instrumental in the production of legal experts who can guide social governance. Since any legal education system is a conscious response to the needs of a particular society, legal education tends to produce experts with professional skills and the mind-set suited for indigenous needs. Any attempt to transplant a legal education developed in a foreign jurisdiction is, therefore, likely to create friction in the recipient jurisdiction. Analysis of this friction can illuminate the unique legal landscape of a recipient jurisdiction and, in turn, that of a donor jurisdiction.

Teaching Legal Principles or the Power of Legal Reasoning?

The core of twentieth-century American legal education is the case method, introduced at Harvard Law School in 1871 by Christopher C. Langdell. From its outset the case method was Janus-faced. It had two aspirations: to provide students with the professional skills necessary to discover unchangeable principles of common law, and to emphasize the power of legal reasoning. These two aspirations coexisted in the early years of the case method, during the last part of the nineteenth century. Early practitioners of the case method, such as Langdell and William Keener,[1] seem to have put more emphasis on the discovery of unchangeable common law principles. However, James B. Ames, who succeeded Langdell as dean of Harvard Law School, seems to have promoted the second aspiration. The aspiration to promote the power of legal reasoning gradually became the leading motive of the case method and dominated American legal education by the early decades of the twentieth century.[2]

Dean Ames's advocacy of the case method had one remarkable characteristic. He emphasized that the case method does not teach the substantive law of any particular state of the United States, such as Massachusetts law.[3] Instead, he stated that the object of the law degree is to impress upon students "the power of legal reasoning. . . . I am sometimes asked by first-year men what the law of Massachusetts is on the point under discussion, and I always tell them that sitting in this chair I do not know, but that if they speak to me after the hour I will tell them."[4] This is a strong claim that the case method can overcome state boundaries and thus is applicable to varied state laws.

The case method claims its universal applicability, but it does not deny any local variation in common law rules and their interpretations in different states. In contrast, the aspiration to learn the uniform and unchangeable rules and principles of law, as well as the method to reach a unique result, seems to have dominated Japanese legal education since Japan's modernization in the 1860s. This modernization led to the unification of fragmented feudal domains and the creation of a unified set of laws for the nation-state. Japanese teachers and students of law are interested in finding one set of substantive rules for all of Japan. When Japanese scholars learned of the American common law, they did not pay any serious attention to the existence in the United States of local variation of common law rules and their application. To them, local variation simply meant the residue of the old regime under feudalism. Ever since modernization began, the Japanese approach to the nation-building led by the central government has not changed.[5] Legal education has been in the hands of the central government, and major research interest in law has been closely related to this nation-building.

In this intellectual environment, Japan introduced a new system of professional legal education in 2004: the university graduate program. The reform of legal education was part of government efforts to reform the justice system in order to make it more responsive to the people, to enhance the role of the legal profession, and to encourage citizen participation in law.[6] The new system was consciously modeled after the American law school system but, unlike in the United States, retained undergraduate legal education. Thus, the new system of Japanese legal education became a combination of a four-year undergraduate program and a three-year professional program. The new system gradually shifted the focus of professional teaching from the theoretical discussion of law to the discussion of court cases, because the object of professional legal education is, as Justice Holmes said, "the prediction of the incidence of the public force through the instrumentality of the courts."[7]

Under the new Meiji government, Japan accumulated case records and published case reports from 1878.[8] All these cases were available in 2004 from various databases. Leading designers of the new law school system were law professors. They emphasized the critical importance of the Socratic method (i.e., the case method) in professional legal education and enthusiastically recommended the extensive use of this method in teaching and learning. They advocated a radical transition from the one-way lectures to two-way class discussion. However, since the introduction of the new system in 2004, that enthusiasm about the Socratic method has waned, and Socratic dialogue seems to have mostly disappeared from law school classrooms.[9]

Against this background, this chapter compares and analyzes the legal landscape of Japan and the United States to highlight some of the key conditions for the American case method to work effectively. The chapter first looks at the professional practice of legal experts, since professional education is meant for effective practice. Then, it examines the influence of the judicial structure on legal education. More broadly, it suggests that state governance in a unitary state and a federal state seems to assign different missions to the judiciary and, in turn, to legal education. Next, the chapter considers the function of judicial cases. The cases decided by higher courts are the most important source of legal information in both Japan and the United States. Since important cases in the past influence the future decisions made by courts, case analysis occupies the core of law students' professional training and continues to be the essential skill of legal experts in their professional life. This chapter suggests that the skill of case analysis may be taught differently in Japan and the United States and that the use of the case method has different implications for the two jurisdictions. Lastly, this chapter contends that the American case method has a built-in predisposition toward lawmaking and legal innovation by legal experts. This predisposition will not survive for long in a jurisdiction such as Japan, where the aspiration for stable legal rules and principles dominates.

Professional Practice in the Courtroom: Oral Advocacy versus Advocacy by Documents

One of the main stages for legal experts is the courtroom, where they undertake powerful advocacy through oral argument. In many countries, including the United States, advocacy is done through oral argument. However, this is not the case in Japan. The Japanese law of civil procedure does have provisions covering oral argument.[10] For example, Article 87 (1) of the *Code of Civil Procedure*[11] reads: "(1) The parties shall conduct oral arguments before the court in connection with the litigation; provided, however, that for a case to be concluded by a ruling, the court determines whether or not oral arguments should be conducted." Article 148 of the same code provides that "(1) The presiding judge directs oral arguments. (2) The presiding judge may permit a person to speak or prohibit a person who does not comply with the judge's orders from speaking."

However, these provisions are deceptive. Japanese law students who attend a court session of a civil case often report that there was no "oral" argument before the judge. What they hear is the judge's question: "Does the plaintiff argue the case as written in this complaint?" and a short answer by the plaintiff's counsel: "Yes, Your Honor." Then, the judge continues: "Does the defendant argue the case as written in the brief?" "Yes, Your Honor," the defense counsel replies. The judge acknowledges: "Very well." The judge and counsel decide the next date of the session. The session ends in ten minutes.[12]

The official website of the Japanese courts explains oral argument as follows:

> Parties or their statutory agents shall appear on the date for oral argument, make allegations *based on the brief that they have submitted to the court in advance*, and submit evidence in support of their allegations.[13]

Real oral advocacy in the American sense is missing in Japan. Both in the formal and preparatory proceedings of a civil case, Japanese legal experts practice frequent exchanges of documents and briefs under the rubric of oral argument. The preparatory proceedings are not open to the public. In these proceedings, there is one stage to clarify the disputed issues and align the arguments of both parties. At this stage, parties and their counsel submit a series of legal briefs to prepare for the trial. The judge, the lawyers, and the parties meet to clarify parts of the submitted documents and to confirm the relevant parts of the documents. One session of the preparatory proceedings tends to last longer than one session of the formal proceedings. When one party persuades the judge that a particular part of the brief needs clarification, the judge instructs the other party to submit an additional brief by the next court session.[14] Oral exchange is, therefore, supplemental to the exchange of documents.[15] The main function of oral exchange is not advocacy.

The case method, however, assumes real-time oral dialogue before a court as the norm. A law school class in the United States might be a rough approximation of a courtroom in an appellate court. Ideally, both teacher and students are prepared for the class. The teacher plays the role of a judge or opposing counsel. Students are trained through Socratic dialogue to become a competent counsel who can respond to inquiries effectively and construct strong arguments for their client. Students learn how to summarize the facts of the case to develop their own legal argument, with reference to relevant cases. The whole training process consists of a series of prompt oral interactions. In addition, oral argument is a hybrid communication of information and emotion. Lawyers can construct advocacy heavily loaded with emotion to impress the judge and the jury.

In Japan, the case method was transplanted into a legal environment where the exchange of documents forms the basis of professional practice and communication.[16] Proficiency in written advocacy is more significant than oral skills in a professional world of document communication. Furthermore, there is no jury in Japanese civil proceedings. The judge is the sole decision maker on both facts and law. The judge makes decisions based on the principle of the freedom of the judge's own conviction, which allows the judge to determine the value of the evidence in the context of the entire oral argument, such as it is.[17] In actual courtroom practice, judges rarely reveal their emotional response to lawyers' argument. They remain impassive. They rarely interrupt a counsel's argument to ask questions.[18]

The case method reflects a court practice of hearing the oral arguments offered by both sides. Oral advocacy helps the court clarify the law and the scope of cited cases, estimate the value of evidence, and become aware of the parties' subjective senses of justice. These aspects of the case method will not function appropriately in a professional environment dominated by the exchange of documents. The case method in Japan's new law school system has little use outside the classroom.

Judicial Structure and Legal Education

As the expression "judge-made law"[19] suggests, the common law tradition allows judges to make law through adjudication. In fact, American courts—both federal and state—have been known to practice judicial activism. The Continental law tradition, which is dominant in Japan, tends to discourage judicial lawmaking with the doctrine that decided cases will not form the source of law. However, court cases in Japan, particularly those of the Supreme Court of Japan, do control lower courts' decisions and professional practices.

Since any one legal rule cannot give a clear and specific answer to all possible cases, judges must have the freedom to make law within limitations. In the Continental law tradition, this operation is often called the "interpretation" of law. In the common law tradition, it may be referred to as "legal method," which is related to the skill of how to read a case. The critical question for both traditions is how the legal system can control judges' freedom to make (or interpret) law. This section considers four notable differences between the Japanese and American judiciaries to clarify the context of judge-made law and legal education: (1) the notion of jurisdictional independence; (2) judicial independence; (3) uniform application of law; and (4) judicial deference.

The United States has one federal and fifty state jurisdictions. They are more or less independent. The notion that the United States Supreme Court, the highest federal court, aggregates all the judgments of both federal and state courts and, in turn, controls the law throughout the United States is simply false. Each state has the power to design its own judiciary and legal system. This establishes a strong basis for the jurisdictional independence of American courts. The United States has a pluralist legal landscape.

In contrast, the Japanese Supreme Court supervises eight high courts and the numerous lower courts of Japan. It has a judicial management office—the General Secretariat—whose task is to prepare the Rules of the Supreme Court; to represent the judiciary in the lawmaking process; to manage transfers and promotions of judges; to develop the list of judges for reappointment; to prepare the budget of the judiciary; to organize meetings of presidents of high courts, district courts, and family courts; and to conduct research on law and professional practice in Japan and overseas.[20] The Japanese judiciary lives in a monastic and tightly structured world. Jurisdictional independence as experienced the United States does not exist in Japan.

The second notable difference is the function of judicial independence. Japan and the United States share the doctrine of separation of powers: the judicial branch operates independently from the other branches of government. The similarity, however, ends there. Judges of the American federal courts are appointed for life, and most state court judges are elected. The notion of promotion based on seniority and good professional service seems to be nonexistent. The American legal world makes each judge independent and free from any pressure, except for reelection in the case of state courts.

In Japan, the executive branch (the Cabinet) appoints Japanese judges for a term of ten years.[21] The Cabinet appoints them from a list prepared by the Supreme Court. The established practice is that the Cabinet endorses the list submitted by the Supreme Court without alteration. A duly appointed judge cannot be removed from the office except through public impeachment.[22] Rejecting the reappointment of a judge after a ten-year term is very rare.[23] This process has succeeded in protecting each judge's independence from outside pressures. Unlike in the United States, however, control of individual judges within the judiciary is effective because of the transfer and promotion system managed by the General Secretariat of the Supreme Court. The General Secretariat keeps personnel records of each judge prepared by the president of the lower court where the judge works. Judges are transferred from one court to another every three or four years on average. The sense of promotion based on seniority and good professional service is shared by the judges as a group. This transfer-promotion system creates pressure for conformity. In this sense a Japanese judge is less independent compared to an American judge.

The third difference is judicial commitment to the uniform application of law. Given the strong jurisdictional independence of American courts, the legal world of the United States is tolerant of diversity of laws and varied application of rules. In spite of the past efforts of the Uniform Law Commission (established in 1892) and the American Law Institute (established in 1923), the United States has never achieved a system of uniform application of nationally shared rules. The gravitational pull toward diversity and fragmentation is embedded in the law of the United States.

In Japan, with weak jurisdictional independence under a clear court hierarchy, commitment to the uniform application of national rules to every corner of the country dominates the Japanese legal world. Laypeople as well as professionals expect all the courts of Japan to read a rule in the exact same way and to apply a rule in the exact same way. This universal application of national rules is one aspect of justice in Japan. Japanese lawyers often express this sense of universality by using a professional phrase of "established precedents and dominant scholarly opinions." One mechanism fostering the uniform application of law is the publication of leading Supreme Court cases. The Supreme Court has a Cases Committee (判例委員会), which consists of six justices. The committee meets monthly and selects Supreme Court cases for publication in official reports. Its editorial policy is to select cases that have legal issues and facts that have not yet been covered by previously reported cases. The research judges of the Supreme Court (最高裁判所調査官), who are bright and experienced judges, prepare draft issues of the case, create a one-sentence case summary, and outline the relevant statutory provisions of the case.[24] In addition, the Supreme Court publishes commentary on the cases that appear in its official reports. The commentary first appears in the *Lawyers Association Journal* (法曹時報) and later in book form. The commentary draft of a case is prepared by the research judges who were actually assigned to the case and is reviewed by the justice who drafted the judgment. The commentary, therefore, often functions as the de facto official explication of a leading case.

The fourth difference is the function of judicial deference. Japan and the United States share this concept. Given the separation of powers, judicial deference means that the judiciary respects the work of the other branches of government in the context of constitutional review of laws enacted by the legislature, judicial review of agency rules, and interpretations of statutes. However, it seems that the activist United States Supreme Court under Chief Justice Earl Warren triggered a long-lasting controversy about the proper task of the Court in light of the principle of judicial deference. American academic publications on this topic of judicial deference rapidly increased in the 1950s and continues to be an area of great debate.[25]

In Japan, the executive branch, led by the Cabinet, prepares important laws and submits them to the deliberation of the national assembly (the Diet). National ministries and agencies prepare draft laws allocated to their respective fields. The draft laws are developed using the database e-Gov Law Search (e-Gov 法令検索),[26] which enables drafters of legislation to use terms and expressions consistently over time and across the variety of laws. The draft laws are circulated to all ministries and agencies for feedback. The Cabinet Legislation Bureau works with the drafters and reviews the draft laws. Parallel to the drafting work, the ministry in charge of a particular law contacts clients, interested parties, and stakeholders, including political parties, in order to obtain support for the bill. The draft law that has passed review by the Cabinet Legislation Bureau is submitted to the Cabinet, where a unanimous decision is necessary to send the bill to the Diet. After promulgation of a new law, ministry drafters often publish a book that provides detailed commentaries on the law. Local governments and stakeholders often regard the book as the official interpretation and guideline for a particular law. Ministries and agencies accumulate inquiries and responses to the law through communications with local governments and stakeholders. The collections of inquiries and responses are often published for implementation of each provision of a law.

Judicial deference in Japan is responsive to this institutional arrangement.[27] Since its establishment in 1947, the Supreme Court has found a very small number of statutes unconstitutional.[28] In civil law cases, however, courts have been active to improve the law through their decisions.[29]

Lack of jurisdictional independence, judicial independence with a built-in mechanism for internal conformity, commitment to the uniform application of law, and judicial deference to the law made by the legislature and the executive have made the Japanese legal world much less controversial than that of the United States.

In any country, legal education responds to its legal environment. The case method developed by Langdell and Ames at Harvard Law School is an attempt to overcome the challenge of the pluralistic legal world of the United States. It reflects the common law practice of piecemeal legal development through oral advocacy based on the unique facts of each case.[30] In 2004, the American case method came to Japan carrying these echoes of the common law tradition. It struggled to survive in a wholly unfriendly environment. This struggle becomes apparent when we see how case analysis functions in Japan versus the United States.

Approaches to Case Analysis

Langdell stated that "[l]aw, considered as a science, consists of certain principles and doctrines. To have such a mastery of these as to be able to apply them with constant facility and certainty to the ever-tangled skein of human affairs, is what constitutes a true lawyer."[31] He is referring in this statement to the professional skill of common law lawyers, that is, the skill of case analysis: how to read and apply past cases to decide the case at hand.

A "case" is simply a record of a judgment of a court on a past case. A case as a record contains varied information such as the case number, names of judges, attorneys, and parties, facts and arguments submitted to the court from the parties, analysis of facts and arguments by the court, characterization of the case by the court, reasoning underlying the court's decision, and the decision of the court.

When lawyers are consulted by a client about an ongoing dispute, they try to extract useful information from past cases to resolve the dispute for the benefit of their client. In this context, a case does not mean the judgment record itself but rather the information a lawyer's case analysis extracts from past cases. Lawyers learn how to analyze past cases through their legal education. In each jurisdiction, there may be a broadly shared practice of case analysis. According to Langdell, the United States trains lawyers to read and analyze judgments in a particular way so that they find legal principles and doctrines.

A crucial question is whether the American method of case analysis is broadly shared by lawyers of other jurisdictions. It is, however, more likely that lawyers of other jurisdictions practice different methods of case analysis from that of the United States. If case analysis allows different methods, it implies that lawyers extract different information from past cases depending on the method of case analysis they use.

Since case analysis is essential for applying law, the method of choice for case analysis has a significant impact on legal education and practice. Karl Llewellyn points out that there are two approaches to a case: one from the rear, and one from the front. The approach from the rear treats "the decision primarily as a something done and complete, a something which provides an authoritative datum about the state of the law," whereas the approach from the front is "an approach to the case as a problem *for* solution, not as a problem already solved."[32] Llewellyn, as a legal realist, suggests the need to use the approach from the front. He describes how a class looks under the approach from the front:

> What materials were there to work with, before the decision and in the decision?
>
> How could the case, or the materials at hand, have been analyzed, presented, and argued to give cogent reason for deciding for the losing party? How did the winning party arrange his case to win? Or did the court decide for the winner in spite of his blobs in presentation and argument, and, if so, how and why?

Put simply, the problem is presented as one *for* solution, as a problem not with its answer at hand but as one to which possible answers are to be worked out in class.[33]

In a jurisdiction within the Continental law tradition such as Japan, the method of how to analyze a case is heavily influenced by the notion of authoritative text of law. Laws and statutes are enacted by a national assembly, and the text of laws and statutes binds judges as well as the people. Legal discussion, therefore, often focuses on how to understand particular terms of a particular provision. Though past cases may help lawyers clarify the meaning of a legal text, they remain servants to the legal text. In contrast, the American discussion of the codification movement during the nineteenth century demonstrates a strong aversion to the statutory text enacted by the legislature. James Carter, a strong opponent of the codification movement, wrote that "the characteristic feature of a written and enacted rule is that it governs *all* cases falling within the scope of its language, whether they are novel or otherwise. . . . Their real purpose is to stop the processes of reason and to substitute in the determination of particular cases the simple inquiry 'what has been written?' in the place of 'what is right?'"[34]

Carter's view is echoed in the Restatement of Law movement led by the American Law Institute. The first Restatement attempted to restate the law developed by courts in a statutory-law style. The Restatement, however, is not intended to be binding; instead it tries to be persuasive by collecting and summarizing important cases that support the black-letter law collected in the Restatements.[35] Both Carter and the Reporters of the Restatements shared the view that cases are the real basis of legal principles. The metaphor of the written legal text as a floating leaf on a river of cases may be appropriate here. It is not the text of statutes but the cases that control the real meaning of law. This reveals one aspect of the common law approach to statutory law.

The Japanese approach to statutory provisions is very similar to the one criticized by Carter. The statutory provisions cover all cases falling within the scope of its language. Though the drafters of law might have drafted provisions with typical as well as problematic cases in mind, the written text has its own life. It is not the practice to ask what sort of facts and cases the drafters considered at the time of legislative drafting. The written text is taken as a general and binding rule applicable to many unknown fact situations for the future.

When unexpected cases come to the court, the judge is forced to interpret the text of the provision to decide the case. Though a decision on a novel case is, in its substance, an example of judicial law-making, it is still characterized as interpretation of statutory law. For example, Article 968 (1) of the *Japanese Civil Code* allows testators to create a valid will by writing the entire text, the date, and their name in one's own hand and by affixing one's own seal to the document.[36] The Supreme Court heard a case where the testator had used his own fingerprint instead of his seal and announced that the fingerprint satisfied the requirement of the seal.[37] The court consistently discussed the issue from the perspective of how to read the statutory term "seal" and whether the term could include a fingerprint. The court did not make any reference to creating a new principle to fill a gap in the law.

Japan uses what Llewellyn called "the approach to the case from the rear." The court's interpretation of a statutory provision does not imply judicial lawmaking. Rather, the implication is that the case helps the court clarify a legal text or the meaning of a term to solve a legal question. Legal experts tend to regard the combination of the provision and the cases interpreting it as "an authoritative datum about the state of the law."[38] Japanese legal databases provide information in a format that links cases to the relevant statutory provisions. Therefore, "Article 968 (1)" is an effective search term to identify all relevant cases relating to that article. Since important Supreme Court cases are selected by the Supreme Court to reduce ambiguity and unclear aspects of a provision,[39] cases appear to control judicial lawmaking over time and to produce more specific rules, rather than to encourage legal innovation. The drive for innovation that exists in the approach from the front is under control in this legal environment.

If the case method adopts the approach from the front, it encourages students to analyze the facts of the case and to develop a solution. It is training for innovative lawyering. If the case method uses the approach from the rear, it encourages students to view court decisions as announcing specific rules that will clarify black-letter law further. Studying cases is not an invitation to creativity but an invitation to understand the authoritative announcement of more specific rules. Japanese legal education takes the approach from the rear, which produces students who want professors to tell them what the rule of a case is.

Conclusion: The Case Method and a Built-in Predisposition toward Legal Innovation

The case method used in the United States seems to adopt the approach from the front. This case method trains students in the skill of problem-solving. It is training not for discovery of a final solution but for innovation for a better solution to a dispute. This training assumes that there is more than one solution to the problem and that it is worth the effort to persuade the court and the jury to choose the particular solution for which the legal expert advocates.[40] The cases decided in the past are a starting point for critical analysis and creative discussion rather than an endpoint for the discovery of the final answer to the problem.

Through training in case analysis, law students soon learn that the rationale (or *ratio decidendi*) of the case does not show itself automatically in a perfect form, and it is not akin to a statutory provision. It is derived from a professional skill that extracts and formulates precedent from a judgment.[41] The starting point for students is to read the facts of the case carefully and formulate the *ratio* on the basis of these facts.[42]

The *ratio* formulated by a student in this way always remains tentative. This is because any formulation of the *ratio* demands a choice of "essential" facts and the abstraction of facts to produce a rule. Choices are always arguable and controversial, since there is no absolute standard for these choices. Suppose there was a case about a dog with the habit of biting other dogs. Does this case establish the *ratio* for dogs with the habit of attacking, dogs in general, or animals in general? This choice of a level of abstraction is not mechanical. Many factors will influence the formulation of the *ratio*. Therefore, even the *ratio* formulated by the most experienced legal experts is not free from this tentativeness. If students understand the tentative nature of the *ratio*, they can see a legal environment full of opportunities for professional innovation. The world of law is not radically different from the world of industry and technology where variation is routine. The case method can highlight the innovative potential of the legal profession.

Statutory provisions stipulate the conditions of their application with general terms. Though the drafters of statutes broadly consider past cases relevant to a provision, statutory provisions—unlike the provisions of the Restatement of the Law—do not report the facts of cases considered by the drafters. It is hard for law students to notice the innovative potential of legal experts when they start from the black-letter law of statutory provisions. But this is not to deny legal innovation in the Continental law tradition. A quick review of the interpretation of the *Japanese Civil Code* would show many cases of judicial lawmaking.

Both the case method in the common law tradition and the interpretation in the Continental legal tradition can be either innovative or suppressive of innovation. The American case method, with its drive for innovation, was transplanted to Japan in the early 2000s. It met the world of document-based advocacy, where there is one Supreme Court dominates the whole jurisdiction, an independent judiciary with an established mechanism for judicial conformity, a national commitment to the uniform application of law, and a clear sense of judicial deference for other branches of government. This world did not need a case method that goes beyond jurisdictional borders and encourages judicial innovation for better social governance. Professional legal education in Japan has been using the approach from the rear and did not succeed in switching to the approach from the front. This chapter has examined the key conditions for the American case method to work. One significant condition is the social arrangement to allow courts to make innovations for better social governance though their decisions.

NOTES

1 Keener says that "the student is taught to look upon law as a science consisting of a body of principles to be found in the adjudged cases." William A. Keener, "Method of Legal Education," *Yale Law Journal* 1, no. 4 (March 1892): 144.

2 Robert Stevens, *Law School: Legal Education in America from the 1850s to the 1980s* (Chapel Hill: University of North Carolina, 1983), 59–64. The case method of 1871 did not spread to other law schools until 1890. The case method spread with the movement of Harvard professors to other law schools. William Keener went to Columbia Law School in 1890, John H. Wigmore to Northwestern Law School in 1893, and Joseph Beale to the University of Chicago Law School in 1900. Through this strategy the case method steadily spread and became *the* method of legal education by the 1920s.

3 The study of the state law is to be done either through practice or so-called cram schools, which prepare law students for a state bar examination.

4 Charles Warren, *History of the Harvard Law School and of Early Legal Conditions in America*, vol. 2 (Chicago: Lewis, 1908), 419–20.

5 See Eugene Kaplan, *Japan: The Government-Business Relationship: A Guide for the American Businessman* (Washington, DC: United States Department of Commerce, 1972).

6 The whole plan is described by the document "Recommendations of the Justice Reform Council: For a Justice System to Support Japan in the 21st Century [司法制度改革審議会意見書—21世紀の日本を支える司法制度のために—]" Justice System Reform Council [司法制度改革審議会], last modified June 12, 2001, www.kantei.go.jp.

7 Oliver Wendell Holmes, Jr., "The Path of the Law," *Harvard Law Review* 10, no. 8 (1897): 457.

8 The principle of governance by precedents has much longer history in Japan. Various collections of precedents were continuously prepared officially and privately during the eighteenth century under the Tokugawa regime. These collections were privately copied and widely shared for general practice.

9 See generally Dan Rosen, "Japan's Law School System: The Sorrow and the Pity," *Journal of Legal Education* 66, no. 2 (January 2017): 267–88. As to the students' interest in foreign laws, see 285–86.

10 As to the process of oral argument, see Carl F. Goodman, *The Rule of Law in Japan: A Comparative Analysis* (Netherlands: Kluwer Law International, 2008), 346–47.

11 *The Code of Civil Procedure* (Act No.109 of 1996).

12 For example, the following web page reports the courtroom experience of the person who seems to be a party to a civil case: "civil lawsuits that cannot be understood by hearing," About Civil Lawsuits, Freedom of Expression in the Internet, www.i-foe.org.

13 Supreme Court of Japan, *Outline of Civil Procedure* (Supreme Court, 2017), 10, www.courts.go.jp (emphasis added).

14 Society for the Study of the Civil Procedural System, ed., *Report on Japan's 2011 Civil Litigation Survey* (Tokyo: Jigakusha, 2014). Reports at page 92 that 39.4 percent of the opinion poll respondents (the people) felt strongly that the judge "listened to your side of the story enough." This response came from the context of frequent exchange of documents supplemented by oral exchange among the parties, the legal counsels, and the judge.

15 As to the practiced oral argument and its criticism, see generally Masako Hatano [波多野雅子], "A Working Paper on the Significance of Oral Argument" [口頭弁論の意義に関する試論], *Sapporo Gakuin Hogaku* [札幌学院法学] 19, no. 2 (2003): 195–247.

16 In 2009, Japan introduced a new system of citizen participation in criminal cases as six lay judges of the nine-judge panel. Oral argument becomes more important in this context, but the training of professional lawyers for this change has not become an important element in law school education.

17 Article 247 of *the Code of Civil Procedure* (Act No. 109 of 1996) provides: "In reaching a judgment, the court decides whether to find allegations of fact to be true based on its freedom of personal conviction, in light of the entire import of oral arguments and the results of the examination of evidence."

18 See http:/bengoshi.shiga-saku.net. One attorney's blog reports that many judges maintain an emotionless mask in the courtroom and explains that this behavior is meant to show the neutrality of the judges.

19 Jeremy Bentham, "Truth v. Ashhurst," in *The Works of Jeremy Bentham*, vol. 5, ed. John Bowring (London: Simpkin, Marshall & Co. 1843), 235.

20 See Muneyuki Shindo [新藤宗幸], *Bureaucrats of the Judiciary: Power-wielders of Courts* [司法官僚：裁判所の権力者たち] (Tokyo: Iwanami Shoten, 2009), 50–52.

21 Articles 79 and 80 of the Constitution of Japan (1946). The chief judge of the Supreme Court is named by the Cabinet and appointed by the Emperor. Section 2, Article 7 of he Constitution of Japan.

22 Article 78 of the Constitution of Japan.

23 "Number of Appointed and Reappointed Judges and Assistant Judges for 2002," www.courts.go.jp. The statistics of the reappointment report that there was only one rejection out of 823 candidates for the period 1998–2002.

24 See Tokiyasu Fujita[藤田宙靖], *The Memoir of the Supreme Court: Seven and a Half Years of a Scholar-Justice* [最高裁回想録：学者判事の七年半] (Tokyo: Yuhikaku, 2012), 194–202.

25 "Judicial deference (choice of American English)," Google Ngram Viewer, https://books.google.com. Though the Google Ngram Viewer is not an accurate indicator, it shows the notable jump in the frequency of use of "judicial deference" since the 1950s.

26 E-Gov, http://elaws.e-gov.go.jp. The government also uses an unpublished database that stores the law data before publication.

27 For a more detailed analysis of the Japanese Supreme Court based on the interviews, see Davis Law, "The Anatomy of a Conservative Court: Judicial Review in Japan," *Texas Law Review* 87, no. 7 (June 2008): 1545–93. Frank Upham argues that Japan designed its legal system to divert major social issues from the judiciary to the executive branch. See Frank Upham, *Law and Social Change in Postwar Japan* (Cambridge: Harvard University Press, 1987).

28 Jun-ichi Sato, "Judicial Review in Japan: An Overview of the Case Law and an Examination of Trends in the Japanese Supreme Court's Constitutional Oversight," *Loyola Los Angeles Law Review* 41, no. 2 (January 2008): 603–28.

29 The accumulated cases on the Civil Code show that the courts changed the meaning of many provisions over time.

30 Ronald Dworkin's characterization of the legal world might be a modern formulation of the mind-set of the common law lawyers. See Ronald Dworkin, *Law's Empire* (Cambridge: Belknap Press of Harvard University Press, 1986).

31 Christopher Langdell, *A Selection of Cases on the Law of Contracts*, 2nd ed. (Boston: Little, Brown & Co., 1879), viii.

32 Karl Llewellyn, "The Current Crisis in Legal Education," *Journal of Legal Education* 1, no. 2 (December 1948): 213 (italics in original).

33 Ibid., 213–14.

34 James Carter, "The Provinces of the Written and Unwritten Law," *American Law Review* 24 (January 1890): 11–12.

35 As to the Reporters' approach to the Restatement, see Deborah DeMott, "The First Restatement of Agency: What Was the Agenda?," *Southern Illinois University Law Journal* 32, no. 1 (September 2007): 31.

36 The relevant provision reads: "To make a will by holograph document the testator must write the entire text, the date, and his/her name in his/her own hand and affix his/her seal." Article 968 (1), the Civil Code (Part IV and Part V), Act No. 89 of 1896. The 2019 amendment of Article 968 created a new paragraph (2) that allows to use the printed list of the testator's estate.

37 Supreme Court Judgment of Feburary 16, Heisei 1 [1989], *Official Report of the Supreme Court* 43–2: 45. [最一小判平成元年2月16日民集43巻2号45頁]

38 Llewellyn, "The Current Crisis in Legal Education," 213.

39 Tokiyasu Fujita[藤田宙靖], *The Memoir of the Supreme Court: Seven and a Half Years of a Scholar-Justice* [最高裁回想録：学者判事の七年半], 194.

40 Ronald Dworkin, *Law's Empire*. Dworkin's claim that there is one right answer to any legal question does not contradict this assumption. What he claims is that the law is a game of legal experts who compete to construct the best answer to the question.

41 Granville Williams, *Learning the Law*, 11th ed. (London: Sweet & Maxwell, 1982), 67.

42 Rupert Cross, *Precedent in English Law*, 2nd ed. (Oxford: Oxford University Press, 1968), 39–43.

11

Legal Education in France Turns Its Attention to the Harvard Model

JEAN-LOUIS HALPÉRIN

For more than a century, all who have compared the Harvard model to legal education in France have noted strong contrasts between the structures, the programs, and the methods of law schools. Since 1804, French law schools—named *écoles de droit* in the founding law of March 13, 1804, then *facultés de droit* since 1806—have been state institutions. They held a monopoly over legal education until 1875; following the recognition of freedom of higher education in 1875, they have possessed a quasi-exclusive position to grant law degrees.[1] Until the end of the nineteenth century, the law schools had to respect national programs that were very detailed and that concentrated on teaching the Napoleonic Code. Lecture courses *ex cathedra* (so-called frontal lecturing) were devoted, for the main part, to the explanation (or recitation) of statutory laws according to the so-called deductive method. Before 1895, professors of civil law were normally obliged to follow the order of the articles of the Napoleonic Code. While the so-called exegesis method was not uniquely French (it was also used by the German Historical School as a good way interpret legal rules), it was certainly followed by law professors in France during the nineteenth century. This method was built on the commentary of statutory laws and left a subaltern role to case law quotations.[2] All of these features of legal education in France evolved from the reforms of the Third Republic, which began in the 1880s, and carried on until the creation of the Sciences-Po Law School in 2009. Among these developments, one cannot speak of any adoption of the Harvard model in France. The story to be analyzed here is how a few French jurists turned their attention toward the Harvard model and Christopher Langdell's case method.

The knowledge of the Harvard model began very discreetly among a small group of specialists of comparative law at the end of the nineteenth century; this occurred before the emergence of the first appraisals of the case method after World War I. Prior to World War II, French jurists—even those interested in American legal education—felt a kind of superiority complex toward American law schools. At the time of Langdell's reforms in 1870, Harvard Law School had four full-time professors and about 150 students, whereas the Paris Law School boasted nineteen professors and 2,500 students.[3] In 1900, when James Barr Ames was dean at Harvard Law School, there were fewer than fifteen professors and 800 students there, whereas Paris had thirty-nine professors and more than 7,800 students During the 1930s, the *Faculté de droit de Paris* (part of the *Université de Paris* since 1896) was the biggest law school in the world in terms of the number of students: more than 11,000.[4] French law professors were convinced of the efficiency of their model of legal education, especially after reforms in the 1880s and the 1900s, which had developed a more scientific approach toward the study of law, adopted in part from the German model. This chapter examines the archaeology of texts showing how the Harvard model was known in France and why it was kept at a distance, even by French jurists who were interested in American legal education.

The Primary Sources of Knowledge about the Harvard Model

In France, the first mention of Langdell's reforms is found in the early issues of a journal devoted to educational reforms, the *Revue internationale de l'enseignement*, which was published from 1881 onward by the *Société pour l'étude des questions d'enseignement supérieur*. This society was created in 1878, with Édouard Laboulaye, a Republican lawyer, serving as president and two law professors, Claude Bufnoir and Paul Gide, on its board. The society favored comparative studies about higher education, aiming to improve French universities in light of foreign experiences. In 1881–1882, Adrien Jacquinot (1827–1883) described Harvard Law School in two papers published in the *Revue*. Jacquinot was a Frenchman who taught as an assistant professor of French language at Harvard beginning in 1876. He began his legal education in France in 1846, then became a tax administrator and eventually emigrated to the United States in 1857. He was not a renowned lawyer or teacher but rather an intellectual adventurer who sought fortune in America. After offering a general introduction to Harvard University in the first issue of the review in 1881,[5] Jacquinot developed a richer analysis of the law school in the second issue of the review in 1882.[6] In explaining the entrance examinations and the three-year program, Jacquinot deemed that Langdell's method was tailored to American law, and he contrasted it with legal teaching in France. Langdell's inductive method, according to Jacquinot, was consistent with customary law—a law that was not based mainly on statutes but was instead decided and modified by case law (*jurisprudence* in French). Jacquinot was aware of the preparatory work undertaken by American law students through the use of casebooks, of the questions asked by American law professors using the "Socratic maieutic," and of the proliferation of the Socratic method among Harvard courses. Jacquinot concluded that he largely approved of these methods: Harvard students felt that they "created" law—that they were reasoning people and not reciting parrots.

Jacquinot's article was probably the first introduction to the Harvard model for French lawyers. With respect to other connections between Harvard and France, the *École libre des sciences politiques* had an exchange program with Harvard. However, while many invitations to visit Harvard were issued to French writers and philosophers, the program was in fact taken up by only one Frenchman in 1910.[7] Jacquinot's article probably found readers among the members of the *Société de législation comparée*, another society founded by Laboulaye in 1869. Laboulaye devoted his teaching in the *Collège de France* to the history of the United States without ever having visited America. This Republican lawyer wanted to promote a liberal model and was the initiator of the Statue of Liberty in New York.[8] The *Société* gathered together French lawyers, judges, and professors interested in comparative law. Its *Bulletin* was an important source of information in Europe about foreign laws and institutions. The *Bulletin* of this comparative law society made several mentions of the *Harvard Law Review*,[9] including comments by Henri Lévy-Ullmann in 1895 that it was one of the most important journals on American law.[10] Born in 1870, Lévy-Ullmann had just passed his doctoral thesis at the time of publishing this comment and was not yet a professor.[11] Notwithstanding his relative inexperience and junior status, this young member of the *Société de législation comparée* published an article in *Harvard Law Review* in 1896. In that article, Lévy-Ullmann described French society with the hope of recruiting Americans.[12]

At the beginning of the twentieth century, the relationship between Harvard and French law schools was insignificant. For example, the presence of American lawyers in the 1900 Comparative Law Congress in Paris was weak and did not include any law professor from Harvard. The only American participant was John Burgess from Columbia University. Similarly, in the 1904 Saint-Louis Congress, the French delegate Georges Blondel was a business school professor and not a jurist. Nonetheless, some years later, French jurists were again informed of the Harvard case system, this time through Alfred Nerincx's book *L'Organisation judiciaire aux États-Unis*, published in 1909. Nerincx was a Belgian professor, and his book addressed the judicial system in the United States. He received some funding from a French institute, *Académie des sciences morales et politiques*, and his book was ultimately published in a prestigious comparative law series that was directed by the public law professor Gaston Jèze. Having visited the United States, and having been well informed about American Bar Association (ABA) reports, Nerincx described and evaluated the replacement of the "recitation system" by the "true revolution" that had been initiated by Langdell. Nerincx presented Langdell's method as "scientific" and judged it as being excellent for teaching legal history (in the sense that the method described the development of case law). Yet Nerincx also argued that the method would be unlikely to contribute to the building of a solid doctrine and saw it as being useful only for elite students and professors. Nerincx also quoted the critical point of view of Simeon Baldwin in an ABA report, probably to reinforce his own critical perspective.[13] Nerincx's book likely attracted little attention from the very small group of French jurists interested in American law prior to World War I, as evidenced by a quoted reference to the book by Édouard Lambert in 1921.[14]

The Impact of World War I: One French Propagandist for the Langdell Method

The American involvement in World War I dramatically improved the relationships between French and American jurists. During wartime, the Parisian law professor Geouffre de La Pradelle visited Columbia University, and Jules Valéry translated an article by Roscoe Pound into French. As the article was about the influence of French Law in America, it flattered French nationalism and supported the French-American friendship as early as 1915.[15] During the period of demobilization from 1917–1918 onward, American soldiers were invited to attend special courses organized at the *Faculté de droit de Paris* and casebooks were sent to France in order to instruct these students.[16] As a new law professor at the Paris Faculty of Law, Henri Lévy-Ullmann began to work on Anglo-American law and quoted Charles Warren's book, *History of the Harvard Law School and of Early Legal Conditions in America*, and *The Centennial History of the Harvard Law School* in a conference before the *Société de Législation comparée* in 1919.[17] In that same year (1919), Édouard Lambert—born in 1866, professor of legal history at the University of Lyon, and one of the most active participants in the 1900 Comparative Law Congress in Paris (among the young collaborators of Saleilles, including Lévy-Ullmann)[18]—published the program of the future *Institut de droit comparé* in Lyon: *L'enseignement du droit comparé. Sa coopération au rapprochement de la jurisprudence française et de la jurisprudence anglo-américaine* (The Teaching of comparative law. Its contribution to bring closer American and French jurisprudences). Quoting Nerincx in a critical manner, along with Josef Redlich's *The Case Method in American Law Schools*,[19] Lambert argued that Langdell's method had triumphed in the United States. He was of the view that Langdell's method had the advantage of enabling the perception that it taught students about economic realities through real cases, even if the use of the method was a little excessive, given that it underestimated the role of statutory laws. In this book, with very ambitious perspectives on French law (suggesting that it was another kind of common law of international legal currency), Lambert was not afraid to compare Harvard Law School with the *École Normale Supérieure* as the ideal place for educating elite law professors.[20]

In 1920, the *Revue internationale de l'enseignement* published an enthusiastic article about the case system and the Socratic method used in American law schools. The author was Pierre Lepaulle, a young lawyer born in 1893. After beginning law courses in France and serving six years in the army (1913–1919), Lepaulle obtained a fellowship to study at Harvard Law School from 1919 to 1922. Lepaulle studied (and even taught some seminars) during his three years at Harvard and was awarded a doctorate (SJD) in 1922 for his thesis about administrative law within international law. He submitted his article before finishing his studies in America (and before obtaining a French doctorate in 1923, on the direction of Lévy-Ullmann). In twenty pages, Lepaulle enthusiastically described the case method as an "original creation of the American spirit"—a method perfectly adapted for giving a "legal spirit" to professional lawyers who were able to practice across the United States. Well informed about the practice and the literature surrounding the case method (he quoted James Bradley Thayer, Redlich, Joseph Henry Beale, and Roscoe Pound), Lepaulle was particularly impressed by the method's propensity to overcome students' complexes through the use of intellectual challenges (*déflegmatiser l'étudiant*) and to trigger an atmosphere of camaraderie and competition through the implementation of clubs and law reviews. Lepaulle was also attentive to details that were new to the French audience: courses limited to fifty minutes, with ten-minute intervals reserved for questions addressed to professors; high work levels for students with the support of a rich library; and practical problems to be resolved in written examinations. Lepaulle did not propose to "adopt en bloc" the case method, characterizing it instead as a transitory and intermediate method.[21] His article was considered to be so revolutionary as to warrant a foreword from Larnaude (the dean of Paris Law School and the general secretary of the *Société pour l'étude des questions d'enseignement supérieur*). Larnaude (who had corresponded with Thayer in 1902 about judicial review)[22] took a different view than Lepaulle. He argued that the French method, with its didactic courses, was superior to Langdell's, and he tried to diminish the novelty of the American method by alluding to practical exercises made by French professors in "conferences" (optional small groups for students) or "seminars" (for the doctorate students).[23] In 1921, when Lambert published his renowned book *Le Gouvernement des juges aux États-Unis* (without having visited the United States), he presented the case method, quoted Nerincx and Lepaulle, and wrote that Lepaulle's enthusiasm was perhaps inconsistent with a scientific attitude.[24]

As he developed the *Institut de droit comparé* in Lyon (also encouraging studies about Egypt and the Soviet Union), Lambert supervised the doctoral thesis of Robert Valeur. Valeur's thesis (*L'Enseignement du droit en France et aux États-Unis*, 1928) compared law teaching in France and the United States. Valeur received a fellowship from the Rockefeller Foundation, visited several universities (among them Harvard), and worked as a "foreign adviser" in the 1927/1928 reform of studies at Columbia Law School. His thesis, a book of more than 300 pages, provides a remarkable history of American law schools, containing a great quantity of facts and figures. Concerning Harvard, Valeur concentrated on Joseph Story's pioneering teaching, which made use of moot courts,[25] and, of course, on Langdell's method. Valeur's point of view was different from Lepaulle's: Valeur was of the opinion that the inductive method was problematic for a "normative science" such as law (according to the German expression used by Redlich) and that it could fuel superficial ideas about precedents.[26] Valeur preferred the more eclectic methods that were proposed at Columbia along with mixed historical perspectives (with Hessel E. Yntema) and sociological approaches (along Max Weber's lines).[27] Valeur remained convinced of the superiority of the French universities, believing that social sciences had triumphed in French law schools thanks to the reforms at the end of the nineteenth century (he quoted the sectioning of the *agrégation* in 1896). Lambert supported Valeur's vision through a text of more than a hundred pages prefacing Valeur's thesis (*L'Enseignement du droit comme science sociale et comme science internationale*). In an extraordinary interpretation of the history of legal education in France (affirming that French law schools had been teaching social sciences forty years before German universities), Lambert argued that the American schools remained in an "inferior situation" and placed his hopes in Columbia professors (Herman Oliphant, Underhill Moore, and Yntema, each of whom were linked with the dissents of Oliver Wendell Holmes and Louis Brandeis); in the development of economic studies by Leon Marshall (at that time a visiting professor at Columbia); and in the future of comparative research about commercial arbitration.[28]

During the interwar period, the publishing of a casebook with French precedents by Henri Capitant in 1924[29] was the only observable point of contact between Langdell's method and France. Whereas French jurists were familiar with the very sophisticated law journals that had been publishing case law since the beginning of the nineteenth century (e.g., the collections of Sirey or Dalloz), Capitant's book was the first casebook written by a professor of civil laws in order to select the leading cases of the civil *jurisprudence* of the Court of Cassation. The case law of the Court of Cassation was essential in French law since its beginning during the French Revolution, and it largely contributed to completing the Napoleonic Code (e.g., the entry about strict liability). Lambert prefaced Capitant's *Espèces choisies empruntées à la jurisprudence* and defended the limited impact of this "nuanced" case method in the *Revue internationale de l'enseignement.*[30] Later, Lambert compared Canadian casebooks with American and French ones in a paper that he wrote with his doctorate pupil Max Judd Waserman. The paper was titled "The Case Method in Canada and the Possibilities of Its Adaptation to the Civil Law," and it was published in the *Yale Law Journal.*[31] Lambert also prefaced E. F. Albertsworth's *Selected Cases and Other Authorities on Industrial Law* (Northwestern University Press, 1928), and his son Jacques Lambert wrote *Les Year Books de langue française* in 1928.[32] All these texts brought French case law closer to English and American case law, but they did not change how French precedents were taught, which was more through commentaries (the so-called *notes d'arrêt* published by the professors in the law reviews) than through pedagogical exercises.

Lepaulle, who organized (with his wife, also a barrister) conferences at the American Bar Association and wrote publications in the field of trusts, remained isolated. In 1938, he published a short paper in the book collection, *Harvard et la France*, for the tercentenary of Harvard. He wrote that Harvard Law School combined different methods for studying law and had made a "definitive step forward" in pedagogy with the "case-system."[33] However, Lepaulle's reputation was tarnished when he supported the anti-Semitic legislation of the Vichy regime through a 1943 article in the *Gazette du Palais* ("L' Aryanisation des entreprises"). This shameful paper did not prevent Lepaulle from being elected in 1969 as president of the Harvard Law School Association of Europe.[34] By contrast, Robert Valeur rallied the Free French and served as director of the French Information Centre in New York (since 1945) and as a lecturer in economics at Columbia.[35]

A New Generation of French Professors Interested in the Harvard Model

At the end of World War II, the relationships between French jurists and Harvard Law School ceased. Both Lévy-Ullmann and Lambert died in 1947. Many law professors were not interested in American law and remained convinced that French legal culture continued to have the capacity to radiate all over the world, notably through the *Association Henri Capitant*. The new generation of comparative lawyers—again a small group—was directed by René David (born in 1906, professor since 1929 at the age of twenty-three), who had worked at Unidroit in Rome and then at Oxford with H. C. Gutteridge. After having served in the Free French Forces (and being gravely wounded), René David taught at the Paris Law School and served as a visiting professor at Columbia University in 1950.[36] He devoted his 1951–1952 course on comparative private law to American law and created a small description of legal education in the United States for his doctorate students.[37] While giving more attention to Columbia than to Harvard overall, David noted Langdell's method and admired the free discussion between professors and students. He also noticed the evolution of American casebooks, which, now titled "Cases and Materials," integrated doctrinal pages with annotations about economic and social problems. David deemed these American books "heteroclite" and "incomplete," preferring the French combination of doctrinal treaties, Capitant's casebook about *civil jurisprudence*, and the guides for practical exercises developed by the Mazeaud brothers beginning in the 1940s.[38] He viewed the case method as offering weak preparation for future professionals (paying too great attention to Supreme Court decisions at the expense of the preparation of routine files) and concluded that the French and English methods were as good as, or better than, American casebooks for educating lawyers.

David acknowledged that he found much information in the manuscript of the book prepared by André and Suzanne Tunc, which was finally published in 1955. Born in 1917, André Tunc became a professor of private law at Grenoble University in 1943. After the war, he had the opportunity to work for three years in the International Monetary Fund in Washington. With his wife, Suzanne Tunc (who had obtained a law doctorate in 1943), he used this time to collect a great bulk of information about American law and to write the first French synthetic book about this subject. About thirty pages of this book are devoted to legal education, with a very rich bibliography (including recent articles from the *Journal of Legal Education* and Albert J. Harno's *Legal Education in the United States*, published in 1953). Focusing on the numerous differences with the French system (notably, the admission of graduates; the absence of any teaching of Roman law, economics, and political science; and the fact that most of the law professors were not doctors of juridical science), André and Suzanne Tunc presented nuanced conclusions about the case method. They were of the view that the method was cumbersome and that, if it was to be adapted to the teaching of legal technique to future professionals, it needed to be combined (after the first year) with the use of textbooks and work in seminars. In addition to expressing these concerns, the Tuncs approved of the introduction of "teaching fellows" for first-year students at Harvard and of the comparative law courses that had been taught since 1949.[39] They also repeated one of the observations that Nerincx had made in 1909: the case method was useful only with excellent professors and excellent students. In a small paper published in 1959 ("Méthodes actuelles de l'enseignement du droit"), André and Suzanne Tunc again argued that the French method, combining lectures *ex cathedra* and "directed works" (*travaux dirigés*, made compulsory through a 1954 reform), had to be maintained.[40] At that time, the biggest courses of law were accompanied by the study of directed works in smaller groups. This practice remains a feature of the pedagogy in French faculties of law today. It was thus not the practice, even for these admirers of American legal culture, to adopt the Harvard model.

In the 1960s and 1970s, the contact between French jurists and Harvard Law School was limited to a very small group of Frenchmen who obtained Harvard degrees. One example was Bernard Audit, who was a student of the HEC business school and then became a doctor in law before obtaining an LLM from Harvard (1969) and becoming a private law professor (1971, now emeritus) and a well-known specialist in conflict of laws. One can also notice the place of the Harvard degree (during the 1970s) in the cursus of Francis Caballero, a lawyer and legal writer (writing about tobacco and drugs), who was at one time a professor at Paris-Nanterre.

At the beginning of the 1980s, Laurent Cohen-Tanugi (one of the alumni of the *École Normale Supérieure*) was a student at Harvard before publishing *Le Droit sans l'État* in 1985 (a book favoring the American model over the French and citing *Critical Legal Studies* with approval) and becoming a renowned lawyer.[41] However, these academic and professional projects (including one by Louis Vogel, LLM Yale Law School, in 1982) had no direct impact on French legal education.

The state law schools obtained more and more autonomy for defining programs (notably through the so-called Bayrou reform in 1997), but they continued to structure the bachelor's (*licence*) and master's degrees through a combination of lectures *ex cathedra* and directed works (*travaux dirigés*) in small groups. The American model nonetheless influenced French universities by prompting the creation of legal clinics, a movement beginning at Grenoble University in 1986 (with *Etujuris*, a students' association) and taking place now in more than twenty law schools. One also sees the publication of English comparative casebooks that can be used for advanced students in France (e.g., the series *Ius Commune Casebooks on the Common Law of Europe*, a comparative contract law casebook, which involved the participation of Denis Tallon (2002) and Bénédicte Fauvarque-Cosson (2010)).

The main initiative that has made reference to the Harvard model was the creation of the Sciences-Po Law School in 2009, which concluded an exchange agreement with Harvard Law School in 2011. The program involves an exchange of students and of professors, with the notable participation of Scott Brewer and David Kennedy. Recruiting graduate students for two years to complete master's degrees (and also preparing them for entrance in the bar and the national competition of the Judges' School), the Sciences-Po Law School competes with the traditional *Facultés de droit* and proposes a pedagogy centered on teaching synthetic and practical knowledge. For example, in his teaching of civil law and through his advocacy in his book *La Cuisine du droit* (2012), Christophe Jamin (the dean of the law school), places great importance on case law and takes account of the advantages, as well as the drawbacks, of Langdell's method (providing the same criticism as René David about the exclusive attention paid to appellate courts' rulings in the studied cases).[42] According to recent sociological inquiries, this method of teaching is not in fact so different from the one practiced in the universities.[43] There is, however, nothing in France than can be compared to the *Journal of Legal Education* and its impact on methodological debates in the United

States. Generally speaking, discussions about legal pedagogy are rare in France. Inside the universities, the faculties of law continue to follow the same scheme of lectures (*cours magistraux*) and directed works (*travaux dirigés*), even if the development of e-learning allows for the development of new forms of communication between professors and students. It remains difficult to extend the methods used for elite groups in Sciences-Po or in business schools into the large classrooms of the faculties of law.

The strong contrast between the structures of legal education in France and in the United States continues to make impossible a transfer of the Harvard model. The knowledge of this model is old, but it has always been restricted to a small group of jurists interested in comparative law who admit that, despite their interest in the Harvard model, it is not transposable into French legal education. It is not to be concluded that historical and cultural pre-understanding are heavily pregnant, because these historical and cultural factors are themselves diverse and always changing. But the combined structure of the legal order and organization of legal education—both being conceived as public law subjects in France—creates strong constraints that limit the opportunity to transplant foreign models.

NOTES

1 Frédéric Audren and Jean-Louis Halpérin, *La Culture juridique française. Entre mythes et réalités (XIXe-XXe siècle)* (Paris: CNRS éditions, 2013). Private universities were, after the 1875 law, Catholic institutions with some capacity for the teaching of law. The students enrolled in these Catholic universities had to pass the state examinations within the public universities, and for this reason these private institutions followed the public programs without great pedagogical innovation.

2 Jean-Louis Halpérin, "V° Exégèse (École)," in *Dictionnaire de la culture juridique*, ed. Denis Alland and Stéphane Rials (Paris: PUF, 2003), 681–85. With respect to all the debates among French jurists in the first half of the nineteenth century concerning the advantages and drawbacks of quoting case law, see Alfons Bürge, *Das französische Privatrecht im 19. Jahrhundert* (Frankfurt am Main: Klostermann, 1995).

3 Jean-Louis Halpérin, ed., *Paris, capitale juridique (1804–1950). Étude de socio-histoire sur la faculté de droit de Paris* (Paris: éditions rue d'Ulm, 2011).

4 One has to take into account of fact that the study of economics was merged with the study of law, but the number of professors and students specialized in economics remained very small. All the students could become lawyers after the

three-year degree of *licence*, even if many of the alumni of the Faculty of Law chose administrative or business careers. Just before World War I, there were around 17,000 law students in France and around 5,000 lawyers (advocates). In 1930, the number of lawyers remained relatively low, with 4,700 advocates.

5 Adrien Jacquinot, "L'université d'Harvard," *Revue internationale de l'enseignement* 1 (1881): 50–69, and Adrien Jacquinot, "L'université d'Harvard, deuxième partie," *Revue internationale de l'enseignement* 2 (1881): 23–35, 224–28 (about Harvard College) and 319–41.

6 Adrien Jacquinot, "L'université d'Harvard, troisième partie: Les Écoles spéciales et les annexes," *Revue internationale de l'enseignement* 4 (1882): 530–51.

7 André Siegfried, "L'Ecole des sciences politiques et l'Université Harvard," in *Harvard et la France, Revue d'histoire moderne* (Paris: Presses Universitaires de France, 1936), 149.

8 Jean-Louis Halpérin, "Laboulaye historien du droit et/ou comparatiste," *Revue internationale de droit comparé* 63, no. 3 (2011): 517–25.

9 See, for example, C. A. Pret, "Comptes-rendus d'ouvrages: section de la langue anglais," *Bulletin de la Société de Législation Comparée* 21, no.3 (1892): 293–94, with a brief mention of *Harvard Law Review*.

10 Henri Lévy-Ullmann, "Harvard Law Review, Revue Juridique d'Harvard," *Bulletin de la Société de Législation Comparée* 24, no. 8, 9 (1895) : 693.

11 Jean-Louis Halpérin, "Henri Lévy-Ullmann (1870–1947): Classicisme et singularités," in *Le Renouveau de la doctrine française: Les grands auteurs de la pensée juridique au tournant du XXe siècle*, ed. Nader Hakim and Fabrice Melleray (Paris: Dalloz, 2009), 95–122.

12 Henri Lévy-Ullmann, "Account of the French Society of Comparative Legislation," *Harvard Law Review* 10, no. 3 (1896): 161–67.

13 Alfred Nerincx, *L'Organisation judiciaire aux États-Unis* (Paris: Giard et Brière, 1909), 120–30.

14 Édouard Lambert, *Le Gouvernement des juges aux États-Unis et la lutte contre la législation sociale aux États-Unis: L'expérience américaine du contrôle judiciaire de la constitutionnalité des lois* (Paris: Giard, 1921), 24.

15 Roscoe Pound, "Étude sur l'influence du droit français en Amérique," *Bulletin de la Société de Législation comparée* 46 (1915): 390–401.

16 Édouard Lambert, "Le Rôle français d'un recueil de cas juridique choisis," *Revue internationale de l'enseignement* 78 (1924): 336–40.

17 Henri Lévy-Ullmann, "Comment un Français d'aujourd'hui peut-il aborder l'étude du droit anglais?," *Bulletin de la Société de Législation Comparée* 48, no. 1 (1919): 97.

18 With respect to Édouard Lambert, see Carlos Petit, "Lambert en La Tour Eiffel, o el derecho comparado della Belle Epoque," in *La Comparazione giuridica tra Ottocento e Novecento. In memoria di Mario Rotondi*, ed. Antonio Padoa-Schioppa (Milano: Istituto Lombardo di Scienze e Lettere, 2001), 53–98. On the correspondence between Lambert and Pound, see Carlos Petit, "Harvard en Lyon: Lecturas

de Roscoe Pound en el Institut de Lambert," in *Temas de Filosofia del derecho*, ed. Andrès Botero Bernal and Sergio Ivan Estrada Velez, 503–54 (Medellin: Editorial Universidad de Medellin, 2003).

19 Josef Redlich, *The Common Law and the Case Method in American University Law Schools: A Report to the Carnegie Foundation for the Advancement of Teaching* (Boston: Merrymount Press, 1914). This report, prepared by a law professor in Vienna, was probably influential on Continental lawyers' conceptions of the case method.

20 Édouard Lambert, *L'enseignement du droit comparé. Sa coopération au rapprochement de la jurisprudence française et de la jurisprudence anglo-américaine* (Lyon: A. Rey and Paris: A. Rousseau, 1919), 79–80.

21 Pierre Lepaulle, "Le système du Case et la méthode socratique dans les écoles de droit américaines," *Revue internationale de l'enseignement* 74 (1920):161–83.

22 Ferdinand Larnaude, "Les Garanties judiciaires qui existent dans certains pays au profit des particuliers contre les actes du pouvoir législatif," *Bulletin de la Société de Législation comparée* 31, no. 3 (1902): 204.

23 Lepaulle, "Le système du Case," 161.

24 Édouard Lambert, *Le Gouvernement des juges aux États-Unis*, 24.

25 Robert Valeur, *L'Enseignement du droit en France et aux États-Unis* (Paris: Giard, 1928), 185.

26 Ibid., 213–16.

27 Ibid., 311–14.

28 Ibid., xxiv–xvii.

29 Henri Capitant, *Espèces choisies empruntées à la jurisprudence* (Paris: Dalloz, 1924).

30 Édouard Lambert, "Le Rôle français d'un recueil de cas juridiques choisis," *Revue internationale de l'enseignement* 78 (1924): 336–40.

31 Édouard Lambert, "The Case Method in Canada and the Possibilities of Its Adaptation to the Civil Law," *Yale L Journal* 39, no. 1 (1929): 1–21.

32 Jacques Lambert, *Les Year Books de langue française* (Paris: Sirey, 1928).

33 Pierre Lepaulle, "L'Ecole de droit de Harvard et ses initiatives," in *Harvard et la France, Revue d'histoire moderne* (Paris: Presses Universitaires de France, 1936), 136.

34 Albert Brunois, "Obituary of Pierre Lepaulle," *Revue internationale de droit compare* 31, no. 3 (1979): 652–53, is also silent about what was more than a detail: Lepaulle wrote his French thesis with Lévy-Ullmann, and the French professor was probably upset by his student's anti-Semitic discourses during the Vichy régime.

35 *Columbia University Bulletin of Information* (1940): 96.

36 Jean-Louis Halpérin, "V° David René," in *Dictionnaire historique des juristes français XII*[e]*-XX*[e] *siècle*, ed. Patrick Arabeyre, Jean-Louis Halpérin, and Jacques Krynen (Paris: PUF, 2015), 307–08.

37 René David, *Introduction au droit des États-Unis*, (Paris: Cours de droit, 1952), 102–14.

38 Henri Mazeaud, *Guide des conférences et exercices pratiques pour la licence en droit* (Paris: Sirey, 1941).
39 André Tunc and Suzanne Tunc, *Le Droit des États-Unis d'Amérique: sources et techniques* (Paris: Dalloz, 1955), 318–21.
40 André Tunc, "Méthodes actuelles de l'enseignement du droit," in *Travaux de l'Institut de droit comparé de l'Université de Paris* (Paris: Sirey, 1959), 247–58.
41 Laurent Cohen-Tanugi, *Le Droit sans l'État. Sur la Démocratie en France et en Amérique* (Paris: PUF, 1985).
42 Christophe Jamin, *La Cuisine du droit* (Paris: Lextenso, 2012), 206–07.
43 Emilie Biland and Liora Israël, "À l'école du droit: les apports de la méthode ethnographique à l'analyse de la formation juridique," *Les Cahiers du Droit* 52, no. 3–4 (2011): 619–58; Liora Israël and Rachel Vanneuville, "Enquêter sur la formation au droit en France," *Revue interdisciplinaire d'études juridiques* 72, no. 1 (2014): 141–62.

12

American Moment(s)

When, How, and Why Did Israeli Law Faculties Come to Resemble Elite US Law Schools?

PNINA LAHAV

Today, Israeli law faculties bear many similarities to their US counterparts. This has not always been the case. As late as 1982, a short article by Joshua Weisman, who was dean of the Hebrew University Faculty of Law at the time, titled "On the Teaching of Law in the United States and in Israel" called to halt the process of Americanization before it became too late.[1] The article warned that "the exposure of law professors in Israel to the conventional methods of legal education in American law schools carries the risk that the teacher who returns to Israel will teach what he has learnt and not what students should study."[2] Let me dwell briefly on this statement. Weisman, an eminent scholar of property law, plainly could not anticipate the Israeli network of law professors that is currently expanding in the United States. He was addressing the then-novel phenomenon that he found worrisome: Israeli graduates who studied in the United States, returned to Israel, and enthusiastically imported American methods. The problem was discussed in the halls of the law school for some time and appeared to be sufficiently insignificant to justify a call to nip it in the bud. I shall return to the methods Weisman rejected, but for now all I wish to record is the moment of open resistance as captured by Weisman's warning. Weisman was speaking for many who disapproved of the American influence on Israeli legal education, believing that the American model was unfit for Israel.

The trend Weisman was hoping to reverse began in the late 1960s, at around the same time as the 1967 war launched a new phase in Israeli history.[3] By sheer coincidence, two rising stars at the Hebrew University Law School were spending their sabbatical year at Harvard Law School during the 1966/67 school year. They returned ready to introduce reforms in legal education at exactly the time that Israel was beginning to reckon with the stunning results of the 1967 war. These were Aharon Barak and Itzhak Zamir.[4] Barak, then thirty, had completed his Ph.D. under professor Gad Tedeschi at Hebrew University. Zamir, then thirty-six, had completed his Ph.D. at the University of London. In time, the two would rise to become justices of the Supreme Court of Israel. Barak gained worldwide recognition for his judicial opinions in the field of political and civil rights, human dignity, and the legal techniques of balancing and proportionality. At Harvard Law School, the two friends—still unknown to the American legal academy—took the school's groundbreaking course on legal process, as well as a course on American legal education. Both presented a different approach to legal thought and legal education. The legal process course, taught by professors Henry M. Hart Jr. and Albert M. Sacks, introduced them to a radically different way of thinking about the law. Instead of the positivist model that dominated their legal education in Israel, they encountered a jurisprudence that viewed precedent and statutory text as only two components among many in the craft of legal praxis.[5] Professor David Cavers's course on legal education introduced them to the building blocks of legal education (reviewed below), as well as to the significance of interdisciplinary study for legal thought.[6]

Barak and Zamir found these courses eye-opening. Upon returning to Jerusalem, they initiated reforms in their law school according to the American model. This was the foundational American moment when seeds of American influence were planted on Israel's legal soil. The implantation did not proceed smoothly and invited skepticism and resistance, but the seeds were germinating. It is safe to say that the close interaction between American and Israeli legal education today can and should be traced to 1967.

Periodization: The History of American Influence on the Israeli Legal Education

From the perspective of periodization, the American influence on Israeli legal education can be captured by four dates along a continuum: 1967—beginnings; 1982—resistance; 1990s—invigoration and acceleration; and 2008—consolidation.[7] Naturally, the conventional caveat should apply: Nothing happened overnight; neither did everything take place on a particular date or year. The process was slow and consisted of small, incremental steps. Only in hindsight do these dates assume any critical significance.[8]

Neither is it the case that American legal education was transplanted wholesale. Much of Israeli legal education is authentic and specific to Israel—for example, the growing role of Jewish law.[9] The influence of substantive English and continental European law has been and is still visible.[10] But significant structural changes were applied through these American moments, and they sent the Israeli law school on a different path.[11] This historical trajectory also justifies the focus of this chapter on the first two law faculties in Israel, which to this day are considered leaders of the pack: the faculty of law at Hebrew University in Jerusalem, and the faculty of law at Tel Aviv University.

Certainly, American influence over Israel's legal system did not begin in the late 1960s. As Assaf Likhovski has shown, a program of collaboration between Israel and Harvard Law School began as early as 1950.[12] Prominent founders of the Israeli legal community obtained their legal education in the United States. For example, Chief Justice Simon Agranat graduated from the University of Chicago School of Law in 1928, just before embarking on a ship to Palestine. Agranat served as professor of criminal law at the law school in Jerusalem from the early 1950s to the mid-1960s, and his approach to criminal law bore the marks of his American legal education.[13]

The late 1960s saw not only the return of Barak and Zamir from Harvard Law School but also the establishment of the law school at Tel Aviv University. Until the 1966/67 school year, the Tel Aviv faculty of law was formally a "branch" of Hebrew University's faculty of law, and many teachers were members of both faculties.[14] Gradually, both faculties considered educational reforms and looked to the United States for inspiration. Competition between the two schools helped enhance the reform.

Three major reforms, beginning at the end of the 1960s, signaled what I call the "American moment": The establishment of a student-run law review, curricular reform, and the introduction of a teaching method based primarily on the insight that good learning requires a dialogue between teachers and students.[15] A lively classroom environment based on discussion was presented as an alternative to frontal lectures. This method, in turn, invited an alternative to the method of examination. Because the classroom invited open discussion, it was reasoned, the examination should not depend on mere knowledge but rather on students' ability to analyze and apply that knowledge. Barak and Zamir, influenced by their experience at Harvard Law School, introduced the open-book examination.

The American moment is primarily the point at which these ideas were consciously put on the table. Some of the suggestions for reform, such as the establishment of a student-run law review, were relatively easily accepted, but others encountered substantial resistance. In hindsight it is evident that the American moment heralded a new era for Israeli Law Schools.

Law Reviews as Educational Tools: Mishpatim and Iyuney Mishpat

Until 1968, the Israeli legal community had two law reviews: *Ha-Praklit* and the *Israel Law Review*. *Ha-Praklit* ("The Attorney"), established in 1943, was published by the Israeli Bar Association and operated by attorneys. It published, in Hebrew, primarily short pieces on doctrinal issues and is now defunct. The *Israel Law Review*, established at Hebrew University in 1966, printed in English and was more ambitious academically. It aimed to showcase Israeli scholarship to the world and to give Israeli scholars the opportunity to publish in English and thereby meet the requirements of publication for purposes of academic promotion. It was run by senior members of the faculty at Hebrew University, peer-reviewed, and assisted by a professional editorial staff. Neither journal involved student participation.[16]

In 1968, the faculty of law at Hebrew University decided to establish a new law review that would be run by students: *Mishpatim*. This was a major step, signaling that there is (or should be) enough legal scholarship to justify a second Hebrew venue, that legal education and scholarship went hand-in-glove, that good students were (or should be) an integral part of the educational and scholarly enterprise, and that the faculty of law at Hebrew University was aspiring to resemble the model of excellence embodied by Harvard Law School.[17]

Indeed, *Mishpatim* did resemble the *Harvard Law Review*. In an interview, Barak remembered that, during his year as a visiting scholar at Harvard Law School, he visited the editorial board of the *Harvard Law Review* at Gannett House, studied their modus operandi, and consulted their bylaws. Upon returning to Israel, he proposed adopting the Harvard model. The faculty at Hebrew University, however, was skeptical of the ability of students to make serious editorial decisions, and many professors were puzzled by the wisdom of submitting their scholarship to the judgment of students. Joshua Weisman, a young professor who followed Barak and Zamir as a visiting scholar at Harvard Law School, felt strongly that the American model was misguided. Weisman was not against a law review but felt that law students lacked the professional skills associated with editorial work. Furthermore, he worried that frequent personnel turnovers among editors would hamper accumulated professional experience. Interviewed in 2008, he felt even more confident that the professional scholar's interaction with the student editors had enough drawbacks to trump the pedagogic advantages.[18]

In 1968, however, Barak applied his formidable persuasive skills, and a student law review was launched. The best students were chosen for the editorial board and were put in charge of reviewing manuscript submissions and making decisions on publication. To alleviate the anxiety of the faculty, Barak volunteered to serve as *Mishpatim*'s first faculty adviser. As a member of that first editorial board, I recall Barak's pivotal role in guiding the students. Some of the board's meetings were held in his small apartment in Jerusalem, sometimes with his young children playing in the same living room where the meetings were held. He provided invaluable advice and certainly exerted weighty influence. In an interview, Barak remembered that he personally wrote the bylaws of *Mishpatim*, hoping to secure editorial independence for the board as it was taking its first steps.

Barak viewed *Mishpatim* as an educational tool, not merely as a venue for faculty publications. The expectation was that the student-editors would develop the capacity to distinguish good from bad scholarship and that their writing skills would improve with the practice of editing. Moreover, there was a clear anticipation that students themselves would make an effort to publish. Barak never tired of repeating that publishing a law review note was the best way to launch a scholarly career.[19]

To ensure autonomy, the law review was registered as an independent company with shares going to the dean, to two senior student-editors, and to the Center for Legislative Studies.[20] Indeed, within a very short time the student-editors did develop considerable independence. The number of rejections of manuscripts was reasonably high. In one case, a lecture submitted by the retired chief justice Simon Agranat was rejected as "unfit for publication in a journal oriented towards a 'professional-legal audience'" (the quotation marks appeared in the original). A handwritten note from the faculty adviser to the dean said: "I am very sorry about this development. I tried to prevent it but my arguments fell on deaf ears."[21] Despite the apparent discomfort with the editors' decision, the freedom of editorial discretion was honored, and evidently this by itself had an impact on the students' confidence. A report to Dean Weisman in 1982 recommended keeping the law review "as a separate and independent entity in order to preserve its autonomy."[22] Despite his reservations, Weisman endorsed the report. This aspect of transplantation was surely successful.[23]

Tel Aviv followed suit two years later. Amos Shapira, a young lecturer intensely interested in legal education, first encountered the institution of the law review at Columbia Law School in 1962. Shapira was very impressed by the law review as an educational tool. He was so captivated by the idea of students integrated into the process of critical editing that he decided to write a seminar paper about it.[24]

Tel Aviv's decision to establish its own law review was more circumspect than Jerusalem's. The faculty did not trust the ability of its students to do the job independently and preferred a more structured supervision.[25] The Tel Aviv law review, *Iyuney Mishpat*, vested the editorial authority in a joint professor/student team. Interestingly, the professor who launched the Tel Aviv law review had little American experience. Professor and district court judge Ze'ev Zeltner, whose legal background was German, was designated editor in chief, and Nili Cohen, then a fourth-year student and later a senior professor at Tel Aviv, served as coeditor.[26] However, there was no torrent of scholarship awaiting consideration, and both law reviews had to work hard to solicit meritorious publications.[27]

Curricular Reform: From Mandatory to Elective Menus

The second major innovation expanding the influence of the American model was curricular reform. Until 1948, there were two law schools in Palestine: the Palestine Law Classes in Jerusalem, and the Higher School of Law and Economics in Tel Aviv. Following the establishment of the State of Israel, the Palestine Law Classes closed, and Hebrew University established a faculty of law.[28] While this new faculty struggled to display its academics as distinct from professional credentials, it also portrayed the Tel Aviv School of Law and Economics as not sufficiently academic, and that school eventually closed.

Unlike the United States and to this day, Israeli legal education confers an undergraduate degree (an LLB) on its graduates. Most students enroll following military service, equipped with some real-life experience but with only a high-school diploma.[29] The curriculum, therefore, had to confront a problem not present in the American context: the lack of undergraduate education among the majority of the student population.

The European curriculum provided an answer to this dilemma. It was based on a linear pedagogic conception, where students first received general knowledge through introductory courses, such as "Introduction to the Theory of Law," and only later were exposed to the "bread and butter" legal subject matters, such as contracts and torts.[30] In the European tradition, the senior professors behaved as if they were monarchs of their fields, and those lower on the hierarchy depended on professors' goodwill for career development. Both universities began to contemplate reform in the late 1960s, when this monopoly of the senior professors over their respective fields slowly faded. Thus, curricular reform reflected not only American influence but also a generational shift. The retirement, or impending retirement, of the old guard opened a window to change and innovation inspired by the American model.[31]

Because Tel Aviv University as an institution was comparatively new, it is reasonable to expect that it was less encumbered by institutional tradition and more open to reform. Amnon Rubinstein, then dean at the newly independent faculty of law at Tel Aviv,[32] found the American way attractive, even though (or perhaps because) he himself was a graduate of the London School of Economics. In an interview, he recalled studying the curricula of the major American law schools while contemplating reform. His agenda was revolutionary: fewer mandatory courses and more electives. Rubinstein was a dynamic dean, eager to lead his young faculty into the modern age. He also enjoyed the advantage that most (not all) of the older guard on the Tel Aviv's faculty of law were full-time practitioners who were not too involved in academic affairs and, therefore, were less motivated to fight the "Young Turks."[33]

From the 1970s to the 1990s, both faculties introduced curricular reform. Several introductory courses were eliminated or became electives, substantive courses such as criminal law and contract law moved into the first year, and electives and seminars were added. The requirement of moot court coupled with instruction on legal argumentation was added.[34] It appears that Tel Aviv pioneered curricular reform and that Jerusalem lagged a bit behind.[35] Uriel Procaccia, appointed dean in Jerusalem in 1990, remembered that the resistance of the senior members of the faculty centered particularly on the fact that the reforms would turn their courses into electives. They feared (rightly) that their courses would lose some of the prestige emanating from the core curriculum. Proccacia recalled that his offer to turn his own course, corporations, into an elective served as an incentive to accept the new plan.

There was no blind imitation of the American model in these reforms.[36] For example, courses such as Property Law and Civil Procedure, which are mandatory in the first-year curriculum of the American law school, did not enter during the first year of the Israeli law school.[37] Also, both Israeli faculties retained a component of liberal arts education in the first-year curriculum. However, the idea of exposing students to substantive law and the emphasis on electives were certainly American.

Teaching Method: From Frontal Lectures to Class Discussion

The third and most contentious innovation was the introduction of a model resembling the Socratic method. Throughout the 1950s and 1960s, the conventional teaching method was frontal lecturing, also known as lectures *ex cathedra*.[38] The professor would generally dictate a lecture that students would diligently write into their notebooks. Only rarely were students invited to question the transmitted knowledge. If someone did raise a question, the answer was usually brief and authoritative. There were no office hours, and face-to-face contact between professors and students was minimal. Professors considered the body of knowledge they were imparting to be fixed and therefore barely changed their lectures from year to year.[39] Professors did recommend a short bibliography but rarely required any reading prior to class. However, the required courses also came with sections attached to them (*Targilim*, or "discussion groups") where attendance could be mandatory (depending on the discretion of the instructor) and where cases were required reading. There were no casebooks or mimeographed materials, and students were expected to read the cases in the library. The sections mostly consisted of dull rehearsals of the facts contained in those cases with some attention to the *ratio decidendi* (holding).[40] A culture developed whereby students did not attend classes but relied on mimeographed materials, which were either sold or passed along. Sometimes a particularly bright or entrepreneurial student would gather the professor's notes and publish them with the university's Students' Publishing House (*Akademon*). In 1956, the young student Aharon Barak published his notes from Gad Tedeschi's course "Introduction to the Theory of Law."[41]

Evidently, it takes one very versed in the old system to understand its limitations. Barak was a gifted teacher, and his experience at Harvard Law School motivated him to adopt a different mode of instruction. Upon returning to Jerusalem, he began to invite a class dialogue. He welcomed and encouraged student participation. These classes were not the typical Socratic method as immortalized by the character Professor Kingsfield in the film *The Paper Chase*. Barak was warm and gentle, and his demeanor always reflected love of knowledge and immense curiosity. Questions were probed in the true spirit of deepening understanding.[42] In the fall of 1967, for the first time, Barak taught a course in tort law (until then the subject was a part of a course known as "obligations," where contracts and torts were taught back to back, as is the custom in continental Europe). To lead his section, Barak chose David Kretzmer, one of his most brilliant graduate students on the faculty, who later distinguished himself as an eminent authority on international law and a leading professor at Hebrew University. Kretzmer's method of instruction fit Barak's style hand-in-glove. Kretzmer distributed sheets with legal problems, required prior reading, and in the classroom proceeded to dissect the problems instead of rehearsing the reading materials.

I have always assumed that the "problem method" of legal instruction was another innovation imported from Harvard Law School by Barak. But I was wrong. The young Kretzmer was unaware of the American pedigree of his method. He borrowed the approach from the property law professor Joshua Weisman. Weisman, a graduate of the second class of the faculty of law at Hebrew University, obtained his Ph.D. from Hebrew University.[43] In an interview, Weisman recalled how he conceived the problem method. Unhappy with the frontal lecture, he searched for ways to enliven the class and encourage analytical thinking. He did not wish to discuss what courts had already resolved but rather to apply legal knowledge to hypothetical problems. Weisman recalled being surprised to realize, upon arriving at Harvard Law School on the heels of Barak and Zamir in the fall of 1967, that the problem method was being implemented there as well.[44] This point deserves emphasis. No one will deny that the American teaching method had a significant influence on Israel. Still, not everything that looks similar, or even identical, was intentionally imported.

At Tel Aviv, the younger faculty was also eager to introduce new teaching techniques. Amnon Rubinstein recalled that while serving as dean he was keen on class discussion and encouraged his colleagues to follow suit.[45] The spirit of reform was in the air and itself became the subject of scholarship.

In 1972, Amos Shapira published an article titled "Changing Patterns in Legal Education in Israel."[46] Shapira was enthusiastically reporting to the world, in English, that Tel Aviv was engaged in curricular reforms, and he called for these reforms to be "coupled with effective teaching." Shapira's description of the ideal method of teaching reflects both the dream and the reality of legal education at both Jerusalem and Tel Aviv at the time: effective teaching "would mean, first and foremost, relinquishing the formal lecture ex cathedra as the principal method of instruction. Lecturing should be replaced by dialogue, by group discussion, by a process of give and take shared by teachers and students. . . . Mechanical note-taking and memorizing should give way to independent thinking and a critical approach."[47] At the time of Shapira's writing, only very few professors introduced class discussions, but he believed he was observing a trend.

The debate continued. To avoid discord, the faculties adopted a variation of Chairman Mao's slogan "let a thousand flowers bloom."[48] The various teaching methods have coexisted since. It is quite reasonable to assume, on the basis of recollections by interviewed faculty members, that the frontal lecture remained predominant, yet pockets of innovation kept growing. New faculty appointments, persons who returned with an SJD or faculty members who visited the United States for extended periods of time experimented with more dynamic teaching methods, adjusting them to the prevailing practice and thereby changing the practice itself.

Resistance, Intimate Links between Teaching, and Legal Thought Exposed

In 1982, this "live and let live" approach was publicly challenged when Joshua Weisman, then dean of the Faculty of Law in Jerusalem, delivered his attack, already mentioned above:

> The exposure of law professors in Israel to the conventional pedagogic approach in law schools in the United States harbors a risk that upon returning to Israel the professor will teach his students what he has studied, not what they should learn.[49]

The reader may remember that it was Weisman himself who had developed the problem method, unaware that it was being developed in the United States at approximately the same time. Evidently, his arrow was not targeted at the problem method. Weisman distinguished between two approaches to legal education: one was technical, doctrinal, and cabined within the four corners of the law as traditionally conceived. Its rival was a discussion based on "broad policy considerations," a discussion that investigated the general principles underlying the technical legal problem and ways to resolve the deeper problems presented by these legal problems. It is safe to say that Weisman was advocating a pedagogic method that would give center stage to arguments internal to the law. In his opening remarks in the article, Weisman conceded that the policy method—allowing external factors to be weighed—was more interesting and appealing to students, but he insisted that professionalism and precision were thereby compromised or even lost.

Weisman did his homework. He put together a list of eight factors distinguishing Israel from the United States that militated against the "policy-oriented" method of deliberation in the law school classroom.[50] Of these eight, I shall focus on the first, which I intuit was also the most important and where the attack on the policy-oriented method is clearest. Weisman contended that in the United States the presence of the written Constitution was critical. Legal professionals were required to evaluate the validity of legislation under the Constitution and consequently had to take into consideration the broad principles embedded in the fundamental document. By contrast, Israel had no constitution, parliament was supreme, and its legal professionals were concerned merely with legislative acts. In the United States, a legal professional would ask, "Does the particular legislative act fit the general principles embedded in the Constitution?" In Israel, professionals only asked, "What does the statute say?" While advocating caution, and while also conceding that policy considerations should occasionally enter the classroom, Weisman was delivering an attack on US legal education as he had experienced it in the 1980s. His eight factors only sharpened the differences between Israel and the United States and therefore underscored the need to chill the reception of American influence on the law faculties.

The key to understanding Weisman's objection is his strategy in framing his question. Weisman framed the difference between the two legal systems in terms of the tasks facing each legal community. Are the tasks of both communities similar? he asked. He answered that they were not.[51] Israelis were charged with merely interpreting legislative acts, whereas Americans had to consider the impact that the United States Constitution has on them. This way of framing the difference allowed Weisman to divert attention from the deeper question: the meaning of law.

Understood in this way, Weisman's attack was not really on the American teaching style but instead on contemporary American legal thought. It was a plea to retain law as a closed system of rules and to restrict discussion to the internal legal arguments, rather than shifting the understanding to law as a social system that reflects and interacts with other social systems. It is here that the connection between teaching methods and scholarship is most evident. Legal scholarship depends on whether one believes law to be a closed or open-ended system. Hidden inside the message that law should be taught as a closed and technical system was also a subtext that true scholarship was the scholarship of "pure law."

In 1982, Weisman was making a heroic effort to clip the wings of a bird that was already airborne. However, a decade before Weisman suggested that there was a distinction between public law and private law, and that private law should be taught as a closed system of rules, Amos Shapira already protested that such an approach was ill-advised:

> It is meaningless . . . to examine currently proposed auto compensation plans separately from economic and sociological questions, such as: how the substitution of fault as a criterion of liability by a principle of strict liability (linked to an insurance scheme of one sort of another) is likely to affect the car industry? The development of new and better safety devices? The number and severity of car accidents? The propensity of drivers and pedestrians to behave more—or less—prudently? The profits of the insurance industry? The caseload of trial courts? The business of the legal profession? The claimed consciousness of accident victims?[52]

One is tempted to think that Dean Weisman was one of the last people standing trying to stop the hostile takeover or that Shapira's eloquent call for interdisciplinary study and a broad understanding of law won the day. But such was not the case.[53] Indeed, Shapira was not alone in his criticism. Dean Amnon Rubinstein at Tel Aviv was a passionate supporter of the "law and . . ." movement, as were many others. And yet Weisman represented a strong camp, skeptical of the American way and determined to underscore the fundamental differences between the Israeli and the American legal systems.

In fact, it is even arguable that Shapira himself did not march to the tune of his own pipe. In an interview, he conceded that, when he was writing in the early 1970s, he was a "true believer" and that he later changed his mind. He might have been co-opted by the predominant culture and the pressure to conform. Be that as it may, more holders of an American SJD degree were joining the ranks of Israel's law faculties, and more faculty members visited the United States and returned eager to implement change.

In 1990, the new dean of the Faculty of Law at Hebrew University, Uriel Procaccia, delivered a speech to the entering class, later published under the title "Legal Bubbles."[54] It was a bold attack—conceded to be polemical by its author—on the "pure theory of law" and included a call to adopt an interdisciplinary approach to law or, "as one of the best scholars in our generation has called it, 'law and . . . .'"[55] Procaccia specifically rejected the position taken by the old guard that law was independent of society, insisting that law was socially constructed and requiring an attention to other social disciplines, from economics (his favorite) to sociology, philosophy, and more.[56] He concluded by welcoming the entering class into the "most interesting profession in the universe, a profession that precisely because of its substantive hollowness, contains everything." Procaccia was promising the new law students a legal education that would be fascinating and exciting, not boring and dull.

What was the difference between Procaccia in the 1990s and Shapira in the 1970s? Only that Procaccia was now dean and had amassed enough support and determination to implement reform. In Tel Aviv, the younger generation was watching, eager to seize the day. Dean Ariel Rosen-Zvi, a scholar committed to innovation even though he had little exposure to the United States, encouraged a young law professor named Menachem Mautner to contribute an article on legal education to a newly established journal.[57] Mautner, a gifted teacher and scholar, accepted the invitation and elaborated on Shapira's themes. He rejected the formalistic approach, extolled the virtues of interdisciplinarity, and called for the adoption of a different paradigm of legal thought.[58] In a footnote, Mautner did mention that his senior colleagues, such as Amos Shapira at Tel Aviv and a few at Hebrew University, had advocated the same thing two decades earlier, but he did not pause to reflect on the reasons why, despite their efforts, the "formalistic" and "traditional" approaches still prevailed.[59] Rather, like Shapira two decades earlier, Mautner (who also grew to modify his position ten years later) simply announced that the "new paradigm" of interdisciplinary studies was rising.

Indeed, the new paradigm *was* growing. By now, a critical mass of young faculty members had joined the ranks, actively expecting change.

Following the publication of his article, Mautner was appointed dean of the Tel Aviv University Faculty of Law and has been credited with having consolidated the ascendance of American influence. Under his leadership, more graduates of leading American law schools were hired, more curricular reforms were introduced, and more interdisciplinary scholarship was produced. It appears that the 1990s were the time of the great leap forward, as Tel Aviv became an intellectual powerhouse on par with any elite law school in the United States.[60]

Ron Shapira, a colleague of Mautner's in the 1990s and later dean of the Bar-Ilan Faculty of Law, responded with a critique of Mautner's thesis. Ron Shapira (to be distinguished from Amos, by now on the verge of retirement) focused primarily on Mautner's article, giving it an economic spin. Behind it, he argued, was an effort by law professors to maintain a monopoly over the field of legal education at the expense of the many lawyers and judges who had thus far been an integral part of the pedagogic enterprise. Ron Shapira also defended formalist legal thought, challenging the thesis that it represented an anachronistic jurisprudence.

Even before the new paradigm advocated by Procaccia and Mautner solidified, however, it encountered opposition in the form of those anxious to maintain the old doctrinal mode of legal research.

Ron Shapira relied on United States Supreme Court Justice Antonin Scalia and Fred Schauer, both Harvard Law School graduates, to sustain his claim. Earlier in his article, he enlisted Judge Richard Posner, another Harvard Law School graduate, in support of his critique of the "policy-oriented" mode of legal analysis. Mere policy arguments, based on generalizations and unsupported by empirical verifications, he declared, were empty and barren and would confuse legal analysis.[61]

Which brings us back to Dean Weisman. It was Weisman who, in 1982, had issued the warning that Israelis should beware of importing the policy-oriented mode of legal instruction. Ron Shapira echoed Weisman and, like Mautner, did not situate the debate as a continuation of any particular Israeli historical tradition. There was, however, a glaring difference between Ron Shapira and Weisman. Weisman had argued that Israel was fundamentally different from the United States, and he painstakingly developed an eight-point list to persuade his audience that adoption of the policy-oriented pedagogy was ill-advised. By contrast,

Ron Shapira's challenge to the "new (American) paradigm" was based on the competing "old-new (American) paradigm" advanced by Antonin Scalia and Richard Posner.[62]

The debate brings us back to Dean Weisman in yet another aspect, which is important for our subject matter: the intimate link between legal education and legal scholarship. The scholar's legal thought affects her teaching method. The call for interdisciplinary study ("law and . . .") was becoming a part of Israel's legal education landscape. Ron Shapira was not calling for a return to the frontal lecture model and did not appear to be troubled by the changing structure of the Israeli law school.

From this perspective, the American moment appeared triumphant. In the twenty-first century, all the participants in the Israeli debate were Americanized.[63] As in the United States, there has been no resolution regarding the preferred legal theory. The debate as to whether law is a closed or open system will likely occupy Israelis for many years to come, just as it occupies Americans. The difference between the late 1960s and the first decades of the twenty-first century is that today both Israelis and Americans draw water from the same intellectual well. For Israeli law students, the US legal landscape is no longer terra incognita. Those who come to the United States to pursue higher study are well equipped to integrate and compete relatively easily.

All three basic features of American legal education—law reviews, curricular reforms, and a shift from frontal lectures to class discussions—have taken root in Israel. Can this turn of events be called a complete triumph of the American moment? I shall return to this question in the conclusion. For now one should recognize that, despite evidence of the predominance of the American model, Israeli legal education still appears to have retained its peculiar and authentic profile (the increasing role of Jewish law is relevant).

Context: Israel as a Willing Importer of American Influence, the United States as an Active Exporter

Up to this point, I have reviewed the migration of American legal education into Israel by focusing on a few individuals. I should add that a few women were also involved in this struggle, even though none obtained positions of formal power and influence. Frances Raday and Orit Kamir at Hebrew University, and Irit Haviv-Segal (deceased) and Leora Bilsky at Tel Aviv, were actively involved in promoting interdisciplinarity.[64] However, without the conditions to facilitate—let alone to encourage—Americanization, the process might well have failed. Below, I briefly suggest some of the external factors driving this project's success.

The Courts

The story must return to Aharon Barak, who in 1967 was eager to transform his faculty of law into an elite institution modeled after Harvard. Barak went on to serve in positions more versatile and powerful than the conventional law professor. From 1980 to 2006, he served as Israel's Attorney General and then as an associate justice, and later as chief justice, of the Supreme Court. He brought to the Court a different way of thinking about the law, as well as an interest in the relevance of American law.[65] He used such doctrines as balancing of interests and purposive interpretation in order to make Israeli decisional law less authoritarian and more liberal. Along the way, he also made it less formalistic. Utilizing two basic laws authored by Amnon Rubinstein (when Rubinstein served as a member of the Knesset), Barak launched a constitutional age in Israel. This new era invigorated the idea that Israel was not a pure majoritarian democracy but rather a polity striving to honor political and civil rights, especially those of minorities. Concepts such as freedom of expression, gender equality, gay rights, and more entered the Israeli legal discourse.[66] Judicial opinions affected scholars, teachers, and students. This was another method by which US law influenced Israeli thought.

The Legal Profession

The legal profession has also undergone considerable change. Whereas the equivalent of the American law firm—large, bureaucratized, and regimented—barely existed in Israel during the 1950s and 1960s, the 1990s saw such firms proliferate, mainly due to closer relationships with the United States and the wish to maximize profits.[67] A process of cross-fertilization has been taking place between the law schools and the legal profession to produce and facilitate this change.

The Privatization of Law Schools

In 1967, Israel had two law schools situated inside two established universities; today there are thirteen law schools, seven of which are private.[68] The idea of the private law school was pioneered simultaneously by Daniel Friedmann, who founded the School of Law at the College of Management in Rishon Le-Zion, and Uriel Reichman, who established the Interdisciplinary Center in Herzelia. Israel has seen an exponential rise in the number of law students as well as of attorneys. One reason for the growing number of law schools in Israel is the fact that the leading law faculties, particularly in Jerusalem and Tel Aviv, recognized their status as elite schools and raised the admissions requirements. For a while, an entry ticket to either school was so desirable that it became harder to gain admission to law school than to Israel's highly competitive medical schools. Students who could not meet the admissions criteria sought legal education abroad, particularly in England. The opening of more law schools diverted their tuition revenue back to Israel.[69]

The rising status of the legal profession, coupled with the increasingly privatized market in Israel, are symptoms of the watershed changes that Israel has experienced since the late 1960s and are closely tied to the American influence on Israel in general.

Globalization/Americanization

Globalization barely needs elaboration. Israel has effectively transformed itself to meet the challenges.[70] Structural economic changes as well as social and cultural modifications have swept the land and the legal community. Lawyers, according to political scientist Gad Barzilai,

> became more engaged in politics as agents of the liberal economy and have significantly contributed to the economic liberalization of the state and afterward to its interactions with the global economy. Economic privatization . . . has altered the basic relationship between state power foci and lawyers, since the liberal maze of economic transactions requires the veil of certainty that legal knowledge may provide.[71]

A correlation between these trends and the American influence on Israeli legal education appears to be strong.[72] The more Americanized and globalized Israel becomes, the more its institutions are likely to resemble American institutions.

Conclusion

In a previous version of this chapter, I suggested that perhaps the American influence on Israeli legal education has been somewhat modified by the rising influence of the European Union, and Germany in particular, on Israeli legal academia. So far, however, that turn has not come to pass. A committee convened in 2014 by the Israeli Council for Higher Education to study the condition of Israeli law schools concluded:

> Whatever the reason and whatever the extent, many Israeli academics believe that there has been an "Americanization" of Israeli legal education. The composition of this committee, with one Israeli member, one Italian member, and four US members, is consistent with this view.[73]

This situation is unlikely to change in the near future. A recent decision by the Israeli Council for Higher Education to allow instruction in English (but not in other languages) describes its goal as "improving the country's international reputation," but it also signals further leaning toward US culture.[74] The leading Israeli law schools celebrate their ties to the American law and economics movement and continue to nurture a relationship with American law schools.

Israeli legal academics continue to nurture ties with Europe, but the dominant American influence remains vibrant. At the same time, American law schools have also opened to outside influence, comparative law is no longer an exotic stranger, and US ties to European and Asian law schools are visible and active. Another factor, not to be underestimated, is the Americanization of legal education elsewhere in the world, making the American legal vocabulary a common tool of communication among scholars and members of the legal profession.[75] Only time will tell how these factors may change the face of the Israeli faculty of law.

Nevertheless, the Israeli law school increasingly acquires a distinctive authentic flavor. Israeli law schools are more open to social and ethnic diversity. The twenty-first century saw the appointment of an Israeli Palestinian as dean of the faculty of law in Jerusalem,[76] and a Palestinian woman who is an expert on Islamic law is a member of the law school in Tel Aviv.[77]

Another unique feature of the Israeli law school is religious law. Jewish law is seriously and extensively studied. At the Tel Aviv law school, the theoretical and historical foundations of Muslim law are taught by an internationally recognized scholar.[78]

An important and highly controversial proposal is to introduce gender-based segregation into the law schools, a move that reflects the rising power of traditional religion on Israeli politics and culture. At least one private Israeli law school offers gender-segregated law classes.[79] Recently, the Israeli Council for Higher Education passed a resolution permitting other universities to hold segregated classes. A petition challenging this separate-but-equal plan is pending before the High Court of Justice.[80] If indeed this process takes root, it may signal fundamental changes in the fabric of society and cast doubt on the continuing Americanization of law school culture. These are only budding developments, and their impact is yet unclear.

NOTES

This chapter was written during my fellowship with the Institute for Advanced Studies (IAS) at the Hebrew University of Jerusalem. I wish to express my gratitude to the IAS and its staff for their gracious hospitality. I also wish to thank members of the Legal History workshop at Tel Aviv University, members of the workshop at the Faculty of Law of the Netanya College, members of the workshop at Boston University School of Law, and members of my research group at the IAS for valuable comments and suggestions. I also wish to thank Olga Frishman for her research assistance and Ron Harris, Assaf Likhovski, Roy Kreitner, Leora Bilsky, Dafna Hacker, Sandy Kedar, Celia Wasserstein-Fassberg, Daphne Barak-Erez, Laura Kalman, David Sugarman, Yifat Gazit Holzman, Ori Shwartz, and Gail Hupper for their specific comments. I thank professor Ron Harris and Dean Michael Karayanni for their help in addressing their law school's current policies toward the integration of Israeli Arabs. Thanks, too, to Dean Yofi Tirosh of the Sapir College law faculty for her input. The responsibility for the contents of this chapter is mine alone. The current version of this chapter updates the information discussed herein, but it is also drastically cut, and much information has been excluded in order to make it a readable book chapter. I thank Ariela Rivkin, my research assistant at Boston University, for her expert and invaluable help in shortening the original document so that the current version meets the publisher's requests.

1 Joshua Weisman, "On the Teaching of Law in the United States and in Israel," *Mishpatim* 12 (1982): 425 (Hebrew). First published in English as part of a symposium on legal education conducted at the Tel Aviv Faculty of Law. Joshua Weisman, "The Relevance of the American Experience to Legal Education in Israel," *Tel Aviv University Studies in Law* 5 (1980–1982): 55.

2 Weisman, "On the Teaching of Law."

3 For example, Hebrew University's law faculty, located on the Givat Ram campus, spearheaded the campus's relocation to Mount Scopus, as Israel reasserted its sovereignty over the mountain and celebrated its capital's reunification. See Mordechai Kremnizer, "From the Peak of Mount Scopus," *Mishpatim* 2 (1970): 3 (Hebrew) ("the faculty of law ascended the mountain. . . . [A] project of renovation and the joy accompanying it"). US Jewry's growing interest and pride in Israeli affairs after 1967 resulted in handsome donations that facilitated academic meetings and encouraged interest in the Israeli legal academic enterprise.

4 In 1975, after a year as dean, Barak was appointed Attorney General in Yitzhak Rabin's (first) government. His decision to indict Rabin's wife for illegally holding a bank account in the United States led to Rabin's resignation. However, Barak did share Rabin's admiration for the American political system and culture. In 1978, Barak was appointed to the Supreme Court, and in 2006 he retired as its chief justice. See Nomi Levitzki, *Kvodo* (Jerusalem: Keter, 2001) (Hebrew). Zamir followed Barak to the deanship and later served as Attorney General in Menachem Begin's government. He, too, was appointed to the Supreme Court, serving between 1994 and 2001.

5 Barak, Zamir, and professor Ruth Gavison taught the legal process course together at Hebrew University in the early 1970s. On the impact of legal process thought on Israeli scholarship, see Pnina Lahav, *Judgment in Jerusalem: Chief Justice Simon Agranat and the Zionist Century* (Berkeley: University of California Press, 1995).

6 I could not locate Cavers's syllabus at Harvard Law School. His ideas are captured in his scholarship. See, e.g., "Remarks by David F. Cavers to Duke Students Concerning the Origin of and Vision for Law and Contemporary Problems," *Law & Contemporary Problems* 51 (1988): xxiii.

7 Israel's Supreme Court Justice Daphne Barak-Erez, a former law professor at Tel Aviv Law School, suggests that there were in fact two American moments. She thinks the major shift in legal education, particularly at the Tel Aviv Faculty of Law, occurred in the 1990s and should be recognized as an independent "American Moment."

8 I do not carefully trace independent developments in each of these institutions but point to major developments that occurred in one or the other. In the beginning, Jerusalem served as a model, which Tel Aviv sought both to emulate and deviate from to emphasize its separate identity. This chapter is based mainly on printed articles and interviews and includes some study of internal protocols. A more intensive study awaits another work.

9 The old Israeli guard was European-oriented and uncomfortable with the "spirit of the 1960s," which it identified with American culture. Of course, the spirit of the 1960s was not exclusively American, even though the civil rights movement, the antiwar movement, and the feminist movement were particularly American.

10 For an interesting analysis of the various schools of legal thought, including documentation of the Israeli contribution within each school, see Gad Barzilai, "The King Is Not Naked—Why Law Is Political," *Din U-Dvarim* 4 (2008): 1 (Hebrew).

11 There has been an American presence in Israeli higher education from the very beginnings of the Hebrew University of Jerusalem in the 1920s. See, e.g., Walter Ackerman, "The Americanization of Israeli Education," *Israel Studies* 5 (2000): 228, 235 (reviewing the influence of John Dewey's work on Israeli educators and stating that "several generations of curriculum workers and students in Israel have been taught a conception of curriculum—and, by extension, of teaching and other aspects of schooling—which is peculiarly American"). Similarly, the Department of Economics at Hebrew University had a strong American presence since the late 1940s, due primarily, but not exclusively, to the fact that Don Patinkin, a graduate of the University of Chicago, served as its energetic and influential dean. See Nachum Gross, "'Economics' at the Hebrew University before the 'Patinkin Age'" (Maurice Falk Institute for Economic Research in Israel, Discussion Paper No. 00.05, 2000); and Nachum Gross, "The Department of Economics at the Hebrew University during the 1950s" (Maurice Falk Institute for Economic Research in Israel, Discussion Paper No. 04.06, 2006). I thank Ephraim Kleiman for directing me to these materials.

12 See Assaf Likhovski, "Argonauts of the Eastern Mediterranean: Legal Transplants and Signaling," *Theoretical Inquiries in Law* 10 (2009): 619. Also, in 1958, an International Lawyers Convention was held in Israel, and Harvard law professor David Cavers was a guest of honor. Ibid., 641.

13 He taught scores of students, including Barak and Zamir. Another example is Justice Shneur Zalman Cheshin, a founding father of Israel's Supreme Court, who received his law degree at New York University School of Law.

14 The current building serving as a home to the faculty was the first on the Tel Aviv campus. Originally it was home to the Higher School for Law and Economics in Tel Aviv, which was closed down to give way to the "branch." See Assaf Likhovski, "Legal Education in Mandatory Palestine," *Iyuney Mishpat* 25 (2001): 291 (Hebrew).

15 Olga Frishman, "Curricular Trends in Law Schools—The Case of Tel Aviv University" (unpublished seminar paper, Tel Aviv University, on file with author, 2007) (Hebrew). This seminar paper is based on faculty protocols and is recommended for a study of the period. I thank Ron Harris for bringing this paper to my attention and Olga Frishman for sharing it with me.

16 There was very little interest in Israeli law outside of Israel throughout the 1950s and 1960s, and US and UK law reviews rarely accepted Israeli scholarship. Because Israeli scholars were required to publish in English for promotional reasons,

they felt obliged to publish either comparative pieces (of little interest at the time) or scholarship related to either American law or the common law. It could also be that the American editorial boards of students did not recognize the Israeli scholars and therefore were less likely to have incentive to publish their work. Note, also, the decision to publish in English, signaling anticipation of dialogue with English-speaking countries.

17 In his foreword to the first issue, Dean Reuven Yaron stated that *Mishpatim*'s main purpose was "to serve as an important educational tool, first and foremost to the best students who are its editors, and beyond them to the many who will use it as a venue to publish their scholarship." Reuven Yaron, foreword to *Mishpatim* 1 (1958): 3 (Hebrew).

18 Weisman conceded that a student-run law review had its advantages. However, his experience has been that each submission to the law review leads to scholars writing a second "article" in response to the editors' feedback, elaborating reasons why their feedback reflects lack of sufficient understanding of the field. Joshua Weisman, interview with the author, Jerusalem, April 10, 2008. (Relevant interviews were conducted in 2008, the year the author worked on this project; this chapter is a rendition of an article from that period.) Criticism of student editors judging scholarship that they lack the skills to evaluate is widespread in the United States as well. In his foreword to the first volume of *Mishpatim*, Dean Yaron responded to this reservation: "The frequent change of editors will prevent sinking into the conventional and will promise a fresh approach that does not hesitate to introduce necessary and useful reforms." Yaron, foreword at 3.

19 Aharon Barak, interview with the author, Herzlia, March 13, 2008. From a report to the university comptroller: "The journal *Mishpatim* is published by a registered company . . . [and] the university established a special fund to support the expenses involved in publication." Report to University Comptroller, April 1, 1982, box 35/1, MP/3877, Hebrew University Faculty of Law Archive.

20 *Mishpatim*'s first issue contained eight student notes.

21 Letter from editors Tal Band and Shirley Renner to Chief Justice Agranat, October 28, 1983; undated handwritten note on the letter from faculty adviser Uriel Procaccia to Dean Weisman, box 35/1, Hebrew University Faculty of Law Archive.

22 A 1978 report to the dean states that of twenty-six submissions, sixteen were accepted, seven were rejected, and three were pending: box 35/1, Hebrew University Faculty of Law Archive.

23 Report to Dean Weisman, May 17, 1982, box 35/1, Hebrew University Faculty of Law Archive.

24 "I was an uncritical fan," Amos Shapira remembered in an interview. Shapira obtained his SJD from Yale Law School, working with Ronald Dworkin, Guido Calabresi, and Leon Lipson. Earlier, Shapira received an MCL (Master in Comparative Law) from Columbia University School of Law. Upon return he never tired of talking about the "way we do things at Columbia." Amos Shapira, interview with the author, Tel Aviv, April 13, 2008. Michael Riesman joined the Yale Law School

faculty. Arie David was a member of the faculty of law at the Hebrew University and returned to the United States. Yuval Levy founded a prosperous law firm in Tel Aviv but continued teaching.

25 As some of my interviewees indicated, perhaps the level of the average Tel Aviv law student in the early 1970s (but not today) was lower than that of the average student in Jerusalem.

26 Cohen pursued her PhD at Tel Aviv University, then spent a postdoctoral year at the University of Pennsylvania School of Law. Nili Cohen, interview with the author, Tel Aviv, March 3, 2008. Following her retirement, Cohen was appointed president of the prestigious Academy of Sciences and Humanities.

27 The Tel Aviv faculty went through a series of experiments concerning the editorial board's composition. It started with a joint faculty/student team, then changed into a system where the teacher was the editor and the students were "vice editors." Later, a member of the faculty served as the editor in chief, and an editorial board of students worked under their authority. Nili Cohen, "Iyuney Mishpat Is Thirty Years Old," *Iyuney Mishpat* 30 (2008): 5 (Hebrew).

28 The Hebrew University had already offered a program in legal studies concentrating on Jewish Law and International Law.

29 See Uri Cohen, *Ha-Har Ve-Ha-Giva* [The Mountain and the Hill] (Tel Aviv: Am Oved, 2007) (Hebrew); and Nathan Feinberg, *Reminiscence 144* (Jerusalem: Sifrey Mabat, 1985) (Hebrew). Feinberg was the Hebrew University law faculty's first dean.

30 Israeli students are more mature than American law students, due to their military experience, but are less roundly educated because they lack education to the liberal arts.

31 See Asher D. Grunis, "Legal Education in Israel: The Experience of Tel-Aviv Law School," *Journal of Legal Education* 27 (1975): 203 (providing a historical overview and a comparison of the curricula at Jerusalem and Tel Aviv).

32 Amnon Rubinstein, interview with the author, Herzlia, April 13, 2008. Rubinstein studied law and economics at the Hebrew University and expressed admiration for the rigorous and interactive pedagogy of the faculty of economics. The faculty of economics, the reader should recall, was formed and led by a graduate of the University of Chicago. In the Tel Aviv Faculty of Law archives, attached to the report on curricular reform there is a collection of documents from the law schools at the Universities of California (Berkeley), Stanford, Pennsylvania, Virginia, Chicago, George Washington, Illinois, and Wisconsin. Curiously, the curricula of the Harvard and Yale law schools do not appear in this collection. This may be an archival omission or based on the familiarity of the reformers with these curricula. At the Hebrew University the reform was less extensive. See note 12.

33 Rubinstein was also a public intellectual and soon established a political party. His public profile appealed to students who were attracted to law's connection with politics. Rubinstein's retirement may have left the Tel Aviv law school to the influence of the continental European tradition and stymied the process of Ameri-

canization, but not before he had instituted significant reform, as documented by Grunis, "Legal Education in Israel."

34 Frishman, "Curricular Trends in Law Schools," 18–20, 31.

35 Professor Procaccia, email to the author, June 18, 2008. In addition to curricular reform, Procaccia also introduced a grading reform and integrated the idea of commitment to the public interest as a part of legal education. Procaccia observed a connection between these reforms and the slow shift from formalist scholarship to a recognition that "black-letter law erudition is not at the heart of our project." Procaccia also presented himself as "exhibit A" of the changes that Israeli legal scholars had undergone since the 1970s. As a young lecturer in the early 1970s, he recalled, he was not aware that there were other ways of thinking about the law (despite his graduate work at the law school of the University of Pennsylvania). When he embarked on a joint research project with David Kretzmer (then a young lecturer, the only person on the faculty familiar with theories of law and economics), he heard Kretzmer announce that a particular legal rule was not "efficient." Procaccia remembered being startled by this characterization, as he did not know how efficiency was relevant to the legal analysis at hand. Thereafter, Procaccia studied economics at the Hebrew University, published scholarship within this discipline, and founded the field of law and economics in Israel. (Kretzmer, an expert on a number of legal fields, went on to establish himself as a renowned authority on international law and human rights.) Proccacia's influence may explain the fact that today the faculty of law in Jerusalem is particularly strong in analytical jurisprudence and law and economics. The component of analytical jurisprudence, clearly an English (Oxfordian) legacy, represented by such luminaries as Ruth Gavison, Hanina Ben-Menachem, and Alon Harel (it should be added that Oxford-based philosopher Joseph Raz, an international authority on jurisprudence, is a graduate of the Hebrew University Faculty of Law and taught there briefly as a young lecturer in the late 1960s), may have contributed to the antipathy to "law and . . ." courses at the Hebrew University during the 1970s and 1980s.

36 One interesting difference is the focus on comparative law. Comparative law has been a central aspect of Israeli legal education and scholarship long before it was discovered in the United States. For a thoughtful analysis, see Ron Harris, "Rethinking the Rationale for Teaching Comparative Law in Israel," *Iyuney Mishpat* 25 (2001): 443 (Hebrew).

37 The field of civil procedure is an interesting example of the differences that separate the Israeli and US models. Federalism makes the teaching of civil procedure in the first year an important part of students' introduction to the distinction between federal and state law. This difference also appears as one of the factors Weisman listed for rejecting the American teaching method. Weisman, "On the Teaching of Law."

38 Latin for "from the chair," denoting the professor's chair, but also the authority with which the text is delivered. The term is used in Catholic theology to denote

the infallibility of the Pope. By implication, its use designates the infallibility of the professor.

39 The professors would delegate the study of new cases to the sections.

40 If professors felt they could not complete the lectures due to time constraints, they would sometimes ask the teaching assistant (the *metargel*, known in US colleges as the section leader) to shift to lecture mode. In an interview with Amos Shapira, I learned about the title *me-sha-nen*, which he thought meant "tutor." Shapira, interview. Literally, it means "repeater" or "rehearser" and conveys the emphasis of memorization. Barak did not recall this term but conceded that this was the nature of the instruction. Barak interview.

41 Gad Tedeschi, *Introduction to the Theory of Law*, comp. Aharon Barak (Jerusalem: Akademon, 1956) (Hebrew). Other examples are Shalev Ginossar, *Evidence*, comp. Eliahu Harnon (Jerusalem: Mifaal Ha-Shichpul, 1956) (Hebrew); and Shalev Ginossar, *Civil Procedure*, comp. Aharon Barak (Jerusalem: Mifaal Ha-Shichpul, 1957) (Hebrew). Generally, the professors did not oppose publication but insisted on the inclusion of the caveat that the professor had not reviewed the text.

42 David Kretzmer, interview with the author, Jerusalem, Mach 27, 2008.

43 Weisman spent a year at the London School of Economics as a doctoral student but did not recall encountering a different teaching method there.

44 Weisman recalled that students did complain bitterly about this novel teaching method, which forced them to read and prepare for class. He acquired the reputation of a "tough teacher." Weisman, interview. This was another aspect of transplantation. The topic of transplantation has grown into a serious industry since Alan Watson's seminal work *Legal Transplants: An Approach to Comparative Law* (Edinburgh: Scottish Academic Press, 1974). In this chapter I am using this term of art lightly and do not address the theoretical complexity it entails.

45 Rubinstein, interview.

46 Amos Shapira, "Changing Patterns in Legal Education in Israel," *Administrative Law Review* 24 (1972): 233; see also Grunis, "Legal Education in Israel."

47 Shapira, "Changing Patterns," 233.

48 The original Mao slogan was "let a hundred flowers bloom, let a hundred schools of thought contend." Barak and Shapira, interviews.

49 Weisman, "On the Teaching of Law." Weisman's attack was delivered the previous year (1982) at an international conference on legal education at the faculty of law at Tel Aviv University. Weisman, "The Relevance of the American Experience." At about the same time, Itzhak Englard, also of the faculty of law at the Hebrew University, denounced the Socratic method as a tool used by evil persons (he referred to the fictitious character Professor Kingsfield in *The Paper Chase*). Englard also opined that teaching methods were secondary to students' ability and motivation and mentioned the frontal lecture approvingly. Englard based his remarks on continental European sources exclusively. Itzhak Englard, "Reflections about the Faculty of Law," *Mishpatim* 12 (1982): 217 (Hebrew).

50 The other seven were, in the following order: (1) federalism, which leads to the operation of American law schools as national schools with minimal emphasis on the technical aspects of any one state's legal system; (2) codification, which is a central part of Israel's private law and requires close attention to legislation; (3) the fact that Israel requires a period of clerkship where young graduates are trained by attorneys prior to taking the bar exams (it is not clear whether this point works to support or challenge Weisman's major idea, but I shall not get into that here); (4) the fact that Israelis, unlike their American peers, come to law school with no college education and therefore are not as equipped to discuss policy issues; (5) the lack, in Israel, of textbooks and casebooks, which facilitate access to knowledge; (6) the fact that American lawyers are allowed to advertise their skills, thereby emphasizing their specialization, whereas in Israel self-advertising is prohibited and therefore the tendency to specialize is weaker; and (7) the little emphasis on comparative law in the United States, whereas Israeli legal culture tends to consult "how other countries have approached the problem." The purpose of this chapter is not to critically examine Weisman's list of factors, and therefore I do not go beyond this description. Some of the factors on his list seem to have lost their relevance.

51 In an interview, Weisman stated that this point may be obsolete, because Israel today does have a form of a constitution. Weisman, interview.

52 Shapira, "Changing Patterns," 237.

53 In fact, their disagreement reflects two stages of globalization. See Duncan Kennedy, "Two Globalizations of Law and Legal Thought: 1850–1968," *Suffolk University Law Review* 36 (2003): 631.

54 Uriel Procaccia, "Legal Bubbles," *Mishpatim 20* (1990): 9 (Hebrew).

55 Ibid., 10, 17. Procaccia relied on the seminal article by Yale Law professor Arthur Allen Leff, "Law and," *Yale Law Journal* 87 (1978): 989.

56 Procaccia, "Legal Bubbles," 11. Procaccia specifically referred to two senior professors. Avigdor Levontin and S. Z. Feller, the latter known for referring to the "law and . . ." approach as "parasitology." It could be that professor Feller's origins in communist Romania, where he taught law before arriving in Israel, made him think of law scholars drawing on other disciplines as parasites, similar to individuals exploiting other workers' labor.

57 Ariel Rosen-Zvi, a family law scholar, was an erudite and broad-minded man whose commitment to a more meaningful system of legal education and better scholarship cannot be sufficiently recorded here. His untimely death prevented him from fulfilling his potential as a leader and reformer. Menachem Mautner, "The Law School: Between the University, the Bar and the Courts," *Yearbook of Israeli Law* 1 (1992–1993) (Hebrew).

58 Ibid.

59 Ibid., 28.

60 Other energetic deans who participated in this process, from Uriel Reichman, who was dean in the 1980s (and went on to establish the formidable university

called the Interdisciplinary Center in Herzlia), to Ariel Porat, now president of Tel Aviv University, to Hanoch Dagan, who built on these changes and took the law school in new directions. See particularly the innovative graduate school developed by Dean Dagan, The Zvi Meitar Center for Advanced Legal Studies, at "Home," The Buchmann Faculty of Law, Tel Aviv University, https://en-law.tau.ac.il. As I noted earlier, some believe that there were two American moments and that the moment of the 1990s should be seen as distinct. (This idea was suggested to the author by Justice Dafna Barak Erez during a workshop on this article in 2008; see note 8.) In my view, a rejection of the origins of the American moment in the 1970s and the insistence that the 1990s were "totally new" is an example of the tension between memory and history. Mautner justly recalls the excitement and energy produced by his 1992 article, but his ability to publish in a new journal and his invitation to present the work at various legal workshops across Israel are themselves indications that legal education was following the American model, adopting such features as journals and workshops.

61 Ron Shapira, review of *On Legal Education*, by Menachem Mautner, *Iyuney Mishpat* 27 (2004): 821 (Hebrew).

62 Of course, there are fundamental differences between Scalia and Posner. Ron Shapira was relying on the similarities.

63 Still, this may not mean that the "culture of learning" in the Israeli law school mirrors the culture of learning in any elite American law school. For a devastating critique of the Israeli environment of legal learning, cowritten by eminent scholars well acquainted with the American, the European, and the Israeli legal cultures, see Joseph Weiler and Yaniv Friedman, "On the Education for Superficiality," *Iyuney Mishpat* 25 (2001): 421 (Hebrew). It appears, however, that the best and most motivated Israeli law students have internalized the American method.

64 Three of these four women taught law and feminism and contributed substantially to the development of feminism in Israel and to introducing feminist thought to students. See Leora Bilsky, "Cultural Import: The Case of Feminism in Israel," *Iyuney* 25 (2001): 523 (Hebrew). Many others followed; see, e.g., Daphne Barak-Erez (now Supreme Court justice), Daphna Hacker, and Orit Kamir.

65 Many believe that the rate of Israeli judicial reliance on US law has substantially increased in the twenty-first century. However, a statistical study conducted by Yoram Shachar and others, while conceding that the reliance on US citations has increased, still claims that the status quo has not been destabilized. The study does not distinguish between canonical and ordinary cases. See Myron Gross, Ron Harris, and Yoram Shachar, "Patterns of Citation at the Supreme Court: Quantitative Analysis," *Mishpatim* 27 (1996): 119 (Hebrew). An updated version of this work was published in *Hapraklit* 29 (2007). The update did not fundamentally change the findings of the earlier study.

66 For an exposition of Barak's judicial philosophy, see Aharon Barak, *A Judge in a Democracy* (Princeton: Princeton University Press, 2006). Israeli law students coming to the United States since the late 1980s were puzzled by the strict con-

struction and formalistic opinions emerging from the Rehnquist Court. Little did they know that what they thought of as "the different Israeli approach" was an approach characteristic of the Warren Court and the Burger Court (while Justice Brennan was its intellectual leader) in the United States during the 1960s and 1970s, an approach that migrated to Israel under Chief Justices Meir Shamgar and Aharon Barak. It should also be mentioned that Barak never gave up his academic affiliations. He visited Yale Law School regularly, where he taught and updated himself on cutting-edge scholarship. He is currently a faculty member at the Interdisciplinary Center in Herzlia.

67 Israeli law schools today not only compete for students but also strive to place their graduates with the most prestigious firms and then rely on this data to recruit more and abler students.

68 As of 2018, Israel had thirteen law schools. Four law schools at the major Israeli (State) Universities: Tel Aviv, Hebrew University in Jerusalem, Haifa University, and Bar-Ilan University. Ben-Gurion University does not have a law school. In addition, there are two state-supported law schools, one in Sapir College (serving mostly Israel's southern population) and the other in Zefat College (serving mostly the northern Israeli population). The remaining seven law schools are private: the Interdisciplinary Center in Herzlia, the College of Management in Rishon L'Zion, Shaarery Mishpat College, the College of Law and Business, Netanya Academic College, Peres Academic Center, and Ono Academic College.

69 The flood of new lawyers led the bar to forego the traditional oral examination, where passage was practically guaranteed, and introduce a more rigorous written examination.

70 In the 1950s and 1960s, the self-image of Israelis was captured by a small, cartoonish figure named "Srulik" (a nickname for Israel), a childlike, rather innocent, and vulnerable sabra. In 2004, the Israeli sociologist Oz Almog published a two-volume book titled *Farewell to Srulik*. The book's cover depicted little Srulik, still wearing sandals, but with something new printed on his shirt: an American flag. Almog was describing the process through which Israel abandoned its erstwhile socialist, idealist, and rather autonomous culture and joined the worldwide processes of Americanization and globalization. Oz Almog, *Farewell to "Srulik": Changing Values Among the Israeli Elite* (Ramat Gan: IDF Division of Education, 2004) (Hebrew).

71 Gad Barzilai, "The Ambivalent Language of Lawyers in Israel: Liberal Politics, Economic Liberalism, Silence and Dissent," in *Fighting for Political Freedom*, ed. Terence C. Halliday, Lucien Karpik, and Malcolm M. Feeley (New York: Hart Publishing, 2008), 247, 255.

72 See Kennedy, "Two Globalizations." Kennedy's stages of the globalization of law correspond to the stages described in this chapter.

73 General Report, Committee for the Evaluation of Law Studies in Israel, submitted to Israel's Council for Higher Education, 2015, Professor Ed Rock, Chair. On file with the author.

74 Shira Kaddari-Ovadya, "The Council for Higher Education Will Make It Easier to Hold English Teaching Programs in Academic Institutions," *Haaretz*, December 10, 2018, www.haaretz.co.il.

75 Hanoch Dagan, interview with the author, Tel Aviv, February 2, 2008.

76 Other faculty members are Nadera Shalhoub, Badi Siasi, and Bana Shoughry, the director of the international human rights clinic.

77 Professor Ron Harris, former dean of the Tel Aviv law faculty, interview with the author, Houston, Texas, November 2019. The low number of Palestinian students in the law faculty is related, among other factors, to the high admission requirements coupled with the fact that Palestinian high achievers tend to study computer sciences. (Dean Michael Karayanni, email to the author, January 23, 2019, on file with the author). However, canon law reflective of Greek Orthodoxy—a religion practiced by many Israeli Palestinians—is not taught. For the status of canon law in Israel, see Michael Karayanni, "Multiculturalism as Covering: On the Accommodation of Minority Religions in Israel," *American Journal of Comparative Law* 66 (2018): 831. For a critical Israeli-Palestinian analysis of legal education at Tel Aviv Law School, see Rabea Egabariah, "Arab-Palestinian Students in Israeli Law Schools: A Critical Reading of Legal Education," 9 *Tel Aviv University Journal of Law & Social Change* (*Ma'asei Mishpat*) (2017): 219 (Hebrew), and Hassan Jabareen, "Critique of Israeli Legal Education: The Central and Missing Component," 43 Iyuney Mishpat, forthcoming (Hebrew).

78 Tel Aviv University also copublishes the academic review of Jewish law, *Dine Israel*, whose coeditor is professor Suzanne Last Stone. Stone, a professor at Cardozo Law School, is an international authority on Jewish law and has often taught at both Tel Aviv and Hebrew University law schools. Professor Lana Salaymeh teaches Muslim law and is the author of *The Beginnings of Islamic Law: Late Antique Islamicate Legal Traditions* (Cambridge: Cambridge University Press, 2016).

79 "The Ultra Orthodox (Haredi) Campus," The Ono School of Law, www.ono.ac.il. Formally, law classes are taught in segregated classes.

80 "Segregated Campuses," Haredi Education, https://haredimedu.wordpress.com/english.

13

Catalytic Agents?

Lon Fuller, James Milner, and the Lawyer as Social Architect, 1950–1969

DAVID SANDOMIERSKI

With the rise of the regulatory and administrative state at the beginning of the twentieth century, legal scholars aligned with the Legal Process school eventually began experimenting with and advocating for the idea that law schools should equip students to master a range of legal processes to accomplish human purposes.[1] Lon Fuller, a canonical member of the legal process movement,[2] developed his own gloss on the importance of teaching multiple legal processes. Fuller's preoccupation with the "science, theory, or study of good order and workable social arrangements"[3] led him to articulate the lawyer's responsibility to help solve individual and social problems.[4] The lawyer would become an "architect of social structures,"[5] an expert in relating means to ends.[6] The social-architect ideal reflected Fuller's sense of the lawyer's professional responsibility to contribute to society and his view of that contribution's distinctiveness.[7]

Fuller wrote and spoke voluminously in the 1940s and 1950s on the need to reform legal education.[8] But his most powerful recommendation was to equip the lawyer as social architect to master diverse forms of social order *by providing equal emphasis on the diverse legal processes*. For Fuller, disproportionate emphasis on case law gave the inaccurate picture that law was primarily constituted by the adjudicative process.[9] This point's corollary for legal education is that the lawyer-as-problem-solver should be exposed to multiple legal processes and that overemphasis on adjudication should be avoided.

In a paper emanating from the Inter-Professions Conference on Education for Professional Responsibility in Pennsylvania in April 1948, Fuller more fully developed this idea:

> Adjudication presents the lawyer in his role as advocate, or judge, or office counselor. . . . The legislative process, on the other hand, presents the lawyer in his rule-creating, structure-giving role. It presents him as a planner, negotiator, and draftsman. . . . [L]egal education in this country has almost totally neglected the legislative process, and has dealt with only one aspect of the adjudicative process, that of our appellate courts. . . . [T]herefore, . . . we must assume a responsibility for conveying to the student an understanding of both of the basic processes with which he will be concerned as a lawyer.[10]

Fuller was a philosopher, but he was also practical.[11] While he taught the abstract ideas behind his so-called Principles of Social Order[12] in a class on jurisprudence, he did so through concrete case illustrations.[13] Fuller aimed for students to address "live facts" and to become problem-solvers.[14] In courses such as Contracts, he sought to diversify exposure to multiple legal processes, including, for example, "problems of negotiation and draftsmanship."[15]

This chapter is concerned with the legacy of Lon Fuller's idea that law schools ought to produce social architects by exposing students to a complete range of legal processes, emphasizing problem-solving and informed by his understanding of the diverse Principles of Social Order. More specifically, it details the influence that Fuller had on one Canadian: University of Toronto law professor James Bryce Milner.

Born in 1918 in Amherst, Nova Scotia, Milner studied law at Dalhousie University in Halifax, Nova Scotia (on the eastern coast of Canada), and was a member of the faculty there from 1945 to 1949.[16] In 1949–1950, he completed his LLM at Harvard, where he took jurisprudence under Lon Fuller and studied Fuller's then-recent essay, "What the Law Schools Can Contribute to the Making of Lawyers." These encounters would influence Milner and inform his writings, teaching, and other initiatives while at the University of Toronto throughout the 1950s and 1960s. Milner would attempt to transplant the Fullerian social architect seed through his teaching and writing casebooks on contracts and land planning, his leadership of the Association of Canadian Law Teachers (ACLT), and his curricular initiatives within the faculty of law. This chapter attempts to elucidate Milner's efforts, to illustrate a moment when the social-architect vision of legal education might have taken root at the University of Toronto Faculty of Law. It also demonstrates that, much like Fuller's inchoate efforts to produce a fully theorized work on the Principles of Social Order during his lifetime, Milner's Fullerian vision for legal education never did flourish during his tenure at his home university.

Milner and Fuller—an Intellectual Legacy

In the fall of 1949, James Milner studied for a one-year master of law degree at Harvard Law School.[17] He received A's in jurisprudence with Fuller and the legislation seminar with Henry Hart,[18] and both professors clearly made an impression on him. Near the end of his LLM year, he wrote to his soon-to-be dean, Caesar Wright at the University of Toronto, that he "was glad he came to Fuller for jurisprudence" and that he had "been watching Hart's mimeographed materials come out . . . with the greatest interest."[19]

At Harvard, Milner led a graduate seminar on law teaching. The seminar's first guest was Fuller, who presented "What the Law Schools Can Contribute to the Making of Lawyers" on December 5, 1949.[20] Milner wrote to the dean of Harvard Law School, Erin Griswold, at the end of the year: "We owe a particular debt to Professor Fuller, who not only started the ball rolling at the first meeting . . . but who also gave us continuous encouragement and advice throughout the year."[21]

Milner would pay this debt forward for the next two decades, all the while remaining in intermittent contact with Fuller.[22] On Fuller's and Griswold's recommendations,[23] Wright hired Milner to start teaching at the University of Toronto in September 1950. Even before he started at Toronto, Milner anticipated how his Harvard education might apply. Referring to Hart's legislation materials, he told Wright: "I can hardly wait until I can show them to John [Willis]. Hart's idea is that legislation is a fancy name for legal method. I thought I was back in jurisprudence for five weeks, then it gradually developed into statutory interpretation, where we are now."[24]

To say that "legislation is a fancy name for legal method" reflects the idea—which Milner would have encountered in Fuller's Jurisprudence course[25]—that law can be understood as multiple forms of social order, each with distinctive contributions, norms, and methods. The related idea for legal education—that students ought to be exposed to multiple legal processes in order to maximize their capacity to contribute to the attainment of human purposes—would become a pervasive theme in Milner's teaching and casebook writing upon his arrival at Toronto.

Milner's Contracts Teaching: The Fullerian Influence

Before attending Harvard, Milner had taught contracts at Dalhousie. A publication from that era reveals Milner's predisposition to a realistic approach to contract law that considers legislation's importance.[26] Fuller's influence deepened and expanded those initial inclinations. Fuller himself had significantly innovated ways to teach contracts. His seminal articles on the reliance interest broke new ground with their functional analysis, and his innovative 1947 casebook placed the study of remedies first with a similarly functional rationale.[27] A third edition of Fuller's contracts casebook sets out explicitly how contract is one among many forms of social order.[28] Milner's approach to teaching contracts would not only borrow from these innovations but also reflect other Fullerian themes of social order, human relations and purposes, and multiple legal processes.

For example, in the syllabus and supplementary material for his 1951/52 contracts class, Milner writes:

> The second purpose of the course is to give you some insight into the working of contract as a tool for advancing human relations. . . . As a lawyer your job is to know as much as possible about this process of ordering affairs, and this involves your knowing the construction of contracts and the analysis of affairs, just as much as you must understand the attitudes and approaches of courts. Emphasis will, therefore, also be placed on the planning and drafting of contracts.[29]

The idea that litigation ought not to be the sole focus of teaching contracts descends from the idea that diverse legal processes provide distinctive resources for solving human problems. The corollary is that the lawyer ought to have a diverse set of legal tools that track these processes. For example, "planning and drafting" are tools that relate to the legislative process, not the adjudicative.

Presaging an article he would write years later,[30] Milner's 1951/52 contracts syllabus lists a broad range of "procedures" illuminated by case analysis. These include "drafting suitable agreements in advance, . . . legislative correction of the 'law' and . . . negotiation, compromise and arbitration."[31] Milner also provides excerpts from Lon Fuller's *Basic Contract Law* as course readings.[32] The final examination for that year's course included a question on law reform that asked students to draft a memorandum to a law revision committee.[33] Course calendar descriptions referred to "an emphasis on planning and drafting,"[34] and exam questions in subsequent years also refer to Fuller and ask students to identify which legal processes are best equipped to achieve desired ends.[35]

Milner's Casebooks—Carrying the Fullerian Torch

Perhaps the most robust evidence of Fuller's influence on Milner's teaching of contracts is his published casebook on contracts in 1963.[36] His correspondence with others about the book reveals his concern for multiple legal processes, his affinity for the purposive and functional views of Fuller, and his understanding of the diverse and public responsibilities of the lawyer.

Early on, he sought to get information about a contracts casebook planned by Horace Read, who had developed a course in legislation at the University of Minnesota, and Milner would continue similar efforts when he became dean at Dalhousie.[37] In response to Read's statement that Read was "attempting to produce [a book] which will deal principally with the types of transaction most commonly met with today,"[38] Milner asks if he is intending a "Canadian Havighurst" and asks for a copy to see how it "fits into my own ideas."[39] When he hears nothing, he expands on his own plans in a letter to professor Gilbert R Schmitt at the University of Saskatchewan:

> To begin with Damages and other Remedies is a radical departure from tradition but I have found it exceedingly effective. I have also found that the introduction of documents and drafting problems generally are very helpful, particularly as *I like to present Contracts as an exercise in both the judicial and legislative process.*[40]

We see here three distinct Fullerian influences: the inclination to place remedies first, to focus on drafting problems, and a decentering of adjudication.

In a subsequent letter to John Smith, Milner expands: "I have set myself the impossible task of following the principles of Lon Fuller's Basic Contract Law and Harold Havighurst's casebook."[41] The references to Havighurst and Fuller are, in a sense, complementary. Like Fuller, Havighurst was iconoclastic in his organization of materials, grouping cases not according to doctrinal categories but according to their subject matter. Like Fuller, Havighurst's approach envisioned a functional and practical approach to legal education, considering "each situation as a living problem rather than as merely dead material for logical dissection"[42] and emphasizing the "part that relationship, circumstance, and custom play in molding the bargain."[43] Havighurst sought to use cases prospectively, in a way that transcended the conventional limitation of the case method.[44] His second edition in particular contained a series of counseling problems.

Milner embraced Havighurst's forward-looking problem-solving approach, which dovetails with Fuller's conception of the lawyer working prospectively to solve live problems and to fulfill human purposes. And while he was reaching out to other contracts professors to float these views, he was also developing them for an article he would ultimately publish in June 1955 for an audience of UK legal academics.

In "One Canadian View of the Case Methods," an intellectual forerunner to Milner's 1963 casebook, Milner offers a pluralistic idea of the case method as distinguished from the traditional focus on rules and judicial reasoning. His approach uses the case as "a problem of some sort, not as, or merely as, an authority." Cases raise problems across a range of multiple legal processes "in the functioning of the judicial process: in the logical analysis of precedent or in the just settlement of a dispute; in the functional interpretation or amendment of a statute; in the drafting of a clause or section for a contract or a statute; or in some or all of them."[45] Echoing Fuller's 1948 essay, Milner argues against "excessive court orientation":

> In North America . . . the student can easily get the notion that life in the law is a continuous succession of law suits. [A lawyer] will be much more

> often asked to advise on drafting contracts, wills, regulations and statutes, incorporating companies, and generally acting as a catalytic agent to the struggle of mankind to solve his social and commercial problems.[46]

His evocative language—"catalytic agent to the struggle of mankind to solve . . . social and commercial problems"—recalls Fuller's "architect of social structures." And Milner's advice on how to train such catalytic agents also echoes Fuller: "This need can be easily met by organizing the course materials around problems that involve legislative as well as adjudicative processes of law."[47]

Milner's essay concludes with a spirited, optimistic, and realistic picture of legal education: "[T]he case methods contribute most when the cases are regarded as problems in justice, as well as problems in legal and logical analyses and semantics; when positivism is substantially abandoned; and when the educational aim is to free the student for creative and imaginative thought at least as much as it is to restrict him with fixed and settled rules."[48] These are the words of someone contemplating how to put these ideals into practice, in both his teaching and in the eventual publication of his casebook.

By June 1958, when Milner delivers his Presidential Address to the eighth annual meeting of the Association of Canadian Law Teachers, Milner continues to contemplate similar themes. In this address, Milner defends university law schools' liberal aims, invoking Matthew Arnold's invitation to turn "a stream of fresh and free thought upon our stock notions and habits."[49] He states that in "every course . . . [t]he examination and re-examination of problems in the judicial and legislative processes receive lasting and recurrent attention."[50] He refers to multiple legal processes throughout.[51] He invokes the Fullerian functional emphasis on human purposes[52] and uses the Fullerian phrase "form, or principle of order" to categorize subjects of law.[53] He cites Fuller, warning his audience not to ignore "the collaborative articulation of shared purposes," and he calls attention to the limits of adjudication.[54]

After this address, progress on Milner's contracts casebook seems to slow somewhat due to his involvement in a 1960 conference with US and British law teachers (discussed below).[55] By May 1962, Milner began to work in earnest,[56] and in February 1963 he writes to Fuller asking permission to reproduce numerous writings, appending, in a handwritten postscript: "Nowhere above have I said thanks, but for many reasons my gratitude for your kindness and intellectual stimulation is inexpressible anyway."[57]

The Casebook Texts

That gratitude looms large in Milner's 1963 contracts casebook, as he reinforces in the Acknowledgments: "My great debt to Professor Lon Fuller is frequently apparent throughout the book."[58] Fuller's influence coalesces with Milner's evolving attitudes about the case method and legal education in Milner's spirited and "highly personal" Introduction.[59]

Hearkening back to his 1955 essay, Milner writes that there is "no such thing" as *the* case method: "[I]f anything, the reference should be to 'case methods,' in the plural, and you should expect to find as many methods as you have teachers."[60] Milner rejects the idea that cases are primarily important for what they "stand for."[61] Instead, he emphasizes the importance of facts, quoting (as he did in his 1955 article on case methods) the anonymous Supreme Court of Canada justice who said that "I sometimes feel that when I have mastered the facts I have done seventy-five per cent of my job."[62] He invites his students, recalling his 1958 Presidential Address, and with "apologi[es] to Matthew Arnold," to "turn a stream of fresh and free thought upon our stock notions and habits."[63] Recalling Havighurst, he writes that "a client rarely asks a lawyer what the law is . . . he asks . . . what can he do, or not do, in particular circumstances. He wants advice on how to act in a situation that presents a variety of courses of action."[64]

These opening remarks portray the lawyer as a problem-solver whose value lies in giving prospective and proactive advice. The ability to do so requires, in Fullerian language, understanding "the importance to the law of human purposes" that are "many, varied, and conflicting." The law's task, Milner writes, is to "sort . . . out" the purposes and "promote those that should be promoted and suppress those that should be suppressed." This "difficult task of selection [is] the basic problem of justice."[65]

Channeling Fuller, Milner argues that to serve the "complex purposive activity of man,"[66] lawyers must perform a diverse range of activities, "justify[ing] . . . an even greater emphasis on the legislative area than our legal education presently offers."[67] Law requires more than *predicting* outcomes in court.[68] The case method can give the impression that "life in the law is just one continuous lawsuit."[69] Drawing on Fuller's 1948 characterization, Milner ends the introduction's penultimate section by identifying the law's three "basic processes," each with its limitations and strengths.[70]

In the contracts casebook, therefore, Milner (again echoing Fuller[71]) considers that equally emphasizing adjudication and legislation is essential to studying law. Like Fuller, Milner makes the study of *processes*—rather than knowledge, skills, or exposure to interdisciplinary knowledge—legal education's foundation[72]; considers problem-solving to be a key focus of the case method[73]; and believes that understanding diverse legal processes expands the lawyer's range of activities or skills[74] and widens the lawyer's conception of his or her responsibilities to clients and society.[75]

Fuller and Milner: Catalysts for Change in Legal Education?

The self-reflective, iconoclastic, liberal tone of Milner's Introduction, combined with its heightened sense of the lawyer's role in pursuing human purposes at the client and societal levels, captures a moment of deep preoccupation with the objectives of legal education. The early 1940s saw the Committee on Aims and Objectives of Legal Education at the Association of American Law Schools focused on equipping future lawyers with skills of policy-making and "government and public administration."[76] In 1947, Fuller attended one of these meetings[77] and authored the watershed Preliminary Statement of the Committee on Legal Education of the Harvard Law School, which argued, among other things, that law school "does not adequately prepare the lawyer for the problems [that lawyers] will have to solve in practice."[78] In 1954, the executive committee of the ACLT commissioned its own report on the "Objectives of Legal Education," resulting in a detailed memo in 1956 by Wilbur Bowker, dean of law at the University of Alberta. That memo emphasized the importance of multiple legal processes and provided a voluminous survey of the recent literature on legal education, including Fuller's 1948 essay.[79]

This period of "ferment,"[80] characterized by challenges to the conventional case method, the desire for greater integration with social sciences, the exposure to multiple legal processes, and a concern with the lawyer's public duties and diverse roles in society, culminated in an important tripartite conference in 1960. Held at New York University in early September 1960, the conference brought together the who's who of legal academia in the United States, United Kingdom, and Canada. Lon Fuller was the chief organizer. Canadians in attendance included a large contingent from Toronto, including Caesar Wright, Bora Laskin, James Milner, John Willis, and Albert Abel. Horace Read and Ronald St. John Macdonald, future law dean at Toronto, were also in attendance.

This conference, coming at a period of Milner's heightened engagement with Fullerian themes, might have been the perfect vector for the idea of the lawyer as social architect to more profoundly infiltrate the intellectual life at the University of Toronto Faculty of Law. The conference occurred near the beginning of Fuller's 1960–1961 sabbatical, which was partially funded by the Rockefeller Foundation based on Fuller's proposal to "write a book which will probably carry the title, 'The Forms of Social Order.'" Fuller anticipated that the book would consider "the lawyer in his function as 'an architect of social structure'"[81] and would be based on his essay "The Forms and Limits of Adjudication," which (as he pitched it to the Rockefeller Foundation) was concerned with the appropriate allocation of tasks among courts, administrative agencies, planning boards, public corporations, and legislatures.[82] Fuller's working title for this tome was *The Principles of Social Order*, which he never in fact completed.

These ideas, had they figured prominently at the conference, might have made an impression on the other leading figures at Toronto: both Willis[83] and Laskin[84] demonstrated some concern with multiple legal processes, and Wright was both enamored of Harvard and probably had some receptivity to Legal Process views, despite an otherwise fairly conservative understanding of law.[85] However, although the ideas did get somewhat of an airing at the conference,[86] Fuller did not give the social architect/Principles of Social Order vision a full-throated celebration.[87] Rather than taking this signature conference as an opportunity to develop and test his book-length ideas on social architecture, he seems to have given the international platform a pass.

What accounts for this failure to emphasize the forms (principles) of social order, and the related social-architect ideas, at this conference?

In a word: Nixon. In the months leading up the conference, Fuller was spending most of his time working on the Republican candidate for US president Richard Nixon's campaign—so much so that he suggested to the Rockefeller Foundation in November 1960 that the "major distraction" of the campaign might justify him returning some of his sabbatical money.[88]

Fuller's distraction from completing *The Principles of Social Order* appears to have been quasi-permanent. By the time that Fuller's attention returned to academia, he became preoccupied with a completely separate project: the Storrs Lectures at Yale Law School in May 1963, which would ultimately become a signature work, *The Morality of Law*.[89] It was a copy of *this* book that Fuller would ultimately deliver to the Rockefeller Foundation in recognition of its financial support.[90] As Kenneth Winston notes, *The Principles of Social Order* never coalesced into a book in Fuller's lifetime.[91] Fuller's ideas on social architecture would remain more or less buried in his writings and speeches on legal education, taken up by a few select acolytes such as Milner but never really reaching the mainstream.

Milner, moreover, did not seem to be a particularly effective advocate for their uptake at his own faculty. Despite his efforts in casebooks and speeches, his attempts largely floundered.[92] Milner and Willis brought forward a proposal in 1962 to institute first-year tutorials on legislation: these were "unfavourably received."[93] Several years later, Milner advocated for a first-year course on legislation, so that "our students accept statute law and the legislative process on a footing with the judicial process"[94]; this invitation, too, was not embraced.

Ironically, it was not until the year of Milner's death (1969) that ideas about diversifying legal processes in teaching law began to take root at the University of Toronto Faculty of Law. In May 1969, a newly constituted Curriculum Committee, chaired by Dick Risk, proposed as its "major recommendation"[95] a first-year course titled "Introduction to the Legislative and Administrative Process" that aimed to "remedy" the distortion caused by "the emphasis on cases, the common law, and the adjudicative process."[96] The rationale for the new changes reflected a vision of legal education squarely in line with the ferment of the 1940s and 1950s, echoing Fuller's concern for producing lawyers adept at solving social problems: Risk cites Karl Llewellyn to the effect that "law government is a service institution: in service lies its soul—service for client or cause or class, or for some dream which embraces all classes and even a world."[97] The report is redolent with Fulleresque quotes, both with respect to the objectives of professional legal education[98] and the lawyer as problem-solver.[99]

Yet, despite this affinity with ideas promoted by Fuller and Milner, there is no mention of Fuller anywhere in the document. In recent times, Dick Risk has remarked on the "general lack of awareness" of Fuller within the faculty at the time.[100] Neither is there any specific mention of Milner. Given Milner's repeated emphasis on decentering adjudication in teaching law, that is, on cultivating lawyers who are prospective problem-solvers and planners, it is striking that his name is absent from the curriculum report that finally reflects these ideas.

To the extent the social-architect vision percolated into the consciousness of the University of Toronto law faculty in the 1970s, it appears to have done so without widespread acknowledgment of its origins, be they Fullerian or Milnerian. And without these intellectual anchors, they were perhaps destined to fade away. With Milner's death in 1969 this happened on several fronts. First, although the late 1960s and 1970s would see the institution of the "Introduction to the Legislative and Administrative Process" course and a continuation of the upper-year course on legal process, more radical changes to the first-year law school curriculum do not appear to have taken root. Current offerings, with their continued focus on teaching case law through the case method, reflect the "standard fare of law schools everywhere."[101] Around the time of the 1969 memo, comments made to Dick Risk by a colleague who taught during that first year and was supportive of the new direction, that instruction in contracts, property, and torts would "bury alive" the legislative and administrative process course, seem to have been prescient: The course changed names twice in the 1970s, was reduced in credit weight, was even discontinued for several years, enjoyed one last gasp under the title "Public Law" in the early 1980s, and eventually it disappeared altogether.[102]

Milner's attempts to incorporate Fullerian themes *within* the core course of Contracts likewise seem to have faded away after his death. Milner's signature casebook (*Milner's Cases and Materials on Contracts*) was taken over by Stephen Waddams, a young professor who had graduated with distinction from the faculty in 1967.[103] As recounted elsewhere, in three successive editions Waddams effected a gradual distancing from the Fullerian views contained in the first edition. In 1977, Waddams published his own contracts textbook, the preface of which signaled an enchantment with the adjudicative method—the opposite of Milner's Fullerian views on decentering adjudication.[104] Waddams, who started studies at the University of Toronto in his second year and thus did not study contracts under either Milner or Risk (the year he *would* have been in first year, 1964/65, both were teaching the course),[105] would restore the centrality of adjudication to his own casebook, which finally replaced *Milner* definitively in 1994.[106]

The other threads of Fuller's social-architect influence seem likewise to have faded from the mainstream of faculty consciousness. Milner and Laskin, for example, had contemplated writing a book tentatively titled *Introduction to the Study of Law*, which Milner described to Fuller in terms of multiple legal processes and functionalism.[107] That book was never written, but Stephen Waddams did produce a very popular primer of the same title, now in its eighth edition.[108] Waddams's *Introduction*, in a sense, couldn't be further from challenging to the centrality of adjudication. As the young Rod Macdonald wrote of the first edition in 1979, the book communicates the message that "the adversarial, adjudicative processes of the common law are the best, if not the only way for a legal system to operate . . . [and] the lawyer's principal preoccupation is with reading and analysing cases and in preparing for court."[109]

The fervor with which Macdonald writes is itself reflective of perhaps the last vestigial presence of Lon Fuller's social-architect views at the University of Toronto Faculty of Law in the 1970s. In 1974–1975, Macdonald studied at Toronto for his LLM under the supervision of Angela Swan, who convinced him to read Lon Fuller's works.[110] This supervisory intervention would have profound consequences; the final pages of Macdonald's thesis contain the seeds of his eventual theories on "critical legal pluralism" and foreshadow a career as both professor and dean that placed the idea of social architecture at its core.[111] Macdonald's skepticism about conventional forms and sites of normativity would go on to have massive impacts on the institutional and intellectual life of his future academic home, the McGill University Faculty of Law, where he would encourage scores of students and colleagues to think about Fuller's conception of the lawyer as social architect.[112]

At Toronto, no similar critical mass developed among scholars committed to Fuller's views on the Principles of Social Order. Indeed, the converse appears to have obtained. In the early 2000s, a young SJD student at Toronto (and recent McGill law graduate), Sean Rehaag, organized a conference premised on the idea of two distinct strains of Fuller's thought: a Fuller-inspired pluralism at McGill, and a "rule of law" Fuller at Toronto, inspired by *The Morality of Law*.[113] Although it would be too easy to caricature the differences as two solitudes—as one participant stated, the conference showed that there was more commonality than differences[114]—the impulse to organize such a conference illustrates the apparent institutional disjuncture: Fuller's pluralistic legal process views, reflected in his unrealized tome *The Principles of Social Order*, apparently never really took off at Toronto, whereas his more mainstream *The Morality of Law* did. By contrast, at McGill, the towering personality of Rod Macdonald influenced the reverse destiny: Fuller's abandoned ideas took on a new life, thanks to Swan's fateful intervention.

Conclusion: Historical Contingency, Path Dependence, and Legal Consciousness

Might things have been different had Milner lived longer? Certainly there was a core of faculty members at Toronto who might have been intellectually predisposed (in part because of their Harvard training) to combine forces to pursue Fuller's ideas about social architecture. Had Milner continued his casebook and written his primer, might Waddams's publications have taken a different direction? Might Milner and Swan have collaborated in the field of contracts to develop a Fuller-inspired casebook that commanded significant market share?[115] Had Milner lived, might the face of teaching Contracts at Toronto, and across Canada, been different? Might Risk's "Introduction to the Legislative and Administrative Process" course not have been doomed to failure had there been one more ardent voice to help it survive? Might incoming law students have been exposed to an introductory text that posits a plurality of legal processes and the importance of social problem-solving as foundational premises, primed to think of themselves as social architects from the first day of their legal educations? And what might the effect of the intellectual culture have been on other University of Toronto professors had Fuller not worked on Nixon's campaign, stuck to his sabbatical plan, and been working on *The Principles of Social Order* in earnest during the 1960 conference, when Toronto's leading lights were there to listen and learn?

All of these questions are worth asking in order to reflect on the role of historical contingency and path dependence in the intellectual and pedagogical dimensions of the modern-day law faculty. But such reflections should not ignore two integral features of this contingency. First: personality. It may be that Milner simply didn't have a commanding personality and felt more comfortable advocating for his views on legal education through other venues. Risk's remark that Fuller's ideas flew under the radar may be indicative of a shy and retiring personality, of someone who refrained from sharing his deep pedagogical commitments with his colleagues.

At another level, the forces inhibiting the uptake of iconoclastic views such as Fuller's may not be attributable to happenstance alone. Fuller knew quite well in the late 1940s that his views profoundly challenged the status quo. Even during the immediate postwar period, decentering adjudication would have required upending nearly seven decades of settled practices at Harvard Law School, challenging both the case method of teaching and the inherited classical subject-matter categories of law.[116] In writing his landmark Preliminary Report in 1947, Fuller was quite aware of what he was up against. Judged on the merits of his ideas alone, one might expect many and quick converts, but intellectual merit alone does not determine the uptake of ideas. A legal consciousness has its varied and complex sources, not least of which are the implicit commitments shared by those who have progressed through the traditional system. Inasmuch as Fuller's and Milner's advocacy for the social-architect ideal may have been refracted, distracted, inhibited, or extinguished by historical accidents, still they were up against a collectivity of shared practices and commitments, a force that may ultimately be more determinative than any singular event.

The Harvard legacy, even in a place so nearby as Canada, a country that consistently sent its best students to prepare for a career in law teaching, is complex. Fuller, along with Hart and Sacks, reimagined legal education against the Langdellian orthodoxy. Despite the vicissitudes of academic and political life leading Fuller to stray into other fields, his ideas attracted a powerful following. It may be that the Langdellian model remains triumphant in mainstream Canadian legal education.[117] But the efforts of Milner and Macdonald to import Fuller to Canada disrupt any image of hegemony: there are multiple Harvard models and a porous, variable, and contestable reception of them all.

NOTES

This research has been supported by the Social Sciences and Humanities Research Council of Canada, the graduate program at the Faculty of Law at the University of Toronto, and the Faculty of Law and Work-Study Program at Western University. This chapter is an abridged version of the original article, "Catalytic Agents? Lon Fuller, James Milner, and the Lawyer as Social Architect, 1950-69" *University of Toronto Law Journal* 71, no. 1 (2021): 91. Reprinted with permission from University of Toronto Press, DOI 10.3138/utlj-2020-0003, © University of Toronto Press.

1 See Kent Roach, "What's New and Old about the Legal Process," *University of Toronto Law Journal* 47, no. 3 (1997): 368, citing William N. Eskridge Jr. and Philip P. Frickey, "An Historical and Critical Introduction to *The Legal Process*," in *The Legal Process: Basic Problems in the Making and Application of Law*, ed. Henry M. Hart Jr. and Albert M. Sacks (Westbury, NY: Foundation Press, 1994), lxxix; Eskridge and Frickey, "Introduction," liii.

2 See Charles L Barzun, "The Forgotten Foundations of Hart and Sacks," *Virginia Law Review* 99, no. 1 (2013): 9–10; Neil Duxbury, "Faith in Reason: The Process Tradition in American Jurisprudence," *Cardozo Law Review* 15, no. 3 (1993): 632–33; William N Eskridge Jr. and Philip P. Frickey, "The Making of *The Legal Process*," *Harvard Law Review* 107, no. 8 (1994): 2047–49.

3 Lon L Fuller, "Means and Ends," in *The Principles of Social Order: Selected Essays of Lon L. Fuller*, ed. Kenneth I. Winston, rev. ed (Oxford and Portland, OR: Hart Publishing, 2001), 61–62.

4 See, e.g., Lon L. Fuller and John D. Randall, "Professional Responsibility: Report of the Joint Conference," *ABA Journal* 44, no. 12 (1958): 1159–62, 1216–18.

5 See, e.g., Lon L. Fuller, "The Lawyer as Architect of Social Structures," in *The Principles of Social Order: Selected Essays of Lon L. Fuller*, ed. Winston, 285.

6 See Kenneth I. Winston, "Editor's Note," in *The Principles of Social Order*, ed. Winston, 61.

7 See Fuller and Randall, "Professional Responsibility," 1160 and 1217.

8 See Preliminary Statement of the Committee on Legal Education of the Harvard Law School, Harvard Law Library, 1947 (on file with author); also cited in Robert S. Summers, *Lon L. Fuller* (Stanford: Stanford University Press, 1984), 141–44 (especially the text surrounding notes 12, 15, and 17). See, e.g., Lon L. Fuller, "On Teaching Law," *Stanford Law Review* 3, no. 1 (1950): 37; Lon L. Fuller, "What the

Law Schools Can Contribute to the Making of Lawyers," *Journal of Legal Education* 1, no. 2 (1948): 189–204; Lon L. Fuller, "Objectives of Legal Education," *Record of the Association of the Bar of the City of New York* 2, no. 3 (1947): 120–27; Lon L. Fuller, "On Legal Education"; Lon L. Fuller, "The Place and Uses of Jurisprudence in the Law School Curriculum," *Journal of Legal Education* 1, no. 4 (1948): 495–507.

9 Cf. Lon L. Fuller, "The Forms and Limits of Adjudication," *Harvard Law Review* 92, no. 2 (1978): 353–409.

10 Fuller, "What the Law Schools Can Contribute," 192–95, 197, 203.

11 See Barzun, "The Forgotten Foundations," 36.

12 See Lon L. Fuller, *The Problems of Jurisprudence: A Selection of Readings Supplemented by Comments Prepared by the Editor*, temp. ed. (Brooklyn: Foundation Press, 1949), 694.

13 See Fuller, "The Place and Uses," 503–04; Fuller, *Problems of Jurisprudence*, 2.

14 See Fuller, "Objectives," 125.

15 See, e.g., Lon L. Fuller, *Basic Contract Law* (St. Paul: West Publishing, 1947), 424–25.

16 See Clifford Ian Kyer and Jerome Edmund Bickenbach, *The Fiercest Debate: Cecil A. Wright, the Benchers, and Legal Education in Ontario, 1923–1957* (Toronto: University of Toronto Press, 1987), 237.

17 See James B. Milner, "Curriculum Vitae," in Letter from James Milner to Caesar Wright, April 20, 1950, Milner Papers (hereinafter cited as MP), 1992–014/005(161), Clara Thomas Archive (hereinafter cited as CTA).

18 See Examination Results, Harvard Law School, James Bryce Milner (June 1950), MP, 1992–014/005 (161), CTA. See also Letter from Paul Freund, Chairman of the Committee on Graduate Studies, Harvard Law School, to Caesar Wright, March 25, 1952, UAV 512.26.15, box 18, folder "University Law Schools [ULS] (12)," Harvard University Archives (hereinafter cited as HUA).

19 See Letter from Milner to Caesar Wright, May 4, 1950, MP, 1992–014/005(161), CTA.

20 See Memorandum from Milner to graduate students at Harvard Law School, November 28, 1949, MP, 1992–014/005(161), CTA.

21 See Letter from James Milner to Erin Griswold, March 27, 1950, MP, 1992–014/005(161), CTA.

22 See, e.g., Letter from Milner to Fuller, January 15, 1952, MP, 1992–014/005(149), CTA.

23 See Letter from Griswold to Wright, February 15, 1950, Cesar Wright Papers, B1982–0028, box 02, University of Toronto Archives (hereinafter cited as UTA).

24 See Letter from Milner to Wright, May 4, 1950.

25 See Fuller, *Problems of Jurisprudence*, 694, 741.

26 See James B. Milner, "The Law of Contract: 1923–1947," *Canadian Bar Review* 26, no. 1 (1948): 135.

27 See Lon L. Fuller and William R. Perdue Jr., "The Reliance Interest in Contract Damages: 1," *Yale Law Journal* 46, no. 1 (1936): 52–96; Lon L. Fuller and William R. Perdue Jr., "The Reliance Interest in Contract Damages: 2," *Yale Law Journal* 46, no. 3 (1937): 373–420; Fuller, *Basic Contract Law*.

28 Lon L. Fuller and Melvin Aron Eisenberg, *Basic Contract Law*, 3rd ed. (St. Paul: West Publishing, 1972), 93.

29 See Milner, Professor JB—Correspondence, University of Toronto Faculty of Law Records (hereinafter cited as UTFLR), A82/0041, box 023, UTA.

30 James B. Milner, "One Canadian View of the Case Methods," *Journal of the Society of Public Teachers of Law (New Series)* 3, no. 1 (1955): 32–39.

31 See Milner, Professor JB—Correspondence, 1–2.

32 See ibid., 37.

33 James B. Milner, "Annual Examination, Contracts, Question V (Faculty of Law, University of Toronto 1952)," UTFLR, A82/0041, box 018, "Examination Questions—Faculty of Arts & School of Law," UTA.

34 See, e.g., University of Toronto, School of Law, *Calendar* 1954–55, UTFLR, A82/0041, box 018, Faculty of Law—History 4, UTA, 12; University of Toronto, Faculty of Law, *Calendar* 1963–64, UTFLR, A82/0041, box 018, "Faculty of Law—History 4," UTA, 16.

35 See, e.g., James B. Milner, "Annual Examination, Contracts, Question IV (Faculty of Law, University of Toronto, 1956)," UTFLR, A82/0041, box 018, "Examination Questions—Faculty of Arts & School of Law," UTA.

36 James B. Milner, *Cases and Materials on Contracts* (Toronto: University of Toronto Press, 1963).

37 See Horace E. Read and John W. MacDonald, *Cases and Other Materials on Legislation* (Brooklyn: Foundation Press, 1948), vii, quoted in Eric Adams, "The Dean Who Went to Law School: Crossing Borders and Searching for Purpose in North American Legal Education, 1930–1950," *Alberta Law Review* 54, no. 1 (2016): 23; John Willis, *A History of Dalhousie Law School* (Toronto: University of Toronto Press, 1979), 177–78.

38 Letter from Read to Milner, November 30, 1953, UTFLR, A82/0041, box 023, UTA.

39 Letter from Milner to Read, December 9, 1953, UTFLR, A82/0041, box 023, UTA.

40 Letter from Milner to Schmitt, January 14, 1954, UTFLR, A82/0041, box 023, UTA [emphasis added].

41 Letter from Milner to John Smith, March 22, 1954, UTFLR, A82/0041, box 023, UTA.

42 Harold C. Havighurst, "Preface to the First Edition," in *A Selection of Contract Cases and Related Quasi-Contract Cases*, ed. Harold C Havighurst (Rochester, NY: The Lawyers Co Operative Publishing Company, 1934), iii.

43 Harold C. Havighurst, *Cases and Materials on the Law of Contracts*, 2nd ed. (Chicago: Callaghan and Company, 1950), iii.

44 See James Lake, review of *Cases and Materials on the Law of Contracts*, 2nd ed., by Harold C. Havighurst, *Journal of Legal Education* 3, no. 4 (1951): 636–37.

45 Milner, "Case Methods," 32.

46 Ibid., 37.

47 Ibid.

48 Ibid., 39.

49 Matthew Arnold, *Culture and Anarchy*, ed. J. D. Wilson (Cambridge: Cambridge University Press, 1946), quoted in James Milner, "Fact and Fancy in the Idea of a University Law Faculty," *University of Toronto Law Journal* 13, no. 1 (1959): 37.

50 Ibid., 40.

51 Ibid., 37, 41.

52 Ibid., 40.

53 Ibid., 39.

54 Ibid., 42, citing Lon Fuller, "Human Purpose and Natural Law" *Journal of Philosophy* 53, no. 22 (1956): 702.

55 See the discussion in the final section below.

56 Letter from Milner to Wright, May 7, 1962, UTFLR, A82/0041, box 030, "Correspondence 1961–2," UTA.

57 Letter from Milner to Fuller, February 25, 1963, Fuller Papers, box 5, folder 9, Harvard Special Collections.

58 Milner, *Cases and Materials*, xx.

59 See David Sandomierski, *Aspiration and Reality in Legal Education* (Toronto: University of Toronto Press, 2020), chap. 3.

60 Milner, *Cases and Materials*, vii.

61 Ibid.

62 Ibid., ix. See also Milner, "Case Methods," 36. Cf. Fuller, "What the Law Schools Can Contribute," 193.

63 Milner, *Cases and Materials*, xii. See also Milner, "Fact and Fancy," 37.

64 Milner, *Cases and Materials*, xv. Cf. Havighurst, "Preface to the First Edition," v.

65 Ibid., xvii.

66 Ibid., xvi.

67 Ibid., xvii. Cf. Fuller, "What the Law Schools Can Contribute," 195.

68 Milner, *Cases and Materials*, xvii.

69 Ibid., xi.

70 Ibid., xvii–xviii. Cf. Fuller, "What the Law Schools Can Contribute," 192–93. Milner reinforced the importance of the lawyer in mastering multiple legal processes in his update to the Introduction, drafted in 1968 but published posthumously by S. M. Waddams, ed., *Milner's Cases and Materials on Contracts*, 2nd ed. (Toronto and Buffalo: University of Toronto Press, 1971), xxx–xxxi; Sandomierski, *Aspiration and Reality*, chap. 3.

71 See Fuller, "What the Law Schools Can Contribute," 195.

72 Cf. ibid., 196–97, 199, 201.

73 Ibid., 197.

74 Milner, *Cases and Materials*, xvii; Fuller, "What the Law Schools Can Contribute," 197.

75 Milner, *Cases and Materials*, xv; Fuller, "What the Law Schools Can Contribute," 203.

76 George Osborne, "Curriculum and Related Matters," *Proceedings of the Annual Meeting of the Association of American Law Schools* (1946): 110.

77 See Albert James Harno, *Legal Education In the United States: A Report Prepared for the Survey of the Legal Profession* (San Francisco: Bancroft-Whitney, 1953), 161–63.

78 Harvard University, Law School, Committee on Legal Education, *Preliminary Statement of the Committee on Legal Education of the Harvard Law School* (March 1, 1947), iv.

79 See W. F. Bowker, "Association of Canadian Law Teachers Draft Statement of Objectives," May 28, 1956, RG 37, container 7, folder "W.C.J.M. Canadian Law Teachers' Association," McGill University Archives, 3.

80 Harno, *Legal Education In the United States*, 181–87.

81 Letter from Lon L. Fuller to Kenneth W. Thompson, December 4, 1959, Rockefeller Foundation Records, projects, RG 1.2 (FA387), Box 514, Folder 4389, "Harvard University—Fuller, Lon L.—(Social Order)" 1959–61, 1963–64, Rockefeller Archive Center (hereinafter RFR, RAC). Fuller changed the title from "Forms" of social order to "Principles" of social order. See Letter from Lon Fuller to Kenneth Thompson, November 15, 1960, RFR, RAC.

82 Lon L. Fuller, Abstract for "The Forms and Limits of Adjudication," as appearing in RFR, RAC (time stamp of January 25, 1960).

83 Letter from Cecil A. Wright (no recipient), April 21, 1959, UTFLR, A82/0041, box 027, "Faculty—Memos 2," UTA.

84 Letter from James Milner to Lon Fuller, March 3, 1959, James B. Milner fonds, 1992–014/005(149), CTA.

85 See Osgoode Society for Canadian Legal History, Oral History Interview with Richard B. Risk (November 11, 2013), 28.

86 See Walter Gellhorn, "Summary of Colloquy on Administrative Law," *Journal of the Society of Public Teachers of Law (New Series)* 6, no. 1 (1961): 73–74; *British-Canadian-American Conference on Legal Education-Proceedings of the General Sessions New York, N.Y. September 5–8, 1960*, Special Issue, *Journal of Legal Education* 14, no. 1 (1961–1962).

87 See Lon L. Fuller, "The Academic Lawyer's House of Intellect," *Journal of Legal Education* 14, no. 1 (1961): 153–63 (focusing on institutional changes that would lead to greater cohesion between law professors, practicing lawyers, and judges).

88 Letter from Lon Fuller to Kenneth Thompson, November 15, 1960, RFR, RAC.

89 Ibid. See Lon L. Fuller, *The Morality of Law* (New Haven: Yale University Press, 1964).

90 Letter from Kenneth W. Thompson to Lon Fuller, June 15, 1964, RFR, RAC; Letter from Lon L. Fuller to Kenneth W. Thompson, October 10, 1963, RFR, RAC.

91 Lon L. Fuller, "Means and Ends," in *The Principles of Social Order*, ed. Winston, 61–62.

92 See generally David Sandomierski, "Decentering Adjudication at the University of Toronto, 1950–1975," in *Law, Life, and the Teaching of Legal History: Essays in Honour of G. Blaine Baker*, ed. Ian C. Pilarczyk, Angela Fernandez, and Brian Young (McGill-Queen's Press, forthcoming 2021).

93 Committee on Curriculum and Calendar Revision, Faculty of Law, University of Toronto, "Matters For Consideration—1962," UTFLR, A82/0041, box 030, "Law School 1961–62 (5)," UTA, 1.

94 "First Year—Proposed Course on Legislation—Extract from a letter to James Milner," enclosure to John Willis, Memorandum to the Committee on Curriculum and Calendar Revision (December 1, 1966), UL034, "Law School Correspondence 1966–67," UTA.

95 Report of the Curriculum Committee Faculty of Law, University of Toronto (May 1969, Chair R. C. B. Risk), Ronald St. John Macdonald fonds, subseries 36.10, "University of Toronto—Report of the Curriculum Committee," Dalhousie Archives, 22.

96 Ibid., 12, 28.

97 Karl Llewellyn, "The Study of Law as a Liberal Art," in *Jurisprudence: Realism in Theory and Practice* (Chicago: University of Chicago Press, 1962), 391, quoted in Report of the Curriculum Committee, 12.

98 Report of the Curriculum Committee, 13–14, 21 ("The introductory understanding of the legal institutions and processes should be an introduction to the judicial, legislative and administrative processes, and this introduction should include an introduction to the form, functions, and work-products of the institutions.")

99 Ibid., 20, 33 ("The lawyer must and does act; the lawyer must unravel the problems into forms appropriate for decision according to the terms of the legal institutions or processes, and the lawyer must make decisions").

100 Email correspondence with author, August 28, 2019.

101 John Willis, *A History of Dalhousie Law School*, 177–78.

102 See Sandomierski, "Decentering Adjudication."

103 Waddams was the recipient of the Dean's Key in 1967. See Faculty of Law, University of Toronto, *Calendar 1967–68* (Toronto: University of Toronto Press, 1967), 33.

104 See Sandomierski, *Aspiration and Reality*, chap. 3; S. M. Waddams, "Preface to the First Edition," reproduced in S. M. Waddams, *The Law of Contracts*, 7th ed. (student edition) (Toronto: Thomson Reuters, 2017), v.

105 See University of Toronto, *University of Toronto Directory: Students of the University and the Federated Colleges, 1965–1966*, P78–0175.(07), UTA, 142; University of Toronto, *University of Toronto Directory: Students of the University and the Federated Colleges, 1964–1966*, P78–0175.(06), UTA, 174; University of Toronto, Faculty of Law, *Calendar 1964–1965* (Toronto: University of Toronto Press, 1964), 16. Risk did teach Stephen Waddams in real estate in his second year (1965/66). See Faculty of Law, 1965–66, "Prizes," UTFLR, A82/0041, box 031, "Examinations 1964–65," UTA. See Letter from R. C. B. Risk to Caesar Wright, November 7, 1966, UTFLR, A82/0041, box 036 ("1966–67 Correspondence"), UTA.

106 S. M. Waddams, M. Trebilcock, and M. A. Waldron, eds., *Cases and Materials on Contracts* (Toronto: Emond Montgomery, 1994).

107 Letter from James Milner to Lon Fuller, March 3, 1959, James B. Milner fonds, 1992–014/005(149), CTA.

108 Stephen Waddams, *Introduction to the Study of Law*, 8th ed. (Toronto: Carswell, 2018).
109 R. A. Macdonald, review of *Introduction to the Study of Law*, by S. M. Waddams, *University of Toronto Law Journal* 31 (1981): 443, 445.
110 Angela Swan formerly went by the first name John. References to Swan in this chapter are to Angela and use the feminine pronoun.
111 See Angela Swan, "Rod Macdonald: The Perfect Graduate Student," in *The Unbounded Level of the Mind: Rod Macdonald's Legal Imagination*, ed. Richard Janda, Daniel Jutras, and Rosalie Jukier (Montreal, Kingston: McGill-Queen's University Press, 2015), 266–67, quoting Rod Macdonald, "Prolegomena to a Theory of Legal Relevance" (unpublished LLM thesis, University of Toronto, 1975).
112 See generally Janda, Jutras, and Jukier, eds., *The Unbounded Level of the Mind.*
113 The conference was held once at McGill and once in Toronto, in 2005. Although the proceedings of the conference were not published, vestiges of it remain. See, e.g., Sean Rehaag, "Curriculum Vitae," last modified August 1, 2019, 9, www.osgoode.yorku.ca.
114 Conversation with author, September 28, 2016.
115 Swan's Fullerian influence on contracts teaching appears to have made only a minimal mark on the University of Toronto faculty: Waddams's *Milner* and *Waddams* have probably always been considered the "house book," and Swan's early attempts to unite contracts scholars at Toronto under a functionalist banner ultimately resulted in a splintering off into different research agendas. See Barry Reiter and John Swan, *Studies in Contract Law* (Toronto: Butterworth, 1980), 6. See generally Sandomierski, *Aspiration and Reality*, 85. Swan left the University of Toronto definitively in 1988. While Swan's casebook continues to live and breathe, it enjoys a distinctly minority share across Canada, attracting a loyal but decidedly cult following. See David Sandomierski, "Tension and Reconciliation in Canadian Contract Law Casebooks," *Osgoode Hall Law Journal* 54, no. 4 (2017): 1192.
116 Thomas C. Grey, "Langdell's Orthodoxy" *University of Pittsburgh Law Review* 45, no. 1 (1983): 47.
117 See Sandomierski, *Aspiration and Reality.*

14

Legal Teaching and the Reconceptualizing of the State

Global Law and New Legal Education Loci

JOSÉ GARCEZ GHIRARDI

And so immense was the sea and its sparkle that the child was struck dumb by the beauty of it. And when he finally managed to speak, trembling, stuttering, he asked his father: 'Help me to see!'
–Eduardo Galeano, *The Book of Embraces* (1989), 17.

Law schools play a fundamental role in shaping the way that societies think about law. Although often eclipsed by their more practical function of forming legal professionals, this shaping of the social imaginary[1] regarding the legal world is arguably one of their most consequential tasks.[2] Every class on statutes, every lecture on jurisprudence bespeaks a specific understanding—albeit often unspoken—of what law is and of what it should be. Legal education has among its core goals that of shaping students' representation of law[3] and of furnishing them with the predicative structures[4] they will articulate in their professional life.

The veritable revolution brought about by Langdell and the case method, for example, cannot be fully grasped if this connection between teaching law and conceptualizing law is not taken into account. The implications of the pedagogical use of *A Selection of Cases on the Law of Contracts* (1871), Christopher Langdell's landmark textbook that introduced the case method at Harvard Law School, go far beyond the classroom. The rationale it embodies and the class dynamics it assumes articulate a set of beliefs about law that stand in close connection to the conceptual standpoint at the heart of Holmes's seminal *Harvard Law Review* article "The Path of the Law" (1897).

Help Me to See: Legal Education and Images of Law

In the United States in the second half of the nineteenth century, teaching methods and theoretical propositions worked together to advance a different way of thinking about law, its meaning, and its institutions.[5] In his seminal article mentioned above, Holmes states his belief that law is essentially a practical matter, a tool to achieve concrete social ends:

> When we study law, we are not studying a mystery but a well-known profession. We are studying what we shall want in order to appear before judges, or to advise people in such a way as to keep them out of court. . . . The object of our study, then, is prediction, the prediction of the incidence of the public force through the instrumentality of the courts.[6]

This rendering of the object of legal study is in line with his famous contention that experience, not logic, is the life of law.[7] For Holmes, learning law means acquiring the professional skills necessary to successfully counsel clients and to plead in court. Law students, from this viewpoint, are being trained not to be philosophers but practitioners capable of handling the cases that come their way.[8]

Langdell's views on legal education reveal the same belief in the fundamentally practical dimension of law. In the introduction to his pioneering casebook, Langdell declares that he started his deanship at Harvard "with a settled conviction that Law could only be taught or learned effectively by means of cases of some form."[9] This "settled conviction" sprung from his specific understanding of the nature of law:

> Law, considered as a science, consists of certain principles and doctrines. To have such a mastery of these as to be able to apply them with constant facility and certainty to the ever-tangled skein of human affairs, is what constitutes a true lawyer; and hence to acquire that mastery should be the business of every earnest student of law.[10]

Langdell, much like Holmes, believes that law is no mystery, being instead a clearly defined set of principles and doctrines; what is more, it has the equally clear practical function of helping unravel the "ever-tangled skein of human affairs." His concept of law translates effortlessly into his pedagogical creed.

Thus, in spite of their different argumentative paths—Holmes starts from his idea of law to move to pedagogical considerations, whereas Langdell starts from pedagogical considerations to ponder on the nature of law—both authors share core beliefs on the nature of law and the function of its teaching. Their joint effort makes a powerful case for the inextricable connection of the beliefs on what law is, what students should learn, and how they should be taught it. There is an ideological continuum between teaching methods and doctrinal tenets, a circular reinforcement that seems to be at the heart of the Legal Realism movement.

Such understanding programmatically opposed the rival positivist narrative, which offered its own version of the connection between teaching methodologies and visions of law. The main theoretical tenets of positivism in its Kelsenian version—for example, the normative pyramid and the insulation of law from other areas of life—were in line with the dynamics characteristic of the increasingly prestigious Humboltian-style universities.

When the first edition of Hans Kelsen's *Pure Theory of Law* appeared (1934), the German version of higher education was expanding throughout Europe. In Wilhelm von Humboldt's model of higher education,

> Research and Bildung[11] were indissolubly linked. Teachers must also be researchers, because Bildung places the search for truth and understanding, not professional training or the routine absorption of knowledge, at the center of general, liberal education.[12]

This emphasis on the intimate connection between research and teaching, and the value it placed on philosophical speculation at the expense of practical training, bespeaks the same mind-set espoused by Kelsen's goal of establishing a universal theory of law.

In the famous opening lines of his seminal work, Kelsen stresses emphatically that what he intends to offer is "a theory of positive law in general, not an interpretation of specific national or international laws."[13] His concern is diametrically opposed to Holmes's; Kelsen's aim is not to observe the everyday functioning of law, but to grasp the essential, immutable traits of legal normativity.

This type of quest could only be carried out by pure, that is to say, abstract—not applied—research. Abstract research, in turn, required universities whose main function

> was not to pass on recognized and directly usable knowledge such as the schools and colleges did, but rather to demonstrate how this knowledge is discovered.[14]

The Humboldtian model of higher education, one may well suggest, connects to Kelsen's philosophy of law in much the same way as the Langdellian educational stance is aligned with Holmes's understanding of law. Similar claims could be made about the close connection between the pedagogic use of the *debates* in medieval universities and the understandings of law prevailing in that period, or that between the dynamics of the Inns of Court in seventeenth-century England and legal theories under the Tudors and the Stuarts.[15] The ways law is taught and law is conceived are necessarily linked, as Harold Berman has elegantly observed:

> The body of legal learning in which the legal specialists are trained stands in a complex, dialectical relationship to the legal institutions, since on the one hand the learning describes those institutions but on the other hand the legal institutions, which would otherwise be disparate and unorganized, become conceptualized and systematized, and thus transformed, by what is said about them in learned treatises and articles and in the classroom.[16]

The rise of global law as an academic object, and the prestige it now enjoys, seem to spring from a similar interplay among changes in the legal imaginary, a shift in theoretical paradigms, and innovation in legal teaching methodology. Virtually absent from curricula at the beginning of the twenty-first century, the phrase "global law" and its variations (e.g., "global lawyer," "global governance," "global rule of law") are nowadays omnipresent. Oftentimes the central theme of courses, seminars, and dissertations, the idea that the key challenges to legal normativity today are too large for individual states to handle arguably shapes the debate in every field in law schools. As a result, even those professors whose courses focus on domestic law can hardly avoid promising to examine it from a *global perspective*.

Unsurprisingly, the structure and methodology of law schools have changed *in tandem* with this novel conception of the relations among law, the state, and universities. Bill Readings forcefully makes this argument in *The University in Ruins*:

> The current shift in the role of university is, above all, determined by the decline of the national cultural mission that has up to now provided its raison d´être. . . . In short, the University is becoming a different kind of institution, one that is no longer linked to the destiny of the nation-state by virtue of its role as producer, protector and inculcator of an idea of national culture. The process of economic globalization brings with it the relative decline of the nation-state as the prime instance of capital around the world. For its part, the University is becoming a transnational bureaucratic corporation.[17]

The rise of globalization, and the socioeconomic changes that it represents, have therefore required a new type of law (global law), implemented and interpreted by a new type of lawyer (global lawyer) within a new political space (global world). This overcoming of national barriers as the necessary framework for the practice of law has called into question the traditional parochial perspective of most law schools, which offered their educational services to those willing to practice in a specific national jurisdiction.

Global law, however, is meant to be practiced globally. It is thus possible, maybe even desirable, for legal education institutions to try to attract as global a group of students as possible. New technologies make this appeal to global audiences feasible, while the job prospects for global lawyers makes it attractive. Legal education has gone beyond national borders to become a global issue.

Online courses, virtual universities, and the opening by top institutions of teaching centers abroad (mainly in the so-called developing countries) are a testimony to this shift that has made legal education a global business—in more than one sense—that aims at preparing students to act in this new global arena. The Law Schools Global League, with more than two dozen members in five continents,[18] as well as the course offerings in China by New York University and the plethora of "abroad programs" offered by top law schools worldwide,[19] mean to tackle exactly this challenge.

This chapter suggests that these curricular and methodological changes are embedded in and reinforce a broader intellectual movement that postulates either the "end" of the nation-state,[20] its "demise,"[21] or its "withering away."[22] It is argued that legal education has become a primary tool in fulfilling this post-state prophecy in that it helps develop and naturalize a worldview in which states have ceased to be the central actors in political life. The remainder of this chapter is divided in two sections, apart from this introduction: "Study Local, Teach Global: The Rise of Global Legal Education," which discusses the main characteristics of *global law* programs; and "Teaching for a Post-state World?: Brazilian Legal Education in the Age of Globalization," which presents the impact of this new global perspective on the education of lawyers in Brazil.

Study Local, Teach Global: The Rise of Global Legal Education

Global law programs have mushroomed during the twentieth century: from the United States to India,[23] from the Netherlands[24] to Brazil, from Portugal to Mexico, law schools all over the world have developed strategies to offer nationals and interested foreigners the possibility of learning law from a supranational viewpoint.[25] Their necessary differences notwithstanding, these programs seem to share some important features:

1. They are usually offered by prominent institutions whose previous academic record has granted them national, regional, and/or international prestige;
2. they are presented as innovative, both in content and in methodology;
3. they justify their existence by making reference to a new global reality that requires transformations in law;
4. they suggest that this transformation not only affects the international arena but also impacts the dynamics and contents of national legal systems;

5. they aim to form lawyers capable of proficiently practicing in this new system; and
6. they are offered in English.

It is argued here that these characteristics seem to represent the educational counterpart of post-state theories which have gained momentum since the beginning of this century. They deserve, therefore, closer analysis.

The fact that these programs are offered by prestigious universities—some of the first universities to offer global programs were world-class institutions, based mainly in the United States[26] and the European Union[27]—lends immediate credibility to global law as a sound academic object. As these institutions serve as de facto benchmarks of quality for legal education, their decision to invest so much energy in these programs sends a powerful message to law schools around the world that this global perspective is worth pursuing. These reverberations follow the broader pattern of cultural exchanges between the so-called developed and developing worlds, where the adoption of the practices by the former is considered to be a sign of improvement for the latter.

Reinforcing the same dynamics, these new courses are not presented as a mere alternative perspective but as an innovative perspective, that is to say, there is a suggestion that they are an improvement over previous models. The idea of innovation embodies a qualitative aspect, as it supposes a better solution to problems than those offered by the theories, practices, or products it aims to replace.

This innovative drive is seen not as whimsical or unmotivated. On the contrary: it is portrayed as the necessary response to a broader movement. Globalization is perceived as an inescapable fact that, though dependent on no one anywhere, forces everybody everywhere to adapt to it. Its network nature and the fluid rapports it promotes make it even more uncontrollable, as its source of power remains elusive. Its effects, however, are clearly perceptible and have to be dealt with.

One of the key functions of academia would be to provide answers on how to best respond to such effects. A new approach to law is fundamental to performing this task, as Tilburg's University home page announcement to prospective students aptly illustrates: "Global Law offers a new point of view when it comes to law: it puts 'global' before 'local' by going beyond the limits of one judicial system and considering solutions from other jurisdictions or from international law."[28]

Precisely because the consequences of globalization take place within national borders, this inexorable phenomenon imposes changes on domestic legal systems. Countries face the challenge of either adjusting to the new dynamics or falling behind competitors. As the categories in the World Bank's influential *Doing Business* rankings clearly demonstrate, this adjustment has in law its prime tool and object. The project claims that it has been responsible for the implementation of 294 business regulatory reforms in 115 economies between 2018 and 2019.[29] Contract, labor, and investment rules, for example—key legal areas—have to be altered so as to enhance the viability of countries in a setting of global competition. Court structures and forms of adjudication—as exemplified by the rise of alternative dispute resolution (ADR) methods—must also be renewed as a result of globalization.[30]

Such alterations will not take place in the absence of professionals capable of designing and implementing them. That is why, unsurprisingly, the education of global lawyers has become a key factor in the quest for success in the global arena. Given the domestic nature of law and legal institutions, these professionals can hardly be imported because they must have in-depth knowledge of their country's legal structures—and, hopefully, good local connections to make these changes politically viable. They must therefore become proficient in establishing a meaningful dialogue between global and local normative systems: they have to be global lawyers.[31]

The language of this dialogue is English. This apparently pedestrian observation has, nevertheless, momentous implications. On the one hand, it acts as a social hurdle within individual countries for large numbers of professionals willing to become global lawyers. This is so because the level of linguistic mastery required for legal work in an international setting is far from negligible. Global lawyers are constantly required to discuss cases with peers and clients, revise or draft documents, litigate in international courts, and participate in ADR settlement conferences. In most cases, the possibility of successful performance in each of these tasks is linked to near-native-speaker language skills. In countries that do not have English as a first or second language, this degree of proficiency is usually within reach of only a tiny fraction of the small fraction of the population with access to university educations.[32]

On the other hand, given the fact that law *is* language, uneven degrees of mastery affect the odds of successfully advocating different positions. In addition, legal terminology does not appear in a vacuum. It is not only that the concepts used are rendered in English: they have a history within English-speaking legal traditions, which are mostly common law. And this tradition is inextricable from the semantic value—and thus legal import—of individual concepts. Although meanings can be (and often are) renegotiated as new players come into the game, the background against which this renegotiation is made is the English-speaking legal tradition.

Understandably, national law is not the core of these courses. As sketched above, there are plenty of good reasons for this international focus: supporters and critics of globalization converge in the recognition that the field of battle is now the global arena. This is the horizon against which professional expertise in law is now perceived. Domestic law is often assessed in terms of its ability to adequately responding to this new scenario.

As Jacques Chevallier observed in *L'État post-moderne* (The Postmodern State),[33] this responsive stance is often at odds with traditional readings of the state, especially the key concept of sovereignty, which implies a state's capacity to act on its own terms—even if this capacity was, in many instances, a mere rhetorical claim. But the very fact that it could function as a rhetorical strategy stresses the received wisdom that international relations are initiated in the interest of a sovereign state that then parleys, as an equal, with the other members of the community of nations.

This seems no longer to be the case. The relevant international community today has been greatly expanded and made much more complex: a vast array of international organizations, both public and private, global corporations, and NGOs, alongside a variety of supranational communities (such as the European Union and the many economic blocs) appear to have pushed the nation-state to the status of one more player as opposed to the major player it used to be.

Mirroring the fate of King Lear, the nation-state sees its commands less likely to be enforced as its economic and political power wanes.

Some of the most consequential issues affecting the lives of their nationals—for example, climate change, immigration, terrorism, and cybersecurity—require actions that are out of reach for national governments. At the same time, such governments struggle ever more fiercely to find the resources they need to meet even the most ordinary demands of their populations, as the Base Erosion and Profit Shifting phenomenon grows in importance and erodes tax revenues.[34]

National governments are thus rapidly becoming a much less powerful player than they had been in the centuries after the Westphalia Treaty of 1648. As a result, the authority of domestic law—the very heart of national political power—also wanes, as it must now struggle to accommodate itself to other normative, global systems that vie for control of very concrete aspects of national life.

The consequences of this shift in viewpoint are not restricted to global law programs: it affects legal education as a whole, including, most noticeably, undergraduate courses. The following section aims at presenting one example of this shift and examines the case of a novel law school in Brazil.

Teaching for a Post-state World? Brazilian Legal Education in the Age of Globalization

Brazil is a prime locus to discuss the impact of globalization on legal education. Since the 1990s, the country's political and economic life has been transformed radically, and its relevance as a global player has changed substantially. Globalization has been a key element in this transformation.[35]

The return to democratic rule and the enactment of a progressive new Constitution (1988) have provided Brazil with an institutional framework that allowed it to make the most of the global economic expansion of the early twenty-first century. The neoliberal policies of the 1990s and the market-friendly policies of the 2000s were equally dependent on the country's enhanced participation in the global arena. The positive economic results triggered, and were reinforced by, the implementation of a vast array of cash-transfer and social programs that narrowed the continuing mind-boggling gap between the rich and the poor. The combination of all these policies made Brazil one of the so-called BRIC[36] countries (Brazil–Russia–India–China), whose perceived success translated into international praise and national pride.[37]

BRIC status was in crucial aspects the result of a profound redesigning of the country's previous normative landscape and lawyering practices. The successive processes of privatization and economic deregulation as well as incentives for Brazilian corporations to become world leaders in specific sectors necessitated expertise in approaching law (e.g., contracts, adjudication, business models, and investment rules) in the way favored by those engaged in global exchanges. Brazil lacked legal professionals capable of responding to this challenge.[38]

The initial ad hoc solution of hiring foreign lawyers and sending Brazilian professionals to receive training abroad (mainly in American LLM programs) appeared obviously insufficient to guarantee long-term success.[39] The need for local training of global lawyers became evident and soon translated into a radically new approach to legal education. The new approach would use American law schools as a model. Such a choice is hardly surprising, as it springs from a long trend in Brazilian cultural history toward the American paradigm, which has been reinforced by the more recent phenomenon of US-led globalization.

Mainly after World War II, Brazil's economy became more dependent on the United States, gradually shifting from the European countries whose legal systems previously had been referential to Brazilian business.[40] American companies established subsidiaries in Brazil and pressed those who did business with them to adopt the managerial and lawyering styles that matched those practiced at their headquarters.[41] As Jayanth Krishnan, Vitor Dias, and John Pence observe, from the early decades of the twentieth century onward, there has been a steady flow of US lawyers to Brazil who partnered with the local professional elite to reshape the practice of law in the country.[42]

Globalization acted to intensify and broaden this process of adjustment to the US legal model.[43] Multinational corporations—which have been the key players in reshaping the economic landscape of the twenty-first century—adopt American law and lawyering styles as the blueprint for their legal structuring and transactions.[44] This globalization of the US legal mind-set, and the significance it has for economic integration and success, required the creation of education centers to produce the professionals that the new global setting required. Law school innovations, which followed transformation in law at large, started occurring all over the world.[45]

In Brazil, the pioneer experiment in new legal education methodology and curricular reform was sponsored by the Getulio Vargas Foundation (FGV), which in 2002 opened law schools in São Paulo and in Rio de Janeiro. The fact that it was FGV that accepted the challenge to break away from the traditional modes of legal education is no accident. FGV was created in the late 1940s by the Brazilian government to create the professional expertise it needed to face the deeply changed international scenario that emerged in the wake of two world wars. Its role as a think tank designed to provide the data needed for the development of efficient government policies imprinted on the institution a technical ethos that it retains to this day. It also created an acute awareness of international practices, standards, and theories, as Brazil's internal stability has always been directly related to its foreign exchanges.

These characteristics (i.e., its technical and international perspective) allowed FGV to perceive, more rapidly compared to other players, the impact that the global scenario had on the country and the crucially strategic role played by law in the country's effort to survive—and profit from—the changed global circumstances. Innovation in Brazilian law schools would be proposed not by the traditional legal elites but by those with in-depth knowledge of Brazil's economic dynamics and prospects.[46]

Both the new curriculum and the new methodology mirrored FGV's technical ethos and international perspective. Contrary to the widespread traditional model based on lecturing and on commentary on the law in the books, FGV schools adopt the case method, favor the analysis of law in action, and demand that students have sound knowledge of economics and management. Class dynamics are based on the model used in top US law schools, where a substantial number of FGV faculty members have studied.[47]

Most of the subjects the schools offer are unprecedented in the Brazilian experience and reflect this new viewpoint: law and economics; arbitrage and mediation; legal English; mergers and acquisitions; and, especially relevant to the topic of this chapter, global law (which, significantly, replaced the traditional international law course). Participation in international moot competitions is strongly recommended, and courses taught in English by foreign professors are offered regularly.

Controversial at first—given the break with deeply entrenched academic practices and understandings of law—these pioneer law schools have asserted their place among the most prestigious in the country. New schools are being created according to this model, and traditional institutions are responding by adjusting to this new perspective.

A major feature of this transformation is a new understanding of law among Brazilian professionals. The neatly established political and theoretical boundaries that have for decades characterized the hegemonic versions of legal positivism (e.g., the boundaries between law and other disciplines) and of the traditional nation-state (e.g., between national/international; public law/private law; legislation/adjudication) are seen as increasingly problematic. In fact, it could be argued that a major force shaping this kind of legal education is the critique of such boundaries. This critique is consistent with the broader movement of post-state theory, which problematizes the permanence of traditional national institutions at a time when national governments—even the most powerful—have limited control over events that directly impact life within their borders.[48]

Students are comfortable with such a scenario. After all, their everyday lives are informed by the same forces that have been shaping globalization. At university, their resistance is to the static, confined nature of the old model, not to the fluid, open nature of the new one. As new generations living in this transformed world are trained in these new theoretical tenets, a new normal is bound to appear, one in which the central figure is no longer the state.

Conclusion

Taken together, the rise of global law programs and the creation of new, US-style law schools around the globe—as exemplified by FGV Law Schools—suggest that a broad reconceptualizing of legal institutions and of their social meaning is taking place. This affects the way that the legal community thinks about, practices, and teaches law. Key features of this transformation are the assumptions of a new role for the state, of more fluid borders between diverse legal systems, as well as a novel understanding of sovereignty. The relevance of these assumptions and of the departure they represent from traditional conceptual frameworks can hardly be exaggerated. They seem bound to become the new normal upon which discourses on law are based.

Law schools are fundamental both in the construction of this normal—in its gradual embedding in the social imaginary[49] that shapes practices and expectations in any given society—and in the teaching of the skills necessary to think and act within the new everyday context that this imaginary bespeaks. Changes in curricula, teaching methodologies, and organizational formats are thus loaded with political significance and go far beyond academic concerns. They are responses to deeper social, economic, and political transformations and should be seen as such. Current changes in legal education, with increasing attention being paid to regulation, governance, and ADR procedures, suggest a gradual lessening of the normative relevance of state-centered statutory law, government, and court procedures, thereby reinforcing narratives of the rise of a global order in which states have ceased to be the central actors.

NOTES

1 I adopt here the concept of social imaginary as developed in Charles Taylor, *Modern Social Imaginaries* (Durham: Duke University Press, 2004), 23–30.

2 As David Clark observes: "Legal education, particularly when dispensed in universities, is tied to a nation's cultural history. The systematic ebb and flow of ideas ripple through law faculties and influence the socialization of students, many of whom take up positions of political importance in society. As a result, the nature of a modern society's legal profession, including its characteristic modes of thought and discourse, is intimately related to the method and manner of training its member jurists." David S. Clark, "The Medieval Origins of Modern Legal Education: Between Church and State," *American Journal of Comparative Law* 35, no. 4 (1987): 653.

3 See Serge Moscovici, *Social Representations: Explorations in Social Psychology* (New York: New York University Press, 2001).

4 Paul Ricoeur, "The Metaphorical Process as Cognition, Imagination, and Feeling," *Critical Inquiry* 5, no. 1 (1978): 143–59.

5 Daniel Coquillette and Bruce Kimball., "Dean Langdell, First Casebooks, and Justice Holmes: 1870–1881," in *On the Battlefield of Merit: Harvard Law School, the First Century* (Cambridge: Harvard University Press, 2015), 304–43; Fernando Muñoz León, "Langdell's and Holmes's Influence on the Institutional and Discursive Conditions of American Legal Scholarship / La influencia de Langdell y Holmes sobre las condiciones institucionales y discursivas de la producción académica jurídica en los estados Unidos," *Revista Chilena De Derecho* 38, no. 2 (2011): 217–37.

6 Oliver Wendell Holmes, "The Path of the Law," *Harvard Law Review* 10, no. 8 (1897): 457.

7 Edmund Fuller, "Oliver Wendell Holmes, Jr.," Encyclopedia Britannica, www.britannica.com.

8 This is not to say that Holmes did not value philosophical speculation: his own work proves otherwise. His understanding of law as an object of study, however, carries a marked, and theoretically proficuous, attention to the practical aspects of law.

9 Christopher Columbus Langdell, *A Selection of Cases on the Law of Contracts: With References and Citations* (Boston: Little, Brown, 1871), vii.

10 Ibid., viii.

11 Referring to "the concept of *Bildung*—which can mean simply 'education' . . . but also signified an ideal of self-development through the pursuit of truth." R. D. Anderson, *European Universities from the Enlightenment to 1914* (Oxford: Oxford University Press, 2004), 52.

12 Ibid., 56.

13 Hans Kelsen, *Pure Theory of Law* (Berkeley: University of California Press, 1967).

14 Walter Rüegg, ed., *A History of the University in Europe*, vol. 3, *Universities in the Nineteenth and Early Twentieth Centuries* (Cambridge: Cambridge University Press, 2004), 5.

15 Margaret McGlynn, *The Royal Prerogative and the Learning of the Inns of Court* (Cambridge: Cambridge University Press, 2003).

16 Harold J. Berman, *Law and Revolution* (Cambridge: Harvard University Press, 1983), 8.

17 Bill Readings, *The University in Ruins* (Boston: Harvard University Press, 1996), 3.

18 The information is available at "Members," Law Schools Global League, https://lawschoolsgloballeague.com.

19 A few examples include Harvard ("Semester Abroad," International Legal Studies, Harvard Law School, https://hls.harvard.edu), Cornell ("Study Abroad," International Law at Cornell, Cornell Law School, www.lawschool.cornell.edu), Columbia ("Semester Study Abroad Programs," Study Abroad and Dual Degree Programs, Columbia Law School, www.law.columbia.edu), Georgetown ("Semester Abroad Opportunities," Transnational Programs, Georgetown Law, www.law.georgetown.edu), and Northwestern ("Study Abroad," Global Opportunities, Northwestern Pritzker School of Law, www.law.northwestern.edu).

20 Jean-Marie Guéhenno, *The End of the Nation-State* (Minneapolis: University of Minnesota Press, 2000), 1; Kenichi Ohmae, *The End of the Nation State: The Rise of Regional Economies* (New York: Free Press, 1995), 7. John Bendix et al., "Going Beyond the State?," *American Political Science Review* 86, no. 4 (1992): 1007–21.

21 Martin Carnoy,"The Demise of the Nation-State?," Theoria: A Journal of Social and Political Theory 97 (June 2001): 69–81.

22 David Held, *Democracy and the Global Order: From the Modern State to Cosmopolitan Governance* (London: Polity Press, 1995), 233.

23 A great example of this is Jindal Global Law School, India's first Global Law School, founded in 2009.

24 Tilburg University is the most obvious example, but there are various degrees of "curriculum globalization."

25 The members of the Global Law League offer a good example of this geographical variety. See "Law Schools Global League," Law Schools Global League, https://lawschoolsgloballeague.com.

26 Some examples are: Stanford ("W. A. Frank Global Law Program," Stanford Law School, https://law.stanford.edu), Notre Dame ("Global Law," Programs of Study, Notre Dame University Law School, https://law.nd.edu), and Harvard's institute for global law and policy ("Home," Institute for Global Law and Policy, Harvard Law School, http://iglp.law.harvard.edu).

27 Some examples are Tilburg University ("LLB Global Law," Bachelor's Programs, Tilburg University, www.tilburguniversity.edu), Universidad de Navarra ("The Global Law Program," Universidad de Navarra School of Law, www.unav.edu), and the Global Law Series from Cambridge University Press ("Global Law Series," Cambridge Core, Cambridge University Press, www.cambridge.org).

28 "Programs and Courses LLB Global Law," Global Law, Tilburg University, www.tilburguniversity.edu.

29 "Business Reforms," Doing Business, The World Bank, www.doingbusiness.org.

30 See William Ratliff and Edgardo Buscaglia, "Judicial Reform: The Neglected Priority in Latin America," *Annals of the American Academy of Political and Social Science* 550 (1997): 59–71.

31 Sida Liu, "The Legal Profession as a Social Process: A Theory on Lawyers and Globalization," *Law and Social Inquiry* 38, no. 3 (2013): 670–93.

32 This factor has led to the creation of Legal English courses all over the world. The University of Cambridge offered for some time the ILEC (International Legal English Certificate), which was later discontinued. See "Cambridge English: Legal (ILEC)," Exams and Tests, Cambridge English,www.cambridgeenglish.org. In Brazil, both FGV and PUC offer such a course (see "Inglês Jurídico," FGV Online,www5.fgv.br) and "Inglês Jurídico," Especialização e MB, PUC-SP, www.pucsp.br). Temple University offers a Legal English course at the Tokyo Campus (see "Legal English," Courses, Temple University Japan Campus, www.tuj.ac.jp). Yale offers the Law Seminar, which is a course that introduces the American Legal System and includes communication skills in Legal English (see "Law Seminar," Yale Summer Session, Yale Center for International and Professional Experience, https://summer.yale.edu).

33 Jacques Chevallier, *L'État post-modérne* (Paris: LGDJ, 2017).

34 Martin Hearson, "The Challenges for Developing Countries in International Tax Justice," *Journal of Development Studies* 54, no. 10 (2018): 1932–38.

35 See Luciana Gross Cunha et al., *The Brazilian Legal Profession in the Age of Globalization: The Rise of the Corporate Sector and its Impact on Lawyers and Society* (Cambridge: Cambridge University Press, 2018).

36 BRIC, the acronym for Brazil, Russia, India, and China, is believed to have been created by Jim O'Neill, a former chairman at Goldman Sachs.

37 "Brazil Takes Off," *The Economist*, November 12, 2009, www.economist.com.

38 Luciana Gross Cunha and José Garcia Ghirardi, "Legal Education in Brazil," in *The Brazilian Legal Profession in the Age of Globalization: The Rise of the Corporate Legal Sector and Its Impact on Lawyers and Society*, ed. Luciana Gross Cunha et al. (Cambridge: Cambridge University Press, 2018).

39 David Trubek, "Reforming Legal Education in Brazil: From the Ceped Experiment to the Law Schools at the Getulio Vargas Foundation," University of Wisconsin Legal Studies Research Paper No. 1180 (December 2011), https://ssrn.com.

40 See Luiz Carlos Bresser-Pereira,. *Economic Crisis and State Reform in Brazil: Toward a New Interpretation of Latin America* (Boulder: Lynne Rienner, 1996).

41 Celso Lafer, "Brazil and the World," in *Brazil: A Century of Change*, ed. Ignacy Sachs, Jorge Wilheim, and Paulo Sérgio Pinheiro and trans. Robert N. Anderson (Chapel Hill: University of North Carolina Press, 2009); Paulo Singer, "Economic Evolution and the International Connection," in Sachs, Wilheim, and Pinheiro, *Brazil: A Century of Change*, 55–100.

42 Jayanth K. Krishnan, Vitor M. Dias, and John Pence, "Legal Elites and the Shaping of Corporate Law Practice in Brazil: A Historical Study," *Law and Social Inquiry* 41, no. 2 (2016): 363–65.

43 Nelly P. Tromquist, "Internationalization as a Response to Globalization: Radical Shifts in University Environments," *Higher Education* 53, no. 1 (January 2007): 81–105; John Flood, "Legal Education in the Global Context Challenges from Globalization, Technology and Changes in Government Regulation," University of Westminster School of Law Research Paper No. 11–16 (2015), https://papers.ssrn.com.

44 Daniel R. Kelemen and Eric C. Sibitt, "The Globalization of American Law," *International Organization* 58, no. 1 (2004): 103–136; Martin Shapiro "The Globalization of Law," *Indiana Journal of Global Legal Studies* 1, no. 1 (1993): 37–64.

45 Frank Upham, "The Internationalization of Legal Education: National Report for the United States of America," *American Journal of Comparative Law* 62, no. S1 (2014): S97–126.

46 Diego Rafael Ambrosini and Natasha Schmitt Caccia Salnias, *Construção de um sonho: Direito GV: inovação, métodos, pesquisa, docência*, ed. Antônio Angarita (São Paulo: FGV, 2011).

47 Gabriel Lacerda, Joaquim Falcão, and Tânia Rangel, eds., *Aventura e Legado no ensino jurídico—Adventure and Legacy in Legal Education* (Rio de Janeiro: FGV, 2012).

48 Jacky Hummel, *Carl Schmitt: L'irréductible réalité du politique* (Paris: Michalon, 2005), 95–103.

49 Taylor, *Modern Social Imaginaries*, 23: "By social imaginary, I mean something much broader and deeper than the intellectual schemes people may entertain when they think about social reality in a disengaged mode. I am thinking, rather, of the ways people imagine their social existence, how they fit together with others, how things go on between them and their fellows, the expectations that are normally met, and the deeper normative notions and images that underlie these expectations."

15

Socratic Method, Philippine-style

To Unhave or Uphold?

EMILY SANCHEZ SALCEDO

The Philippines became an American territory at the conclusion of the Spanish-American War, when Spain ceded its archipelago colony (as well as Puerto Rico and Guam) to the United States pursuant to the Treaty of Paris signed on December 10, 1898. Amid escalating tensions with a growing independence movement, an American-style system of government was established, with English as the official language for legislation and the courts. An American-style education system was also adopted. And in 1908, the University of the Philippines (UP) was established in Manila; three years later it opened the UP College of Law, inspired by American legal traditions.

The architect of the new College of Law was the American lawyer George Malcolm, a University of Michigan graduate, who would later be appointed to the Supreme Court of the Philippines by US president Woodrow Wilson. The very first set of faculty members consisted of nine Americans and twelve Filipinos.[1] The new law school would later be admitted to the Association of American Law Schools, a membership it was able to keep until 1957, more than a decade after the Philippines gained independence from the United States on July 4, 1946.

Owing much of its origins to the United States, Philippine legal education readily embraced the Socratic method of instruction, and those who are able to successfully navigate this unique rite of passage and become a lawyer proudly wear an imaginary badge of superiority over other, uninitiated professionals.[2] Ironically, while the Socratic method has lost its luster in the United States, it continues to grip the imaginations of Filipino law students.[3]

Today, there are more than a hundred accredited law schools operating in the Philippines. Ranking those institutions used to be a matter of popular perception based on various factors such as location, costs of tuition, size of the student population, the popularity of leading faculty members, and the roster of distinguished alumni. With the sole exception of UP, law schools operated by religious congregations generally enjoyed greater prestige in a country that is predominantly Christian. Since that initial ranking system, however, the Legal Education Board started awarding citations to the ten highest-ranked law schools according to percentage of graduates who successfully pass the annual bar examination. The top three positions are consistently occupied by UP, the Ateneo de Manila School of Law (Ateneo), and the San Beda College of Law (San Beda).

The Socratic Method, Philippine-style

The Socratic method of instruction, introduced at Harvard Law School by dean Christopher Langdell in the 1870s,[4] had been a defining element of American legal education until it started to decline, after decades of distinction, with the realization that it is (or can be) cruel and psychologically abusive to law students.[5]

Under the traditional Langdellian Socratic method of instruction,

> the professor selects a single student without warning and questions the student about a particular judicial opinion that has been assigned for class. Often the professor begins by asking the student to state the facts of the case and then asks the student to explain how the court reasoned to an answer. The professor might then test the student's understanding of the case by posing a series of hypotheticals and asking the student to apply the reasoning of the case to the new fact patterns. The purpose of this questioning is to explore the strengths and weaknesses of various legal arguments that might be marshalled to support or attack a given rule or decision. To that end, the professor's inquiries are often designed to expose the weaknesses in the student's responses.[6]

The UP College of Law employs a "modified Socratic method" described as a "question-and-answer method accompanied by discussion . . . to enable the student to understand the vital points of the assignment, to develop analytical faculty, and to engender a critical attitude with respect to rules, conclusions, or theories."[7]

The Ateneo de Manila School of Law also employs a modified Socratic method of instruction referred to as "recitation," which is "a system found to be most effective in developing the student's power of analysis, reasoning ability and facility of expression."[8] It is more specifically described on the school's official website as follows:

> Daily assignments on codal provisions, court decisions, and authorities are given by the professor, and the student is called upon to recite to determine whether he/she has properly and correctly assimilated the law, its philosophy, and its application.
>
> Faculty members assist the students in the determination of the correct interpretation and practical application of the legal theories and provisions of law by judiciously supplementing the recitation method with occasional lectures designed to clarify whatever doubts the student may have on the subject. Lectures are also delivered by the professor to harmonize seemingly conflicting provisions of law, to point out recent court rulings, and to integrate the student's knowledge of the course under study.[9]

For its part, San Beda College of Law describes its method of instruction as "based on the combined lecture-quiz and question-and-answer recitation system, more commonly known as the Socratic Method."[10] San Beda similarly claims that this combination has been proven to be "most successful in effecting the harmonious development of the student's potential in reasoning and exposition."[11] San Beda's description does not digress too far from that of the Ateneo:

> The restatement of codal provisions is followed by a discussion of the basic philosophy underlying the same, and winds up with an analysis of the classic jurisprudence exemplifying the application of the legal doctrines involved. The professor lectures on the fine as well as the doubtful points of the laws, and the proper interpretation, construction, harmonization and application of apparently conflicting legal theories.[12]

What the foregoing do not include is a description of how the actual use of the Socratic method often subjects law students to serious ridicule and grave humiliation that can result in lifelong scars.

The Socratic Method and Women Law Students

The Socratic method has an even greater debilitating impact on women law students. Several studies at top law schools in the United States, such as Harvard and Yale, showed that women manifested lower class participation, less self-confidence, lower grades, less representation on the law review, and less probability of graduating with honors compared to their male counterparts.[13]

The groundbreaking study by Lani Guinier, Michelle Fine, and Jane Balin with Ann Bartow and Deborah Lee Satchel titled "Becoming Gentlemen: Women's Experiences at One Ivy League Law School" concluded that the University of Pennsylvania School of Law provided a hostile learning environment for a disproportionate number of its female students.[14] According to this article, many women felt "excluded from the formal educational structure of the Law School."[15] The study also found that "[o]ften, these women refuse to engage in discussion and opt for a strong stance of silence. . . . In other words, some women are disengaged from law school because they find its adversarial nature, its focus on argumentation and competition, and its emphasis on abstract as opposed to contextual reasoning to be unappealing and disengaging."[16] Women law students do not thrive in an environment of "ritualized combat."[17]

Other feminist legal scholars have shown support for the observation that Socratic classrooms are "male-oriented, competitive environments" where women feel "threatened and alienated."[18] Women law students often feel that they have "nothing to contribute and their voices were excluded from the debate," resulting in a "sense of inadequacy which may cause them to underperform on the examinations that later determine career prospects."[19] This chapter attempts to explore the extent of this phenomenon within the Philippine legal academy.

Methodology

What are the effects of the Socratic method on women law students in the Philippines? Does it foster the same feelings of threat and alienation? Does it similarly result in exclusion? Does it eventually lead to underperformance in law school and, thereafter, in legal practice?

In terms of raw student numbers, gender parity in Philippine law school admissions was not achieved until the turn of the twenty-first century. And while concepts of diversity and inclusivity may have started to become popular, it remains doubtful whether they have been fully embraced, as women are still constrained to assimilate to the predominantly masculine legal academic culture. As a result of this phenomenon, women today continue to lag behind their male counterparts in partnership positions at top law firms, in the faculty of top law schools, as well as in all levels of the judiciary. Does the Socratic method deserve part of the blame for this situation?

This chapter attempts to answer those questions through a parallel study of eighteen women lawyers who earned their basic law degrees from the three most prominent Philippine law schools: the state-funded UP, the Ateneo (headed by Jesuit priests), and the San Beda (operated by Benedictine monks).[20] This limitation in scope is partly due to the fact that these three law schools are considered trailblazers in the Philippine legal academy—the rest of the law schools in the country dutifully follow whatever innovations are implemented by any or all of these three. Admittedly, it is also partly due to limited time and resources.

Of the eighteen respondents, eight were graduates of UP, five were graduates of Ateneo, and five were graduates of San Beda. Half of the respondents are junior associates in medium- to large-size law firms; they attended law school between 2006 and 2016. The other half of the respondents held more senior positions in various fields of legal practice: two respondents were partners in small- to medium-size firms, three were professors of law, two were trial court judges, one was a corporate counsel, and one was a government administrator; they attended law school between 1995 and 2005, a period when women law students finally reached equal numbers with men. Only one of the junior associates was married with one child, while six of the senior lawyers were married with either one or two children. Three respondents earned their basic law degree with honors, and six earned advanced degrees in law under prestigious international scholarship grants; together these nine individuals represent 50 percent of respondents.

The De La Salle University Research Ethics Office granted clearance for this author to ask respondents to share personal experiences with the Socratic method and to gauge its effectiveness in enhancing both academic performance and professional achievements. More specifically, respondents were asked exploratory and open-ended questions to elicit comprehensive narratives on four areas:

1. How professors conduct the Socratic method of instruction and the general response of students in their particular law school;
2. their significant personal experiences in a Socratic classroom;
3. how their Socratic experiences may have affected their academic performance; and
4. how their Socratic experiences may have affected their early career.

Questionnaires were originally sent to twenty women lawyers, who responded positively to a request to participate in this research project. However, only eighteen responded with comprehensive answers within the relevant data-gathering period. Follow-up interviews were conducted to seek further clarification and/or elaboration on some of these answers.

Despite the diversity of their backgrounds as described above, the respondents who welcomed the opportunity to share personal experiences and opinions were observed to have commonality of interest and/or engagement in the areas of human rights, antidiscrimination legislation, and/or gender-equality initiatives. This common denominator turned out to be extremely helpful in this exploratory study, as it contributed to the respondents' more nuanced understandings and assessments of the effects of their individual Socratic experiences on their academic performances and early career options.

Results

The results obtained clarified the main points of inquiry in this study. Below I describe how the Socratic method works, respondents' personal experiences in the classroom, and the effects on academics and early careers. Respondents' direct quotations have been lightly edited for clarity.

How Professors Conduct the Socratic Method and the General Response of Students

The respondents were unanimous in their description of how professors conducted the Socratic method of instruction in their particular law schools: terrifying and humiliating. One respondent described with eloquence how each class usually starts:

> The professor would enter the door with a stern look on his face, much like an army general about to give orders to his soldiers. Smiles are very rare. Students immediately drop everything, sit straight, and focus their attention on the professor. Some make the sign of the cross and whisper an often-futile prayer. Some would instinctively curse; often louder than the prayer of the nearest classmate. Books are frantically [put] aside, but last-minute notes are kept handy in the hope that a quick side-glance will save the day.
>
> The professor would sit down, fix his tie or clean the lens of his spectacles ever so slowly, while heartbeats start racing ever so quickly. He takes out a stack of student cards, starts to shuffle then randomly, [and] picks the "chosen one." Once a card is picked, the "lucky" student immediately stands at attention and prepares to answer while the rest of the class is temporarily relieved. The "grilling" starts, which can last for a few minutes or for a full hour, sometimes depending on the substance of the student's answers, oftentimes depending on the professor's whim.

A typical professor will ask students to enumerate the salient facts of a particular case, spot the issue(s) to be resolved, state the decision of the court, and explain the legal basis for the ruling. While this requirement appears reasonable at first glance, most professors require an inordinate volume of reading assignments for each hour of class, so it is common for students to attend sessions with varying degrees of unpreparedness. Many depend on sheer luck or seek deliverance through prayer. This includes such things as the professor coming to class late, dismissing the class early, or arriving in a good mood; being called on to recite a familiar statute or to explain a decision that can be argued based on simple common sense; and being seated next to a classmate who is willing to whisper keywords to help refresh one's memory. Half of the respondents also recalled the times when they decided that the best recourse was not to attend class at all.

One respondent described everyone in her class to be in a "state of panic," while another respondent described the classroom atmosphere to be like "hell":

> The students are scared. You can feel the tension when the professor is shuffling the cards. You can hear the sigh of relief when someone else's name is called. On the other hand, the pressure upon the reciting student is double. Some tremble with fear. It is common to hear nervous voices stuttering or cracking, especially when the professor starts swearing. It is typical for professors to ridicule a student's answers, accent, physical appearance, or even the school where a student earned his or her prelaw degree. Oftentimes, the professor gets irritated when a student sounds uncertain on his or her initial reply to a question and makes him/her sit down immediately with no further chance to redeem oneself. Of course, the student would accept all these in silence. There is no room for any form of protest.

Significant Personal Experiences in the Socratic Classroom

All but one of the eighteen respondents disclosed that they personally experienced humiliating treatment at one point or another in law school. These experiences occurred either during their first or second year. A couple of respondents specifically pointed out the underlying power relations within the Socratic classroom. According to one:

> The professors wield so much power over the students. They ask arbitrary questions. They choose who to call and mock for the day. They laugh at imperfect answers as if they have never been through the stage of naivete that we were at.
>
> Students are rarely encouraged to ask questions or disagree with the professor's interpretation of the law. Then they are given grades according

to the professors' mood. They don't respect students and they portray themselves as gods.

One respondent shared that she "initially blamed [her]self for being so dumb" when she was not able to understand a vague question propounded to her by one professor. She was asked "what [she] read for the day." Thinking that it was only an introductory question, she replied candidly that she read "books, articles, magazines, and opinions from various fields," for which she received a furious scolding and a humiliating order to shut up and take her seat. She was not asked any other substantive question but received a failing mark for that day's recitation. Now an esteemed trial judge, the respondent reflected on this incident:

> On second thought, I felt that I was not given my day fairly and as honestly as possible. He was, to my mind, unprepared to ask for a more specific intelligent question at the first instance that he wanted me to start off and keep the ball rolling for him. It was not fair for me to get a failing mark for that recitation that to me [had] never begun after all. The succeeding questions [asked to other students], if asked of me, I honestly knew I could have very well answered if given the chance. The embarrassment I felt weighed in much less than the feeling of being deprived of expressing my modest knowledge on the topic for the day.

Another respondent shared her sad experience over a similarly worthless question:

> I particularly remember a professor who grilled me for the entire sixty minutes of class. He was looking for an answer that I could not come up with—it was not in the cases he assigned, it was not in the law. He asked me why the principle of stare decisis is not always followed. I gave all the answers I could intelligently think of—because no two cases are exactly the same in background facts and circumstances or because the pieces of evidence presented in the cases being compared were not of the same probative value, etc. He finally gave up on me when the bell rang. Indicating so much frustration in my apparently wrong answers, he said, "The Supreme Court makes mistakes because it is a human institution." I felt that he wasted the time of the entire class.

The rest of the respondents agreed that many professors use the Socratic method of instruction to disguise their own lack of preparation to conduct meaningful classes, as in the case of the above examples. While some questions can be as vague as these, there are also professors who take joy in asking minute details of the case that are not important in the resolution of the central issue before the court—for the simple reason that these kinds of questions can trip up even the most prepared student.

Other respondents have even more unfortunate stories to tell. For instance, sexist language is common fare in the Socratic classroom:

> It felt like my heart [would] explode. My heart was always pounding so fast during class. No matter how prepared I thought I was, I always felt nervous. One time there was this professor who ridiculed me for changing my answer. He said, "Women are really fickle-minded." When it was a male classmate who changed an answer, he said, "You must be gay because you are like these women who always change their minds—what a weakling."

Another respondent shared that she resented her decision to pursue law school because the Socratic method "demeaned" her. She lamented being "subjected to the mercy of some supreme being who can hurl personal attacks, crack sexist jokes, and give malicious examples that we have no choice but to accept."

> I was once asked during recitation what the acronym "ONS" stands for. I racked my brains but cannot recall having encountered the said acronym from the many government offices mentioned in the cases assigned for the day. It turned out that he meant "one-night-stand," a concept totally alien to the legal issues and factual scenarios we were discussing. It did not end there. He also asked one classmate about the profession of her boyfriend. She replied that he just earned his degree in management engineering. The professor said, "Oh, management of erection," to which our male classmates roared in laughter, but the women in the class were quiet as we did not find it funny at all.

Two other respondents separately shared that they often heard professors commenting on female students that, while they were "beautiful," it would be "much better if they also studied well." They identified one professor who commented on a female student's well-kept hair by saying, "Now I know why you have such long, black and shiny hair; it suck [*sic*] up all the contents of your head." Another professor called another female student "*Inday*," a name typically associated with housemaids, because she was wearing a plain-looking blouse over pants, had no make-up on, and tied her hair back in a simple ponytail.

Sadly, sexism is also evident in the evaluation of recitation performance. The respondents pointed out specific male professors during their time that gave higher recitation marks to female students who wore short skirts and make-up compared to those who came to class looking plain and ordinary. One respondent even claimed that an ageing professor, a retired magistrate, typically gave high recitation marks to well-dressed female students. Because he is hard of hearing, he had the tendency to give high grades to students who spoke loud and clear, regardless of substance, and gave low grades to students who were not as confident and eloquent.

Effects of the Socratic Experience on Academic Performance

The respondents were unanimous in acknowledging that the Socratic method was effective in ensuring that students come to class adequately prepared. The downside, however, is that they "study out of fear rather than being positively engaged." They are motivated to study to "avoid humiliation rather than to quench a genuine thirst for knowledge."

The quality of learning acquired in the classroom is also far from optimal. The majority of respondents acknowledged that, while they gained and retained a deeper understanding of the legal concepts and doctrines they were required to discuss during recitations, they failed to acquire the same level of learning by listening to exchanges between the professor and their classmates. This is because when a student is reciting, the rest of the class is barely listening. Practically all other students are busy scrambling to reread their hurried notes in anticipation of the possibility of being the next victim. Only those who have been recently called feel a reprieve for not being on deck at least for the rest of the hour or until the next class. Even worse, most students prefer to skip classes altogether when they feel unprepared, thereby resulting in further degradation of the opportunity to learn. In any event, the respondents believed that their performances during recitations were neither instrumental in getting passing marks in written examinations nor accurately accounted for in the computation of their final grades.

At least five respondents observed that most professors were not transparent with their grading system, so a recitation that went awry does not necessarily affect the students' final grade:

> Most professors claim that the final grade consists of one-third recitation, one-third midterm exam, and one-third final exam. That is often not followed. Many students never get good recitation grades or fail to pass either the midterm exam or the final exam, if not both, but most professors do the "bell curve" and for as long as you are within the average, you're safe.

At least five respondents recalled that there were notorious professors in their respective law schools who did not release students' grades promptly. When pressed by university administrators, most of these professors simply give a generic passing mark for everyone.

It is interesting that, while a good number of the younger respondents shared that being put on the spot during recitations forced them to think on their feet, some older respondents said that recitations mostly required the ability to recall what they have read and not necessarily the ability to analyze and understand the materials. They said there were many professors who simply elicit answers to "what" questions but fail to make the students understand the "how" and the "why" behind a legal doctrine. Many students therefore receive passing marks during recitations through memorization and not necessarily through critical analysis and sound reasoning. They eventually pass their written examinations not because the Socratic method taught them well but because their woeful recitation scores drove them to dedicate further time and energy toward reading textbooks on their own. Some respondents created small study groups and tried to analyze and understand more complex assignments with the help of close friends.

Two of the respondents who became law professors surmised that law school professors who use the Socratic method to instill fear in students probably never underwent any teacher-training workshops and had no idea how learning takes place in the human mind. Such professors still adhere to the "antiquated notion that harsh language is part of the training to toughen their students and prepare them for real-world practice, but we know now that this can be achieved even without resorting to humiliation or downright verbal abuse." Thus, for these respondents, the result was low morale and lack of motivation. They recalled how they "lost their enthusiasm for law and legal learning." They simply "went with the flow, managed to survive one day at a time, passed each course, and eventually got away from law school." As one respondent who earned her prelaw degree with honors strongly opined:

> I earned double baccalaureate degrees, *magna cum laude*. I wanted so much to finish law school with the same distinction and . . . knew I had all the potential, but I failed because the Socratic recitation, or at least the way that it was conducted by petty tyrants in law school, is far from my idea of how an effective method of instruction should be. I spent every single day reading as much as I could from the bottomless list of assigned materials, but how can one remember all the facts, ruling and rationale of all fifty cases assigned for a single hour of recitation? And this quantity is more or less repeated every course, every day, every semester! I felt that we were set up to fail. And to fail miserably because every wrong word we said, every small detail forgotten, every pause we had to make to dissect a question in our mind before blurting out an answer would be met by mocking laughter or sarcastic comments from the professors. Law school crushed my self-esteem. I used to excel academically, but law school made me resort to mediocrity to retain my sanity. Just aim for a 70 to pass the course and move on to the next. What do you need extra points for?

Two other respondents echoed this view and claimed they won prestigious international scholarships that allowed them to earn advanced degrees in law through their excellent undergraduate record, not because of high grades in law school or their Socratic experiences. They added that their experiences attending foreign universities made them realize the inherent mistakes in the Philippine version of Socratic questioning.

Effects of the Socratic Experience on Early Careers

It is customary for honor graduates of the top-three law schools to receive invitations to join the leading law firms in the country after graduation. Examinees who received the ten highest scores in the bar examination likewise enjoy the same privileged treatment, especially if they earned their law degrees from that trio of law schools. The rest of the graduates of the top three law schools still enjoy a more esteemed status compared to graduates of other law schools, including those who graduated with honors. They find themselves competing for jobs in smaller firms, in private corporations, and in government service. One of the respondents recalled:

> Only the top twenty students of the graduating class receive invitations from the big firms, so I did not even try to apply there. There were plenty of smaller firms anyway who were happy to have me because I am an Ateneo graduate.

The majority of the respondents agreed that academic achievements played a major role in getting job interviews and eventually landing a job. However, this is limited to initial work opportunities. On second and subsequent jobs, employers already give greater consideration to experience and skills. In any event, many honor graduates hired by big firms eventually leave for various reasons, the most common being burnout:

> I received several invitations from big firms. I chose the firm that specialized in a field of law that I found very interesting. However, after spending my first year of practice in that firm, I left for government service, as I can't stand the pressure and exhaustion required from junior associates.

Another respondent confirmed the stress at big law firms, something that became intolerable when she started raising a family:

> I was hired as a junior associate in a very popular law firm with international affiliation. I was assigned to [the] tax and corporate practice division. If law school demanded long hours of study, working in a big firm

> demanded even more. I would say that the discipline that I developed in law school helped me go through the transition. However, after a little over a year, I realized it was not what I really wanted. I did not want to be a slave of the billable hours system forever. My husband and I were planning a family, and I can't imagine spending more time in the firm than with my children. When my daughter was born, I knew it was time to go.

Another respondent shared the fact that she declined a position in a large firm altogether:

> I received an invitation to join the country's biggest law firm, but I opted not to. I joined a small firm led by a highly respected human rights advocate. I was sick and tired of the vicious competitive atmosphere in law school and knew that the same pervades the huge law firms. I am not going to live every single day of my life comparing my billable hours with that of my colleagues. Besides, I am really inclined toward human rights and public interest law practice.

When respondents were asked if the Socratic method prepared them well for their first or subsequent employments, the majority responded in the negative. At best, they shared how their experiences in the Socratic classroom gave them more confidence in the courtroom. More specifically, they said it became easier to argue before the court or against an opposing counsel because the courtroom atmosphere duplicated the tense feelings that pervaded the Socratic classroom, something they had already managed to endure for four years. One respondent claimed that meeting arrogant judges or prosecutors in the courtroom was no longer intimidating because they resembled her law school professors. Nonetheless, they all agreed that one does not succeed in litigation without doing the preparatory work. Cases are not won on confidence alone. Moreover, a good number of the respondents, who were not or were no longer litigating, shared how the Socratic method was of little or no relevance to their current careers:

> The Socratic method, when employed in the proper way, can be useful in instilling discipline, work ethic, logical and critical reasoning, [and] thinking on one's feet. However, as we know, the "modified Socratic

method in the Philippines" is far from how Socrates intended it to be. I don't think our brand of recitation is the only way to instill these values or to learn these skills. For instance, clinical legal education can also instill similar values. Besides, my subsequent jobs did not require courtroom work but other skills—lobbying, negotiations, [and] policy and institutional reform—that have no use for the Socratic method anymore.

Another respondent shared her experiences as a litigator who valued alternative dispute resolution (i.e. settlement negotiations, arbitration, etc.), where her Socratic experience of combative argumentation had no relevance:

I was thrown into litigation early on as I joined a small firm. I agree that rigorous recitation in law school gave me a good introductory practice, so to speak, for my future job of appearing and arguing in court. However, my boss was a firm believer in alternative dispute resolution. He used to tell his associates that sometimes the best lawyer is the one who keeps his client out of court and that's because in every courtroom [is] full of litigants, [and] regardless of the brilliance of the lawyers arguing for each one of them, half are destined to be losers. The other half who will eventually be winners may have spent too much time, money, and effort that the victory may already be meaningless. So, we start each and every case review with an eye for possible amicable resolution of the specific conflict(s) that our clients were facing. Part of our advice was always to try to negotiate first, to see if there's greater value at proposing a compromise instead of gearing up for a protracted litigation. True enough, many of our clients were better served by that approach. You see, the Socratic method, which attempts to enhance a lawyer's skills at argumentation, sometimes bordering on arrogance, often has no place on the negotiation table.

Finally, a couple of respondents shared their interesting observations on how the job market for new lawyers is affected by influence-peddling. In particular, they pointed out that law school fraternities maintain a formidable circle of influence not only in law firms but also in private companies and government offices, thereby putting their members at a huge advantage over nonmembers. For these male law students, academic achievements in law school are secondary to fraternity affiliation when they are hunting for their first jobs and as they rise through the ranks. As a result, whether or not the Socratic method of instruction had any effect on their academic performance becomes totally irrelevant in their careers:

> I had this realization when I was looking for my first job: affiliation matters. To begin with, graduates of UP and Ateneo form one huge preferred group over graduates of other law schools. Those who graduated in the top twenty [of their class] form an elite subgroup. But there are other subgroups that are often more important than being in the top twenty. For instance, there are two major fraternities in our law school. It is widely believed that members of these fraternities receive preferential treatment from professors who are also members of the same fraternities. After graduation, fraternity members customarily seek referrals from their "senior brods"[21] who are well-placed in the judiciary or in the legislature to secure employment. Of course, law firms where partners are "senior brods" also prioritize the hiring of their "junior brods." So when there are two contenders for a particular position, one being an academic achiever but nonmember and another who is intellectually average but a member of the fraternity, the hiring decision is often in favor of the "brother." This privilege is customarily extended to the wives of these "brothers." I think this is a shameful reality.

Some Unexpected Implications

In addition to the observations noted above, two unexpected but certainly important implications arise from the information gathered from the eighteen respondents. First, women law students tend to lose a significant part of themselves in law school. And second, some women lawyers nonetheless eventually become accepting of, or even grateful for, their law school experiences.

The extended hours that the respondents devoted to studying for daily recitations not only meant less sleep but also led to less time for extracurricular activities that could have further enriched their law school experiences. They also had less time to be with family and friends outside the law school community. All but one respondent claimed "losing their weekends," as these had to be devoted to reading assignments instead of spending time for themselves or with loved ones. One respondent who used to work as a part-time researcher while in law school shared this anecdote:

> I was preoccupied with the everyday grind at work and daily rigors of law school, so I didn't really have the time to reflect on this. Back then, I didn't feel that I was missing out on things or that I was deprived of anything except sleep. However, looking back, I feel that I sacrificed time for myself since I was dividing my time between work, law school, and family obligations. I didn't have time for hobbies, sports, or other personal pursuits.

Another respondent shared that she regretted the decision to get married while attending law school because it was "doubly stressful to start a family while studying." After suffering a miscarriage, she and her husband decided to postpone having children until after she was able to earn her license.

But losing time for oneself is only one aspect of the downside. The humiliating experiences in law school can significantly erode a student's self-esteem. One respondent shared how the "daily dose of humiliation" during recitations diminished her self-worth:

> I was a consistent honor student during my younger years, but in law school I had my first taste of failing marks during recitation and midterm exams. I studied very hard and prayed even harder. But one can never be completely ready for recitation. The professors will always find a way to put you down. I started doubting my abilities. With [this] daily dose of humiliation, my self-confidence was soon replaced by a relentless feeling of not being good enough. This eventually crept into my personal life. I had a very domineering husband who practically controlled every aspect of my life. [It was] ironic that I was studying law but could not assert myself. The feeling of being worthless was the same in school and at home. Thankfully, when I became a lawyer, I was able to gather enough courage and resources to annul that marriage.

Nonetheless, the majority of the respondents suggested that going through the tedious requirements of law school is a necessary process of refinement that was eventually for their own good. One respondent shared this:

> A bad recitation would haunt me for days, and it would take some time before I [was] able to forget the incident and move on. As years passed by, I learned how to cope and deal with such situations and just consider it as a learning experience to do better next time. I think this experience in law school taught me to be more resilient and helped me adjust more when I was already working.

Humiliation became easier to accept because it was the result of a personal choice and a shared experience:

> At first it was unnerving, but after witnessing almost everyone in class having the same experience, my nerves slowly began to ease and I no longer seemed to mind the embarrassment that much. As a matter of fact, I think my friends and I became closer because of the endless hours that we spent studying and crying together. I learned to accept and appreciate this as part and parcel of law school life. I wanted to be a lawyer, so I have to embrace the process of becoming one.

A couple of respondents went on to express gratitude for their law school experiences, which helped them develop stronger personalities and made them better advocates for their clients.

Conclusion

The undesirable effect of the Socratic method on women law students in the Philippines does not necessarily manifest through underperformance in the academy and, subsequently, in the practice of the legal profession (as it does in the United States) for several reasons.

First, Philippine society is hierarchical. Law students silently embrace the sacrifices demanded by law school because they were trained since childhood that submissiveness to authorities is a valuable trait. Filipino families generally raise children in a culture of respect and obedience. First and foremost, children obey their parents without protest, lest they receive various forms of corporal punishment. This tough-love ethos is explained as the parents' way of instilling discipline that will mold children into responsible adults. Other authority figures in the life of a Filipino child include schoolteachers and/or the parish priest. During the Spanish colonial era and shortly thereafter, these authority figures were merged into one as schools were run by religious congregations; Ateneo and San Beda are good examples. Corporal punishment was also widely practiced in schools even as the Family Code contains a clear proscription that nonetheless carried no penalties. In 2017, the Philippine government launched a five-year multisectoral road map designed for the progressive reduction of violence against children in different settings, including, first and foremost, both home and school environments. Unfortunately, a comprehensive bill that aimed to bring this plan into fruition was vetoed by President Rodrigo Duterte in 2019.

Thus, even in law school, where students are already majority age, disobedience to authority (e.g., failure to study the materials assigned by the professor) still elicits admonition. Students readily accept professors' exercise of power and authority over them even when instructors cross the bounds of decency.

Second, the humiliating experience during recitations is universal in Philippine law schools. Professors see to it that all students are called on and grilled to the point of embarrassment as some sort of rite of passage. The possibility for men to dominate the discussion and for women to feel alienated is unlikely because there is little opportunity, if at all, for students to volunteer for recitations or to join an ongoing discussion between the professor and a classmate. The respondents unanimously confirmed that everyone wants to avoid the embarrassing experience as much as possible, but there is very little success in guaranteeing that outcome.

Third, there is an apparent disconnect between the Socratic experience and measurable academic performance. As shared by the respondents, the marks they received during recitations rarely affected final grades because of the arbitrariness of the grading system employed by most professors. As to whether the Socratic experience wields influence over the quality of learning, the results are diverse. While a few respondents claimed that rigorous recitations taught them to think on their feet, a greater number claimed that the stressful recitation experience was not an effective way to achieve a deeper level of understanding of the legal concepts and doctrines being discussed in class. At the end of the day, most respondents acknowledged that their unsatisfactory recitation grades drove them to study harder for written examinations. It is this greater amount of devotion to studying on their own, or in the safe company of their friends, that resulted in their being able to pass their courses and eventually graduate from law school.

Fourth, in view of the irrelevance of the Socratic method to measurable academic performance, there appears to be a greater disconnect between the Socratic experience and early employment options—and even more so on subsequent opportunities for career development. The respondents' insights on the old-boys network and the culture of patronage that animate the job market for legal practitioners in the Philippines further muddle whatever remaining connection there might be.

Nonetheless, by perpetuating patriarchal traditions, the Socratic method of instruction has brought harm not only to women in particular but also to society in general. Present-day Philippine society is still patriarchal due to three centuries of Spanish colonization, which brought with it the romantic notion that women are designed and destined for marriage and motherhood. Prior to the Philippines becoming an American territory, education was reserved for men, and the only options available to women outside the home were entering the convent or teaching young children. For decades since the UP College of Law was founded in 1911, women constituted a very small minority among the law school population. The same was true after Ateneo opened its doors to women in the 1970s and San Beda in the 1980s.

Thus, even when women law students started to enter law school in greater numbers and attain parity (in numbers) with men at the turn of the twenty-first century, they are still confronted today with the ideal that the legal profession is designed for men with strong and assertive personalities who are hardworking and willing to devote extended hours to its pursuit. The courtroom is akin to a battlefield where lawyers must be trained like warriors in order to succeed. Toward this end, legal education must provide both intellectual training and appropriate character formation, and the means widely believed to be most effective in doing so is the Socratic method of instruction. If women desire to fit into this ideal, they must think and act like these men. They must devote all their time and attention to law school assignments, even if it means giving up personal needs and desires and losing a significant part of themselves in the process. Ironically, at the end of the day, they are expected to be grateful for the "refining" experience. Hearts were set afire among the eighteen women lawyers who participated in this project, but the need to please the demigod, pass the course, and earn the degree muted whatever brewing revolt there was—until their liberating disclosures in the narratives shared here.

The Socratic method of instruction, long considered integral to the system of legal education in the Philippines, has not been adequately scrutinized in the past to determine whether it truly and effectively facilitates learning. Worse, the profanities and sexual innuendos that are shameful hallmarks of the method are simply dismissed by most male law students as trivial and accepted by some female law students as normal. If Philippine law schools are inclined to keep the Socratic method as part and parcel of legal education, then a collective effort must be undertaken to examine how it has deteriorated into the dreadful classroom exchange that it represents today. Law schools should revert to their original design: to foster a deeper intellectual discussion in the classroom and, above all, transform the classroom experience into a more respectful exercise. Acceptance of and appreciation for humiliation in the classroom is both unfortunate and inappropriate.

Finally, law schools should genuinely accommodate women, not force them to assimilate masculine norms. When the training ground for women lawyers—upon whom society should be able to depend for a stronger resolve in upholding gender equality—is itself entrenched in oppressive and discriminatory practices, we can only expect a genuinely inclusive society to be an obscure and distant dream. Law schools should breed equity from within before they can produce guardians of justice for society at large.

NOTES

1 George A. Malcolm, "The College of Law University of the Philippines," *Philippine Law Journal* 1, no. 1 (August 1914): 6.

2 Andres D. Bautista, *Reinventing Philippine Legal Education* (Bangkok: ASEAN Law Association, 2006), 7.

3 Ibid.

4 Robert Stevens, *Law School: Legal Education in America from the 1850s to the 1980s* (Chapel Hill: University of North Carolina Press, 1983), 51–72.

5 Orin S. Kerr, "The Decline of the Socratic Method at Harvard," *Nebraska Law Review* 78, no.1 (1999): 113, 118.

6 Ibid., 114.

7 "Methods and Materials of Instruction," University of the Philippines College of Law, http://law.upd.edu.ph.

8 "Methods of Instruction," Ateneo de Manila School of Law, http://ateneo.edu.

9 Ibid.

10 San Beda College of Law, *Students' Handbook* (2017), 19–20.

11 Ibid.

12 Ibid.

13 E.g., Adam Neufeld, "Costs of an Outdated Pedagogy? Study on Gender at Harvard Law School," *American University Journal of Gender, Social Policy & the Law* 13, no. 3 (2005), and Catherine Weiss and Louise Melling, "The Legal Education of Twenty Women," *Stanford Law Review* 40, no. 5 (May 1988): 1299–1369.

14 Lani Guinier et al., "Becoming Gentlemen: Women's Experiences at One Ivy League Law School," *University of Pennsylvania Law Review* 143, no. 1 (November 1994): 1–110.

15 Ibid., 5.

16 Ibid., 65.

17 Ibid.

18 Kerr, "The Decline of the Socratic Method at Harvard," 121.

19 See ibid., 121–122, citing Lani Guinier et al., "Becoming Gentlemen," 46–51 (discussing the results of a study suggesting that the Socratic classroom is a particularly hostile environment for women law students, who are less able to learn in competitive milieus than are men); Jennifer Jaff, "Frame-Shifting: An Empowering Methodology for Teaching and Learning Legal Reasoning," *Journal of Legal Education* 36, no. 2 (June 1986): 249, 258–61 (asserting that the Socratic method is patriarchal); Carrie Menkel-Meadow, "Portia in a Different Voice: Speculations on a Women's Lawyering Process," *Berkeley Women's Law Journal* 1, no. 1 (September 1985): 39, 45–49 (discussing women's emphasis on relationships rather than issues when problem-solving); Deborah L. Rhode, "Missing Questions: Feminist Perspectives on Legal Education," *Stanford Law Review* 45, no. 6 (July 1993): 1547, 1557 (arguing that the method "runs counter to feminism's most basic insights, which stress learning through empathetic and collaborative exchange"); and Susan H. Williams, "Legal Education, Feminist Epistemology, and the Socratic Method," *Stanford Law Review* 45, no. 6 (July 1993): 1571, 1573 (arguing that knowledge is a socially constructed collective experience, which cannot be attained via reasoning within one student's own mind).

20 There are currently two basic programs of law study in the Philippines: the Bachelor of Laws (LLB) degree and the Juris Doctor (JD) degree. Either degree qualifies a graduate to sit for the national bar examination.

21 Fraternity members colloquially refer to themselves as "brods," a shortened form of the word "brothers."

PART 3

US Perspectives

16

Rethinking Assumptions about the Global Influence of US Legal Education

SUSAN D. CARLE

A collection of country studies is contained in this important volume. As brilliantly conceived by Susan Bartie and David Sandomierski, these studies, as well as the related 2018 symposium and subsequent Law and Society session dedicated to these studies, highlight the emergence of an exciting new field for legal scholarship, which we might preliminarily define as "critical comparative legal education histories." My assigned role as commentator to this project is to provide perspective from my vantage point as a critical scholar of US legal profession history. I thus provide some tentative observations in this chapter, hoping that they may serve the purpose of sparking further critique.

This collective project started out as an investigation into the influence of US legal education on other legal education systems around the globe. What I believe we discovered through our symposium and the case studies that make up this volume, however, is that US legal education has had *less* influence around the world than traditional narratives assume. A second general lesson that emerges from the case studies is one well known to legal historians—namely, that to understand the extent of the influence of a legal transplant, it is important to trace the specific lines of the transmission of ideas such as those surrounding legal education, the topic of this volume.[1] It is not enough simply to lay two systems of legal education side by side and look for similarities. As this volume teaches, even ideas with identical labels, such as the "Socratic method" and the "case method," turn out, when examined closely, to refer to disparate practices in different legal education systems. A third lesson is that, to the extent that American law professors have had something of an outsized influence, that influence has occurred inside the sphere of academia and post-JD studies rather than in basic legal education. Finally, I will further propose, comparative analysis of the case studies in this volume points to the importance of financial resources to the dissemination and influence of legal ideas. Put simply, more resources generally allow for louder voices.

From the perspective of one scholar currently residing in the United States, I end this essay with a focus on the consequences that the current downturn in the financial health of US law schools portends. The long-term fallout from these changes remains uncertain but poses an interesting topic for scholars of comparative legal education. If my tentative hypothesis is correct, the US legal education's shrinking affluence should reduce the amplification of US legal academics' voices. At the same time, prospective new law students in the United States are voting with their feet in eschewing law for other studies, especially business. These emerging trends, too, present further promising topics for future comparative studies.

What We Learned

It is not a coincidence that the idea for this project arose when it did: during a period in which the international influence of the United States is on the wane, in part due to the policies of the Donald Trump administration and in part due to a longer process of shifting global political and economic tectonics. What better time to assess the history of old regimes of US dominance than during a transition period in which those regimes are being replaced with as-yet unclear new sets of relations and influences? The founding question of the collective project reflected in this volume thus becomes: What was the history of US legal education's global influence, as seen from the perspective of the current period characterized by a fading regime of US supremacy?

To investigate that question empirically, one must first ask what characteristics distinguish US legal education from non-US systems. Investigating that question proves much more difficult than one might imagine, as the contributions to this volume illustrate. Indeed, virtually every contributor imagines US legal education as something different. The concept of US legal education ends up as a symbol or a mythology, a fable that may in fact reflect a passing regime of dominance of US ideas in the transnational legal academy rather than the reality of relevant practices on the ground. As we discussed during the symposium, several characteristics of US legal education present themselves as potentially distinctive, though on closer examination none turn out to be unique to the United States. For example, since the late 1800s, US legal education has been primarily university-based.[2] Bruce Kimball discusses this feature of US legal education in his contribution to this volume (chapter 1) as well as in his definitive biography of Christopher C. Langdell, the founder of the so-called Harvard method.[3] As Kimball points out, Langdell took the university-based model for legal education from the German system; it was by no means uniquely US-based.

Relatedly, US legal education is an academic program, as opposed to a vocationally based scheme. European-based systems share that feature, too, and they developed it long before the United States did;[4] it is not a feature US legal education can claim as a unique contribution to the development of legal education.

Another related feature we discussed at the symposium is that legal education should be of high quality; this again is hardly a distinctively US-based idea. To the extent that US legal education can claim to be of particularly high quality—and it is hard to make that claim today given the impressive innovation in legal education methods occurring in many part of the world—the richness of US law school offerings arises from the inordinately abundant resources that historically have been available to the US legal education system, for reasons I will discuss below.

On another related point, US legal education involves a long period of study prior to be being licensed to practice. This, too, is a feature shared by many legal systems, though systems vary in the ways in which they organize their periods of classroom study, such as whether it occurs at the undergraduate or graduate level. Systems likewise vary in the ways they handle apprenticeships. Apprenticeships involve a post–law school period of training in many systems, but they do not exist in the US system. Their absence arguably contributes to the present problems US law students face in finding employment after law school; thus, their absence is hardly a feature of US legal education other systems have wanted to emulate. In his contribution, Philip Girard (chapter 3) compares the Canadian experience to that of the United States, explaining that the Association of American Law Schools (AALS) and American Bar Association opposed the idea of apprenticeships for newly minted

US lawyers.[5] Now, in a tighter economic climate, legal clients are loathe to subsidize the early years of apprenticeship-like training overpaid new US law firm associates previously received. Students who graduate without being practice-ready find it difficult to obtain desirable first jobs.[6] Finally, a notable feature of US legal education that we discussed at the symposium is that it tends to cater to the elite; again, that feature is not particularly US-based.

Another group of characteristics that US legal education might claim as distinctive are those traceable to the Langdellian or so-called Harvard model that professor Kimball writes about so well.[7] Again, closer inspection shows that these features are not unique to the United States. For example, traditional US legal educators use the so-called Socratic method, by which they mean a practice in large-classroom teaching in which professors ask students questions about legal texts, usually appellate cases, that students have been assigned in preparation for class and are expected to discuss in a back-and-forth with the instructor.[8] As we learned through this collective project, however, many legal systems have experimented with disparate versions of law teaching that they label the "Socratic method." For example, as Emily Sanchez Salcedo explained in her conference presentation (see chapter 15), in the Philippines the Socratic method involves teachers requiring students to stand in class to recite case facts and holdings, often accompanied by a certain amount of strictness, harshness, or even humiliation from the teacher in response.[9]

In Japan, as Yoshiharu Matsuura described in his symposium presentation (chapter 10), law professors tried their own version of the Socratic method in the early 2000s, only to find this experiment to be an abysmal failure so that they quickly abandoned this method. In US law schools today, teachers use the Socratic method as a means of generating lively classroom discussions by eliciting a range of voices from students around the room.[10] In other words, the concept of a Socratic method of teaching does not appear to be a useful distinguishing characteristic of US-influenced teaching because there is so much variation in the meanings attributed to that teaching practice, both within the United States and around the world.

The same problem emerges in examining the concept of the case method. In Langdellian terms, this teaching method involves studying rules contained in appellate cases and developing the ability to extract, synthesize, and apply these rules.[11] An alternative definition of the case method, however, involves teaching the common law method of reasoning by analogy from facts in one case to outcomes in the next case. This second kind of teaching of the common case method of legal reasoning is not specifically Langdellian or American. It is what all common law courts do and, therefore, what legal educators in common law systems must teach law students to do as well. Yet another potential meaning of the case method involves the business school method of teaching through the study of detailed case studies.[12] Again, teaching by the case method is not at bottom a distinguishing feature of US-influenced legal education.[13]

Another idea that emerged from several presentations at the symposium involves the difference between teaching law with a focus on general or universal—or perhaps merely dominant—rules and principles versus teaching the specifics of the law in particular localities and contexts.[14] In her symposium presentation, Susan Bartie rightly critiqued the tendency of Australian legal education to focus on rules shared throughout common law systems rather than the particulars of the Australian experience as reflected in law emerging in its local jurisdictions. José Garcez Ghirardi (chapter 14) presented a complimentary argument critiquing the trend among elite law schools to institute "global law" programs that transmit a dominant ideology emphasizing the inexorability of globalization and the withering away of the power of nation-states to control their own destinies.[15] To be sure, these observations capture important trends in legal education conceived of on a global scale, but they do not describe trends attributable to US influence in particular. Instead, both Bartie and Garcez Ghirardi describe phenomena related to first world domination more generally.

And even when US influences can be detected, this project shows that their import must be carefully analyzed. This lesson emerges from Bartie's contribution to this volume (chapter 4), which is different from her symposium presentation. In her chapter, Bartie traces how, in the 1950s and 1960s, US legal ideas offered a modest contribution to progressive Australian scholars' movement away from traditionally dominant English jurisprudence—in Australian legal education and legal scholarship alike. As Bartie points out, it was not that US legal ideas had a particularly large influence on developing Australian jurisprudential models; instead, progressive members of a "first community" of full-time Australian law professors sought alternative ideas, which happened to be American, to provide a counterbalance to traditional English legal thought. Through her clever analysis of book reviews, Bartie shows that many ideas caught these Australian legal scholars' attention. These ideas included not only the "spirit" of Legal Realism and legal functionalism but also, even more significantly, the US Legal Process School. That school provided ideas about presenting many types of legal materials, rather than solely appellate cases, to students in legal textbooks and thus rejected the Langdellian method in favor of richer and more varied understandings of law and how to teach it.[16] Likewise, David Sandomierski (chapter 13) writes about the influence not of the Langdellian method but of the Legal Process School in Canadian legal education.[17]

Bartie and Sandomierski specifically trace the specific line of the transmission of ideas, a type of analysis I have encouraged as a particularly rewarding and illuminating way of understanding cross-cultural influences. In both Australia and Canada, that transmission occurred mostly through legal academics' participation in US graduate programs to obtain LLM and SJD degrees. Bartie captures the patronizing attitude of Harvard Law School dean Erwin Griswold toward Australian law schools. Griswold may have mistakenly thought that Australian law schools should look more like American ones, but that does not mean that Australian law professors agreed. Indeed, by most measures Australian law schools have by now outpaced US ones in adopting innovative best practices and skills-based training. In other words, US legal academics may have believed they had or should have an outsized influence on legal education in other legal systems, but that does not mean they actually did or should have such influence.

Thus we learned from this project that foreign influence from crossovers among systems is not inevitable or predictable. An example is France, as Jean-Louis Halpérin reports (chapter 11). According to Halpérin, in France's centuries-old legal education system there has been virtually no US influence despite some French scholars' interest in transcontinental dialogue on matters of legal theory.[18] Merike Ristikivi's symposium contribution, and Irene Kull, Merike Ristikivi, and Aleksei Kelli's country report on Estonia (chapter 8), further illuminate this point. Proximity, geography, shared traditions, and history resulted in Germans and Scandinavians having the dominant influence on the development of a new profession following the coming of a new political and legal system to Estonia in 1991. The takeaway of this illuminating contribution is, in essence, that US law professors' attempt to impart their influence on the new Estonian legal system was simply too little, too late.[19] In that post-Soviet regime, there is virtually no US influence on methods of legal education (although, it bears noting, this is less true of some other post-Soviet nations in which US legal academics were active after the fall of the Iron Curtain). And in Japan as well, as professor Matsuura explains, even though law schools explored borrowing from the US model, that experiment utterly failed.[20]

In short, this project exposes the somewhat jumbled mythology that exists as to what US legal education is and how it influenced legal education globally. Some of the many important takeaways this project offers include the importance of not exaggerating US influence on global legal education, decentering the Langdellian model, and specifically tracing the transmission of ideas across legal systems as well as the details of their transformation as legal transplants in new systems. Only after doing this work can one reach well-grounded conclusions about cross-system influences.

The preceding case studies further suggest that the specific situation in which US influence emerges most clearly is in the transmission of financial resources, and associated ideas and conditions, to support capacity-building around legal education in a number of nations in Africa. On that continent as well, results were disparate and country-specific. For example, the Ford Foundation injected funds in both Ghana and Nigeria though its SAILER project.[21] However, as John Harrington and Ambreena Manji's contribution (chapter 5) explains, in Ghana the rise to political power of Kwame Nkrumah wiped out the influence of US law professors who had worked there under Ford Foundation funding.[22] Nigeria's political history produced less stark results, as we learn from Josephine Dawuni and Rebecca Badejogbin's contribution (chapter 6). As they explain, in the current period, international organization funding, especially through the World Bank, encourages a worldwide search for best practices in legal education rather than anything specifically US-based.[23]

In sum, as one looks more closely and region-specifically at the extent of US influence on legal education globally, one finds two distinct realities. First, it is not pervasive. And second, in order to trace the transmission of ideas about legal education, it is necessary to look in detail at particular contexts and search for specific lines of transmission, which may or may not exist *or* persist.

A Tentative Hypothesis

The stories of Ghana and Nigeria help illuminate possible general hypotheses about when and why US influence on legal education occurred. In keeping with the theme of financial resources, I want to suggest that the real influence of US legal education—and specifically, US legal academia—has come from the abundant resources that US law schools have commanded, at least traditionally.

Much of what has made US law schools look like the Cadillac version of what legal education can offer comes from the outsized resources US law schools enjoyed until the past decade. Unlike legal education in many other countries, which is primarily government-funded, the majority of US law schools are private nonprofit institutions.[24] The best-funded of these private nonprofits have large endowments and the capacity to lavish resources on law schools and their faculties.

In visiting law schools in the US and many other countries, I have been struck especially by the physical differences between the primarily publicly funded law schools in other countries and the law schools in the United States. In many other countries, law schools look like publicly funded institutions that are working to stretch every taxpayer-provided dollar to maximum effect. In contrast, many US law schools—especially those in the most elite tier—are attached to historically prosperous nonprofit institutions of higher education. One is immediately struck by their impressive physical plants, funded through generous endowments. Large and comfortable libraries sit next to classrooms full of state-of-the-art technology. Students stroll through verdant campuses across well-manicured lawns that must cost a small fortune to maintain. They relax in plush student centers and work out in well-equipped campus gyms.

Law professors, too, have fancy private offices, expert and speedy library services, and sometimes school-funded private dining facilities. Indeed, in the United States, law professors are regarded as the "fat cats" of academia.[25] Tenure-track law professors make higher salaries than professors in any other discipline except business.[26] Salaries for tenured law professors remain comparatively high; in 2019, the average salary for a tenured professor in a private institution in legal studies (which includes both law and other law-related disciplines, so is likely understated) was US$168,742, compared to an overall average in all disciplines of US$100,000.[27] These salaries rest on the high tuitions that privately funded US law schools charge, which in turn were historically supported by statistics showing high future earning power for law school graduates.[28]

High student tuitions and large endowments historically have supported generous funding for professors' scholarship. Professors at higher-ranked schools enjoy relatively low teaching loads, frequent sabbaticals, school-funded research assistants, and generous conference travel funding. School-supported, student-edited law reviews further reflect this abundance of resources, as professor Pnina Lahav astutely focuses on in her contribution (chapter 12).[29] The plethora of student-edited law reviews in most US law schools serve as reliable publication outlets for faculty scholarship.[30] In addition, US law schools have somehow convinced their law students that the menial labor of producing these many law reviews is an especially prestigious undertaking. Top law students thus work for free for legal scholars publishing in US student-edited law journals. Despite their amateur status, students choose the articles they want to publish. Being bright novices without long acculturation in their academic discipline, they have tended in prior periods to be more open-minded in their judgments. This has allowed US legal scholarship more room for experimentation. Students attracted to emerging trends in legal scholarship create room for new scholarly movements such as critical legal studies, critical race studies, law and narrative, clinical scholarship, and more.

At the same time, as professor Girard's chapter aptly points out, the AALS has convinced US bar associations that law should be an academic discipline rather than a vocational training program.[31] Law professors have further convinced their university administrations that only law graduates can judge the quality of legal scholarship, thereby further increasing freedom from oversight constraints for legal scholarship in comparison to other disciplines.

In short, I propose, to the extent that US legal ideas have had an outsized influence, it is because US law professors have had an outsized opportunity to project those ideas. Much of the perceived influence of US legal academia comes from this: US law professors' voices can be louder because they benefit from resources that help them project their voices more broadly. It is not that US teaching methods at the basic legal education level have been particularly influential; it is that US academic voices, most important in teaching at the LLM, SJD, and PhD levels, can be stronger due to the resources that undergird their academic work.

Yet the funding structure that supports the perceived dominance of US legal academia is in fairly grave jeopardy today. US law schools today are suffering the effects of harder times for the US legal profession. US law firms face clients that demand more economical billing and, especially in the realm of Big Law, greater global competition. Statistics show that the employment market for lawyers is still suffering the lingering effects of the 2008–2009 Great Recession; job prospects for new law graduates remain bleaker than in the decades before.[32] Median wages for students who find good jobs continue to climb, but fewer new graduates have found such jobs within the first nine or ten months after graduation than was the case two decades earlier.[33] The effects of the current COVID-19 pandemic are not yet clear but certainly will not improve new graduates' job prospects given the likely lingering effects of economic dislocation and widespread hardship.

The law school admissions market has (belatedly) caught up with the last decade's job-market news. One group of researchers estimates that the aggregate annual tuition revenue for all accredited US law schools has fallen by more than US$1.5 billion from its inflation-adjusted peak in 2011–2012.[34] Fewer students have been applying to law schools[35] (with the exception of a slight, unexpected "Trump bump" in law school applications in 2017–2018, which was not repeated the year after).[36] As a result, law schools must compete much harder for students. Today the so-called merit financial aid pool (i.e., the total amount of tuition discounting used to "buy" students with the highest entering credentials as defined by *US News & World Report* rankings, which receive great weight in the United States) has grown exponentially. Law schools in the middle of the hierarchy ranking imposed by *US News & World Report* are feeling this competitive squeeze the most.[37] But law schools at all rungs of this hierarchy are facing budget constrictions and, with these, reductions in hiring, travel funding, new building construction, and program and research support. As the researchers earlier quoted conclude: "It would be no exaggeration to call these changes [to the finances of legal education] sudden, enormous, and drastic."[38]

Changed economic conditions have fueled institutional rivalry both within and between tiers of elitism in US legal education. Some significant voices have called for so-called lower-tier law schools to transform themselves from traditional outlets for US legal education, focused on teaching students critical thinking and logic skills, into quasi-professional schools turning out graduates who can function in quasi-professional roles.[39] It is no accident, I submit, that the voices making these proposals often come from the more elite schools facing the danger of being under-enrolled as students shop as increasingly savvy consumers, choosing between high-sticker-price elite education or better-value, more modestly decked-out schools.

In the face of all this ongoing transformation in US legal education, it helps to keep in mind the important discoveries of Bryant Garth and others involved in the longitudinal "after the JD" study of outcomes for US law students. As Garth and Ronit Dinovitzer found, students who enter law school from lower socioeconomic rungs end up being the happiest lawyers.[40] For these students, getting a law degree represents an important step up the socioeconomic ladder in comparison to their families of origin. In other words, obtaining the most prestigious and elite job does not predict future happiness in law; instead, moving into the professional class from more modest starting places does. Since *US News & World Report* rankings correlate most highly with the socioeconomic privilege of law schools' student bodies,[41] these findings suggest that the *best* investments in the future of US legal education from a utilitarian perspective are investments in the schools that educate students from lower socioeconomic backgrounds (i.e., less-elite schools).

US legal education is very much in a state of flux. US law schools are attempting to introduce new best practices, borrowing from business schools, for example, in introducing case study and problem-solving approaches to law teaching (indeed, once again Harvard Law School is one of the pioneers of these ideas).[42] At the same time, as a recent AALS study documented, the very "top" students in the United States—

defined as the ones with the highest grades and the highest capacity to do well in standardized testing, who thus have a variety of professional school options open to them—are going to law school at appreciably lower rates than they used to do.[43] Why have those top students largely vanished from the law school applicant pool? What studies have found is that these versatile top students now report most interest in going into business schools and master's degree programs such as economics rather than to law school.[44]

In thinking about the global future of legal education in conjunction with its history, I want to propose that we should delve more deeply into the potentially changed zeitgeist among law students today. In the United States, for example, important studies have shown that today's generation of elite prospective professional school students appears most interested in becoming social entrepreneurs and working in fields such as economics and business rather than entering law.[45] It appears that these are the fields in which they see the most creative energy and the chance to make a difference through their careers. Their role models appear to be Jeff Bezos of Amazon, Steve Jobs of Apple, and others in this mold—creative business persons with (some) social conscience. I went to law school holding as my heroes figures such as Thurgood Marshall and Ruth Bader Ginsburg—lawyers I had read about who devoted themselves to a vision of progressive social change through law. To me, going into law seemed at the time the best way to have a socially significant career on the fairness issues that mattered most to me. In contrast, a new generation of prospective professional school students in the United States appears, for a host of complex reasons, to be focused on other routes for having a meaningful professional impact. US legal educators are starting to focus more on breaking down disciplinary barriers and merging legal education with the problem-solving tools of a range of other disciplines, responding both to prospective student demand and to the quickly growing range of emerging cross-disciplinary employment sectors in which students are starting to move in search of jobs.[46]

Postscript: Possible Future Projects

Of course, what is happening in the United States may by no means be happening in other systems: since law is primarily an undergraduate degree in most other countries, and since the United States produces more lawyers than most other systems, the trends in the United States probably do not portend trends elsewhere. But I nevertheless think it is important, in thinking about the history of global legal education in relation to its future, for comparative legal education scholars and legal educators alike to study, document, analyze, and compare emerging trends in new generations' professional aspirations in different sociolegal systems. As globalization continues, what aspirations do new generations share? In what ways do their aspirations differ? And what are the implications of this demand-side analysis to the future of legal education from a global perspective? If I am right in the hypothesis I pose here, the voices of US academics will become less prominent as the resources traditionally poured into US legal education decline. As critical comparative legal education historians, we should be on the lookout for what new influences will arise and how they will shape the intertwined futures of legal education systems across the world.

NOTES

1 John Henry Schlegel, *American Legal Realism and Empirical Social Science* (Durham: University of North Carolina Press, 1995) (demonstrating this point in tracing the spread of ideas about empirical analysis from other disciplines into legal theory).

2 Robert Stevens, *Law School: Legal Education in American from 1850s to the 1980s* (North Carolina: University of North Carolina Press, 1983), 21–22.

3 Bruce A. Kimball, "The Proliferation and Transformation of Harvard's Case Method in the United States, 1870s-1990s," chapter 1 in this volume; Bruce A. Kimball, *The Inception of Modern Professional Education: C. C. Langdell, 1826–1906* (North Carolina: University of North Carolina Press, 2009).

4 Jean-Louis Halpérin, "Legal Education in France Turns Its Attention to the Harvard Model," chapter 11 in this volume.

5 Philip Girard, "American Influences, Canadian Realities: How 'American' Is Canadian Legal Education?," chapter 3 in this volume.

6 National Association for Law Placement, *Jobs & JDs, Employment for the Class of 2017—Selected Findings*, last modified August 2, 2018, www.nalp.org. According to the National Association for Law Placement, 71.8 percent of graduates from

US law schools in 2017 had bar passage–required jobs in 2017, 12.3 percent had JD-advantage jobs (meaning jobs for which having a JD was an advantage but bar passage is not required), 7.7 percent were unemployed and seeking work ten months after graduation, and smaller percentages fell in other categories.

7 Kimball, *Inception*.

8 Kimball, *Inception*, 140–45.

9 Emily Sanchez Slacedo, "Socratic Method Philippine Style: To Unhave or Uphold?" (presentation at the conference "Beyond Harvard: Transplanting Legal Education," Osgoode Hall Law School, Toronto, June 5–6, 2018).

10 For contrasting visions of the Socratic method in US law school teaching, compare Peter M. Cicchino, "Love and the Socratic Method," *American University Law Review* 50, no. 3 (2001): 533, 534 (arguing that the core of the Socratic method is "a learning context of genuine affection and concern"), with Jamie R. Abrams, "Reframing the Socratic Method," *Journal of Legal Education* 64, no. 4 (2015): 562, 565 (citing three elements of the Socratic method of law teaching, including a casebook approach to learning through appellate cases, Socratic inquisitive dialogue, and a large lecture hall format).

11 Kimball, *Inception*, 164.

12 "Since the Harvard Business School began to publish them in 1925, business case studies of actual cases have been widely used by business schools to provide students with a context in which to learn basic business principles. In some ways, the business case studies parallel the use of the ubiquitous 'hypothetical' in law school classrooms. However, case studies may be more effective than hypotheticals, because they involve real-life, often well-known, scenarios or stories where the players face issues that require resolution, thus providing students with a chance to test their book learning and to make decisions on how to provide advice to their clients." Celeste M. Hammond, "Borrowing from the B Schools: The Legal Case Study as Course Materials for Transaction Oriented Elective Courses: A Response to the Challenges of the MacCrate Report and the Carnegie Foundation for Advancement of Teaching," *Transactions: Tennessee Journal of Business Law* 11, no. 1 (2009): 9, 10–11.

13 Todd D. Rakoff and Martha Minow, "A Case for another Case Method," *Vanderbilt Law Review* 60, no. 2 (2007): 597–607 (arguing that law schools should use business school–type case studies in teaching to challenge students to engage in creative problem-solving).

14 Susan Bartie, "Look Over There: US Distractions in Australian Legal Education," presentation at the conference "Beyond Harvard: Transplanting Legal Education," Osgoode Hall Law School, Toronto June 5–6, 2018.

15 José Garcez Ghirardi, "Legal Teaching and the Reconceptualizing of the State: Discussing Global Law Programs," presentation at the conference "Beyond Harvard: Transplanting Legal Education," Osgoode Hall Law School, Toronto, June 5–6, 2018.

16 Susan Bartie, "Functionalism, Legal Process, and the Transformation (and Subordination) of Australian Law Schools," chapter 4 in this volume.

17 David Sandomierski, chapter 13 in this volume.

18 Jean-Louis Halpérin, "Legal Education in France Turns to the Harvard Model," presentation at the conference "Beyond Harvard: Transplanting Legal Education," Osgoode Hall Law School, Toronto, June 5–6, 2018.

19 Merike Ristikivi, Iren Kull and Alexksei Kelli, "Transplants in Legal Education in Estonia," presentation at the conference "Beyond Harvard: Transplanting Legal Education," Osgoode Hall Law School, Toronto, June 5–6, 2018).

20 Yoshiharu Matsuura, "American Socratic Method in the Context of New Japanese Professional Law Schools," presentation at the conference "Beyond Harvard: Transplanting Legal Education," Osgoode Hall Law School, Toronto, June 5–6, 2018.

21 Jayanth K. Krishnan, "Academic SAILERS: The Ford Foundation and the Efforts to Shape Legal Education in Africa, 1957–1977," Digital Repository @ Maurer Law (2012), www.repository.law.indiana.edu. SAILER is the acronym for Staffing of African Institutions of Legal Education and Research.

22 John Harrington and Ambreena Manji, "Pericles and the Professors: Legal Education in Ghana 1957–1966," presentation at the conference "Beyond Harvard: Transplanting Legal Education," Osgoode Hall Law School, Toronto, June 5–6, 2018.

23 Josephine J. Dawuni and Rebecca E. Badejogbin, "International, Domestication and the Transformation of Legal Education in Nigeria, 1962–2016," presentation at the conference "Beyond Harvard: Transplanting Legal Education," Osgoode Hall Law School, Toronto, June 5–6, 2018.

24 Illana Kowarski, "See the Price, Payoff of Law School before Enrolling," *US News and World Report*, last modified March 12, 2019, www.usnews.com (reporting on tuition and future earning potential for US law students). In 2018, 106 of the 188 ranked law schools in the United States were private and 82 were public.

25 Laura Kalman, "Professing Law: Elite Law School Professors in the Twentieth Century," in *Looking Back at Law's Century*, ed. Austin Sarat, Bryant Garth, and Robert A. Kagan (Ithaca: Cornell University Press, 2002), 335, 339 ("Social scientists and humanists have long found common ground in sniping that law professors receive twice the pay for half the teaching").

26 Jacqueline Bischel et al., "Faculty in Higher Education Annual Report: Key Findings, Trends, and Comprehensive Tables for Tenure-Track, Non-Tenure Teaching, and Non-Tenure Research Faculty; Academic Department Heads; and Adjunct Faculty for the 2018–19 Academic Year," last modified March 2019, 24, www.cupahr.org.

27 Ibid., 76.

28 Illana Kowarski, "See the Price." In 2018–2019, the average annual tuition and fees at private law schools in the United States was $49,095 US.

29 Pnina Lahav, "American Moment[s]: When, How and Why Did Israeli Law Faculties Come to Resemble Elite US Law Schools?," presentation at the conference "Beyond Harvard: Transplanting Legal Education," Osgoode Hall Law School, Toronto, June 5–6, 2018.

30 According to a search in the well-respected *Washington and Lee Law Journal Rankings* database, there are 950 student-edited law journals in the United States.

"W&L Law Journal Rankings," Washington and Lee School of Law, January 20, 2020, https://managementtools4.wlu.edu.

31 Girard, "Canadian Realities."

32 National Association of Law Placement, *Jobs & JDs: Employment and Salaries of New Law Graduates, Class of 2017* (Washington, DC: NALP, 2018), 13 (noting that the number of jobs for which bar passage is required had gone down by about 6,700 jobs from 2007).

33 In 1997, for example, the total of all graduates employed nine months after graduation was 93 percent. National Association of Law Placement, "The Stories behind the Numbers: Jobs for New Grads over More than Two Decades," last modified December 2016, www.nalp.org. Until the Great Recession of 2009, employment rates for graduating lawyers hovered in the 88–90 percent range. Ibid. By 2013, this number had decreased to 84.3 percent, with no increase occurring in 2014 and 2015. NALP, *Jobs & JDs*, 12. In 2017, this number rose slightly from previous years, to 88.6 percent. Ibid.

34 Bernard Burk, Jerry Organ, and Emma Rasiel, "Competitive Coping Strategies in the American Legal Academy: An Empirical Study," *Nevada Law Journal* 19 (2019): 583–646.

35 *See* Illana Kowarski, "Less Competitive Law School Admissions a Boon for Applicants," *US News & World Report*, last modified August 8, 2017, www.usnews.com (reporting that "US News data reveal that the average number of applicants at [top] law schools was 20.6% lower for the entering class of 2016 than it was for the entering class of 2008, and the average number of applicants at lower-ranked schools plunged 52.3% between 2008 and 2016").

36 Stephanie Francis Ward, "The 'Trump Bump' for Law School Applicants Is Real and Significant, Survey Says," *ABA Journal*, last modified February 22, 2018, www.abajournal.com.

37 Burk et al., "Competitive Coping Strategies," 631–32 (summarizing effects on US law schools of the contraction in the job market for new law graduates).

38 Ibid., 600.

39 Mark A. Cohen, "Law Schools Must Restructure. It Won't Be Easy," *Forbes*, last modified May 15, 2017, www.forbes.com (arguing that "[l]aw schools should specialize and focus on training students for a particular market segment").

40 Ronit Dinovitzer and Bryant G. Garth, "Lawyer Satisfaction in the Process of Structuring Legal Careers," *Law & Society Review* 41 no. 1 (2007): 1, 3, 23 41 (noting that data show lawyers from less elite socioeconomic backgrounds report highest satisfaction levels in their careers).

41 Ibid.

42 "The Case Studies," Harvard Law School, January 20, 2020, https://casestudies.law.harvard.edu.

43 Association of American Law Schools, *Before the J.D.: Undergraduate Views on Law Schools* (Washington, DC, AALS, 2018), 24; Benjamin H. Barton,

Fixing American Law Schools: From Collapse to the Trump Bump and Beyond (New York: New York University Press, 2019), 83 (graph showing precipitous decline in law school matriculation corresponding with a large rise in business school and modest rise in public policy matriculation from 2010 to 2014).

44 Ibid.

45 Ibid.

46 Susan D. Carle, "The Current Anxiety about JD Advantage Jobs: An Analysis and Recommendations," *San Diego Law Review* 57, no. 3 (2020) 675–755.

17

The Harvard Models in Their Native Habitat and Abroad

Reflections

ROBERT W. GORDON

When one sees paths of influence, transplants, or borrowings, one wants to know not only what is borrowed but why. What was it about the Harvard model—or rather models, since the Harvard experiment had many facets and mutated significantly over time—that has attracted its imitators. Or failed to attract them?

Let me approach this by asking what made the Harvard models appealing on their own ground. To start with: What considerations inspired the original Harvard Law School experiment? C. C. Langdell, the dean who, with the support of Harvard University president Charles W. Eliot, launched the prototype in 1871, came to legal education out of New York City practice, which had disgusted him: he thought the practice rewarded cunning, chicanery, and corruption. He wanted law to be a learned profession, rewarding education and intellect, and selecting its leaders by academic merit. (In this he differed from some of the other elite reformers of the day, who simply wanted the bar to be staffed with men of exemplary "character," by which they meant native-born gentlemen of Anglo ethnicity.) Langdell made a bet that a lengthy, rigorous, highly competitive law school program would attract ambitious men of talent to apply and that senior lawyers in practice would want to hire such men. (Women were not on the law school's radar and would not be admitted until 1950.) Thus the structure: a postgraduate program (eventually requiring a college degree to enter) of sequenced, mostly required, courses encouraging active learning by inducing students to prepare by reading primary materials (cases), to form independent views of what the cases meant, and to defend those views in arguments with the teachers and classmates. Langdell's goal was to establish law as a learned discipline—a science—worthy of university study (the model for this ideal was, obviously, Germany), investigated by a full-time faculty with time for research. He also wanted the discipline to be autonomous of other university disciplines and departments such as political science, sociology, and economics; and to be apolitical—thus the near-total exclusion of public law and the fixation on private law. The school's faculty aspired to teach a national, general common law; this was continuous with Harvard's earlier history as a school that recruited applicants from all over the country and sent them back to spread the word. Paradoxically, the ultimate focus of law teaching and scholarship as an *academic* pursuit, its raison-d'être and animating purpose, was to be the reform and improvement of legal *practice*: to produce abler, more learned advocates and counselors, judges, and legislators informed by the scholarly products of the schools—treatises, articles, and, when called upon, codifications of bodies of private law. Subjects like legal theory and legal history were not academic side ventures but part of the project of rationalizing and systematizing private law to make it accessible and useful to practitioners and lawmakers.[1]

The bet paid off: after decades of slumping enrollments and financial difficulties, the school attracted enough applications to become more selective and raise entry requirements. By 1900–1920, its primary target—the new law firms of the New York corporate bar—were hiring its graduates in preference to those of its archrival, Columbia; and both Columbia and Yale thought they had to Harvardize—by which they mostly meant adopting the case method, the sequenced curriculum, full-time faculty, and ultimately the college-degree requirement for entry. (Columbia, though not Yale, eventually sought divorce from its public law and social science faculty as well.) Although the school's aim was to reform and elevate practice, it actually taught very little of direct relevance to practice, especially the newly emerging forms of New York corporate practice, which were focused on restructuring the finances of bankrupt corporations. The gamble, however, was that graduates certified as super-smart, competitive, and compulsively hardworking could pick up any legal skill on the fly.

The model seemed to work for elite schools and elite firms that could afford to train new associates in firm specific practice skills and therefore didn't mind that hires arrived in practice innocent of such skills.

The mystery is why it should have been able to spread all over the country to schools producing graduates for very different practice jobs, such as solo or small-firm lawyering, which provided only rudimentary if any apprentice training. There are several plausible explanations. One is that the model was cheap—you could admit hundreds of students and educate as many as 150 at a time in large classrooms, and universities welcomed the flow of tuition money.[2] Also, you could hire bright young lawyers who knew nothing much about law to teach it, using the casebooks produced in the elite schools. Above all, the model conveyed prestige: Harvard by 1900 was considered the center of legal learning by many scholars in the Anglo world and often outside it as well. So, you can see why local university presidents, and local bar leaders with ambitions, might welcome it—even though it faced strong competition from night schools with less stringent entry requirements. It spread very slowly, but inexorably, and by the 1950s had displaced its rivals such as apprenticeship and night schools in almost every state.

You can also see why many would resist it. The projects of Harvard and the other elite schools were an audacious bid to take control of the entry requirements and intellectual formation of the *profession* by vaguely associating law practice with the prestige of university-based science. This project was possible, as Philip Girard points out (see chapter 3),[3] only because American guilds had been weakened earlier in the nineteenth century: in countries such as England, where the bar maintained a stranglehold on prescribing qualifications and controlling entry, the schools were relegated to a decidedly subordinate and peripheral status. The American schoolmen often rubbed bar leaders the wrong way because many of them were law reformers, too—persistent if mild critics of the established bench and bar, not hesitating to say where they thought common law decisions or procedures had gone off the rails of principle. They did not aspire to be Continental jurisconsults, lawgivers, or supremely authoritative glossators—they wanted to be taken seriously as expert counselors on the best interpretation of law. Some prominent judges, the ones they wrote for, accepted them in this role and cited their articles, treatises, and the "Restatements" they helped write for the American Law Institute. Yet many practicing lawyers and bar leaders, perhaps especially in the United States, were and still are antipathetic to intellectuals and theoretical training and are strongly averse to being criticized and seeing their traditional practices made into objects of reform.[4] As the academic wing of the profession drifted to the left of its practicing wing, resistance among the practitioners sharpened.[5]

After the founding years of 1871–1900, the law schools' conception of their mission gradually shifted during the 1920s, 1930s, and 1940s. The primary teaching task for the university law school remained, of course, that of training future private practitioners: Harvard and schools like it continued to sort, rank, and certify graduates as smart competitive workhorses to staff corporate law firms. By the 1950s, Harvard had complacently accepted its reputation as Wall Street North. Yet beginning in the 1920s, its scholarship slowly began to reflect the influence of Progressive legal movements and Legal Realism; and in the 1930s, along with Yale and Columbia, it became Washington North as well, as some of its faculty, and many of its graduates, went off to join the New Dealers. A fair proportion of those were Jewish lawyers who had been excluded from the elite firms, as well as some women and African American lawyers. Ronen Shamir has described this new orientation in scholarship as a "collective mobility project" of the center-left wing of the profession[6]—more critical of the conservative bar and conservative judges, favoring its own judge-heroes like Holmes, Brandeis and Cardozo and more attuned to law as policy as well as law as doctrine, addressed as much or more to legislatures and administrators as to common law judges and given to consequentialist thinking about legal rules. These movements incorporated consideration of the "social element" of law into legal thought and practice. (More of the intellectual pioneers of these movements were at Yale and Columbia than Harvard; but Harvard graduates supplied more bodies.) The Realists and New Dealers wanted to turn out not only government policymakers but also a new kind of private practitioner, one attuned to the functional nature of legal rules and the consequences of legal planning of business affairs.

After World War II, the New Deal agency lawyers moved into the elite law faculties, and in their teaching and scholarship they exemplified the postwar synthesis: still basically doctrinal rationalization, but now with an awareness that law is a pragmatic tool for fulfilling social valued purposes, with considerations of policy made explicit (if usually rather briefly and off to the side) in judicial reasoning. These more Progressive-minded elements at Harvard of 1930–1970 were the Harvards encountered by Canada's Caesar Wright, Bora Laskin, and John Milner[7] and by Israel's Aharon Barak and Itzhak Zamir[8].

In the 1960s and 1970s, a new element entered the mix: the constitutional law of the Rights Revolution and equal protection and, with it, new forms of practice: "public interest" practice and poverty law. Some professors were active in these reform movements, even among the leaders of them, such as Tommy Emerson of Yale, Tony Amsterdam of Stanford and New York University, and Ed Sparer of Pennsylvania. The schools gradually incorporated their perspectives into their faculties and curricula; and these perspectives infiltrated private practice by means of pro bono commitments. Clinical legal education came in as well, thanks to the Ford Foundation; and clinics have spread throughout the world in recent years.

The 1980s and 1990s are, of course, the Age of Theory—the multiplication of interdisciplinary perspectives and a new audience for the professors besides practitioners and policymakers: that is to say, the academy, the rest of the university. The best manifesto I know for this turn is by a Canadian law teacher, Harry Arthurs's *Law and Learning*,[9] though this report was never as well known outside Canada as it should have been. The turn was toward more academic law, more often taught by faculty with PhDs in other fields and limited practice experience.

Throughout all these changes, the elite law schools—still led by Harvard—kept feeding the Borg, shoveling their graduates into corporate practice in New York and other major American cities and in a whole bunch of foreign capitals as well, where they helped turn American law, law firm organization, and dispute-settlement procedures into major export commodities. The graduates repaid the favor by shoveling donations back into the schools.

What were the features of this multifaceted model of legal education that might have encouraged entrepreneurs and missionaries to try to export it and legal professionals or government officials or reformers in other countries to adopt it? The chapters in this volume address and help to answer that question. Many foreign legal systems, of course, found nothing useful and ignored or rejected it. Not surprisingly, countries sharing a common British ancestor, such as Canada (see Girard's chapter and Sandomierski, chapter 13), Australia (Bartie, chapter 4), and to a limited extent the mother country, England itself (Sugarman, chapter

2), have been more open to American influence;[10] while countries that earlier adopted or received civil law systems have found little or no use for a model of legal education based on analyzing and arguing case law, such as France (Halpérin, chapter 11) and Estonia (Kull, Ristikivi, and Kelli, chapter 8)[11] and, to the extent they borrow from foreigners, find codes much easier to assimilate. (This kinship of legal cultures, however, by no means guarantees reception. Brazil, a civil law country, has been much more receptive to having its corporate lawyers trained in US law schools than India, a former British colony.)[12]

Sometimes attempted transplants do not take hold because American teaching methods cannot find analogs in national legal systems, as with (in Matsuura's account, chapter 10) the failure of case method teaching in Japan.[13] Langdell conceived of the case method as a tool for teaching the skills, and improving the quality, of appellate argument, but Japanese courts have little lawmaking discretion and do not hear oral arguments. As Matsuura also points out, Americans think of common law method as a medium for creative lawmaking by judges and creative argument by lawyers—a view not likely to be well received in a jurisdiction that thinks of law as a closed system of rules and principles defended by dogmatic reasoning.[14] Pnina Lahav (chapter 12) tells us of Israeli scholars returning from a year or two at Harvard as evangelists for its policy- and purpose-oriented scholarship and teaching but meeting resistance from Israeli colleagues committed to a more formalist jurisprudence and rule-based teaching.[15] Often, missionaries hoping to export their models do so under illusions about possible impacts (Kroncke, chapter 7 on China[16]), collide with post-colonial political priorities (Harrington and Manji on Ghana[17]), or are vulnerable to rejection by nationalist revolts against foreign influences.

The critical and reformist aspects of American models—the idea that well-trained lawyers can be not only a force for preparing a competent bar and bench but also agents of social and political change—have attracted reformers in other countries. In Latin America, groups of young lawyers educated in US law schools have sought to transplant aspects of US legal education—especially full-time law faculties, as well as instrumentalist forms of legal reasoning as a branch of policy science—to their home countries as a lever for creating cadres of Progressive reformers. This process has created organizations of lawyers devoted to promoting international human rights and fighting corruption. One of the more successful instrumentalist export commodities of the US legal academy, however, has been law and economics, with its promise of instilling a means of thinking about law, designing law, and proselytizing for law as an instrument of economic development—an enterprise materially assisted by "rule of law" funding from agencies such as the World Bank and USAID. The work of Bryant Garth and Yves Dézalay has shown that aspiring lawyers in developing countries—excluded from traditional legal career ladders dominated by family-based elites—have, like economists, used US graduate training to acquire independent credentials that help them bypass local legal establishments and qualify them for newly established technocratic ministries in fields like antitrust and telecommunications and for private practice serving multinational clients.[18] Much of this work has bolstered reforms, but of a distinctive—and inevitably controversial—kind: neoliberal reforms designed to privatize state functions and enterprises, weaken state bureaucracies, and enable capitalist markets.[19] But other models of lawyering partly pioneered in the United States have been exported too: international human rights, public interest law, constitutional rights litigation, class actions seeking structural remedies, and judicial review of administration.

Back at the start of it all, in 1871–1900, the professors in the reinvigorated American law schools had a more or less clear idea of the relation of their teaching and research to practice—though they may have been at least in part deluding themselves. So did their successors, the Progressives and New Dealers. What is the current theory of that relation—besides, of course, the sorting and certifying by "academic merit," meaning, as a practical matter, the ability to perform rapid-fire issue-spotting on examinations? Some of the law-and-economics faculty think they have an idea—that their theoretical knowledge passes the test of good theory, that it can be applied in, inform, and improve practice. But for the most part, current law faculties do not seem to direct much reflection or research toward thinking about what their students will do after graduation or preparing them to do it better (even if they knew how to do so). The schools are concerned about appearing to applicants and bar regulators as if they can produce "practice-ready" graduates, offering more opportunities for clinical training, document-drafting, negotiation, and importing more adjuncts from practice to teach specialty skills. But there is still very little research into what lawyers actually do. To the extent there is a professional or policy audience for academic research, it tends to be in bar committees, law reform commissions, legislatures, agencies, and think tanks and social movements rather than private practice.

Some Gloomy Concluding Reflections

The Harvard model–based US system of legal education, as Susan Carle (chapter 16) points out, was always an elite model.[20] Its requirement of three postgraduate years on top of four undergraduate years of schooling always made it difficult to access.[21] Its insistence on a full-time academic faculty paid enough to recruit professors out of practice and given time for research—a model markedly different from most of the rest of the world's, where law is commonly taught, as it once was in the United States, by part-time practitioners[22]—makes it expensive. Now tuitions at private US law schools exceed $60,000 per year, and state subsidies for public law schools have steeply declined. That is bad news for law as a profession open to socially mobile talent; and in fact elite law schools are largely populated with children of the wealthy and upper-middle-class professionals. Without parental subsidies, law school is really financially viable only for students admitted to the top half of the rankings whose graduates can hope to attain practice jobs that will enable them to repay their student loans. Has legal education become much like the US system of civil litigation—a luxury good only affordable by corporations and the wealthy and far too cumbersome for everyday use?

Clearly, many foreign countries think so. The American model is still much in demand by foreign law students who want to work for American corporate law firms, or for home-country corporate law firms patterned on American law firms and representing multinational clients, and for lawyers working in-house for large corporations. (It also remains in demand by foreign law teachers seeking a prestigious credential to bolster their résumés.) But the easiest way for a foreign country to acquire such lawyers is to send them abroad for graduate training, not to try to build American-style law schools on their home ground. The United States took a schooling model intended for elites and made it into a requirement for every aspiring lawyer. Brazil—to cite a contrasting example—inverts the model, maintaining a cheaper, mass-education undergraduate law curriculum geared toward the bar exam while outsourcing training of its corporate-legal elite to the United States (and a few domestic imitators such as the FGV law school in São Paulo).[23] Meanwhile, the LLMs flocking to US law schools (Georgetown admits about 500 of these each year, Harvard about 180, NYU about 450) help to keep the top-heavy American model afloat.

US students burdened with $300,000 or more of debt want to know: What are law schools good for? Many voices predict a shakedown—reductions in number of years of schooling (perhaps from seven to five), in the size and compensation of faculties, and in the number of schools, especially those ranked in the bottom tiers. The schools are also experiencing pressures from bar associations and practitioners to strip down to a strictly practice-oriented, vocational curriculum—though they often disagree about what such a program to produce "practice-ready" lawyers should look like. Yet most of the experiments that are likely to produce really valuable results—such as supervised live-client clinics, joint faculty-practitioner seminars, and legal problem solving courses using factually complex business school–style cases—are labor-intensive and thus even more expensive than traditional legal education.

There is also reason to worry that the pressures toward a more instrumentalist and vocational curriculum will drive out some of the more genuinely innovative and valuable aspects of American legal education—its critical and reformist elements and its orientation toward public values and goals as well as preparation for private practice. US law schools to their credit have never been slaves to professional orthodoxies or uncritical servants of the state or legal establishments; they have always looked beyond the immediate instrumental tasks of turning out lawyers for practice to larger projects of legal and also broader social reform: the promotion of the rule of law and a more just social order. In the 1920s and 1930s, the professors criticized the premises of orthodox classical law and political economy and helped to theorize the reforms of the New Deal. In the 1960s and 1970s, they helped provide the legal frameworks for the Rights Revolution. In this respect they are very unlike, for example, business schools, which do not as a rule undertake much questioning of the premises of capitalist order. Scholarship that is attentive to broader social goals rather than helping practitioners make more money is always likely to invite hostility and derision from conservative and anti-intellectual elements in the bar and in political life and therefore is to be among the casualties of vocationalist reforms. How can we help to save the vital research functions and critical standpoints of the academy while doing a better job of serving the practical needs of its graduates to make a living?

NOTES

1 On the original Harvard experiment, the indispensable sources are Robert B. Stevens, *Law School: Legal Education in America from the 1850s to the 1980s* (Chapel Hill: University of North Carolina Press, 1987); William LaPiana, *Logic and Experience: The Origin of Modern American Legal Education* (New York: Oxford University Press, 1994); and Daniel R. Coquillette and Bruce A. Kimball, *On the Battlefield of Merit: Harvard Law School, the First Century* (Cambridge: Harvard University Press 2015). My own (minor) contributions to this literature are "The Case For (and Against) Harvard," *Michigan Law Review* 93, no. 6 (1995): 1231–60, and "The Geologic Strata of the Law School Curriculum," *Vanderbilt Law Review* 60, no. 2 (2007): 339–69.

2 See Bruce A. Kimball, "The Proliferation and Transformation of Harvard's Case Method in the United States, 1870s–1990s,"chapter 1 in this volume. Other countries have found this feature useful as well. In Ontario, for example, university-based law schools triumphed in their battle with the benchers for control over legal education because the bar's Law Society–sponsored school was unable to handle the flood of postwar aspirants to legal careers. See C. Ian Kyer and Jerome E. Bickenbach, *The Fiercest Debate: Cecil A. Wright, the Benchers, and Legal Education in Ontario, 1923–1957* (Osgoode Society, University of Toronto Press, 1987). But we should not exaggerate the advantages of the Harvard model for large-scale instruction. In many countries, law is taught by lectures to hundreds of students massed in large auditoria. The teachers are spared the burden of evaluating students because they leave examination to outside authorities.

3 See Philip Girard, "American Influences, Canadian Realities: How 'American' Is Canadian Legal Education?," chapter 3 in this volume.

4 Chief Justice William Howard Taft, for example, wrote letters to law school deans complaining bitterly that decisions of the Supreme Court were being criticized in law review articles, and he refused to cite academic writings in his opinions. See Robert Post, "The Supreme Court Opinion as Institutional Practice: Dissent, Legal Scholarship, and Decision-making in the Taft Court," *Minnesota Law Review* 85, no. 5 (2001): 1364–74.

5 See Jerold Auerbach, "Enmity and Amity: Law Teachers and Practitioners, 1900–1922," in *Law in American History*, ed. Donald Fleming and Bernard Bailyn (Boston: Little Brown, 1971).

6 See Ronen Shamir, *Managing Legal Uncertainty: Elite Lawyers in the New Deal* (Durham: Duke University Press, 1995), 141–57.

7 See Girard, "American Influences, Canadian Realities"; David Sandomierski, "Catalytic Agents? Lon Fuller, James Milner, and the Lawyer as Social Architect, 1950–1969," chapter 13 in this volume.

8 Pnina Lahav, "American Moment[s]: When, How and Why Did Israeli Law Faculties Come to Resemble Elite US Law Schools?," chapter 12 in this volume.

9 Social Sciences and Humanities Research Council of Canada, *Law and Learning / Le droit et le savoir. Report of the Consultative Group on Research and Education in Law* (Ottawa: The Council, 1983) [Arthurs Report]; see also Richard Posner, "The Decline of Law as an Autonomous Discipline, 1962–1987," *Harvard Law Review* 100, no. 4 (1987): 761–80.

10 See Girard, "American Influences, Canadian Realities"; Sandomierski, "Catalytic Agents?"; Susan Bartie, however, suggests that Australia was open to American legal influence in part as a strategy to assert its independence from English legal influence. See Susan Bartie, "Functionalism, Legal Process and the Transformation (and Subordination) of Australian Law Schools," chapter 4 in this volume. Also David Sugarman, "How America did (and didn't) influence English Legal Education, circa 1870–1965," chapter 2 in this volume. .

11 See Jean-Louis Halpérin, "Legal Education in France Turns its Attention to the Harvard Model," , chapter 11 in this volume; Irene Kull, Merike Ristikivi, and Alexksei Kelli. "Transplants in Estonian Legal Education—Influences from United States Legal System," chapter 8 in this volume.

12 David B. Wilkins and Vikramadytia S. Khanna, "South by Southeast: Comparing the Development of In-House Legal Departments in Brazil and India," in *The Brazilian Legal Profession in the Age of Globalization*, ed. Luciana Gross Cunha et al. (Cambridge: Cambridge University Press, 2018), 114–17.

13 Yoshiharu Matsuura, "The American Case Method and New Japanese Legal Education," chapter 10 in this volume.

14 Matsuura, "The American Case Method." Emily Sanchez Salcedo, by contrast, reports that classroom bullying by "Socratic" teachers does to some extent replicate the adversarial conditions of courtrooms, but is so demoralizing as to be counterproductive as preparation for practice. Emily Sanchez Salcedo, "The Socratic Method, Philippine-style: To Unhave or Uphold?," chapter 15 in this volume.

15 Lahav, "American Moment[s]."

16 Jedediah Kroncke, "Model, System, or Node? Understanding Legal Education Reform in 20th Century China and Beyond," chapter 7 imn this volume.

17 John Harrington and Ambreena Manji, "Conservatives, Nationalists, and American Romantics Debating Legal Education in Kwame Nkrumah's Ghana," chapter 5 in this volume.

18 See generally Bryant Garth and Yves Dézalay, *The Internationalization of Palace Wars: Lawyers, Economists, and the Contest to Transform Latin American States* (Chicago: University of Chicago Press, 2002).

19 See José Garcez Ghirardi, "Legal Teaching and the Reconceptualizing of the State: Global Law and New Legal Education Loci," chapter 14 in this volume (documenting how "global legal" programs teach lawyers how to operate in privatized international legal networks that dispense with or work around governments of nation-states).

20 See Susan D. Carle, "Rethinking Assumptions about the Global Influence of US Legal Education," chapter 16 in this volume.

21 In 1910, the first year for which reliable census estimates are available, less than 3 percent of the entire US population had graduated from an institution of higher learning. In 1950, only about 8 percent of the civilian labor force been graduated from college. Those proportions have increased, however, to the point when, in 2011, 30.5 percent of the workforce were college graduates. (I am grateful to Kevin Rothenberg of the Stanford Law Library for extracting these data from *Statistical Abstracts of the United States.*)

22 See Stevens, *Law School: Legal Education in America*, chap. 1.

23 See Luciana Gross Cunha and José Garcez Ghirardi, "Legal Education in Brazil: The Challenges and Opportunities of a Changing Context," in Cunha et al., *Brazilian Legal Profession*, 247–63.

ACKNOWLEDGMENTS

We would like to acknowledge the Social Sciences and Humanities Research Council of Canada, the American Society of Legal History, Osgoode Hall Law School (York University), Western University, and the University of Tasmania for generously supporting a symposium, along with research assistance, that provided the foundation for this collection. We are grateful for the superb editorial assistance of Osgoode Hall Law School students Emma Baumann, Annalise Beube, and Sarah-Jane Nussbaum, as well as Western University Faculty of Law students Madeleine Douglas, Kara Kristoffersson, Tyler Mäkinen, Victoria Ostrovsky, and, especially, Emily Denomme. We would like to thank our contributors for all the considerable work they have put into this volume and would especially like to thank Professor Philip Girard for supporting our funding applications and providing mentorship and also Professor David Sugarman for helping us secure the interest of such a strong group of scholars.

ABOUT THE CONTRIBUTORS

Rebecca Emiene Badejogbin LLB (Jos) LLM (Jos) LLM (Research) (Pretoria) PhD (UCT) is a lawyer and currently Director of Academics at the Council of Legal Education at the Nigerian Law School, where she commenced her academic career in 2001. She is the Head of Academics and the Head of Department of the Property Law Practice Department at the Yola Campus of the Nigerian Law School. She taught Constitutional Law over the years and teaches Property Law Practice, Professional Ethics, and Legal Skills. Her research interests include customary law, property law, wills and succession, constitutional law, legal education, the legal profession, and judicial appointments. Over the years, she has carried out extensive empirical and doctrinal research on customary law, courts, and the judiciary in Nigeria and South Africa. She is published in peer-reviewed journals and is the coauthor of *Law in Practice: Professional Responsibilities and Lawyering Skills in Nigeria* (2014).

Susan Bartie is a lecturer in law at the University of Tasmania. She has previously been a lecturer in law at the University of Adelaide, a commercial litigator, and began her career as an associate to a Federal Court Judge. She has won a number of awards and prizes including a *Dean's Commendation for Doctoral Thesis Excellence* for her PhD, a *Citation for Outstanding Contribution to Student Learning* from the Commonwealth Department of Education and Training (national award) for her teaching, and a *British Chevening Scholarship* to complete a Masters in Law at the University of Cambridge. She is a member of the Working Group on the Legal Profession that is part of the International Sociology Association. She is also part of a group of international scholars writing on gender and careers in the legal academy. She is the author of several articles on the history of legal education and the role of lawyers in society. Her recent book *Free Hands and Minds—Pioneering Legal*

Scholars reveals the central ideas that underpinned the birth of modern Australian university legal education.

SUSAN D. CARLE is Professor of Law at American University Washington College of Law. She teaches and writes about civil rights, legal history, employment discrimination, labor and employment law, legal ethics, and the history and sociology of the legal profession. She has served as the law school's first Associate Dean for Scholarship, as chair of the Association of American Law Schools Section on Professional Responsibility and its Professional Development Committee, as W. M. Keck Fellow in Legal Ethics at Georgetown University Law Center (1995–97), and as Visiting Professor of Law at Harvard Law School (2006). She holds a JD from Yale Law School, where she served as an editor of the *Yale Law Journal*, and she is a former clerk of the United States Court of Appeals for the Third Circuit. She is the author of *Defining the Struggle: National Organizing for Racial Justice, 1880–1915* (Oxford University Press, 2013), for which she received the 2014 Organization of American Historians' Liberty Legacy Award for "the author of the best book by a historian on the civil rights struggle from the beginnings of the nation to the present."

J. JARPA DAWUNI is an Associate Professor of Political Science at Howard University, Washington, DC, and the Founder and Executive Director of the Institute for African Women in Law. She holds an LLB from the University of Ghana and qualified as a Barrister-at-Law before the Ghana Superior Courts of Judicature. She holds a Doctorate in Political Science from Georgia State University, Atlanta. Her primary areas of research include women and the legal professions, judicial politics, women and the law, international human rights, women's civil society organizing, and democratization. She is the editor (with Akua Kuenyehia) of *International Courts and the African Woman Judge: Unveiled Narratives* (2018) and editor (with Gretchen Bauer) of *Gender and the Judiciary in Africa: From Obscurity to Parity?* (2016).

JOSÉ GARCEZ GHIRARDI is an Associate Professor at FGV SP Law School (Brazil). He has also been a visiting scholar at the Collège de France (Chaire État Social et mondialisation) (2017) and Wayne State

University (1998) and part of the Adjunct Faculty at Gonzaga Law School (2010). He served as a member of the Board of Directors of the Brazilian Association for the Teaching of Law—ABEDi (2016–2018). He holds a BA, MA, and PhD from University of São Paulo and is a lawyer accredited at the Brazilian Bar. His publications include *The Brazilian Legal Profession in the Age of Globalization: The Rise of the Corporate Legal Sector and Its Impact on Lawyers and Society* (2018)

Philip Girard is a professor at Osgoode Hall Law School. Prior to joining Osgoode, he was University Research Professor and Professor of Law, History & Canadian Studies at Schulich School of Law, Dalhousie University. At Dalhousie, he served as the Law School's Acting Dean (1991–1993) and Associate Dean (Graduate Studies and Research, 2002–2006). In 2010–2011, he was Visiting Scholar, Centre for Criminology & Sociolegal Studies, University of Toronto. In 2011, he was made an honorary fellow of the American Society for Legal History, the first Canadian to be so recognized. His publications include *Lawyers and Legal Culture in British North America: Beamish Murdoch of Halifax* (2011), winner of the Clio-Atlantic Prize awarded by the Canadian Historical Association; *Bora Laskin: Bringing Law to Life* (2005) (for which he was awarded the Champlain Society's 2006 Floyd S. Chalmers Award for best book published on Ontario history in the previous year, and shortlisted for the 2006 John A. Macdonald Prize for best book published on Canadian history in 2005). He is also editor (with Jim Phillips) of two collections on Nova Scotia legal history: *The Supreme Court of Nova Scotia, 1754–2004: From Imperial Bastion to Provincial Oracle* (2004) and *Essays in the History of Canadian Law: Volume III, Nova Scotia* (1990). Professor Girard is the author of numerous refereed journal articles and book chapters and is a member of the Bar of Nova Scotia.

Robert W. Gordon is Professor of Law at Stanford University and Chancellor Kent Professor of Law & Legal History, Emeritus, at Yale University. He is a graduate of Harvard's College and Law School and a member of the Massachusetts Bar. He began his law teaching career at SUNY/Buffalo and the University of Wisconsin Law Schools; since 1984 he has taught primarily at Stanford and Yale, with visits to Harvard, the University of Toronto, and Oxford law faculties. He is the author of *Tam-*

ing the Past: Law in History and History in Law (2017) and more than a hundred articles, essays, and reviews on the history of legal thought, the legal profession and legal education, and contract law. He is at work on a history of law as a public profession in the United States.

JEAN-LOUIS HALPÉRIN is a Professor (exceptional class) at the École Normale Supérieure (Paris). He is a member of the Institut Universitaire de France (2013–2018) and director of the Unité mixte de recherche 7074—Centre for Legal Theory and Analysis (CNRS—University Paris X-ENS and EHESS). He was a nominated professor at the University of Lyon III (1988–1998), then professor at the University of Burgundy (1998–2003), and became Dean of the Law Faculty from 2000 to 2003. In 1994, he was elected the junior member of the Institut Universitaire de France. He has been a law professor at the École Normale Supérieure since September 2003 and was elected senior member of the Institut Universitaire de France in October 2013. He has published numerous articles in both French and English including "The Concept of Law: A Western Transplant?" (*Theoretical Inquiries in Law*, 2009); "Western Legal Transplants in India" (*Jindal Global Law Review*, 2010); "Law in Books and Law in Action: the Problem of Legal Change" (*Maine Law Review*, 2011); "Transplants of European Normativity in India and in Japan: A Historical Comparison" (*Rechtsgeschichte*, 2014); and "For a Renewed History of Lawyers" (*American Journal of Legal History*, 2016). He is the author of several research monographs, including, with Naoki Kanayama, *Droit japonais et droit français au miroir de la modernité* (2007); *Histoire du droit des biens* (2008); *Profils des mondialisations du droit* (2009); *Portraits du droit indien* (2012); with Frédéric Audren, *La culture juridique française. Entre mythes et réalités (XIXe-XXe siècles)* (2013); *Five Legal Revolutions since the 17th Century: An Analysis of a Global Legal History* (2014); and *Histoire de l'état des juristes. Allemagne XIXe-XXe siècles* (2015).

JOHN HARRINGTON is Professor of Global Health Law and Director of the Centre for Law and Global Justice at Cardiff University and Director of the ESRC Doctoral Training Programme in Wales. He holds degrees in law from Trinity College Dublin and Oxford University. He held previous appointments at Liverpool, Warwick, and the Free University of Berlin, as well as fellowships at the African Population and Health Research Center (Nairobi), University of Melbourne, European University Institute, and the University of Dar es Salaam. His books include *State Formation in Global Health: Development, Security and Sovereignty* (forthcoming), *Global Health and Human Rights: Legal and Philosophical Perspectives*, and *Towards a Rhetoric of Medical Law*, which was the runner-up for the SLSA Legal Theory Book Prize (2017).

ALEKSEI KELLI is a Professor of Intellectual Property Law in the Faculty of Law, University of Tartu. He is Chair of Legal Committee of CLARIN ERIC (Common Language Resources and Technology Infrastructure). Kelli is responsible for the management of intellectual property rights (IPRs) of digital language resources at the University of Tartu and the Institute of the Estonian Language. He holds a doctorate (PhD in Law) from the University of Tartu (2009). He acted as the Head of an Expert Group on the Codification of the Intellectual Property Law (2012–2014, Ministry of Justice of Estonia). He has taken part in several EU and Estonian R&D projects as a leading expert in IP, innovation, knowledge transfer, industry-academia cooperation, open science and open data, personal data protection, and cultural heritage protection. Kelli has published numerous works on intellectual property, innovation, personal data protection, knowledge transfer, cultural heritage, and related issues.

BRUCE A. KIMBALL is a historian and philosopher of education and a Professor at The Ohio State University. He is the recipient of fellowships from a number of organizations, including the Rockefeller Foundation, Luce Foundation, Spencer Foundation, American Council of Learned Societies, and Guggenheim Foundation. He has held appointments at the University of Rochester, Yale University, and the University of Houston. He has authored numerous books that have won a range of prestigious academic prizes, including the History of Philanthropy Book Prize (2017), the Outstanding Book of the Year in Postsecondary Education (2010), and the Frederic W. Ness Book Prize (1987). His books include *The Intellectual Sword: Harvard Law School, the Second Century* (2017, with Daniel R. Coquillette), *On the Battlefield of Merit: Harvard Law School, the First Century* (2015, with Daniel R. Coquillette), *The*

Liberal Arts Tradition: A Documentary History (2010), and *The Inception of Modern Professional Education: C. C. Langdell, 1826–1906* (2009).

JEDIDIAH J. KRONCKE is an Associate Professor of Law at the University of Hong Kong. He earned a BA in Asian Studies and Legal Studies from the University of California, Berkeley, a JD from Yale Law School, and a PhD in Social and Cultural Anthropology also from the University of California, Berkeley. After graduate school, he was awarded the Ruebhausen Fellowship at Yale Law School, the Golieb Fellowship in Legal History at New York University Law School, and the Berger Legal History Fellowship at Harvard Law School. Previously, he was a professor at FGV São Paulo School of Law, and before then he was the Senior Fellow at the East Asian Legal Studies Program at Harvard Law School. Dr. Kroncke's research centers on international legal history and the study of alternative labor and property institutions. His interdisciplinary work draws on the US, Chinese, and Brazilian legal experiences and is devoted to the productive indigenization of comparative legal analysis. His first book, *The Futility of Law and Development: China and the Dangers of Exporting American Law* (2016), explores the role of US-China relations in the formation of modern American legal internationalism and the decline of American legal comparativism. He is the first Associate Editor on comparative and non-Western history for the *Law & History Review* and an inaugural Associate Editor for the *Journal of Law and Political Economy*.

IRENE KULL is a Professor of Civil Law and holds the position of Head of the Department of the Civil Law at the University of Tartu. She participated in the Study Group of a European Civil Code (SGCCE) and was a member of the Expert Group on a Common Frame of Reference in the area of European Contract Law (CESL). She has been a member of the drafting commission on the Estonian Law of Obligations Act and one of the editors and leading authors of comments on the Estonian Law of Obligations, General Part of Civil Code, and Property Law Act. She has taken part in several EU and Estonian research projects and has published a number of works on private law areas. From 2003 to 2008 she acted as Vice Dean in teaching matters and has been an adviser of the civil chamber of the Estonian Supreme Court for more than twenty years.

PNINA LAHAV is a Professor at Boston University School of Law. She has published nearly fifty journal articles and three books, including the critically acclaimed *Judgment in Jerusalem: Chief Justice Simon Agranat and the Zionist Century* (1997). Winner of Israel's Seltner Award (1998) and the Gratz College Centennial Book Award (1998), *Judgment in Jerusalem* was offered as a selection by the History Book Club in the United States and was the subject of a symposium at the Tel Aviv University Faculty of Law in 1999. She has earned fellowships from the Rockefeller Foundation, a grant from the Lipsitt Faculty Research Fund at Boston University, and, for the 2000–2001 academic year, a fellowship at the Stanford Center for Advanced Study in the Behavioral Sciences. She also served as a Fellow at the Center for Advanced Studies at the Hebrew University in Jerusalem in the spring of 2008 and as a Religion Fellow at Boston University School of Theology (2010, 2011). Professor Lahav has also delivered several endowed lectures, including the Lapidus Lecture at Princeton University in March 2015. Professor Lahav was the recipient of the BU Law Melton Prize for excellence in teaching in 2011. She has taught at Hebrew University, Tel Aviv University, the Center for Interdisciplinary Studies in Herzlia, Oxford University, and Université Jean Moulin Lyon 3 in Lyon, France.

AMBREENA MANJI is a Professor of Land Law and Development at Cardiff (since 2014). Before that, she was seconded to Nairobi as the Director of the British Academy's British Institute in Eastern Africa (2010–2014). Ambreena's research focuses on Law and Society in Africa. It is strongly interdisciplinary and collaborative. Her most recent book is *The Struggle for Land and Justice in Kenya* (2020). Ambreena has been invited to teach doctoral and postdoctoral classes in Nairobi, Johannesburg, Cape Town, Dakar, Addis Ababa, and Bogota. She was President of the African Studies Association UK (2018–2020) and is Coeditor of the journal *African Affairs*.

YOSHIHARU MATSUURA is a Professor Emeritus and Designated Professor for a special graduate program at Nagoya University Graduate School of Law. He has worked in comparative legal history, legal theory, and law and computers. He was educated at Osaka University Graduate School of Law and Yale Law School. He has taught at Chukyo, Osaka, and Nagoya universities as a regular faculty member and was a visiting professor at the University of British Columbia Faculty of Law and the University of Wisconsin Law School. He was the Dean of Nagoya University Graduate School of Law (2006–2008) and the Director of the Nagoya University Library (2009–2012). He has published many books and articles, including "Law and Metaphor" (1991) and "Legal Informatics" (1999) in Japanese and "Law and Bureaucracy in Modern Japan" (Review Essay: Upham, Law, and Social Change in Postwar Japan) (1989) and "Toward a New Generation of Comparative Law: A Framework for Bilateral Collaboration in Law & Development Projects in Asia" (2005) in English.

Kjell Å Modéer is a Professor Emeritus of Legal History at Lund University, Sweden. He holds an LLM and Jur.dr from Lund University. He was the holder of the Söderberg Foundations Professorship to the Memory of Samuel Pufendorf from 2005 to 2007. He has been a visiting scholar at the University of Virginia School of Law (1984–1985) and at Stanford University School of Law and the University of California, Berkeley Law School. He holds honorary doctorates from the University of Greifswald Law Faculty, University of Lund Theological Faculty (2004), and University of Helsinki Law Faculty. He is a member of several scientific academies and associations in Sweden, the Nordic Countries, Europe, and the United States. His main research and publications, written in Swedish, English, and German, concentrate on early modern and modern legal history, comparative legal cultures and traditions, and law and religion. His latest monograph is *Det förpliktande minnet: Juridiska fakulteten i Lund 1666–2016*, [*The Binding Memory: The Lund University Faculty of Law, 1666–2016*] (2017).

Merike Ristikivi is an Associate Professor of Legal History in the Faculty of Law, University of Tartu. She has studied law (PhD 2010) and classical philology (MA 2006). Her main research interests are the professionalization of Estonian female lawyers, legal linguistics and discourse analysis, Latin legal terminology, law journals and periodicals, and Roman law and its reception. She is the author of the books *Latin for Lawyers* (several editions, 2000–2019) and *Latin terms in the Estonian*

Legal Language: Form, Meaning, and Influences (2010) and coauthor of *Latin-Estonian Legal Dictionary* (2005), *Latin-Estonian Dictionary* (2002), *Juristernes latin. Suum cuique* (2019), and *Fontes iuris Romani* (2019). She has published numerous articles on legal language, legal education, and women in law.

EMILY SANCHEZ SALCEDO teaches at the Commercial Law Department of De La Salle University in the Philippines. She earned the degree Doctor of Juridical Science at the Indiana University Maurer School of Law, where she was a Fulbright scholar, an International Fellow of the American Association of University Women, and a World Fellow of the Delta Kappa Gamma Society International. Her dissertation "Neither a Pedestal nor a Cage: In Pursuit of Genuine Gender Equality in the Philippine Workplace" won the Best Doctoral Dissertation Award in 2014. It was published as a book in 2015 and became a finalist for the National Book Awards in 2016. Professor Salcedo's current research undertakings are in the areas of human rights, labor migration, and antidiscrimination legislation, which grew out of her earlier research projects as a visiting scholar both at the University of Manitoba and at Queen's University in 2015. Professor Salcedo also holds special interest in gender and the legal profession. Her article on pioneering women law professors in the Philippines is to be published in an international comparative compilation on gender and careers in the legal academy. Professor Salcedo is also a member of the Philippine Bar and the New York State Bar.

DAVID SANDOMIERSKI is an Assistant Professor in the Faculty of Law at Western University in London, Ontario. He holds an SJD from the University of Toronto Faculty of Law, where his dissertation received the Governor General's Academic Gold Medal. Sandomierski has received the Peter Oliver Prize from the Osgoode Society for Canadian Legal History, as well as the Scholarship of Teaching and Learning Award from the Canadian Association of Law Teachers. He is a founding codirector of the Collaborative Research Network on Legal Education of the US Law and Society Association. His recent book *Aspiration and Reality in Legal Education* (2020) explores the relationship between realist and formalist ideas in Canadian law teaching.

David Sugarman is Professor Emeritus of Law, Lancaster University Law School; Senior Associate Research Fellow, Institute of Advanced Legal Studies, University of London; and Senior Associate, Centre for Socio-Legal Studies, University of Oxford. He has authored, coauthored, and edited twenty books and has written more than ninety articles and book chapters. He has also published articles in a broad range of outlets, including *The Times*, *The Guardian*, *The Santiago Times* (Chile), *Open Democracy*, *The North American Congress on Latin America* (NACLA), *Amnesty International* (Chile), and *El Mostrador* (Chile). He has undertaken research for governments, intergovernmental organizations, and NGOs, most recently the European Court of Justice, the European Court of Human Rights, the European Union Parliament Women's Rights and Gender Equality Committee, and the Law Society of England and Wales. He is a Fellow of the Royal Historical Society, a Fellow of the Academy of Social Sciences, and an Honorary Fellow of the American Society for Legal History. He has been a visiting professor in Canada, Germany, Japan, Spain, and the United States and has delivered more than 300 invited lectures in more than twenty countries. He has acted as a consultant to, and occasionally appeared on, a wide range of documentary and television and radio programs on legal history and international human rights topics, including CNN, Channel Four News, BBC Radio 4, BBC News 24, BBC World Service, Deutsche Welle, and Austrian Public Radio.

INDEX

Page numbers with (t) refer to tables.

Lightning Source UK Ltd.
Milton Keynes UK
UKHW011829150622
404479UK00003B/73/J

9 781479 803583